INFINITE RICHES

By Leo Rosten

PASSIONS AND PREJUDICES
THE POWER OF POSITIVE NONSENSE
O K*A*P*L*A*N! MY K*A*P*L*A*N!
THE 3:10 TO ANYWHERE
THE LOOK BOOK (ED.)
A NEW GUIDE AND ALMANAC TO THE RELIGIONS OF
    AMERICA (ED.)
DEAR "HERM"
LEO ROSTEN'S TREASURY OF JEWISH QUOTATIONS
ROME WASN'T BURNED IN A DAY: THE MISCHIEF OF
    LANGUAGE
PEOPLE I HAVE LOVED, KNOWN OR ADMIRED
A TRUMPET FOR REASON
THE JOYS OF YIDDISH
A MOST PRIVATE INTRIGUE
THE MANY WORLDS OF LEO ROSTEN
CAPTAIN NEWMAN, M.D.
RELIGIONS IN AMERICA (ED.)
THE STORY BEHIND THE PAINTING
THE RETURN OF H*Y*M*A*N K*A*P*L*A*N
A GUIDE TO THE RELIGIONS OF AMERICA (ED.)
THE DARK CORNER
SLEEP, MY LOVE
112 GRIPES ABOUT THE FRENCH (WAR DEPARTMENT)
HOLLYWOOD: THE MOVIE COLONY, THE MOVIE MAKERS
DATELINE: EUROPE
THE STRANGEST PLACES
THE WASHINGTON CORRESPONDENTS
THE EDUCATION OF H*Y*M*A*N K*A*P*L*A*N

INFINITE RICHES

Gems from a Lifetime of Reading

LEO ROSTEN

McGraw-Hill Book Company

| New York | St. Louis | San Francisco | London |
| Mexico | Sydney | Toronto | Düsseldorf |

1 2 3 4 5 6 7 8 9 0 B P B P 7 8 3 2 1 0 9

Library of Congress Cataloging in Publication Data

Main entry under title:
Infinite riches.
Includes index.
1. Anthologies.   I. Rosten, Leo Calvin, date
PN6014.I48   808.8   78–8623
ISBN 0–07–053983–9

ACKNOWLEDGMENTS AND THANKS TO:

George Allen & Unwin, Ltd., for excerpts from:
  Gandhi—His Own Story by Mohandas K. Gandhi, translated and edited by
  C. F. Andrews.
  Human Society in Ethics and Politics by Bertrand Russell.
  The Impact of Science on Society by Bertrand Russell.
American Scholar, Autumn 1971, for excerpts from "The Rehabilitation Myth"
by Albert Nussbaum. Copyright © 1971 by the United Chapters of Phi Beta
Kappa.
Asahi Broadcasting Corporation for excerpts from *Here Is Japan*.
Copyright © 1963 by Asahi Broadcasting Corporation.
Atheneum Publishers, Inc., for excerpts from:
  African Genesis by Robert Ardrey. Copyright © 1961 by Literat, S.A. Re-
  printed by permission of Atheneum Publishers.
  The Image by Daniel J. Boorstin. Copyright © 1961 by Daniel J. Boorstin.
  Reprinted by permission of Atheneum Publishers.
  Who Killed Humpty-Dumpty? by Donald Barr. Copyright © 1971 by Donald
  Barr. Reprinted by permission of Atheneum Publishers.
  Day of Trinity by Lansing Lamont. Copyright © 1965 by Lansing Lamont.
  Reprinted by permission of Atheneum Publishers.
Luigi Barzini for excerpts from an article in the *Times Literary Supplement*,
October 3, 1975, by Luigi Barzini.
Basic Books, Inc., Publishers, for excerpts from:
  The Interpretation of Dreams by Sigmund Freud, translated by James Strachey.
  Published in the U.S. by Basic Books, Inc., Publishers, by arrangement with
  George Allen & Unwin, Ltd., and The Hogarth Press, Ltd.
  "The Public Household: On 'Fiscal Sociology' and the Liberal Society,"
  Chapter 6 in *The Cultural Contradictions of Capitalism* by Daniel Bell. Copy-
  right © 1976 by Daniel Bell.
  The Collected Papers of Sigmund Freud, Vol. 2, translated by Joan Riviere.
  Published by Basic Books, Inc., Publishers, by arrangement with The Hogarth
  Press, Ltd., and the Institute of Psychoanalysis, London.

(*continued on page 550*)

C. 2

For future reading
by
Joshua, Pamela, Benjamin,
Carrie, Seth and Alexander

TO THE READER

I bring you treasures: the most arresting, profound or enchanting passages I found in the kingdom of print through which I have wandered for over fifty years.

My assemblage is, I confess, shamelessly diverse—and often downright peculiar. This does not surprise me: I was born a slave to the djinns of curiosity. I am a hopeless *naïf*, spellbound by the history of the umbrella or the floating lanterns of Japan. I become transfixed by Lytton Strachey's description of the death in Khartoum of "Chinese" Gordon, or by a chemist's description of what really happens when you strike a match. You can hold me in thrall by explaining the way snowflakes are formed of crystal droplets in their six-mile voyage down to earth, or the way doges and courtesans paraded during the golden age of Venice, or why in March, in Mesopotamia, dogs literally are red and yellow and blue. I am moved to tears by Masefield's account of the embarkation of England's shining youth to the horrors of Gallipoli and moved to horror by the "human towers" that dotted the plains of Asia in the wake of the Mongol horde. My free will is simply paralyzed by Eddington or Machiavelli, Einstein or Freud.

So this is a book of soaring variety. It is an album for browsing, a sampler of human genius and human folly, a chronicle of splendor and passion and utter lunacy. It is *exactly* the bedside reader I so often wished someone would give me on my birthday.

I think you will find my garnering a succession of surprises: astonishing facts, stupendous ideas, hair-raising scenes, and a cast of characters who simply border on the impossible. What novelist could invent a Leonardo da Vinci, or Caligula, or Isaac Newton? Which playwright could hope to equal von Frisch's discovery of the language-dance of the bees—or the protocol that required 383 (!) noblemen to serve Louis XVI his dinner? What mortal imagination could bring forth the arrogant absurdities of Lord Raglan, the genius of Galileo or Faraday, the cruelties of the Empress Tz'u Hsi, Burton's derring-do in Arabia, the erotic carnival of Catherine the Great, or the obsession that drove Heinrich Schliemann to learn seventeen languages, walk the Andes, hurry to the

Gold Rush, become a U.S. citizen in Indianapolis, then go to unearth, in Anatolia, seven layers of buried cities down to Homer's Troy? History makes fiction look anemic.

I have not included excerpts from poetry, nor from many novels, nor from Shakespeare, nor from the Bible. Our libraries are already crammed with such anthologies.

I have excluded passages and witticisms which have become so familiar as to seem shopworn. Hence the absence from these pages of pages and pages I greatly admire in, say, Aristotle, Gibbon, de Tocqueville, Plutarch, Churchill, Freud. I *do* offer excerpts from these authors, but they are passages that, to my mind, are usually neglected.

I take special pleasure in my selections from writers who are little read today: Livy and Eusebius, Erasmus and Chesterton, James Anthony Froude and the incomparable Voltaire.

I have enlivened the text with some of the funniest one-liners I ever read and some of the funniest paragraphs. I hope you will be as grateful as I am for the laughter tendered us by the likes of H. L. Mencken, Josh Billings or George Mikes (pronounced "Mik-esh").

I have edited some of the longer passages very freely, because I am certain that the excision of outdated references and deadly details suddenly endow a style with a pungency that was strangled in translation. I take full blame for my surgery. Why, in reading Scripture, I even skip right over the "begat"s.

Please do not send me irate complaints about my failure to include *even one word* from Millard Fillmore, who certainly excelled in breathing, or Shmerel Kalyika, who invented the knuckle. And please do not ask me to justify my many excerpts from the great Macaulay, or Bamber Gascoigne, or Ronald Hingley—and merely one line from Theophrastus Bombastus ("Paracelsus"), or the Comtesse du Farfel. You must resign yourself to the fact that this treasury is entirely and intensely arbitrary. *De gustibus* et cetera.

Please do not leap to nasty conclusions when you see how sparse is the number of entries under, say, *Thomas Jefferson* or *Edmund Burke*. Their insights are strewn throughout this work, but under

Democracy, Freedom, Power, and so on. The same arrangement applies to Plato, Rochefoucauld, peerless Mark Twain.

Finally, I call your attention to certain unorthodox headings, which I dreamed up because the selections I wanted to use just did not fit well anywhere else: *Acerbities,* for instance, gave me a perfect basket for epigrams on everything from Darwin to evening gowns, from writers as far removed as "Kin" Hubbard and Madame de Staël. *Incredibilities* is a dandy catch-all for mind-boggling deeds.

And so: Good reading to you, good browsing, good gawking —and frequent laughter. An essay I once wrote, "Creativity and Science," began:

> The history of man's politics is a shameful chronicle of violence and vanity—laced with endless greed, inflated ambitions and parochial fears.
> The history of man's beliefs is an absurd story of ignorance, credulity, infantile terrors and magical beguilements.
> The history of man's ideas is a story of stupendous stupidity, relieved by the occasional, sparkling eruption of original minds.

In one sense, the book you hold in your hands is a tribute to the occasional and sparkling eruptions that have enriched the human race.

LEO ROSTEN

Ward 7
New York

To hold our interest you must tell us something we believe to be true about the men who once walked the earth. It is the fact about the past that is poetic; just because it really happened, it garners round it all the inscrutable mystery of life and death and time. Let the science and research of the historian find the fact, and let his imagination and art make clear its significance.

—GEORGE MACAULAY TREVELYAN,
The Present Position of History

THE ABACUS

Sometime after World War II, there was a public contest between an electronic computer and a Japanese abacus. The abacus won all phases of the contest with the exception of division, where the abacus required a person of remarkable skill, while the electronic computer could be operated by anyone with ordinary technical skill. However, the use of electronic computers has become widespread in Japan.

—Here is Japan, guidebook published by
Asahi Broadcasting Corporation

ACERBITIES

Her features didn't seem to know the value of teamwork.

□

She's the kind of woman who is used for augmenting the grief at a funeral.

□

"Whom are you?" said he, for he had been to night school.

—George Ade

The man was so small he was a waste of skin.

□

What's on your mind? If you'll forgive the overstatement.

—Fred Allen

Minneapolis: a suburb—according to St. Paul.

—Anon.

Population explosion: when people take leave of their census.

—Anon.

It is amazing how nice people are to you when they know you're going away.

—Michael Arlen

There is something about saying "O.K." and hanging up the receiver with a bang that kids a man into feeling that he has just pulled off a big deal, even if he has only called to find the correct time.

—ROBERT BENCHLEY

Bore: someone who talks when you want him to listen.

□

Epitaph: an inscription on a tomb, showing that virtues acquired by death have a retroactive effect.

□

Take not God's name in vain; select a time when it will have effect.

—AMBROSE BIERCE

It is the little things that fret and worry us; you can dodge an elephant, but not a fly.

□

Nature never blunders; when she makes a fool she means it.

—JOSH BILLINGS

His mind is open—so open that ideas simply pass through it.

—F. H. BRADLEY

How holy people look when they are sea-sick!

□

There should be asylums for habitual teetotalers, but they would probably relapse into teetotalism as soon as they came out.

□

'Tis better to have loved and lost than never to have lost at all.

—SAMUEL BUTLER

A yawn is a silent shout.

—G. K. CHESTERTON

You couldn't tell if she was dressed for an opera or an operation.

—IRVIN S. COBB

I have never wanted to see anybody die, but there are a few obituary notices I have read with great pleasure.

□

When I was a boy I was told that anybody could become President; now I'm beginning to believe it.

—CLARENCE DARROW

He has not a single redeeming defect.

—DISRAELI, of Gladstone

Man is ready to die for an idea—provided the idea is not quite clear to him.

—PAUL ELDRIDGE

He's so mean he won't let his boy have more than one measle at a time.

—EUGENE FIELD

A diplomat is a man who always remembers a woman's birthday but never remembers her age.

☐

The reason worry kills more people than work is that more people worry than work.

—ROBERT FROST

He's not worth her wiles.

—JOHN GALSWORTHY

He wasn't hostile to facts; he was apathetic about them.

—WOLCOTT GIBBS

No one can have a higher opinion of him than I have, and I think he is a dirty little beast.

☐

Saturday afternoon, although occurring at regular and well-foreseen intervals, always takes this railway by surprise.

—W. S. GILBERT

Grammar school never taught me anything about grammar.

—ISAAC GOLDBERG

I never said all Democrats were saloonkeepers; I said all saloonkeepers were democrats.

—HORACE GREELEY

Acting: John Wayne demonstrating facial isometrics, based on newly discovered manuscripts of Calvin Coolidge.

—Harvard *Lampoon*

Generally, he is insane, but he has lucid moments, when he is merely stupid.

—HEINRICH HEINE

Don't stop me if you've heard this one before. There is no reason why a joke should not be appreciated more than once. Imagine how little good music there would be if, for example, a conductor refused to play Beethoven's Fifth Symphony on the ground that his audience might have heard it before.

—A. P. HERBERT

Only the young die good.

—OLIVER HERFORD

There's one thing about baldness: It's neat.

—DON HEROLD

The average man's judgment is so poor, he runs a risk every time he uses it.

—EDGAR WATSON ("ED") HOWE

Wrong no man and write no woman.

—ELBERT HUBBARD

Nobody ever forgets where he buried a hatchet.

☐

The safest way to double your money is to fold it once and put it in your pocket.

☐

There's somebody at every dinner party who eats all the celery.

—FRANK MCKINNEY ("KIN") HUBBARD

The three major administrative problems on a campus are sex for the students, athletics for the alumni, and parking for the faculty.

—ROBERT M. HUTCHINS

Many a man in love with a dimple makes the mistake of marrying the whole girl.

—STEPHEN LEACOCK

He was born stupid, and greatly increased his birthright.

□

He was dull in a new way; that made many think him great.

□

This man [Lord Chesterfield] I thought had been a Lord among wits, but, I find, he is only a wit among Lords.

—SAMUEL JOHNSON

Freedom of the press is guaranteed only to those who own one.

—A. J. LIEBLING

If this is coffee, please bring me some tea; but if this is tea, please bring me some coffee.

—ABRAHAM LINCOLN

An idea isn't responsible for the people who believe it.

□

A hypocrite is a person who—but who isn't?

□

He is so unlucky that he runs into accidents which started out to happen to somebody else.

—DON MARQUIS

It is a sin to believe evil of others, but it is seldom a mistake.

□

It is hard to believe that a man is telling the truth when you know that you would lie if you were in his place.

—H. L. MENCKEN

To my embarrassment, I was born in bed with a lady.

—WILSON MIZNER

I despise the pleasure of pleasing people whom I despise.

—LADY MARY WORTLEY MONTAGU

In Ireland there is so little sense of compromise that a girl has to choose between perpetual adoration and perpetual pregnancy.

—GEORGE MOORE

Kleptomaniac: a person who helps himself because he can't help himself.

—HENRY MORGAN

No man is lonely while eating spaghetti—it takes so much attention.

—CHRISTOPHER MORLEY

[He] is one of those people who would be enormously improved by death.

—H. H. MUNRO (SAKI)

He writes his plays for the ages—the ages between five and twelve.

—GEORGE JEAN NATHAN

A gentleman never heard the story before.

□

An Englishman thinks while seated; a Frenchman, standing; an American, pacing; an Irishman, afterward.

—AUSTIN O'MALLEY

You can lead a horticulture, but you can't make her think.

—DOROTHY PARKER

Artificial insemination: copulation without representation.

—*Playboy*

The ignorance of French society gives one a rough sense of the infinite.

—JOSEPH ERNEST RENAN

We often forgive those who bore us, but we cannot forgive those whom we bore.

—ROCHEFOUCAULD

Everybody is ignorant, only on different subjects.

□

The only time people dislike gossip is when you gossip about them.

—WILL ROGERS

I heard him speak disrespectfully of the equator.

—SYDNEY SMITH

While he was not dumber than an ox he was not any smarter either.

—JAMES THURBER

He charged nothing for his preaching, and it was worth it.

□

His money is twice tainted; 'taint yours and 'taint mine.

—MARK TWAIN

The art of medicine consists of amusing the patient while Nature cures the disease.

—VOLTAIRE

He is every other inch a gentleman.

—REBECCA WEST

He has not an enemy in the world, but none of his friends like him.

□

She is a peacock in everything but beauty.

—OSCAR WILDE

I could see that, if not actually disgruntled, he was far from being gruntled.

□

The butler entered the room, a solemn procession of one.

—P. G. WODEHOUSE

Early in life, I had to choose between honest arrogance and hypocritical humility. I chose honest arrogance, and have seen no reason to change.

—FRANK LLOYD WRIGHT

ACTORS

The scenery in the play was beautiful, but the actors got in front of it.

—ALEXANDER WOOLLCOTT

On the stage he was natural, simple, affecting; it was only when he was off that he was acting.

—OLIVER GOLDSMITH

Actors are the only honest hypocrites. . . . They wear the livery of other men's fortunes: Their very thoughts are not their own.

—WILLIAM HAZLITT

They are part of the geology of dreams that made Joan Didion, meeting John Wayne for the first time, realize with a start that his face was more familiar than her husband's. . . . These larger-than-life people have spent their lives as professional incarnations of our fantasies, and have at last earned the right to be incarnations of themselves.

—JACK KROLL, *Newsweek,* October 27, 1975

People you can identify by the glazed look that comes into their eyes when the conversation wanders away from themselves.

—MICHAEL WILDING

ADAM AND EVE

I cannot help feeling disappointed in Adam and Eve. That is, in their temperaments. Not in *them,* poor helpless young creatures—afflicted with temperaments made out of butter; which butter was commanded to get into contact with fire and *be melted.* What I cannot help wishing is, that Adam and Eve had been postponed, and Martin Luther and Joan of Arc put in their place—that splendid pair equipped with temperaments not made of butter, but of asbestos. By neither sugary persuasions nor by hell fire could Satan have beguiled *them* to eat the apple.

There would have been results! Indeed, yes. The apple would be intact to-day; there would be no human race; there would be no *you;* there would be no *me.* And the old, old creation-dawn scheme of ultimately launching me into the literary guild would have been defeated.

—MARK TWAIN
"The Turning Point of My Life,"
Harper's Bazaar, 1910

Adam and Eve had many advantages, but the principal one was that they escaped teething.

—MARK TWAIN

ADOLESCENCE

Don't laugh at a youth for his affectations; he is only trying on one face after another to find his own.

—LOGAN PEARSALL SMITH

Some adolescents temporarily take a perverse kind of pride in making no sense to anyone—least of all to those immediately concerned with them. Always, however, they secretly strive to make sense to some people of their own choice, even if these persons are somewhere on the "undesirable" periphery of their family, their class, or their neighborhood. This is often misunderstood as aimless rebellion or mere egotism, while in many ways it is a search for new loyalties and for new techniques of living.

—ERIK H. ERIKSON and KAI T. ERIKSON,
in *Psychoanalysis and Social Science,*
ed. H. M. RUITENBECK

The old believe everything, the middle-aged suspect everything, the young know everything.

—OSCAR WILDE

Adolescent: a teen-ager who acts like a baby when you don't treat him like an adult.

—ANON.

The adolescent, though given to aggression and lust, is emotionally cold, and ratiocination can be a substitute for feeling.

ANTHONY BURGESS, *Urgent Copy*

Since adolescents are too old to do the things kids do and not old enough to do things adults do, they do things nobody else does.

—ANON.

A child's suffering can be very real and very deep and all the worse since a child has neither the wisdom nor the resources of mature men and women. His misery fills the whole of his world, leaving no space for other things. He has only emotions with no cynicism or resignation to dull the edges of his jealousy or suffering. Those people who think of adolescence as a happy, carefree time either possess deficient emotions or inadequate memories.

—Louis Bromfield, *The Wild Country*

... The married adolescent was to become one of the most prominent types of our time, dictating its values, its appetites and its customs. Thus our society has passed from a period ... ignorant of adolescence to a period in which adolescence is the favorite age. We now want to come to it early and linger in it as long as possible.

□

To every period of history, there corresponded a privileged age and a particular division of human life: "youth" is the privileged age of the seventeenth century, "childhood" of the nineteenth, "adolescence" of the twentieth.

—Philippe Ariès, *Centuries of Childhood*

An adolescent in his round of joyless promiscuity is no more a revolutionary than a pickpocket is a socialist; he is merely taking adult prerogatives without taking adult responsibility, taking without earning.

Adolescents have always dreamed of this erotic utopia—and, of course, most of them still confine themselves to dreams—but there are more youngsters now who act them out, and they are subject to fewer recriminations from adults than ever before in America. In fact, these youngsters are surrounded by adults crying encouragement—and crying the fantasy wares of sex. Fashion, movies, popular music, fiction both popular and serious, advertising—the environment is dosed with aphrodisiac.

Yet this utopia, like all utopias, is joyless. These "free" youngsters giggle and strut like any youngsters. They ape frustration, ape urgency, ape conquest. They go through the motions of emotion. But there is something inanimate about their pleasures.

—Donald Barr, *Who Killed Humpty-Dumpty?*

ADRIANOPLE: The Harem of the Grand Vizier

The roof was painted with all sorts of flowers, falling out of gilded baskets, that seemed tumbling down. On a sofa, raised three steps, and covered with the fine Persian carpets, sat the kiyaya's (deputy's) lady, leaning on cushions of white satin, embroidered; and at her feet sat two young girls, the eldest about twelve years old, lovely as angels, dressed perfectly rich, and almost covered with jewels. But they were hardly seen near the fair Fatima (for that is her name), so much her beauty effaced everything. I have seen all that has been called lovely in England or Germany, and must own that I never saw anything so gloriously beautiful, nor can I recollect a face that would have been taken notice of near hers. She stood up to receive me, saluting me after their fashion, putting her hand upon her heart with a sweetness full of majesty, that no court breeding could ever give.

□

She was dressed in a *caftan* of gold brocade, flowered with silver, very well fitted to her shape, and showing to advantage the beauty of her bosom, only shaded by the thin gauze of her shift. Her drawers were pale pink, green and silver, her slippers white, finely embroidered, her lovely arms adorned with bracelets of diamonds, and her broad girdle set round with diamonds; upon her head a rich Turkish handkerchief of pink and silver, her own fine black hair hanging a great length in various tresses, and on one side of her head some bodkins of jewels. I am afraid you will accuse me of extravagance in this description. I think I have read somewhere that women always speak in rapture when they speak of beauty, but I cannot imagine why they should not be allowed to do so.... For me, I am not ashamed to own I took more pleasure in looking on the beauteous Fatima than the finest piece of sculpture could have given me.

□

Her fair maids were ranged below the sofa, to the number of twenty, and put me in mind of the pictures of the ancient nymphs. I did not think all nature could have furnished such a scene of beauty. She made them a sign to play and dance. Four of them immediately began to play some soft airs on instruments between a lute and a guitar, which they accompanied with their voices, while the others danced by turns. This dance was very different from what I had seen before. Nothing could be more artful, or more proper to raise certain ideas. The tunes so soft!—the motion so languishing!—accompanied with pauses and dying eyes! half-falling back, and then recovering themselves in so artful a manner that

I am very positive the coldest and most rigid prude upon earth could not have looked upon them without thinking of something not to be spoken of. I suppose you may have read that the Turks have no music but what is shocking to the ears; but this account is from those who never heard any but what is played in the streets, and is just as reasonable as if a foreigner should take his ideas of the English music from the bladder and string, and marrow-bones and cleavers. I can assure you that the music is extremely pathetic; 'tis true I am inclined to prefer the Italian. . . .

When the dance was over, four fair slaves came into the room with silver censers in their hands, and perfumed the air with amber, aloeswood, and other rich scents. After this they served me coffee upon their knees in the finest Japan china, with *soucoupes* of silver, gilt. The lovely Fatima entertained me all this time in the most polite agreeable manner, calling me often *Guzel sultanum*, or the beautiful sultana, and desiring my friendship with the best grace in the world, lamenting that she could not entertain me in my own language. . . . I retired through the same ceremonies as before, and could not help fancying I had been some time in Mahomet's paradise.

—LADY MARY WORTLEY MONTAGU,
*The Letters and Works of
Lady Mary Wortley Montagu*

ADVERTISING

. . . What is needed is a constant intelligence service to outline all the latest tricks in the game, so that people do not get too excited by offers which end up like that "bathing suit 50% off" which turned out to be topless, and the "simple and elegant coathanger" which turned out to be a nail.

—DAVID FROST and ANTONY JAY, *The English*

ADVICE

When a man comes to me for advice, I find out the kind of advice he wants, and I give it to him.

—JOSH BILLINGS

I would tell a man who was drinking too much "Be a man," but I would not tell a crocodile who was eating too many explorers "Be a crocodile."

—G. K. CHESTERTON

People in prosperity so overflow with wisdom (however inexperienced they may be), that they take every offer of advice as a personal insult; but in adversity, they know not where to turn, but beg for counsel from every passer-by.

—BARUCH SPINOZA, *Tractatus Theologica Politicus*

The only thing to do with good advice is to pass it on; it is never of any use to oneself.

□

Never buy a thing you don't want merely because it is dear.

—OSCAR WILDE

"Be yourself!" is the worst advice you can give some people.

—TOM MASSON

A good scare is worth more to a man than good advice.

□

Instead of loving your enemies, treat your friends better.

—EDGAR WATSON ("ED") HOWE

Always do right; this will gratify some people and astonish the rest.

—MARK TWAIN

Of two evils, choose neither.

—CHARLES HADDON SPURGEON, *John Ploughman*

AGNOSTICISM

Another source of conviction in the existence of God . . . follows from the extreme difficulty, or rather impossibility, of conceiving this immense and wonderful universe, including man . . . as the result of blind chance or necessity. When thus reflecting I feel compelled to look to a First Cause. . . .

I deserved to be called a Theist. This conclusion was strong in my mind about the time ... I wrote the "Origin of Species"; and it is since that time that it has very gradually ... become weaker. But then arises the doubt: Can the mind of man, which has, as I fully believe, been developed from a mind as low as that possessed by the lowest animals, be trusted when it draws such grand conclusions?

I cannot pretend to throw the least light on such abstruse problems. The mystery of the beginning of all things is insoluble by us; and I for one must be content to remain an Agnostic.

—CHARLES DARWIN, *Letters of Charles Darwin*

AGRIPPINA (15?–59 A.D.)

Agrippina's passion for power carried her so fast that at midday, the time when food and drink raised Nero's temperature, she several times appeared before her inebriate son, finely dressed and ready for incest. Their companions observed the sensual kisses and evil caresses.

Seneca, supposing that the answer to a woman's enticements was a woman, called in the ex-slave Acte, but she feared for Nero's reputation—and her own safety. She was instructed to warn Nero that Agrippina was boasting everywhere of her intimacy with her son, and that the army would never tolerate so sacrilegious an emperor.

—TACITUS, *The Annals of Imperial Rome*

AGRIPPINA'S DEATH

The murderers closed around her bed. First the captain struck her head with a truncheon; then as the lieutenant drew his sword, she cried: "Strike here!" pointing to her womb. Blow after blow fell, and she died.

Some say Nero inspected his mother's corpse and praised her figure; but that is contested. She was cremated that night, on a dining couch, with but meagre ceremony. . . .

This was the end Agrippina had anticipated for years. The prospect had not daunted her. When she had asked astrologers about

Nero, they answered that he would become emperor but would kill his mother. Her reply was, "Let him kill me—provided he becomes emperor!"

—*Ibid.*

AKBAR THE GREAT (1542–1605): Emperor of Hindustan

As his reign progressed Akbar continued to make deliberate concessions to Hindu customs—introducing their festivals at court and having newly washed and painted cows brought into his presence after Diwali, letting his hair grow long in a Hindu fashion and adopting a Rajput style of turban, even on occasions wearing the *tilak*, the Hindu sectarial or ornamental mark made on the forehead—until the more orthodox Muslims became convinced that the emperor had abandoned their faith.

There were, of course, sound political reasons for all this. Akbar could look back on nine successive Muslim dynasties in India before his, which had lasted on average less than forty years each, and he was shrewd enough to see that any stable rule in India must enjoy the consent of both religious groups.

—BAMBER GASCOIGNE, *The Great Moghuls*

AKHENATON (1388–1358 B.C.) (Amenhotep IV)

[James H.] Breasted called him the "world's first individual," and this has a useful meaning. Even when allowance is made for continuity in Akhenaton's social environment, family origins, and historical setting, the art and scripts of his reign suggest that he was so original, so unlike any predecessor known to have been similarly situated, that he must have experienced an intense and sustained sense of his own uniqueness, of his unusual mission, and probably of his historical "failure."

One can hardly avoid conceiving him as a highly self-conscious person, vividly aware that his own nature compelled him to follow strange paths, for he sought to uproot one religion and to establish another; he built a new capital at Amarna to symbolize this change and, though supremely powerful, he refused to make war to save his Empire. He may have been a neurotic epileptic and politically weak; he certainly displayed originality of an order for which there is no precedent in the known records.

—LANCELOT LAW WHYTE,
The Unconscious Before Freud

AKIBA (40–135) (Rabbi Akiba Ben Joseph)

Akiba was found guilty and condemned to death. Still attended by his faithful Joshua, he retained his courage and his strength of mind until the very end. The popular story tells that the Romans killed him by tearing his flesh from his living body. As he lay in unspeakable agony, he suddenly noticed the first streaks of dawn breaking over the eastern hills. It was the hour when the Law requires each Jew to pronounce the *Shema*. Oblivious to his surroundings, Akiba intoned in a loud, steady voice the forbidden words of his faith, "Hear, O Israel, the Lord is our God, the Lord is One. And thou shalt love the Lord thy God with all thine heart, and with all thy soul, and with all thy might."

Rufus, the Roman general, who superintended the horrible execution, cried out: "Are you a wizard or are you utterly insensible to pain?"

"I am neither," replied the martyr, "but all my life I have been waiting for the moment when I might truly fulfill this commandment. I have always loved the Lord with all my might, and with all my heart; now I know that I love him with all my life." And, repeating the verse again, he died as he reached the words, "The Lord is One."

The scene, indelibly impressed on the eyes of Joshua ha-Garsi, became part of Jewish tradition. The association of the *Shema* with the great martyr's death made its recitation a deathbed affirmation of the faith, instead of a repetition of select verses; and to this day the pious Jew hopes that when his time comes he may be sufficiently conscious to declare the Unity of his God, echoing with his last breath the words which found their supreme illustration in Akiba's martyrdom.

—LOUIS FINKELSTEIN, *Akiba*

ALAMOGORDO: July 16, 1945

A pinprick of a brilliant light punctured the darkness, spurted upward in a flaming jet, then spilled into a dazzling cloche of fire that bleached the desert to a ghastly white. It was precisely 5:29:45 A.M. (July 16, 1945).... Across the test site everything suddenly became infinitely tiny. Men burrowed into the sand like ants. Oppenheimer in that blinding instant thought of fragments from the sacred Hindu epic, Bhagavad-Gita:

> If the radiance of a thousand suns
> Were to burst at once into the sky,
> That would be like the splendor of the
>   Mighty One...
> I am become Death,
> The shatterer of worlds.

For a fraction of a second the light in that bell-shaped fire mass was greater than any ever produced before on earth. Its intensity was such that it could have been seen from another planet. The temperature at its center was four times that at the center of the sun and more than 10,000 times that at the sun's surface. The pressure, caving in the ground beneath, was over 100 billion atmospheres, the most ever to occur at the earth's surface. The radioactivity emitted was equal to one million times that of the world's total radium supply.

No living thing touched by that raging furnace survived. Within a millisecond the fireball had struck the ground, flattening out at its base and acquiring a skirt of molten black dust that boiled and billowed in all directions. Within twenty-five milliseconds the fireball had expanded to a point where the Washington Monument would have been enveloped. At eight-tenths of a second the ball's white-hot dome had topped the Empire State Building. The shock wave caromed across the roiling desert.

Human response may have been the same as on that first dawn in the basement of time when Man discovered fire; fright at first, giving way to impetuous curiosity, then an awed realization of the phenomenon and, finally, primitive glee.

Men turned to look at the fireball, inflated now a half-mile wide, and wondered if it would ever stop growing. In their excitement many threw off their dark glasses and instantly lost sight of what they had waited years to see. At Base Camp there were silent hand-clasps and murmurs of amazement; at South-10,000, a squabble of excited voices that rose to a deafening din; and on Compania Hill, a piercing whoop followed by a mad jig that suggested to one observer the fire rites of prehistoric savages.

—Lansing Lamont, *Day of Trinity*

... While man the scientist was developing his first aerial bomb—a bomb that would one day be charged with enough explosive to wipe out 100,000 people—the tiny flea wiped out ten million in India alone.

—James Clark, *Man is the Prey*

POPE ALEXANDER VI (1431–1503) (Rodrigo Borgia)

Alexander's character has undoubtedly gained by the scrutiny of modern historians. It was but natural that one accused of so many crimes, and unquestionably the cause of many scandals, should alternately appear as a tyrant and a voluptuary. Neither description suits him. The groundwork of his character was extreme exuberance of nature. The Venetian ambassador calls him a carnal man, not implying anything morally derogatory, but meaning a man of sanguine temperament, unable to control his passions and emotions. This perplexed the cool unimpassioned Italians of the diplomatic type then prevalent among rulers and statesmen, and their apprehensions have unduly prejudiced Alexander, who in truth was not less but more human than most princes of his time. This excessive "carnality" wrought in him for good and ill. Unrestrained by moral scruples, or by any spiritual conception of religion, he was betrayed by it into gross sensuality of one kind, though in other respects he was temperate and abstemious. ... On the other hand his geniality and joyousness preserved him from tyranny in the ordinary sense of the term. ... As a ruler, careful of the material weal of his people, he ranks among the best of his age; as a practical statesman he was the equal of any contemporary. But his insight was impaired by his lack of political morality; he had nothing of the higher wisdom which comprehends the characteristics and foresees the drift of an epoch, and he did not know what a principle was.

—RICHARD GARNETT,
in *The Cambridge Modern History*, Vol. I

Besides this refined tactical wisdom, and the resolution that betokened the man of action, his experience inclined him towards that spirit of tolerance which—the age being in many respects a fiercely barbarous one—was to win him much sympathy, and mitigate the spiteful verdicts pronounced on him. Rodrigo was to demonstrate this characteristic in the political arena, over matters regarding freedom of thought, and at the level of ordinary day-to-day news —protecting Rome's Jewish refugees, showing remarkable patience in his attitude to Savonarola (though the friar's obstinacy produced a clash in the end), annulling the condemnation pronounced by Innocent VIII against Pico della Mirandola, and allowing Rome's poisonous scandalmongers to decry him as they chose. "Rome is free territory, and Romans have a habit of saying and writing whatever takes their fancy. Even if they speak ill of His Holiness, they are not silenced"—the words are those of Alexander VI himself.

—CLEMENTE FUSERO, *The Borgias*

ALEXANDER I OF RUSSIA (1777–1825)

Alexander I [reached] the summit of his career on 19 March 1814, when he rode into Paris acclaimed by many peoples for his martial prowess and magnanimity in victory. Hailed as an Agamemnon among kings and as the savior of Europe, the Russian Emperor was above all the conqueror of Napoleon, to whose defeat he had perhaps made a larger contribution than any other individual. The Tsar entered Paris with princes, generals and statesmen from many parts of Europe, all of whom he far outshone in the splendor of his achievement and imperial presence. Tall, fair, blue-eyed, imposing and celebrated for his good looks, he rode the light gray mare Eclipse—Napoleon's present from the days of their alliance—and was flanked by the glittering Cossacks of his escort. The event was all the more spectacular in marking so dramatic a reversal of fate, taking place as it did less than eighteen months after Napoleon's

own victorious ride into Moscow of September 1812. But the
Russian's was the more brilliant triumph. In Paris, Alexander was
surrounded by international pageantry at its most splendid, not
by empty streets, burning buildings and the smell of future defeat.
The girls of Moscow had never mobbed Napoleon, but excited
Parisiennes pressed through Alexander's escort and persuaded his
officers to hoist them on the cruppers of their horses so that they
could see the Russian Emperor....

At the Congress of Vienna, Alexander played the role of victor-
in-chief in a dazzling pageant of negotiations, receptions, banquets
and intrigues both diplomatic and amorous. On the European stage
he had graduated from inexperienced *jeune premier* to seasoned
matinee idol, well equipped to put such veteran performers as
Metternich, Talleyrand and Wellington in the shade. Napoleon
himself paid tribute to the Tsar's histrionic talents ... Napoleon
further stressed Alexander's subtle deviousness in negotiation by
calling him a Byzantine Greek; and also paid the more dubious
compliment of saying that if Alexander had been a woman, then
he, Napoleon, would have fallen in love with him.

—RONALD HINGLEY, *The Tsars*

AMBIVALENCE

The mother or nurse not only indulges the infant and the young
child, but denies; hence the mother is both "good" and "bad" to
the child (whose attitude is thus ambivalent). The basis of depression is laid when the child is deprived of the loved one (as by
death), and responds regressively, that is, by seeking to substitute
fantasy for reality. The "good" mother is fondly remembered as
the perfectly indulgent mother; but at the same time the rage at
the "bad" mother is turned against the self. Hence the individual
in extreme cases punishes a part of his personality on behalf of another part of his personality. When children undergo great deprivations during phases of great ambivalence, they often respond
through this depressive mechanism. Subsequently they love persons
after the ambivalent patterns of infancy; and if they are not constantly supplied with love, rage gets the upper hand, but this rage
is internalized in the form of depression and perhaps even suicide.

—HAROLD D. LASSWELL,
Politics—Who Gets What, When, How

AMERICAN GUILT

The feeling of guilt has aptly been termed one of America's few remaining surplus commodities. Ubiquitous and repeated allegations that the West is responsible for the poverty of the so-called Third World both reflect and strengthen this feeling of guilt. Yet while such allegations have come to be widely accepted, often as axiomatic, they are not only untrue, but more nearly the opposite of the truth. Their acceptance has nevertheless paralyzed Western diplomacy, both toward the Soviet bloc and toward the Third World, where the West has abased itself before groups of countries which have negligible resources and no real power.

—PETER BAUER, *Commentary*, January 1976

THE AMERICAN INDIAN

... despite vast study by scientists and a voluminous literature of modern knowledge about Indians, still common are ignorance and misconceptions, many of them resulting from the white man's continuing inability to regard Indians save from his own European-based point of view.

Today most Indians on both continents have been conquered and enfolded within the conquerors' own cultures; but the span of time since the various phases of the conquest ended has been short, and numerous Indians still cling to traits that are centuries, if not millennia, old and cannot be quickly shed. Many Indians, for instance, still do not understand or cannot accept the concept of private ownership of land; many do not understand the need to save for the future, a fundamental requirement of the economies of their conquerors; many find it difficult, if not impossible so far, to substitute individual competitiveness for group feeling; many do not see the necessity for working the year round if they can provide for their families by six months of work, or the reason for cutting the earth-mother with a plow and farming if they can still hunt, fish, and dig roots. Many yet feel a sacred attachment to the land and a reverence for nature that is incomprehensible to most whites. Many, though Christian, find repugnance in the idea that man possesses dominion over the birds and beasts, and believe still that man is brother to all else that is living.

Such ideas, among a multitude that continue to hold numerous Indians apart from non-Indians, are either unrecognized or frowned upon by most whites today. Those who are aware of them are more often than not irritated by their persistence, yet the stubbornness of the white critics' own culture to survive, if a totally alien way of life, like that of the Chinese Communists, were to be forced upon them, would be understood.

—ALVIN M. JOSEPHY, JR.,
The Indian Heritage of America

AMERICANS

America is incredibly likable as a nation, which is in itself a triumph for a land of such power. The British in their heyday were never likable, except as individuals. To tell the French that they are likable, even today, is to insult them, whereas the Germans would greet the allegation with disbelief, and the Russians would submit themselves to self-criticism to find out where they had slipped up. Only the Americans consider such a claim as normal—in no way complimentary.

—PETER USTINOV, *Saturday Review*, December 13, 1975

America: a country whose youth is one of her oldest and most hallowed traditions.

—OSCAR WILDE

AMERICA'S NAME

Strange, that the New World should have no better luck—that broad America must wear the name of a thief. Amerigo Vespucci, the pickle-dealer at Seville, who went out, in 1499, a subaltern with Hojeda, and whose highest naval rank was boatswain's mate in an expedition that never sailed, managed in this lying world to supplant Columbus and baptize half the earth with his own dishonest name.

—RALPH WALDO EMERSON, *Collected Works*, Vol. V

AMUSEMENTS OF THE MIGHTY

Among Anne's [niece of Peter the Great] favorite amusements was the ordering of whimsical marriages, and one of these contributed an especially gaudy splash of color to her reign. Though the groom bore a proud name as one of the many Princes Golitsyn, he served the Empress as a buffoon, and she thought it amusing to marry him to another court butt—an outstandingly hideous Calmuck woman.

For this purpose Anne ordered the construction of an ice palace on the frozen Neva. With its glacial columns, statues and balcony, it was over twenty feet high and nearly three hundred feet long. Ingenious *tableaux* wrought in colored ice graced the scene and included a life-sized elephant mounted by an ice man in Persian dress, with a real man hidden inside to simulate the creature's trumpetings. Lit by countless candles, blocks of ice covered with blazing oil and ice dolphins spewing fire, the crystalline edifice offered a scintillating spectacle, but cold comfort to a bride and groom immured inside for the night after the ceremony with sentries posted to prevent escape. It says much for their ability to take a joke that both survived the rigors of the nuptial slab. A lavish carnival accompanied this grotesque pageant, vividly illustrating the length to which Anne could carry expensive buffoonery—and a reminder that her court was spending over half of the national income. Perhaps it was fortunate that an Empress with such tastes left the ruling of Russia to others, however harsh and grasping.

—RONALD HINGLEY, *op. cit.*

ANCESTRY

Snobs talk as if they had begotten their ancestors.

—ALFRED ADLER

Every king springs from a race of slaves, and every slave has had kings among his ancestors.

—PLATO, *Theatetus*

Certain it is, birth makes no more difference between one man and another than between an ass whose sire carried dung and an ass whose father carried relicks. Education makes a great difference, talents make a greater, and fortune the greatest of all.

—VOLTAIRE, *Observations on History*, tr. T. SMOLLETT, T. FRANCKLIN, others, 1762

ENGLAND

The great distinction between the English aristocracy and any other has always been that, whereas abroad every other member of a noble family is noble, in England none are noble except the head of the family. In spite of the fact that they enjoy courtesy titles, the sons and daughters of lords are commoners.... The descendants of younger sons, who, on the Continent would all be counts or barons, in England have no titles....

□

Ancestry has never counted much in England. The English lord knows himself to be such a very genuine article that, when looking for a wife ... [he seeks] large tracts of town property more than Norman blood. He marries for love and is rather inclined to love where money is; he rarely marries in order to improve his coat of arms.

—NANCY MITFORD, "The English Aristocracy," in *Encounter*, Fall 1955

ANESTHESIA

... anesthesia proved to be a mixed blessing. With totally unconscious subjects to work on, surgeons became excessively daring and their work actually declined in finesse.

... filthy procedure was typical treatment for accident victims, through whose begrimed limbs, wrote Dr. Stephen Smith, one-time New York City health commissioner, "the surgeon was apt to pass his knife ... conveying to the deepest part of the wound, matters of untold septic virulence."

—OTTO L. BETTMAN, *The Good Old Days*

AN ANTARCTIC BLIZZARD

There is something extravagantly insensate about an Antarctic blizzard at night. Its vindictiveness cannot be measured on an anemometer sheet. It is more than just wind: It is a solid wall of snow moving at gale force, pounding like a surf. The whole malevolent rush is concentrated upon you as upon a personal enemy. In the senseless explosion of sound you are reduced to a crawling thing on the margin of a disintegrating world; you can't see, you can't hear, you can hardly move.

—RICHARD E. BYRD, *Alone*

ANTONY AND CLEOPATRA

... Caesar and Pompey knew her when she was but a young thing, and knew not then what the world meant; but now she went to Antonius at the age when a woman's beauty is at the prime, and she also of best judgment. So she furnished herself with a world of gifts, stores of gold and silver, and of riches and other sumptuous ornaments, as is credible enough she might bring from so great a house and from so wealthy and rich a realm as Egypt was. But yet she carried nothing with her wherein she trusted more than in herself, and in the charms and the enchantment of her passing beauty and grace.

—PLUTARCH,
The Lives of the Noble Grecians and Romans,
tr. THOMAS NORTH

I do not weep because I have lost you. I shall be joining you soon enough. No, what hurts me is that such a great general as I should be surpassed in courage by a woman.

—MARK ANTONY to CLEOPATRA, in *ibid.*

APOSTLES

Some of the most beautiful passages in the apostolic writings are quotations from pagan authors.

—HENRY T. BUCKLE, Introduction,
The History of Civilization in England

ARCHIMEDES (287–212 B.C.)

It is said that Archimedes, full of pride in his machines, cried, "Give me a place to stand, and I will move the world!" [But] there is no fixed place in the universe: all is rushing about and vibrating in a wild dance. But not for that reason only is Archimedes' saying pontifical. To move the world would mean contravening its laws; but these are strict and invariable.

—MAX BORN, *Physics in My Generation*

ARGUMENT

If you lose in an argument, you can still call your opponent names.

—ELBERT HUBBARD

I hate a quarrel because it interrupts an argument.

—G. K. CHESTERTON

THE ARISTOCRACY

It is almost impossible to picture the deference, the adulation, the extraordinary privileges accorded to the nobility in the first half of the nineteenth century. A peer was above the laws which applied to other men. He could run up debts, and no one could arrest him. When a famous set of roués and spendthrifts, including Beau Brummel, came to grief, only one, Lord Alvanley, survived, "invulnerable in his person from being a peer," wrote Greville. He could commit a criminal offense and no ordinary court had jurisdiction over him.

And the strange, the astonishing fact was that public opinion accorded these privileges not merely with willingness but with enthusiasm. Foreigners were struck by the extraordinary and eager deference paid by the English to their aristocracy. It was, as Richard Monckton Milnes wrote, "a lord-loving country." Honest British merchants quivered with excitement in the presence of a peer, as if they were susceptible young men in the presence of a pretty girl.

☐

The wind of revolution that had blown from France seemed to have died away and in England rank and privilege had never appeared more firmly entrenched. Flattered, adulated, deferred to, with incomes enormously increased by the industrial revolution, and as yet untaxed, all-powerful over a tenantry as yet unenfranchised, subject to no ordinary laws, holding the government of the country firmly in their hands and wielding through their closely knit connections an unchallengeable social power, the milords of England were the astonishment and admiration of Europe.

—Cecil Woodham-Smith, *The Reason Why*

Offending is the aristocratic pleasure.

—Montesquieu

ENGLAND

For all their dissipation there was nothing decadent about these eighteenth-century aristocrats. Their excesses came from too much life, not too little. And it was the same vitality that gave them their predominance in public life. They took on the task of directing England's destinies with the same self-confident vigor that they drank and diced....

Rakes and ladies of fashion intersperse their narratives of intrigue with discussions on politics, on literature, even on morals. For they were not unmoral. Their lapses came from passion, not from principle; and they are liable at times to break out in contrite acknowledgment of guilt and artless resolutions for future improvement....

Though they were worldly, they were not sophisticated. Their elaborate manners masked simple reactions. Like their mode of life, their characters were essentially natural: spontaneous, unintrospective, brimming over with normal feelings, love of home and family, loyalty, conviviality, desire for fame, hero worship, patriotism. And they showed their feelings too. Happy creatures! They lived before the days of the stiff upper lip and the inhibited public-school Englishman. A manly tear stood in their eye at the story of a heroic deed.... It never struck them that they needed to be inarticulate to appear sincere. They were equally frank about their less elevated sentiments....

The Augustan aristocracy, Whig and Tory alike, said what they thought with superb disregard for public opinion. For if they were not original they were independent minded.... They took for granted that you spoke your mind and followed your impulse. If these were odd, they were amused but not disapproving. They enjoyed eccentrics: George Selwyn, who never missed an execution, Beau Brummel, who took three hours to tie his cravat. The firm English soil in which they were rooted, the spacious freedom afforded by their place in the world, allowed personality to flourish in as many bold and fantastic shapes as it pleased.

—DAVID CECIL, *The Young Melbourne*

ARISTOTLE

... Aristotle maintained that women have fewer teeth than men; although he was twice married, it never occurred to him to verify this statement by examining his wives' mouths. He said also that children would be healthier if conceived when the wind is in the north. One gathers that the two Mrs. Aristotles both had to run out and look at the weathercock every evening before going to bed. He states that a man bitten by a mad dog will not go mad, but any other animal will (*Hist. Am.*, 704a); that the bite of the shrew-mouse is dangerous to horses, especially if the mouse is pregnant (*ibid.*, 604b); that elephants suffering from insomnia can be cured by rubbing their shoulders with salt, olive oil, and warm water (*ibid.*, 605a); and so on and so on. Nevertheless, classical dons, who have never observed any animal except the cat and the dog, continue to praise Aristotle for his fidelity to observation.

—BERTRAND RUSSELL, *The Impact of Science on Society*

He did not consult experience, as he should have done, in the framing of his decisions and axioms; but, having first determined the question according to his will, he then resorted to experience, and bending her into conformity with his precepts, led her about like a captive in a procession.

—FRANCIS BACON, *Novum Organum*

ART

Art is a higher type of knowledge than experience.

—ARISTOTLE

Every time I paint a portrait I lose a friend.

—JOHN SINGER SARGENT

All art is a kind of subconscious madness expressed in terms of sanity.

—GEORGE JEAN NATHAN, *The Critic and Drama*

Pictures must not be too picturesque.

—RALPH WALDO EMERSON, *Essays*

Only an auctioneer should admire all schools of art.

—OSCAR WILDE

Art is long, life short, judgment difficult, opportunity transient. To act is easy, to think is hard; to act according to our thought is troublesome. . . . It is but a part of art that can be taught; the artist needs it all.

—GOETHE, *Wilhelm Meister*

I fail to see . . . how the use of novel materials helps, such as glass, tin, strips of lead, stainless steel, and aluminum. The use of these materials may add novel and pleasing effects in connection with architecture but adds nothing to the essential meanings of sculpture, which remain fundamental. The spirit is neglected for detail, for ways and means.

—JACOB EPSTEIN

I do not know why distinctions are made between ancient art and modern art. There is nothing but art. . . .

It does not matter whether a statue was hewn by an archaic Greek or a modern Frenchman. Its only importance is that it should give us here and now the aesthetic thrill and that this aesthetic thrill should move us to work.

—SOMERSET MAUGHAM, *The Summing Up*

Pop art is advertising art advertising itself as art that hates advertising.

—HAROLD ROSENBERG

EXPLANATIONS OF

Everyone wants to "understand" art. Why not try to understand the song of a bird? Why do we love the night, flowers, everything around us, without trying to understand? . .·. Above all, an artist works out of necessity; he himself is only a trivial bit of the world, and no more importance should be attached to him than to many other things which please us in the world, even though we can't explain them. People who try to explain pictures are barking up the wrong tree.

—PABLO PICASSO

Shall I tell you what I think are the two essential qualities of art? It must be indescribable and it must be inimitable.

—PIERRE AUGUSTE RENOIR

Beyond a certain point great art is best accepted, like miracles, without explanation.

—JOHN CANADAY

To analyze a work of art into its elements is as useless as throwing a violet into a crucible.

—PERCY BYSSHE SHELLEY

ART AND ABSURDITY

Not so long ago there was spectacular publicity for a "silent concert" by an unknown pianist. On the announced day the concert hall was full. The virtuoso of silence sat in front of the piano and seemed to play, but the strings had all been taken out, and no sound was produced by the hammers. The listeners looked out of the corners of their eyes at their neighbors.... But their neighbors were impassive, and so they kept their puzzlement to themselves.

After two hours of silence the pianist got up and bowed and, amid loud applause, the concert came to an end.

The next day the pianist told the story on television. "I wanted to see how far human stupidity would go.... There is no limit."

Weakness, I should call it, rather than stupidity. The listeners knew perfectly well that they were listening to nothing, but they were afraid to protest lest they seem to be "squares."

—ANDRÉ MAUROIS, *Open Letter to a Young Man*

ARTISTS:

ARTISTIC TEMPERAMENT

The artist, like the neurotic, had withdrawn from an unsatisfying reality into this world of imagination; but, unlike the neurotic, he knew how to find a way back from it and once more to get a firm foothold in reality. . . . What psychoanalysis was able to do was to take the interrelations between the impressions of the artist's life, his chance experiences and his works, and from them to construct his constitution and the impulses at work in it—that is to say, that part of him which he shared with all men.

—SIGMUND FREUD, *Collected Works*, Vol. II

The artistic temperament is a disease that afflicts amateurs. It is a disease which arises from men not having sufficient power of expression to utter and get rid of the element of art in their being. It is healthful to every sane man to utter the art within him; it is essential to every sane man to get rid of the art within him at all costs. Artists of a large and wholesome vitality get rid of their art easily, as they breathe easily, or perspire easily. But in artists of less force, the thing becomes a pressure, and produces a definite pain, which is called the artistic temperament. Thus, very great artists are able to be ordinary men—men like Shakespeare or Browning. . . .

The great tragedy of the artistic temperament is that it cannot produce any art.

—G. K. CHESTERTON, *Heretics*

THE ATOM

The air in your lungs at this instant is made of atoms—about 10,000,000,000,000,000,000,000 of them. This will do as a figure to end all figures. It is, for example, a good deal more than the number of cells in the brains and bodies of all the 2,500,000,000 inhabitants of the world today, added together. It reminds us that the scale of the pictures we have just drawn is very large, that the atom is very small, and that it has no trouble in getting anywhere.

—JACOB BRONOWSKI, *ABC of the Atom*

ATOMS, STARS AND US

A drop of water contains several thousand million million million atoms. Each atom is about one hundred-millionth of an inch in diameter. Here we marvel at the minute delicacy of the workmanship. But this is not the limit. Within the atom are the much smaller electrons pursuing orbits, like planets around the sun, in a space which relative to their size is no less roomy than the solar system. Nearly midway in scale between the atom and the star there is another structure no less marvelous—the human body.

Man is slightly nearer to the atom than to the star. About 10 atoms build his body; about 10 human bodies constitute enough material to build a star. Man can survey the grandest works of Nature with the astronomer, or the minutest works with the physicist. . . . I ask you to look both ways. For the road to a knowledge of the stars leads through the atom; and important knowledge of the atom has been reached through the stars.

—ARTHUR EDDINGTON, *Stars and Atoms*

SAINT AUGUSTINE (354–430)

I came to Carthage, where an unholy cauldron seethed and bubbled all around me. I was not in love, but I was in love with love. To love, and to be loved, was sweet to me, all the more when I enjoyed the body of the one I loved. . . . I polluted the spring of friendship with the filth of concupiscence; I clouded its lustre with the slime of lust.

☐

I fell abruptly, then, into the love in which I longed to be ensnared. . . . I secretly arrived at the bond of enjoying; and was joyfully bound . . . that I might be scourged with the burning iron rods of jealousy, suspicion, fear, anger, and strife.

☐

I cannot totally grasp all that I am. Thus the mind is not large enough to contain itself: But where can that part of it be which it does not contain? Is it outside itself and not within? How can it not contain itself? As this question struck me, I was overcome with wonder and almost stupor. Here are men going afar to marvel at the heights of mountains, the mighty waves of the sea, the long courses of great rivers, the vastness of the ocean, the movements of the stars, yet leaving themselves unnoticed. . . .

—AUGUSTINE, *Confessions*, Book X

MARCUS AURELIUS (121-180)

Every morning I must tell myself that before the day is over I shall have to deal with a bore, an ingrate, a brute, an imposter.

□

I learned not to busy myself with trifling things, and not to give credit to what was said by miracleworkers and jugglers about incantations and the driving away of demons and such things ... and to endure freedom of speech; and to become intimate with philosophy.

□

The time is at hand when you will have forgotten everything; and the time is at hand when all will have forgotten you. Always reflect that soon you will be no one, and nowhere.

—MARCUS AURELIUS, *Meditations*

AUTHORITY

The question, "Who ought to be boss?" is like asking "Who ought to be the tenor in the quartet?" Obviously, the man who can sing tenor.

—HENRY FORD

Man, whether he likes it or not, is a being forced by his nature to seek some higher authority.

—ORTEGA Y GASSET, *The Revolt of the Masses*

Let every soul be subject unto the higher civil powers. For there is no power but of God; the powers that be are ordained of God. Whosoever therefore resisteth the power, resisteth the ordinance of God; and they that resist shall receive to themselves damnation.

—MARTIN LUTHER, *Table Talk*

AUTOBIOGRAPHY

All good writers of their confessions, from Augustine on, remain a little in love with their sins.

—ANATOLE FRANCE

There is no hiding place so impenetrable as autobiography. ...
The man who hides in silence is never so puzzling as the man who

hides in a perpetual flow of talk ... and any man who is in danger of attention from posterity, and wishes to hide certain things, will find no better hiding place than under the arc-lights of autobiography.

—THOMAS BURKE, Introduction to De Quincey, *Ecstasies*

There's nothing a man can do to improve himself so much as writing his memoirs.

—MAYNARD PRINTING

I believe it is impossible for a man to tell the truth about himself or to avoid impressing the reader with the truth about himself.

I made an experiment once. I got a friend of mine—a man painfully given to speak the truth on all occasions—a man who wouldn't dream of telling a lie—and I made him write his autobiography for his own amusement and mine. He did it. The manuscript would have made an octavo volume, but—good, honest man that he was—in every single detail of his life that I knew about he turned out, on paper, a formidable liar. He could not help himself.

It is not in human nature to write the truth about itself.

—RUDYARD KIPLING, *From Sea to Sea*

AUTUMN

The sable shadows of my well-beloved darkness walked beside me. I was returning from the gipsy camp, rustling with my steps the dun and giltern leaves of October. It was the leafage that suggested other folios to my youthful mind.

—*The Book Without a Name: Being the Journal of an Unmarried English Lady to Her Natural Son*

BABUR (1483–1530) (Or BABAR or BABER)

Babur's remarkable autobiography, based on notes taken throughout his life but for the most part written in his last years in India, gives a vivid account of what he calls these "throneless times" with his small band of adventurers in search of food, wealth and a kingdom. Rarely can such a sophisticated mind have recorded so wild an existence, which combined to an extraordinary degree the romantic and the sordid. . . . A chance encounter with a rival group when out foraging would end almost invariably in bloodshed, and heads were severed and carried away on the saddle for trophies.

☐

In later life he strongly disapproved of any practice of homosexuality among his followers, but his own first love affair, unconsummated, was for a boy in the camp bazaar, and he describes it with an almost Proustian subtlety of self-analysis. He mooned about the orchards and gardens, bare-headed, barefoot, dreaming and composing couplets, but whenever he actually met his love . . . he was covered in confusion and unable to look at him. On the rare occasions when the boy was sent for into his presence, the situation was even worse: "In my joy and agitation I could not thank him for coming; how was it possible for me to reproach him for going away?"

—BAMBER GASCOIGNE, *The Great Moghuls*

BACK INTO TIME

The crack was only about body-width and, as I worked my way downward, the light turned dark and green from the overhanging grass. Above me the sky became a narrow slit of distant blue, and the sandstone was cool to my hands on either side. The Slit was a little sinister—like an open grave, assuming the dead were enabled to take one last look. . . .

I ignored the sky, then, and began to concentrate on the sandstone walls that had led me into this place. It was tight and tricky work, but that cut was a perfect cross section through perhaps ten million years of time. I hoped to find at least a bone, but I was not quite prepared for the sight I finally came upon. Staring straight out at me, as I slid farther and deeper into the green twilight, was a skull embedded in the solid sandstone, . . . the white bone gleaming there in a kind of ashen splendor, water worn, and about to be ground away in the next long torrent.

It was not, of course, human. I was deep, deep below the time of man in a remote age near the beginning of the reign of mammals. I squatted on my heels in the narrow ravine, and we stared a little blankly at each other, the skull and I. . . .

It was the face of a creature who had spent his days following his nose, who was led by instinct rather than memory, and whose power of choice was very small. Though he was not a man, nor a direct human ancestor, there was yet about him, even in the bone, some trace of that low, snuffling world out of which our forebears had so recently emerged. The skull lay tilted in such a manner that it stared, sightless, up at me as though I, too, were already caught a few feet above him in the strata and, in my turn, were staring upward at that strip of sky which the ages were carrying farther away from me beneath the tumbling debris of falling mountains. The creature had never lived to see a man, and I, what was it I was never going to see?

—LOREN C. EISELEY, *The Immense Journey*

ROGER BACON (c. 1214–1294)

Reasoning draws a conclusion—but does not make the conclusion certain, unless the mind discovers it by the path of experience.

□

A man who should prove by adequate reasoning that fire burns and injures things and destroys them, his mind would not be satisfied thereby, nor would he avoid fire, until he placed his hand or some combustible substance in the fire, so that he might prove by experiment that which reasoning taught.

It is generally believed that the diamond cannot be broken except by goat's blood, and philosophers and theologians misuse this idea. But fracture by means of blood of this kind has never been verified. . . . Moreover, it is generally believed that hot water freezes more quickly than cold in vessels, and the argument that is advanced is that contrary is excited by contrary, just like enemies meeting each other. But it is certain that cold water freezes more quickly for anyone who makes the experiment.

—ROGER BACON, *Opus Magus*

BAGHDAD: The Caliph Rides Forth (12th century)

In the Caliph's palace [Baghdad] are great riches and towers filled with gold, silken garments, and all precious stones. He does not issue forth from his palace save once in the year, at the feast which the Muhammadans called El-id-bed [*sic*] Ramazan, and they come from distant lands that day to see him. He rides on a mule and is attired in the royal robes of gold and silver and fine linen; and on his head is a turban adorned with precious stones of priceless value, and over the turban is a black shawl as a sign of his modesty, implying that all this glory will be covered by darkness on the day of his death.

He is accompanied by all the nobles of Islam dressed in fine garments and riding on horses, the princes of Arabia . . . Togarma . . . Daylam (Gilan) and the princes of Persia . . . [and] the land of Tibet, which is three months' journey distant, and westward of which lies the land of Samarkand.

He proceeds from his palace to the great mosque of Islam which is by the Basrah Gate. Along the road the walls are adorned with silk and purple, and the inhabitants receive him with all kinds of song and exultation, and they dance before the great king which is styled the Caliph. They salute him with a loud voice and say "Peace unto thee, our Lord the King and Light of Islam.". . . Then he proceeds to the court of the mosque, mounts a wooden pulpit, and expounds to them their law.

Then the learned ones of Islam arise and pray for him and extol his greatness and his graciousness. . . . Afterwards he gives them his blessing, and they bring before him a camel which he slays, and this is their passover sacrifice. He gives thereof unto the princes and they distribute it to all, so that they may taste of the sacrifice brought by their king; and they all rejoice.

Afterwards he leaves the mosque and returns alone to his palace by way of the river Hiddekel. The grandees of Islam accompany him in ships on the river. . . . He does not return the way he came; and the road which he takes along the riverside is watched all the year through so that no man shall tread in his footsteps. He does not leave the palace again for a whole year. He is a benevolent man.
—RABBI BENJAMIN BEN JONAH of Tudela (1165–73),
in *Jewish Travellers*, ed. ELKAN N. ADLER

BANQUETS IN LIBYA

In social meetings among the rich Libyans, when the banquet is ended, a servant carries round to the several guests a coffin, in which there is a wooden image of a corpse [of Osiris, god of the underworld] carved and painted to resemble nature as nearly as possible, about a cubit or two cubits in length. As he shows it to each guest in turn, the servant says, "Gaze here, and drink and be merry; for when you die, such will you be."

—HERODOTUS, *History*

BASEBALL

CAN A BASEBALL REALLY CURVE?

As the pitcher releases the baseball, he imparts a spinning motion to it which causes it to rotate about a vertical axis on its path plateward. As the ball whirls, air is carried around with it by friction. On one side of the ball this air moves *with* the current of air caused by the forward motion of the ball, while on the other side it moves in *opposition* to it. This causes the air speed on one side of the ball to be greater than on the other. The ball must curve, therefore, toward the side having the greater air speed and, consequently, the lower static pressure.

—WILLIAM C. VERGARA, *Science in Everyday Things*

THE BASTILLE AS TRINKETS

The Bastille should be demolished. The contract was awarded to a builder named Palloy.... He received no payment.... But by using volunteer labor to pull down the building and by turning it into souvenirs he made a fortune. He carved miniature prisoners out of the stones, turned the bolts into snuffboxes and inkpots, and the chains into medals for the politicians. The marble mantelpiece of the governor's house became a domino set with which the little Dauphin afterwards played in prison. Individual stones were bought by householders who fancied the idea of treading beneath their feet a relic of the bad old past.

—JOHN FISHER, *Six Summers in Paris*

BATHS

The Victorians ... seldom bathed. Glorification of the bathroom is a modern fetish. In 1882 only 2 percent of New York's homes had water connections, and these in all probability were leaky and, if attached to a stove, dangerous. Bathing was considered harmful by some doctors, and one, C. E. Sargent, described it as "a needless waste of time."

—OTTO L. BETTMAN, *The Good Old Days*

BEAUTY

To a toad, what is beauty? A female with two pop-eyes, a wide mouth, yellow belly and spotted back.

—VOLTAIRE

If our sight were longer or shorter, what now appears beautiful would seem misshapen, and what we now think misshapen we would regard as beautiful. The most beautiful hand seen through a microscope will appear horrible.... Things regarded in themselves ... are neither ugly nor beautiful....

—BARUCH SPINOZA, *Letter to Hugo Boxel*

BEHAVIOR BEFORE NOBILITY (England)

[Never] talk to Lordship and Ladyship. Never speak to them—not one word and no matter how urgent—until they speak to you, the head gardener told me on my first day.

Ladyship drove about the grounds in a motorchair and would have run us over rather than have to say, get out the way. We must never look at her and she never looked at us. It was the same in the house. If a maid was in a passage and Lordship or Ladyship happened to come along, she would have to face the wall and stand perfectly still until they had passed.

None of the village people were allowed into the garden. Definitely not. Tradespeople came to their door and never saw the main gardens. Work in front of the house had to be done secretly. About seven in the morning we would tiptoe about the terrace, sweeping the leaves, tying things up, never making a sound, so that nobody in the bedrooms could hear the work being done. This is what luxury means—perfect consideration. We gave, they took. It was the complete arrangement. This is luxury.

—A gardener, in RONALD BLYTHE, *Akenfield*

BEHAVIOR IN REVOLUTIONS

Revolution brought many calamities on the cities, which occurred and always will occur so long as human nature remains the same. . . .

When civil strife had once begun in the cities . . . men changed the conventional meaning of words as they chose. Irrational daring was held to be loyal courage; prudent delay, an excuse for cowardice; sound sense, a disguise for unmanly weakness; and men who consider matters in every aspect were thought to be incapable of doing anything. Frantic haste became part of a man's quality; and if anyone made safety the condition for conspiracy, it was a specious pretext for evasion. The lover of violence was always trusted, and his opponent suspected. If anyone succeeded in a plot, he was shrewd; if he detected one, even more clever; but if anyone took measures in advance to make plots or detection superfluous, he was regarded as a man who broke up his own party in terror of the opposition. In a word, it was praiseworthy to strike first, while your enemy was meditating an injury, and to incite a man to strike who was not thinking of it.

—THUCYDIDES, *History of the Peloponnesian War*

BELIEFS

. . . If we are told that we are wrong we resent the imputation and harden our hearts. We are incredibly heedless in the formation of our beliefs, but find ourselves filled with an illicit passion for them when anyone proposes to rob us of their companionship. It is obviously not the ideas themselves that are dear to us, but our self-esteem, which is threatened. We are by nature stubbornly pledged to defend our own from attack, whether it be our person, our family, our property, or our opinion.

—JAMES HARVEY ROBINSON, *The Mind in the Making*

It is a sin to believe evil of others, but it is seldom a mistake.

—H. L. MENCKEN

We are inclined to believe those whom we do not know, because they have never deceived us.

—SAMUEL JOHNSON

BELLS

One sound rose ceaselessly above the noises of busy life [in the Middle Ages] and lifted all things into a sphere of order and serenity: the sound of bells. The bells were in daily life like good spirits, which by their familiar voices now called upon the citizens to mourn and now to rejoice, now warned them of danger, now exhorted them to piety. They were known by their names: big Jacqueline, or the bell Roland. Everyone knew the difference in meaning of the various ways of ringing. However continuous the ringing of the bells, people would seem not to have become blunted to the effect of their sound.

What intoxication the pealing of the bells of all the churches, and of all the monasteries of Paris, must have produced, sounding from morning till evening, and even during the night, when a peace was concluded or a pope elected.

—JOHN HUIZINGA, *The Waning of the Middle Ages*

BELLS' CODE

The language of bells, too, has very largely joined other mourning customs in the gallery of historical curiosities. Although the solemn pealing of the passing-bell is a familiar sound in country districts, this is all that remains of a whole broadside of peals in the campanological armory of the Middle Ages. Any reasonably intelligent hearer could tell by listening to the funeral bells the age and sex of the person being buried, and whether or not it was a child. Another charming custom which survived into the present century was the ringing of the bells not only to warn St. Peter that a soul was on its way but to frighten off the devils which might impede its passage.... When the Duke of Wellington died in 1852 the Dean of his old parliamentary constituency at Trim ordered that the bells be tolled in a full peal. No sooner had the ringers begun than the tenor bell, the pride of the church, shattered. When it was examined, it was found to have been cast in 1769, the year the Duke was born.

—AMORET and CHRISTOPHER SCOTT,
in *The Saturday Book*, #26, ed. JOHN HADFIELD

BELLS AND DEATH: SUFFOLK

The bells tolled for death when I was a boy. It was three times for a man and three times two for a woman. . . . Then the years of the dead person's age would be tolled and if the bell went on speaking, "seventy-one, seventy-two . . ." people would say, "Well, they had a good innings!" But when the bell stopped at eighteen or twenty a hush would come over the fields.

This practice was continued up until the Second World War, when all the bells of England were silenced. It was never revived.

—A bellringer (tower captain),
in RONALD BLYTHE, *Akenfield*

BIRTH CONTROL

It should be emphasized that fertility rates declined in the West long before contraceptive technology had approached the convenience or effectiveness demanded today, long before family planning services were readily available, when, in fact, publication of information about contraception could bring imprisonment. At a time when national population policies were unheard of . . . birth rates were falling almost as rapidly as death rates.

☐

As long as demographers and economists seek to solve the population problem by emphasizing birth control exclusively, success in limiting population growth will prove elusive. Integrated programs of nutrition, sanitation, and public health services must be incorporated into a country's overall program for family planning.

If we wish to limit population growth, the primary thing we must do is to lower infant and childhood mortality rates. When these remain at high levels, fertility will remain high, but when mortality rates decline visibly, fertility will fall within a few years. The most effective way to lower infant mortality rates is to improve nutritional levels. Therefore, the best birth control program is, simply, to feed the children.

—ROY BROWN and JOE WRAY,
"The Starving Roots of Population Growth,"
in *Natural History*, 1974

BISEXUALITY

[Among] the Batak people of northern Sumatra, all males between the ages of nine or ten and nineteen function as homosexuals, then successfully (and apparently with no accompanying trauma) switch to predominantly heterosexual activity. The experience of the Batak, [John] Money has commented, suggests "a bisexual capability which is either *culturally* encouraged or suppressed."
—paraphrase of JOHN MONEY
by MARTIN JOHN DUBERMAN,
New York Times, November 9, 1975

BLASPHEMY

Blasphemy depends upon belief, and is fading with it. If anyone doubts this, let him sit down seriously and try to think blasphemous thoughts about Thor. I think his family will find him at the end of the day in a state of some exhaustion.
—G. K. CHESTERTON, *Heretics*

I am sometimes shocked by the blasphemies of those who think themselves pious—for instance, the nuns who never take a bath without wearing a bathrobe all the time. When asked why, since no man can see them, they reply: "Oh, but you forget the good God." Apparently they conceive of the Deity as a Peeping Tom, whose omnipotence enables Him to see through bathroom walls, but who is foiled by bathrobes. This view strikes me as curious.
—BERTRAND RUSSELL, *Unpopular Essays*

THE BODY

The body is but a pair of pincers set over a bellows and a stewpan, and the whole fixed upon stilts.
—SAMUEL BUTLER

...the Greeks represented their statues without pubic hair because in real life they had adopted the oriental custom of removing the hairs. We compel our sculptors and painters to make similar representations, though they no longer correspond either to realities or to our own ideas of what is beautiful and fitting in real life.

□

In no civilized country has the artist ever chosen to give an erect organ to his representations of ideal masculine beauty. It is mainly because the unaesthetic character of a woman's sexual region is almost imperceptible in any ordinary and normal position of the nude body that the feminine form is a more aesthetically beautiful object of contemplation than the masculine.

□

Only second to the pelvis and its integuments as a secondary sexual character in women we must place the breasts. Among barbarous and civilized peoples the beauty of the breast is usually highly esteemed. Among Europeans, indeed, the importance of this region is so highly esteemed that the general rule against the exposure of the body is in its favor abrogated, and the breasts are the only portion of the body, in the narrow sense, which a European lady in full dress is allowed more or less to uncover.

—HAVELOCK ELLIS, *Studies in the Psychology of Sex*

The chief function of the body is to carry the brain around.

—THOMAS A. EDISON

BOOK BURNING IN ATHENS (c. 432–400 B.C.)

About 432 B.C. or a year or two later, disbelief in the supernatural and the teaching of astronomy were made indictable offenses. The next thirty-odd years witnessed a series of heresy trials which is unique in Athenian history. The victims included most of the leaders of progressive thought at Athens—Anaxagoras, Diagoras, Socrates, almost certainly Protagoras also, and possibly Euripides. In all these cases save the last the prosecution was successful. . . . All these were famous people. How many obscurer persons may have suffered for their opinions we do not know. But the evidence we have is more than enough to prove that the Great Age of Greek Enlightenment was also, like our own time, an Age of Persecution —banishment of scholars, blinkering of thought, and even (if we can believe the tradition about Protagoras) burning of books.

—E. R. DODDS, *The Greeks and the Irrational*

BOOKS

When Gutenberg announced that he could manufacture books, as he put it, "without the help of reeds, stylus or pen but by wondrous agreement, proportion and harmony of punches and types," he could scarcely imagine that he was about to become the most important political and social revolutionary of the Second Millennium.

The Protestant Reformation would probably not have occurred if not for the printing press. The development of both capitalism and nationalism were obviously linked to the printing press. So were new literary forms, such as the novel and the essay. So were new conceptions of education, such as written examinations. And, of course, so was the concept of scientific methodology, whose ground rules were established by Descartes in his *Discourse on Reason.*

—Neil Postman, "The Politics of Reading," in
The Myth of Cultural Deprivation

Whenever the shelves in the Library of Heaven were entirely full, and a new, worthy book appeared, all the books in the celestial collection pressed themselves closer together, and made room.

—Hebrew legend

Here is the history of human ignorance, error, superstition, folly, war and waste, recorded by human intelligence for the admonition of wiser ages still to come. Here is the history of man's hunger for truth, goodness and beauty, leading him slowly on, through flesh to spirit, from war to peace.

—inscriptions on library at University of Rochester

"This is the best of me; for the rest, I ate, and drank, and slept, loved, and hated, like another; my life was as the vapour, and is not; but this I saw and knew; this, if anything of mine, is worth your memory." That is his "writing"; it is, in his small human way, and with whatever degree of true inspiration is in him, his inscription, or scripture. That is a "book."

—John Ruskin, *Sesame and Lilies*

Books are the magic wand whose touch has broken for me that trance of the transient in which so many of us are frozen. They

are also a magic wand to bear me away from the doldrums of despair.... These [the Great Books Series], often apparently so dry or so difficult, become, when studied to the point and very edge of love, a mighty fortress against the invasion of the barbarians.
— CLIFTON FADIMAN, in MORTIMER J. ADLER,
Philosopher at Large

THE BOREDOM OF TERROR

During that brilliant, burning spring of 1794 yet one more change had come over the minds of the citizens of Paris. Since the beginning of May they had seen more people than ever before "sneezing into the sack" or "putting their heads on the windowsill"—which in current slang meant being guillotined.... The authorities, in order to maintain the rule of Terror, had begun to guillotine teen-age prisoners as well as veterans in their seventies. Even Frenchmen whose patriotism was undoubted began to be bored with the monotonous repetition of public death, and the public reached the point of preferring an acquittal to a conviction....
— JOHN FISHER, *op. cit.*

CAESAR BORGIA (1476–1507)

The Count of Larin, a vassal of the King [of Navarra] ... reinforced, turned upon him. Caesar's few troops fled; Caesar, with only one companion ... fought until he was cut down and killed (March 12, 1507). He was thirty-one years old.

It was an honorable end to a questionable life. There are many things in Caesar Borgia that we cannot stomach: his insolent pride, his neglect of his faithful wife, his treatment of women as mere instruments of passing pleasure, his occasional cruelty to his enemies —as when he condemned to death ... Giulio Varano.... Usually he acted on the principle that the achievement of his purpose justified any means. He found himself surrounded with lies, and managed to lie better than the rest until Julius II lied to him. He was almost certainly innocent of his brother Giovanni's death.... He lacked—perhaps through illness—the strength to face his own misfortunes with courage and dignity. Only his death brought a gleam of nobility into his life.

But even he had virtues. He must have had extraordinary ability to rise so rapidly, to learn so readily the arts of leadership, negotiation, and war. Given the difficult task of restoring, with only a small force at his command, the papal power in the Papal States, he accomplished it with surprising rapidity of movement, skill of strategy, and economy of means. Empowered to govern as well as to conquer, he gave the Romagna the fairest rule and most prosperous peace that it had enjoyed in centuries. Ordered to clear the Campagna of rebellious and troublesome vassals, he did it with a celerity that Julius Caesar himself could hardly have surpassed. . . . But his victories, his methods, his power, his dark secrecy, his swift incalculable attacks, made him the terror instead of the liberator of Italy. The faults of his character ruined the accomplishments of his mind.

—Will Durant, *The Renaissance*

THE BOURGEOISIE

The bourgeoisie . . . has been the first to show what man's activity can bring about. It has accomplished wonders far surpassing Egyptian pyramids, Roman aqueducts and Gothic cathedrals. . . . The bourgeoisie draws all nations . . . into civilization. . . . It has created enormous cities [and] rescued a considerable part of the population from the idiocy of rural life. . . . The bourgeoisie, during its rule of scarcely one hundred years, has created more massive and more colossal productive forces than have all preceding generations together.

—Karl Marx and Friedrich Engels, *The Communist Manifesto*

BREAKFAST WITH LOUIS XVI

More often than not the King got up twice each morning. Once privately and later semipublicly at his Levee. . . . Five classes of people were admitted to his bedchamber to pay their respects. . . . The King's hands were then bathed in toilet water offered to him on a golden dish. He made the sign of the cross and offered up a short prayer. Then he got out of bed, put on his slippers, and the Great Chamberlain and the First Gentleman handed him his dressing-gown. He put it on and sat down in the armchair in which he intended dressing. At that moment the door of the antechamber opened once more and a third group composed of those who had purchased the right to be present at the ceremony, flocked into the room ... [including] Foreign Ambassadors, Secretaries of State, Marshals of France and other nobles and bishops. ... The Grand Master of the Wardrobe took the right sleeve of his nightshirt and the First Valet of the Wardrobe the left sleeve and the two of them handed it over to an officer of the Wardrobe, while a valet of the Wardrobe brought the King's dayshirt within a white taffeta jacket. ... The Grand Master of the Wardrobe passed the King his waist-coat and jacket. ... Several cravats were offered in a basket and the Master of the Wardrobe tied the one which the King had chosen. Then the valet in charge of handkerchiefs brought in a selection of three arranged on a saucer. ... Finally the Master of the Wardrobe presented the royal hat, gloves and stick to the King. ...

It was at the royal table that the King really came into his own with his three hundred and eighty-three Officiers de Bouche including noblemen serving as pantrymen, cupbearers and car-vers. ... Twenty or thirty people attended to the dish set before the King and supervised the glass that he drank out of. It needed four people to serve him with a glass each of water and wine.

—JOHN FISHER, op. cit.

BRUTUS MADE NO SPEECH

The murder over, Brutus turned to deliver his speech to the Senate. But the curia was empty. ... Then they emerged from the curia, with their togas twisted round their left arms for shields, brand-ishing their bloody daggers in their right hand, bearing aloft on a stick the cap, the symbol of liberty, and shouting to Liberty, to the Republic, and to Cicero, the philosopher of republicanism. But outside they found all was noise and confusion. In the colonnade and the neighboring streets people had taken fright at the sudden emergence of the senators and the appearance of the armed gladiators.

The alarm was raised in an instant and the public took to their heels. The noise of the shouting reached the spectators in the theater of Pompey, who rushed out to join the fugitives.... There was a general rush for refuge into houses and shops, which their owners as promptly closed. The sudden appearance of a crowd of armed men, reeking with blood, increased the disorder in the streets they traversed. It was in vain that, led by Brutus, they shouted and gesticulated to quiet the crowd. Men were far too frightened to listen.... Before long Antony was safely shut up in his house, the conspirators were entrenched in the capitol, the frightened public had retired expectant to their homes, and Rome was wrapped in funereal silence, like a city of the dead.

—GUGLIELMO FERRERO, "The Ides of March," in
The Greatness and Decline of Rome,
tr. ALFRED E. ZIMMERN

WILLIAM JENNINGS BRYAN (1860–1925)

Has it been duly marked by historians that William Jennings Bryan's last secular act on this globe of sin was to catch flies? A curious detail, and not without its sardonic overtones. He was the most sedulous flycatcher in American history, and in many ways the most successful. His quarry, of course, was not *Musca domestica* but *Homo neandertalensis*. For forty years he tracked it with coo and bellow, up and down the rustic backways of the Republic. Wherever the flambeaux of chautauqua smoked and guttered, and the bilge of idealism ran in the veins, and Baptist pastors dammed the brooks with the sanctified, and men gathered who were weary and heavy laden, and their wives who were full of Peruna and as fecund as the shad ... there the indefatigable Jennings set up his traps and set his bait.

□

This talk of sincerity, I confess, fatigues me. If the fellow was sincere, then so was P. T. Barnum. The word is disgraced and degraded by such uses. He was, in fact, a charlatan, a mountebank, a zany without sense or dignity. It was hard to believe, watching him at Dayton, that he had traveled, that he had been received in civilized societies, that he had been a high officer of state. He seemed only a poor clod like those around him, deluded by a childish theology, full of an almost pathological hatred of all learning, all human dignity, all beauty, all fine and noble things.... What animated him from end to end of his grotesque career was simply ambition.

□

From my place in the courtroom, standing upon a table, I looked directly down upon him, sweating horribly and pumping his palm-leaf fan. His eyes fascinated me; I watched them all day long. They were blazing points of hatred. They glittered like occult and sinister gems. . . .

—H. L. MENCKEN, *American Mercury*, October 1925

BUREAUCRACY

The Federal Power Commission sent out a questionnaire to the gas producers which weighed ten pounds and required seventeen thousand accountant man-hours to complete.

—STEWART ALSOP, *Saturday Evening Post*,
November 20, 1965

We have pruned and pruned our bureaucracy, and after four years we have taken a census of the government staff, and we have an increase of twelve thousand.

—LENIN, in Anatole Shub, *Lenin*

Some of the private enterprise bureaucracy [in the U.K.] reaches proportions of Oriental deviousness which would be denounced by *Pravda* if it occurred in Soviet industry. Secretaries have secretaries, personal assistants have personal assistants and secretaries, even press agents have press agents. To reach any department of any firm you have to explain what you want down to the last detail to every person you contact before they will reveal that they are not the right person and pass you on to someone else who is also not the right person.

—ALAN BRIAN, *Spectator* (London), March 1964

EDMUND BURKE (1729–1797)

Burke was a practical and imaginative thinker unpredictable in the range and depth of his insights. In his feats of language . . . he was, as Coleridge said, "almost a poet." A useful approach to his thought, therefore, must look for "sense" instead of "system." The unity in

Burke's thinking is to be sought in its latent character or spirit, in what I have called "practical imagination"—his power to experience the life of a thing in its organic complexity, to discriminate its relations, and to act upon (or reverence) its latent good.

□

At least three respectable judges—Hazlitt, Arnold, and Leslie Stephen—have called Burke the greatest prose writer in English literature. He is one of those great amphibious Englishmen, not quite liberal, not quite conservative, poetically open in his thinking, broadly practical in his poetry, whose diffuse and many-mansioned thought seems always implicit with a coherent and synthetic system which, however, is never achieved. Laski, after a cautious sizing-up from an opposing camp, pronounced Burke the greatest figure in the history of English politics.

—GERALD W. CHAPMAN,
Edmund Burke: The Practical Imagination

To do him justice, it would be necessary to quote all his works; the only specimen of Burke is, all that he wrote.

—WILLIAM HAZLITT, *Political Essays*

BURMA

PAGODAS

The whole pagoda was covered with pure gold leaf and its summit was crowned with a delicate *hti*, an umbrella of gold on whose rings were hung gold and silver jewelled bells which tinkled with every passing breeze. The Shwe Dagon Pagoda was a beautiful and sacred thing. In the early mornings it gave a radiance to the clear air and the blue sky; in the daylight it shone forth like a blaze of gold, burning and pure; in the evenings it glowed softly as the breeze tinkled its bells, and filled the heart with a gentle sadness which is not grief but a sweet perception of unearthly things; and at night the lights flooded it to stand high and illumined above the dark wooded slopes of the hill. At all times and from all parts of Rangoon it could be seen, calm and sublime, with the same smiling look as is seen on the face of the Buddha, not smiling in the eyes or mouth but in the serene expression of inward calm.

—MI MI KHAING, *My Burmese Family*

RICHARD BURTON (1821–1890)

Burton's character was complex. It would be an easy task to assemble an impressive body of evidence to show that he was cruel, dirty-minded, stupid, pretentious and basically evil. But it also would be easy to collect an equally impressive array of evidence (as was done by his wife) to show that he was kind, scholarly, brave, brilliant and badly neglected by the nation he devotedly served. In reality, Burton was all of these things. The man who carefully nursed Speke in the wilds of Africa was the same man who within a few weeks of his death launched a vicious attack on his character. . . . The man who stood in the dark with only a naked sword to face a crowd of wild Somalis intent on his blood was the same man who was afraid of losing his job and pension by being seen in a restaurant outside of his work area. A man of advanced scientific ideas, he was childishly superstitious; an expert on religions, he could find none for himself; a loving husband, he advocated polygamy.

His accomplishments were often so unrelated that it is difficult . . . to imagine that the man who was one of the pioneers in Central African exploration, the discoverer of Lake Tanganyika, was the same man who made the brilliant translation of *The Arabian Nights*, or that the poet of *The Kasidah* and the translator of the great Portuguese poet Camoens was the same man who made the adventurous pilgrimage to Mecca in disguise. Burton was . . . both a man of action and a scholar, and he made significant contributions to the world in both science and literature.

□

He wrote books or published papers on mining, archaeology, poetry, anthropology, military science, commerce, engineering, geography, mountain-climbing, religion, abnormal sexual practices, reptiles, ethnology, slavery, medicine, politics and a host of other subjects. . . . His conclusions and theories were frequently bizarre, heretical or erroneous, but his mind was capable of moving beyond the thoughts of other men. . . . He was an adventurer in the intellectual and the spiritual as well as the physical world and it was this combination of interests, actively followed, which made him . . . one of the rarest personalities ever seen on earth.

—BYRON FARWELL, Foreword, *Burton*

BUSINESSMEN

Businessmen, after all, had never taken culture seriously. They have always rather agreed with Adam Smith when he wrote: "Though you despise that picture, or that poem, or even that system of philosophy which I admire, there is little danger of our quarreling on that account. Neither of us can reasonably be much interested about them."

He could not have been more wrong. It is ideas which rule the world, because it is ideas that define the way reality is perceived; and, in the absence of religion, it is out of the culture—the pictures, the poems, the songs, the philosophy—that these ideas are born.

—IRVING KRISTOL, *Wall Street Journal,*
September 11, 1975

The world does not owe men a living, but business, if it is to fulfill its ideal, owes men an opportunity to earn a living.

—OWEN D. YOUNG, address at Harvard, June 4, 1927

The violence and injustice of the rulers of mankind is an ancient evil, for which, I am afraid, the nature of human affairs can scarcely admit of a remedy. But the mean rapacity, the monopolizing spirit of merchants and manufacturers, who neither are, nor ought to be, the rulers of mankind . . . may very easily be prevented from disturbing the tranquility of anybody but themselves.

—ADAM SMITH, *Wealth of Nations,* Vol. V

BUTTERFLIES

Were a naturalist to announce to the world the discovery of an animal which first existed in the form of a serpent; which then penetrated into the earth and, weaving a shroud of pure silk of the finest texture, contracted itself within this covering into a body without external mouth or limbs, resembling, more than anything else, an Egyptian mummy; and which, after remaining in this state, without food and without motion . . . should at the end of that period burst its silken cerements, struggling through its earthly covering and start in today a winged bird—what think you would be the sensation excited by this strange piece of intelligence? After the first doubts of its truth were dispelled, what astonishment would succeed!

—William Forsell Kirby, *Butterflies and Moths*

GEORGE GORDON, LORD BYRON (1788–1824)

Byron was beautiful, with fierce, clear, blue-gray eyes, a fine straight nose, full lips, and a delicately chiseled chin. He had chestnut hair (which he pinned up nightly) and a fair alabaster complexion. A lifelong tendency to overweight was overcome only by starvation diets and the continuous consumption of laxatives. A little over 5'7", Byron always walked with a limp. Self-conscious, he made great efforts to overcome his physical shortcomings by excelling in sports, including boxing, fencing, riding, cricket, and swimming. . . .

Women chased him, adored him, and tried to possess him. One eccentric blueblood, Lady Caroline Lamb, pursued him everywhere and climaxed her passion with a scene at a masked ball in which she cut herself and fell to the ground in a pool of blood.

Byron's already dubious reputation was further undermined when rumors began to circulate concerning an incestuous relationship between the poet and his half sister. Augusta Leigh was a beauty who was said to resemble her younger half brother closely, and the two had come to know each other only as adults. Though he did absolutely nothing to deny the gossip, Byron became so worried over the state of his own morals that he turned to marriage. The woman he chose was the stunning Anne Isabella Milbanke, a respectable, highly educated mathematician who hoped that she could tame "the wild lord."

Yet on the wedding night Byron told her: "It is enough for me that you are my wife for me to hate you!" Shortly afterwards, she became pregnant, and his conduct toward her bordered on the insane. He tormented her by shooting off guns in her bedroom and demanded that his sister live with them, for Augusta was the only one who could calm his rages.

Lady Byron's request for a separation, following the birth of their daughter, affirmed public belief in the old stories of Byron's incest. Though his poetry was more popular than ever, he was socially ostracized. He chose to exile himself from England. Naturally, he left in truly "Byronic" style. His coach, designed after that of his hero, Napoleon, contained a bed, library, and complete dining and cooking facilities.

—NANCY H. MEDVED, in *The People's Almanac*,
ed. David Wallechinsky and Irving Wallace

BYZANTINE CIVILIZATION

The Byzantines carried the torch of civilization unextinguished at a time when the barbarous Germanic and Slav tribes had reduced much of Europe to near chaos. It is no exaggeration to credit the empire with the preservation of European civilization from Islam in the seventh and eighth centuries. Had the empire fallen before the Arab attacks, Islam would have spread to much of Europe, with unforeseeable consequences, while it was still in an amorphous state. The Slavonic East would doubtless have received the Islamic faith, as would much of central Europe. . . .

—SPEROS VRYONIS, JR., *Byzantium and Europe*

JULIUS CAESAR (102 B.C.–44 B.C.)

His baldness was a disfigurement which troubled him greatly, since it was often the subject of the gibes of his detractors. Because of it he used to comb forward his scanty locks from the crown of his head. Of all the honors voted him by the Senate and people there was none which he received or made use of more gladly than the privilege of wearing a laurel wreath at all times.

They say that he was fantastic in his dress; that he wore a senator's tunic with fringed sleeves reaching to the wrist, and always had a girdle over it, though rather a loose one; and that, they say, was the occasion of Sulla's quip, when he warned the nobles to keep an eye on the ill-girt boy.

□

They say that he was led to invade Britain by the hope of getting pearls, and that in comparing their size he sometimes weighed them with his own hand. He was always an enthusiastic collector of gems, carvings, statues, and pictures by early artists; also of slaves of exceptional figure and training at enormous prices, of which he himself was so ashamed that he forbade their entry in his accounts. . . .

To leave no room for doubt of his evil reputation both for sodomy and adultery, Curio the elder, in one of his speeches, calls him "every woman's man and every man's woman."

He drank very little wine; not even his enemies denied that. There is a saying of Marcus Cato that Caesar was the only man who undertook to overthrow the state when sober.

□

Marcus Brutus declares [that] one Octavius, a man whose disordered mind made him somewhat free with his tongue, after saluting Pompey as "King" in a crowded assembly, greeted Caesar as "Queen." But Gaius Memmius makes the direct charge that Caesar acted as cupbearer to Nicomedes with the rest of his wantons at a large dinner-party. . . . Cicero is not content with having written in sundry letters that Caesar was led by the King's attendants to the royal apartments, that he lay on a golden couch arrayed in purple, and that the virginity of this scion of Venus was lost in Bithynia.

□

He was greatly skilled in arms and horsemanship, and possessed incredible powers of endurance. On the march he always headed his army, sometimes on horseback, oftener on foot, bareheaded both in the heat of the sun and in rain. He covered vast distances with astonishing speed, as much as a hundred miles a day in a carriage, with little baggage, swimming rivers or crossing them on inflated skins, often arriving before the messengers whom he had sent ahead to announce his coming.

In conducting his campaigns, it is a question whether he was more cautious or more daring. He never led his army where ambuscades were possible without first carefully reconnoitering the country. He did not cross the water to Britain without making many personal inquiries about the harbors and the approach to the island . . . when news came that his camp in Germany was besieged, he swiftly made his way to his men, through all the enemies' pickets, disguised as a Gaul. . . .

He joined battle not only after carefully planning his movements in advance but on sudden opportunities, often immediately at the end of a march, sometimes in the foulest weather, when the enemy would least expect him to make a move. It was not until his later years that he became slower to engage a foe, believing that the oftener he had been victor, the less he ought to tempt fate. He thought that he could not possibly gain as much by a success as he might lose by a defeat.

He never put an enemy to flight without also driving him from his camp, thus giving him no place for respite in panic. When a battle was doubtful, he used to send away the horses, his own among the first, to force upon his troops the need of standing their ground by taking away their aid to flight.

☐

In eloquence and in the art of war he either equaled or excelled the glory of the very best. After his prosecution of Dolabella, he was indisputably reckoned one of the most distinguished advocates. And Cicero, reviewing the great orators in his *Brutus*, says that he does not see that Caesar was inferior to any one of them, maintaining that his style is elegant as well as brilliant, even grand and in a sense noble.

—SUETONIUS, *The Lives of the Twelve Caesars*,
tr. Dryden and Clough

. . . we fail to grasp the true significance of Caesar's career till we discern that, like Pompey and Crassus and the other great figures of his day, his mission was primarily destructive—to complete the disorganization and dissolution of the old world, both in Italy and the provinces, and thus make way for a stabler and juster system.

☐

It matters little that in the latter part of his life he displayed more wisdom and moderation than in the earlier; that he attempted in part though with many inconsistencies, to repair as a reformer the mistakes he had committed as a demagogue; that he had at last come to see that a discontented society, blind and breathless in the race for riches and self-indulgence, had set its selfish course, beyond all turning, for the Abyss.

—GUGLIELMO FERRERO, *op. cit.*

[He] was the greatest genius that ever was, and the greatest judge of mankind.

—DAVID HUME, letter, March 19, 1751

Caesar was the complete and the perfect man.

—THEODOR MOMMSEN, *Römische Geschichte*

CALIFORNIA

This is the California where it is easy to Dial-A-Devotion, but hard to buy a book. This is the country of the teased hair and the Capris and the girls for whom all life's promise comes down to a waltz-length white wedding dress and the birth of a Kimberly or a Sherry or a Debbi and a Tijuana divorce and a return to hairdressers' school. "We were just crazy kids," they say without regret, and look to the future.

The future always looks good in the golden land, because no one remembers the past. Here is where the hot wind blows and the old ways do not seem relevant, where the divorce rate is double the national average and where one person in every 38 lives in a trailer. Here is the last stop for all those who come from somewhere else, for all those who drifted away from the cold and the past and the old ways. Here is where they are trying to find a new lifestyle, trying to find it in the only places they know to look: the movies and the newspapers.

—JOAN DIDION, *Slouching Towards Bethlehem*

CALIGULA (12–41 A.D.)

MONSTROUS MADNESS

He was sound neither of body nor mind. As a boy he was troubled with epilepsy; and while in his youth he had some endurance, at times ... he was hardly able to walk, stand up, collect his thoughts, or hold up his head. He himself realized his mental infirmity. ...

It is thought that his wife Caesonia gave him a drug, intended for a love potion, which had the effect of driving him mad. He was especially tormented with sleeplessness. He never rested more than three hours at night, and even for that length of time not quietly,

but terrified by strange apparitions.... [He would] wander
through the long colonnades, crying out from time to time for daylight, longing for its return....

... He began to ... lay claim to divine majesty. He ordered that
statues of the Gods especially famous for sanctity or artistic merit,
including that of Jupiter of Olympia, should be brought from
Greece, in order to remove their heads and put his own in their
place.... He also set up a special temple to his own godhead...
in which was a life-sized statue of the Emperor in gold, which was
dressed each day in clothing such as he wore himself.... At night
he used to invite the full and radiant moon to his embraces and
his bed.

□

He lived in habitual incest with all his sisters. At a large banquet
he placed each of them in turn below him, while his wife reclined
above. Of these he is believed to have violated Drusilla when he
was still a minor.... Afterwards, when she was the wife of Lucius
Cassius Longinus, he took her from him and openly treated her as
his lawful wife.... It is not easy to decide whether in his marriages
he acted more basely in contracting them, in repudiating them, or
in continuing them.

□

The following are instances of his innate brutality. When cattle
to feed the wild beasts he provided for a gladiatorial show were
costly, he selected criminals to be devoured; and, taking a place in
the middle of a colonnade, he reviewed the line of prisoners...
and bade them be led away "from baldhead to baldhead." [Cali-
gula was bald].... Many men of honorable rank were first disfigured with the marks of branding irons and then condemned to
the mines, to work at building roads, or to be thrown to the wild
beasts; or else he shut them up in cages on all fours, like animals, or
had them sawn into pieces.

Not all these punishments were for serious offenses, but merely
for criticizing one of his shows, or for never having sworn by his
Genius.

After inviting Ptolemy to come from his kingdom he received
him with honor, then suddenly had him executed for no other
reason than that when giving a gladiatorial show, he noticed that

Ptolemy on entering the theater attracted general attention by the
splendor of his purple cloak. . . .

. . . there was scarcely any woman of rank whom he did not approach. These he invited to dinner with their husbands, and as
they passed by the foot of his couch, he would inspect them criti-
cally and deliberately, as if buying slaves, even lifting up the face
of any who looked down in modesty. Then, as often as the fancy
took him, he would leave the room and send for the one who
pleased him best. Returning soon afterward . . . he would openly
commend or criticize his partner, recounting her charms or defects. . . . He threw down the statues of famous men . . . and so
utterly demolished them that they could not be set up again with
their inscriptions entire. He then forbade for all time the erection
of the statue of any living man anywhere, without his knowledge
and consent. He even thought of destroying the poems of Homer,
asking why he should not have the same privilege as Plato, who
excluded Homer from his ideal commonwealth.

—SUETONIUS, *op. cit.*

CANADA

The land is virginal, the wind cleaner than elsewhere, and every
lake newborn. . . . The breezes have nothing to remember, and
everything to promise. . . . This is the essence of the gray freshness
and brisk melancholy of this land.

And for all the charm of those qualities, it is also the secret of a
European's discontent. For it is possible, at a pinch, to do without
gods. But one misses the dead.

—RUPERT BROOKE, *Letters from America*

CANDIDATES FOR PUBLIC OFFICE

They will all promise every man, woman and child in the country
whatever he, she or it wants. They'll all be roving the land looking for chances to make the rich poor, to remedy the irremediable,
to succor the unsuccorable, to unscramble the unscrambleable, to
dephlogisticate the undephlogisticable. They will all be curing
warts by saying words over them, and paying off the national debt

with money that no one will have to earn.... In brief, they will divest themselves of their character as sensible, candid and truthful men, and become simply candidates for office, bent only on collaring votes. They will all know ... that votes are collared under democracy, not by talking sense but by talking nonsense.... Most of them, before the uproar is over, will actually convince themselves.

—H. L. Mencken, *Prejudices: Fourth Series*

CANNIBALS

Cannibals have the same ideas about right and wrong that we do. They make war with the same anger or passion. They commit the same crimes: Eating their enemies is only an added ceremonial. The wrong lies not in roasting them, but in killing them.

—Voltaire, to Frederick the Great

CAPITALISM

ACHIEVEMENTS

The capitalist achievement does not typically consist in providing more silk stockings for queens but in bringing them within the reach of factory girls in return for steadily decreasing amounts of effort.

☐

The capitalist process ... progressively raises the standard of life of the masses. It does so through a sequence of vicissitudes, the severity of which is proportional to the speed of the advance. But it does so effectively. One problem after another of the supply of commodities to the masses has been successfully solved by being brought within reach of the methods of capitalist production.

—Joseph A. Schumpeter, *Capitalism, Socialism and Democracy*

DOOMED BY SUCCESS

A socialist form of society will inevitably emerge from an equally inevitable decomposition of capitalist society.... Capitalism is being killed by its achievements.

—*Ibid.*

FALLACIES

A socialist interpretation of history . . . has governed political thinking for the last two or three generations and . . . consists mainly of
a particular view of economic history. The remarkable thing about
this view is that most of the assertions to which it has given the
status of "facts which everybody knows" have long been proved
not to have been facts at all; yet they still continue, outside the
circle of professional economic historians, to be almost universally
accepted as the basis for the estimate of the existing economic
order.

□

Who has not heard of the "horrors of early capitalism" and gained
the impression that the advent of this system brought untold new
suffering to large classes who before were tolerably content and
comfortable? We might justly hold in disrepute a system to which
the blame attached that even for a time it worsened the position of
the poorest and most numerous class of the population. The widespread emotional aversion to "capitalism" is closely connected with
this belief that the undeniable growth of wealth which the competitive order has produced was purchased at the price of depress-
ing the standard of life of the weakest elements of society.

That this was the case was at one time indeed widely taught by
economic historians. A more careful examination of the facts has,
however, led to a thorough refutation of this belief. Yet, a generation after the controversy has been decided, popular opinion still
continues as though the older belief had been true.

□

It is easy enough to find in the early nineteenth century instances
of extreme poverty and to draw the conclusion that this must have
been the effect of the introduction of machinery, without asking
whether conditions had been any better or perhaps even worse
before. . . .

And there is every reason to remember how miserable the majority of the people still were as recently as a hundred or a hundred
and fifty years ago. But we must not . . . allow a distortion of the
facts, even if committed out of humanitarian zeal, to affect our
view of what we owe to a system which for the first time in history
made people feel that this misery might be avoidable. The very

claims and ambitions of the working classes were and are the result of the enormous improvement of their position which capitalism brought about.

—F. A. HAYEK, "History and Politics," in
Capitalism and the Historians

IN CHINA

One of the most amusing and revealing episodes of the Chinese cultural revolution was the fact that when hundreds of thousands of inspired youths flooded Peking in 1966, they found that each contingent wore button badges announcing its city, but some badges were scarcer and thus rarer than others. Immediately and spontaneously a market arose in which different badges were traded at discount. Youths proudly showed off the scarce badges they were able to get by trade—as they demonstrated against the restoration of capitalism. . . .

—GORDON A. BENNETT and
RONALD N. MONTAPERTO (eds.),
Red Guard: The Political Biography of Dai Msiau-ai

ITS "INHUMANITY"

The common charge of inhumanity against the nineteenth century—for that is the popular reading of the policy of laissez faire, is it not?—would be an idle slander if it were not so gross. On three counts at least the indictment is false. The nineteenth century, for the first time, introduced on a broad scale the state policies of public health and public education. The nineteenth century, by turning out cheap goods, made possible the amazing climb of real wages in industrialized economies. The nineteenth century, by permitting the transfer of capital in large amounts, opened up the interiors of backward countries for development and production. For we must not forget that the investments of trading companies, before the nineteenth century, rarely penetrated beyond the seacoasts themselves. Early investments did not lead to capital improvements on a significant scale; the maintenance of trading stations did little to increase the production or transport systems of peoples being reached and therefore the marginal productivity of their labor. The record of Britain in America and India, before the nineteenth century, is clear on this point, as is, indeed, that of France. One exception is to be noted in the West Indies, and that is in the case of plantation wares. But certainly it is plain that British and French capital did not move overseas to any important degree into manufactures, internal transport, and banking until the nineteenth century.

—L. M. HACKER,
"The Anticapitalist Bias of American Historians," in
Capitalism and the Historians

CAPITALISM AND HISTORIANS

It was not among the factory employees but among the domestic workers, whose traditions and methods were those of the eighteenth century, that earnings were at their lowest. It would have provided evidence that it was not in the large establishments making use of steam power but in the garret or cellar workshops that conditions of employment were at their worst. It would have led to the conclusion that it was not in the growing manufacturing towns or the developing coal fields but in remote villages and the countryside that restrictions on personal freedom and the evils of truck were most marked. But few had the patience to go carefully through these massive volumes. It was so much easier to pick out the more sensational evidences of distress and work them into a dramatic story of exploitation.

□

"The clothing of the working people in a majority of cases," Engels declares, "is in a very bad condition. The material used for it is not of the best adapted. Wool and linen have almost vanished from the wardrobes of both sexes, and cotton has taken their place. Skirts are made of bleached or coloured cotton goods, and woolen petticoats are rarely to be seen on the wash line." The truth is that they never had been greatly displayed on the wash line, for woolen goods are liable to shrink. The workers of earlier periods had to make their garments last (second or third hand as many of these were), and soap and water were inimical to the life of clothing. The new, cheap textiles may not have been as hard-wearing as broadcloth, but they were more abundant; and the fact that they could be washed without suffering harm had a bearing, if not on their own life, at least on the lives of those who wore them.

—T. S. ASHTON,
"Treatment of Capitalism by Historians," in
Capitalism and the Historians

CAPITALISM AND MERCHANTS

We are faced here with a principle which runs through the whole history of commerce. For the long-distance trade—for the import and export of goods—the merchant, as an independent class, is indispensable. The sale of goods manufactured within the city, on the other hand, is the exclusive right of the manufacturers—i.e., the artisans. Why indeed should a middleman be allowed to step in and profit from such transactions? The simple artisan, the tailor or the shoemaker, was clearly distrustful of the smooth, slick, cunning Syrian, who might lure his customer away from him.

In the import-export trade, on the other hand, the main emphasis is on the risk, on the pleasure of doing business, and on the prospect of fat profits. It needed courage to furnish a ship, load it at great expense, and then wait for months, and sometimes years, until the captain returned with ship and merchandise. Courage, too, to risk an entire fortune in such an enterprise. A merchant needed confidence in himself, in his abilities, and in his knowledge of people. And he had to enjoy the confidence of others to get them to lend him money, and that, moreover, under the restrictive conditions of marine loans.

Wherever these merchants appeared their competitors grumbled. But their customers received them with open arms. They were delighted to be able to buy goods which did not exist in their own country: foodstuffs and indispensable raw materials, jewelry and ornaments, and sweetly smelling perfumes. Moreover, they could get rid of their own surpluses at excellent prices. That was just what annoyed the local consumer, the man in the weekly market, for naturally the prices rose steeply the moment the foreign buyers appeared. Rulers and police viewed every stranger with great distrust, in case he was a spy of a foreign power, a disguised pirate on reconnaissance, the political agent of a neighbor country, or the emissary of a group of discontented exiles engaged in subversive activity against their own city.

—ERNST SAMHABER, *Merchants Make History*

CAPITALISM AND RELIGION

All revolutions are declared to be natural and inevitable, once they are successful, and capitalism, as the type of economic system prevailing in Western Europe and America, is clothed today with the unquestioned respectability of the triumphant fact. But in its youth it was a pretender, and it was only after centuries of struggle that its title was established. For it involved a code of economic conduct and a system of human relations which were sharply at variance with venerable conventions, with the accepted scheme of social ethics, and with the law, both of the Church and of most European states. . . .

The tonic that braced them for the conflict was a new conception of religion, which taught them to regard the pursuit of wealth as, not merely an advantage, but a duty. This conception welded into a disciplined force the still feeble bourgeoisie, heightened its energies, and cast a halo of sanctification round its convenient vices.

—RICHARD H. TAWNEY,
Religion and the Rise of Capitalism

CAPITALISM AND SOCIALISM

The inherent vice of Capitalism is the unequal sharing of blessings; the inherent virtue of Socialism is the equal sharing of miseries.

—WINSTON CHURCHILL

CAPITALIST PROGRESS AND TURMOIL

Capitalist economy is not and cannot be stationary. . . . It is incessantly being revolutionized *from within* by new "experprise," i.e., by the intrusion of new commodities or new methods of production or new commercial opportunities. . . . Any existing structures and all the conditions of doing business are always in a process of change. Every situation is being upset before it has had time to work itself out. Economic progress, in capitalist society, means turmoil.

—JOSEPH A. SCHUMPETER, *op. cit.*

CAPITAL PUNISHMENT

No matter what can be said for abolition of the death penalty, it will be perceived symbolically as a loss of nerve: Social authority no longer is willing to pass an irrevocable judgment on anyone. Murder is no longer thought grave enough to take the murderer's life, no longer horrendous enough to deserve so fearfully irrevocable a punishment.

When murder no longer forfeits the murderer's life (though it will interfere with his freedom), respect for life itself is diminished, as the price for taking it is. Life becomes cheaper as we become kinder to those who wantonly take it.... If life is to be valued and secured, it must be known that anyone who takes the life of another forfeits his own.

—ERNEST VAN DEN HAAG, *Punishing Criminals*

CARNIVAL IN HAVANA

At last the final chariotload of Venuses sailed by, and a fanfare of trumpets heralded the arrival of a far stranger procession, organized by the Chinese community of Havana. Little men in the costumes of Buddhist priests swelled their cheeks over the mouthpieces of long wind instruments resting on the shoulders of the boys in front of them. A cohort of pikemen followed. They were dressed ... in Chinese armour and they grasped ... long halberds with fantastically shaped blades. After them came standard-bearers with silk banners which were embroidered and tasseled and fringed and charged with gleaming stars and dragons made of paper, lit from inside....

Other light-bearers accompanied them, supporting, in the slots of their baldricks, poles ten or fifteen yards high that poised on their summits many-colored parchment globes.... As they moved along, the light-bearers twirled the staves in their sockets, and the airy palaces and temples, glowing with a soft lustre against the stars, swung and gyrated high over our heads to the sound of bells and trumpets and far-oriental music.

There was something unspeakably charming and almost magical about this flimsy flying architecture. Chinese girls in gold litters came after them, and then ... little piebald horses splendidly caparisoned.... They bore upon their backs fairy-tale Manchu princesses whose heavy silk and gold-embroidered robes, sweeping to the ground with the stiffness of metal, entirely enveloped them. Under winged and pinnacled headdresses, ivory Chinese faces of extreme beauty gazed into the night. ...

The sound of the bugles and bells grew fainter, and the shining edifices receded; a diminishing Chinese Venice floating into the distance on a lagoon of stars.

□

An African sound now struck our ears: The clatter and boom of tom-toms ... and, again in the wake of a forest of lights and escorted by the flames of torches, an interminable but orderly horde of Negroes came dancing down the street. They heaved backwards and forwards with the advance and the recoil of the authentic Negro dance of Cuba, the *Conga*. On they came in hundreds, each dancer evolving alone; surging three paces to the left, stopping with a sort of abrupt choreographic hiccup on a half beat, then three paces to the right (crash!), and then to the left again as all the barbaric instruments underlined the beat....

They were tall, jet-black Negroes and handsome Negro women in the slave costume of the plantations.... Enormous scorpions were hung on scarecrow figures of eighteenth-century plantation owners in powdered wigs. Each of the dancers held in one hand a length of green sugarcane and in the other a cutlass which he flourished in rhythm with his steps. They were singing, a deep repetitive African chant that rose and fell and abruptly ceased and then began all over again in the mode of a Voodoo incantation.

□

Holding hands lest the human currents should carry us off into different maelstroms, we headed back to the *Perla de Cuba*.... Confetti was scattered everywhere and tangled balls of streamers had collected in the gutters. Under a streetlamp at the corner six amazing figures stood in colloquy. They were horses' heads ten feet high, like gigantic chessmen with bared teeth and staring eyes, their lower lips, articulated to mimic the action of speech, hanging inanely loose. Little portholes in their breasts revealed the faces of six Negroes smoking cigars. Intrigued by our three running figures,

the great heads swung ponderously round and followed us out of
sight with their great fatuous eyes. . . .
                    —PATRICK LEIGH FERMOR, *The Traveller's Tree*

CARNIVAL IN VENICE: 18th Century

Carnival began on St. Stephen's day, 26 December, when permission to wear masks was given publicly by a government officer
dressed in old pantomime clothes, in St. Mark's Square. The en-
semble of the black or white mask covering most of the face, with
the *bauta*, a hood of velvet or silk over the shoulders and the rest
of the head, under a three-cornered hat, looked sombre only to
visitors: Under it every woman was a *zentildonna;* class and even
sex were canceled out, and everyone became a secret spectator.
Even servants wore masks when they went shopping. Even beggars
used them. During the masquerades patricians and ordinary citizens
crowded together round the triumphal carriages and threaded their
way through the *calli* singing and dancing.
    The wildest day was Maundy Thursday, when fireworks were
let off in the Piazza in broad daylight, and a bull was beheaded by
members of the Smiths' and Butchers' guilds, in fantastic costumes.
A rope was slung between the top of the Campanile and the doge's
box . . . and an acrobat performed the annual *volo* or flight, to
present a bouquet to the doge. . . . There were puppet shows, fortune tellers, wandering musicians singing to the guitar, there were
quacks and perfumiers. . . .
    After six months of it the celebrations roared to a sudden full
stop: There were red flares and rockets, a mass of masked and
painted and costumed people dancing and joining hands; fireworks
went up continuously, and fell with a thrilling hiss into the water;
the shouting, the beating of drums, the laughter and squeals of
pleasure were such that the city seemed to tremble; sweets, oranges,
ribbons, pumpkin seeds and confetti were trampled on the paving
stones. At midnight the *marangona* and the bell of S. Francesco
della Vigna tolled slowly, and by dawn there was only the coloured
trash in the streets, and an unusually complete silence, with
Venice's typical night sounds, the lapping of water on stone and
the slight boom of boats on their moorings.
                    —MAURICE ROWDON, *The Silver Age of Venice*

GIACOMO CASANOVA (1725–1798)

All my life I was the victim of my senses. Indeed, I enjoyed going astray.... My follies were those of youth, and I laugh at them now, and if you are kind you will laugh at them, too.

□

I sought whatever gave me pleasure; that was always the main concern of my life. I never found any other occupation more important.

I always felt I was born for the opposite sex. I always loved it and I always did all I could to make myself loved by it. I always found that the woman with whom I was in love smelled good; the more profuse her sweat, the sweeter it was to me.

□

I loved truth so passionately that I resorted to lying in order to present truth to mentalities ignorant of its charm.

□

Happy or not, life is the only treasure a man possesses; those who do not love life do not deserve it. Honor is set above life, but only because dishonor betrays life.

—G. Casanova, Introduction,
The Story of My Life

CATALYSTS

Did you ever try to burn a lump of sugar with a match? You can't. But place some cigarette ash on it, and you can. Nothing happens to the ash; it merely makes the chemical reaction of burning possible.

As sugar burns in the presence of ash, so a host of fundamental reactions take place in the presence of substances called catalysts. All chemical reactions involve changes in the reacting materials; the peculiarity of a catalytic reaction is that the catalyst which promotes it is not changed at all. In fact it emerges ready to play its catalytic role all over again.

Catalysts resemble, in a way, the "philosopher's stone," which ancient alchemists dreamed would transmute base metals into gold. Though catalysts cannot change one element into another, they do enable the modern chemist to create new materials by breaking up or rearranging or combining the molecules of others.

—*Chemistry's Secret Agents,*
Standard Oil Company (New Jersey)

CATHERINE THE GREAT (1729–1796)

By no stretch of the imagination could Catherine be called a Russian, having been born as Princess of Anhalt-Zerbst . . . a petty German princedom. However, that only helped commend Catherine to the Empress Elizabeth when she decided to find a bride for her nephew Peter, heir to the Russian throne. . . .

Elizabeth staged a prodigious marriage celebration in St. Petersburg on 21 August 1745 but was so eager to see the union blessed with offspring that she hustled Catherine off to the nuptial couch when the wedding ball was barely underway. The groom, less ardent, arrived two hours later—remarking fatuously that the servant would indeed be astonished to see the two of them in bed together. Still an ignorant and innocent young girl, Catherine vainly awaited enlightenment on her wedding night, for the most eligible bachelor in Europe proved a dismal failure as husband, as at everything else. He even achieved the seemingly impossible feat of being unfaithful and impotent at the same time. Impotent or not—the point has never been established beyond doubt—he had several purported love affairs but has not been proved to have fathered a child in or out of wedlock. According to Catherine's own account, her marriage still remained unconsummated in 1752.

□

To Catherine the six months of Peter's reign were a nightmare. He repeatedly threatened to put her in a convent, while continuing to flaunt his liaison with Elizabeth Vorontsov—a squat, sallow, squinting, pockmarked, rowdy girl, and Catherine's very opposite. For years he had been threatening to marry this soulmate once his wife was out of the way, and as reigning monarch he could now easily dispose of her. Nor could Catherine easily protect herself, being in an advanced state of pregnancy by her latest lover, Gregory Orlov. Though the flowing fashions of the day might help to conceal her condition in early 1762, she hardly felt poised to overturn an empire. But in the event her latest liaison was to bring Peter's downfall.

□

Could Catherine bear her child without the Tsar's knowledge? To this end she employed a stratagem based on Peter's love of watching the fires which so often broke out in his capital. A servant of Catherine's agreed to set light to his own conveniently sited wooden house on receiving a signal from the palace. Labor began, the signal was given, the diversion duly created and the baby safely smuggled away. This took place on 11 April. A month later the drunken Emperor publicly humiliated Catherine at an official banquet, calling her a fool in front of four hundred distinguished guests who included foreign ambassadors.

□

She became a compulsive reader—graduating from novels to historical, political and philosophical works, and paying special attention to two French contemporaries, Montesquieu and Voltaire. Such matters meant nothing to most of Elizabeth's courtiers, but Catherine did come to share the concern of that circle for political intrigue. At first persecuted as an enemy by the powerful chancellor Bestuzhev-Ryumin, she allied herself with him when he realized that she was not an ally of Prussia. She was in fact more the instrument of England, obtaining loans or bribes from one British ambassador in respect of services to be rendered later.

—RONALD HINGLEY, *The Tsars*

[Catherine of Russia] was a fat woman in her sixtieth year, with false teeth and swollen legs; she still had the charm that some women exude to their dying day, but her love affairs, if they can be so called, were reduced to a system. When Potemkin found his powers no longer adequate for her demands, he connived at her having a series of youthful lovers, chosen from among the household guards. If her eye fell upon a handsome young guardsman, he was first given a thorough physical examination by the court physician to see if he was "healthy"; then one of the Empress's ladies of honor, known in court circles as *l'épreuveuse* (the prover), tested his capacity in a practical way. If he passed, he became the Empress's lover. This happened no fewer than thirteen times, since none of these young men could stand it very long. The incumbent during Jones's sojourn in Russia was Zubov, a guards-man in his twenties, and he was doing very well. Thus the Empress had no personal need for Jones; and his one thought after seeing her was to get off to the Black Sea and take over his command.

—SAMUEL ELIOT MORISON, *John Paul Jones*

CELEBRITIES AND HEROES

Since the Graphic Revolution, the celebrity overshadows the hero by the same relentless law which gives other kinds of pseudo-events an overshadowing power. When a man appears as hero and/or celebrity, his role as celebrity obscures and is apt to destroy his role as hero. The reasons, too, are those which tend to make all pseudo-events predominate. In the creation of a celebrity some-body always has an interest—newsmen needing stories, press agents paid to make celebrities, and the celebrity himself. But dead heroes have no such interest in their publicity, nor can they hire agents to keep them in the public eye. Celebrities, because they are made to order, can be made to please, comfort, fascinate, and flatter us. They can be produced and displaced in rapid succession.... We forget that celebrities are known primarily for their well-known-ness. And we imitate them as if they were cast in the mold of greatness.

☐

Our very efforts to debunk celebrities ... are self-defeating. They increase our interest in the fabrication.

... most true celebrities have press agents. And these press agents sometimes themselves become celebrities. The hat, the rabbit, and the magician are all equally news. It is twice as news-worthy that a charlatan can become a success. His charlatanry makes him even more of a personality.

—DANIEL J. BOORSTIN, *The Image*

CHANGE

Human society goes very incompetently about healing its ills. It is so impatient under the immediate irritation which is chafing it that it thinks only of getting rid of this, careless of the cost....

Good does not necessarily ensue upon evil; another evil may ensue upon it, and a worse one.

—MONTAIGNE

In a progressive country change is constant; and the great question is, not whether you should resist change which is inevitable, but whether that change should be carried out in deference to the manners, the customs, the laws, the traditions of the people, or in deference to abstract principles and arbitrary and general doctrines.

—BENJAMIN DISRAELI

... [Melbourne] thought change always ran the risk of disturbing the security of society; while convinced as he was of the futility of most human effort, he did not believe it ever did the good it intended. On the contrary, sensational reforms, like parliamentary reform, did positive harm. For by raising hopes that could never be fulfilled, they left people more discontented than ever.

—DAVID CECIL, *Melbourne*

CHARLES I (1600–1649)

With the assistance of the executioners he [Charles I] put his long hair under a white satin nightcap. He removed his cloak and doublet and laid himself down on the scaffold with his head on the block. For a few minutes he lay there praying, his eye, said a watcher, "as brisk and lively as ever he had seen it." Then he stretched out his hands, and the grizzled executioner brought down the axe and severed his head. The other held it up in silence to the people. A groan of horror rent the stillness. . . .

Then followed a hideous scene. Men and women were permitted —on payment—to dip their handkerchiefs in the King's blood, and his long locks were shorn and sold as keepsakes. The body was put in a plain deal coffin costing six pounds, covered with a black velvet pall, and remained for some days in a Whitehall bedroom.

Then it was embalmed, the head being sewn on, and afterwards removed to St. James's palace. An application to bury it in Henry VII's chapel was refused, but permission was given to lay it in St. George's chapel at Windsor. Thither, on Friday, February 9th, [1649] it was taken ... and placed in the vault which held the remains of Jane Seymour and Henry VIII. No service was read, for the governor of Windsor would not permit the use of the prayer-book.

The prophecy of Merlin was fulfilled, and Charles, who had chosen to be crowned in white, went in white to his tomb.

—JOHN BUCHAN, *Oliver Cromwell*

CHARLES XII OF SWEDEN (1682–1718) AND SULTAN AHMED III

The Grand Vizier [of Sultan Ahmed III] invited King Charles XII, who was in Demotica, to visit him, along with the new Khan of the Tartars and the ambassador from France. But Charles, whose pride had increased with his misfortunes, considered it an intolerable insult that a subject of the Sultan should dare send for him. He ordered his chancellor, Mullern, to go in his stead, and thinking that the Turks might not show him enough respect, the King, who was extreme in everything he did, took to his bed and resolved not to get up out of it as long as he stayed in Demotica.

He stayed in bed, pretending to be ill, for ten months. . . .

It was while Charles XII was spending his life in bed, that he learned of the disastrous fate of all the provinces of his kingdom outside of Sweden.

—VOLTAIRE, *Charles XII of Sweden*

KING CHENG (OR CH'IN) (3rd century B.C.)

King Cheng (or Ch'in) was the terrible genius who built the Great Wall and the fabulous complex of palaces at Hsien Yang, his capital. . . . He standardized the laws, the customs, the written language, the weights and measures, the agricultural tools and even the lengths of cart axles (so that the wheels would always fit the ruts) throughout the empire, and built great strategic highways 250 feet wide to link up the different parts of the country. He worked like a man obsessed, "examining 120 pounds-weight of reports a day."

But, fearful of treachery and heresy, he moved 120,000 leading families of the states he had conquered to the capital, so that they could not plot in peace, and ruled that any man who quoted from the Confucian classics should be executed. Nor was this enough. . . . He sanctioned the atrocious act that has won him the undying detestation of more than 60 generations of Chinese; the burning of the entire body of Chinese literature, with the exception of a few works on agriculture, medicine and divination. The precious heritage of the golden age of Chinese philosophy, which had so strikingly coincided with that of Greece, went up in the flames.

The Chinese did not stand the Ch'in reign of terror for long. ... Ch'in's swift and ephemeral triumphs left behind one vast country named after him: China.

—DENNIS BLOODWORTH, *The Chinese Looking Glass*

THE CHILD

A child is often an innocent by-product.

—ANON

... the most deadly of all possible sins is the mutilation of a child's spirit; for such mutilation undercuts the life principle of trust, without which every human act, may it feel ever so good and seem ever so right, is prone to perversion by destructive forms of conscientiousness.

□

In that first relationship man learns something which most individuals who survive and remain sane can take for granted most of the time.... I have called this early treasure "basic trust"; it is the first psychosocial trait and the fundament of all others. Basic trust in mutuality is that original "optimism," that assumption that "somebody is there," without which we cannot live. In situations in which such basic trust cannot develop in early infancy because of a defect in the child or in the maternal environment, children die mentally. They do not respond nor learn; they do not assimilate their food and fail to defend themselves against infection, and often they die physically as well as mentally.*

—ERIK H. ERIKSON, *Young Man Luther*

If children grew up according to early indications, we should have nothing but geniuses.

—JOHANN WOLFGANG VON GOETHE

* Rene Spitz, "Hospitalism," *The Psychoanalytic Study of the Child*, Vol. I.

CHILD LABOR

"We take them as soon as they can stand up." Not only did they take them, as the Southern manager said in reference to children working in his factory, but running machines late at night they were sometimes kept awake "by the vigilant superintendent with cold water dashed into their faces." "Late" meant two o'clock in the morning in upstate New York, where "mere babies" were found employed in a cannery. In their utter weariness after work, these children often forgot their hunger and fell asleep with food in their mouths.

—OTTO L. BETTMAN, *The Good Old Days*

CHILDHOOD

In medieval society the idea of childhood did not exist: this is not to suggest that children were neglected, forsaken, or despised. The idea of childhood is not to be confused with affection for children: It corresponds to an awareness of the particular nature of childhood ... which distinguishes the child from the adult, even the young adult. In medieval society this awareness was lacking. That is why, as soon as the child could live without the constant solicitude of his mother, his nanny or his cradle-rocker, he belonged to adult society....

There is not a single collective picture of the times in which children are not to be found, nestling singly or in pairs in the *trousse* hung round women's necks, or urinating in a corner, or playing their part in a traditional festival, or as apprentices in a workshop, or as pages serving a knight, etc. The infant who was too fragile as yet to take part in the life of adults simply "did not count": This is the expression used by Moliere....

Until the eighteenth century, adolescence was confused with childhood. In school Latin the word *puer* and the word *adolescens* were used indiscriminately ... there were no terms in French to distinguish between *pueri* and *adolescentes*. There was virtually only one word in use: *enfant*.

—PHILIPPE ARIÈS, *Centuries of Childhood*

Everybody's young days are a dream, a delightful insanity, a sweet solipsism . . . everything is a possibility, and we live happily on credit. . . . The world is a mirror in which we seek the reflection of our own desires. The allure of violent emotions is irresistible. . . . We are not apt to distinguish between our liking and our esteem; urgency is our criterion . . . we are impatient of restraint.

—MICHAEL OAKESHOTT, *Rationalism in Politics*

CHILDREN

Children: natural mimics who act like their parents in spite of every effort to teach them good manners.

—ANON.

The games of children are their most serious business.

—MONTAIGNE, *Essays*

Children and princes quarrel for trifles.

—BENJAMIN FRANKLIN

A boy is, of all wild beasts, the most difficult to manage.

—PLATO

Childhood: that happy period when nightmares occur only during sleep.

—*Changing Times*

We are all geniuses up to the age of ten.

—ALDOUS HUXLEY

BEATING

The majority of men have never invented the device of beating children into submission. Some of the American Plains Indian tribes were . . . deeply shocked when they first saw white people beat their children. In their bewilderment they could only explain such behavior as part of an overall missionary scheme—an explanation supported by the white people's method of letting their babies cry themselves blue in the face. It all must mean, so they thought, a well-calculated wish to impress white children with the idea that this world is not a good place to linger in, and that it is better to look to the other world where perfect happiness is to be had at the price of having sacrificed this world.

—ERIK H. ERIKSON, *Young Man Luther*

REARING THEM

The very title of Dr. [Benjamin] Spock's new book—*Bringing Up Children in a Difficult Time*—has caught one of the fundamental undercurrents of contemporary civilization, namely, self-pity. . . .

"The main lesson in school," we are told, "is how to get along in the world. Different subjects are merely means to this end."

In Dr. Spock's world, everything is subordinated to the end of undifferentiated sociability, served up with the custard of love; and the isolated [student] getting on with his quadratic equations . . . is an image of failure. "The child who doesn't know how to make friends needs help in becoming sociable and appealing." . . .

The Spockian idea that "there's no use knowing a lot if you can't be happy, cannot get along with people, can't hold the kind of job you want" is one that leads straight to the tranquilizer.

—KENNETH MINOGUE, *Encounter*, July 1975

CHILDREN AND DEATH

A child's idea of being "dead" has nothing much in common with ours apart from the word. Children know nothing of the horrors of corruption, of freezing in the ice-cold grave, of the terrors of eternal nothingness—ideas which grown-up people find it so hard to tolerate, as is proved by all the myths of a future life. The fear of death has no meaning to a child; hence it is that he will play with the dreadful word and use it as a threat against a playmate: "If you do that again, you'll die."

[Footnote added in 1909]: I was astonished to hear a highly intelligent boy of ten remark, after the sudden death of his father: "I know father is dead, but what I can't understand is why he doesn't come home to supper."

—SIGMUND FREUD, *Interpretation of Dreams*

CHILDREN AND PARENTS

Parents must confront themselves before their children confront them, and they must learn what they want their children to learn —that time does pass and that the future happiness of their child is more important than the present gratification of their child. They must learn to say "no" as lovingly as they say "yes."

The child who has never been controlled can never control himself. And there is no insecurity like being unable to control oneself. Words like "control," "obedience," "authority," "discipline" offend the sentimental liberalism of too many American parents. But the id can be a much more terrible despot than the superego.

The permissive fallacy is that children learn good things from bad experiences.

—DONALD BARR, *Who Killed Humpty-Dumpty?*

CHILDREN AND SEX

The practice of playing with children's privy parts formed part of a widespread tradition, which is still operative in Moslem circles. These have remained aloof not only from scientific progress but also from the great moral reformation . . . which disciplined eighteenth-century and particularly nineteenth-century society in England and France.

□

Père de Dainville . . . writes: "The respect due to children was then [in the sixteenth century] completely unknown. Everything was permitted in their presence: coarse language, scabrous actions and situations; they had heard everything and seen everything."

This lack of reserve with regard to children surprises us: We raise our eyebrows at the outspoken talk . . . the bold gestures, the physical contacts, about which it is easy to imagine what a modern psychoanalyst would say. The psychoanalyst would be wrong. The attitude to sex . . . varies according to environment, and according to period and mentality. Nowadays the physical contacts described by Heroard would strike us as bordering on sexual perversion and nobody would dare to indulge in them publicly. This was not the case at the beginning of the seventeenth century.

—PHILIPPE ARIÈS, *Centuries of Childhood*

It is commonly believed that the sexual instinct is lacking in children, and only begins to arise in them when the sexual organs mature. This is a grave error, equally serious from the point of view both of theory and of actual practice. It is so easy to correct it by observation that one can only wonder how it can ever have arisen. As a matter of fact, the newborn infant brings sexuality with it into the world; certain sexual sensations attend its development while at the breast and during early childhood, and only very few children would seem to escape some kind of sexual activity and sexual experience before puberty.

□

A younger child is very specially inclined to use imaginative stories such as these in order to rob those born before him of their prerogative . . . ; and he often has no hesitation in attributing to his mother as many fictitious love affairs as he himself has competitors. An interesting variant of the family romance may then appear, in which the hero and the author returns to legitimacy himself while his brothers and sisters are got out of the way by being bastardized.

□

In this way, for instance, the young phantasy builder can get rid of his forbidden degree of kinship with one of his sisters if he finds himself sexually attracted by her.

If anyone is inclined to turn away in horror from this depravity of the childish heart or feels tempted, indeed, to dispute the possibility of such things, he should observe that these works of fiction, which seem so full of hostility, are none of them really so badly intended, and that they still preserve, under a slight disguise, the child's original affection for his parents. The faithlessness and ingratitude are only apparent.

If we examine in detail the commonest of these imaginative romances . . . we find that these new and aristocratic parents are equipped with attributes that are derived entirely from real recollections of the actual and humble ones; so that in fact the child is not getting rid of his father but exalting him. Indeed the whole effort at replacing the real father by a superior one is only an expression of the child's longing for the happy, vanished days when his father seemed to him the noblest and strongest of men and his mother the dearest and loveliest of women. He is turning away

from the father whom he knows today to the father in whom he
believed in the earlier years of his childhoood.

—SIGMUND FREUD,
The Sexual Enlightenment of Children

CHINA

The Chinese pattern has governed more people, over a larger area,
for a greater length of time, than any other. By the first century
B.C. the Chinese emperor ruled an area larger than that of the
Roman Empire at its greatest extent, and at many periods it has
been much larger. No other system of government has maintained
its sway over a state of anything approaching comparable size for
two thousand years in almost uninterrupted succession. It has been
the most viable government yet developed by man.

—HERBERT G. CREEL,
"The Origins of Statecraft in China," in
Midway, Summer 1969

A BABY TOWER

Peasants without a grain of rice left in the home sold their children into domestic service, concubinage, and slavery. More often,
distracted Chinese simply killed off the latest baby in order to have
one less mouth to feed, one less claim on the meager inheritance
to be shared out among the next generation. Sometimes a bucket
of water was kept ready beside the bed of childbirth so that the
period from delivery to death by drowning need only be a matter
of moments.

Somerset Maugham tells us in *The Sights of the Town* how he
came upon a little tower on a Chinese hillside with a single small
hole in its wall, from which came a nauseating odor. This was the
baby tower, and it covered a deep charnel pit into which parents
threw their unwanted children through the aperture or, if they
were more gentle, lowered them in a basket on a piece of stout
string. . . .

Perhaps nothing measures the enormous abyss between Chinese
living and Western understanding than a passage from a Chinese
book of travel . . . in the last century: "England is so short of in-

habitants that the English rear every child that is born. Even prostitutes who bear children do not destroy them."
—DENNIS BLOODWORTH, *The Chinese Looking Glass*

CHINA: A CAPITAL OF CHINA BURNS FOR A LAUGH

... the imperial concubines injected a fine flow of vulgarity into
the veins of the imperial family.... But otherwise their rivalries,
their ambitions, their extravagances, and their whims played the
devil with empire and more than once brought China to the brink
of ruin ... like the lady whose favorite occupation was tearing up
vast quantities of silk, and whose failure to smile proved a national
catastrophe. Determined to wring a laugh from this gloomy beauty,
the infatuated emperor ordered hilltop beacons to be lit in the
recognized alarm signal that the Huns had invaded.

All over the country, men dropped their plows, seized their
swords, and followed their feudal lords in forced marches to defend the frontier and the capital. When the joke was sprung and
the tired, mud-stained feudatories learned they had been the victims of a harmless little hoax, the concubine's merriment knew
no bounds. But sheepish though they may have appeared, they
would not respond twice to the same cry of "Wolf," and when the
beacons had to be fired in earnest shortly afterward, the lords and
their armies stayed at home and let the Huns light the biggest bea-
con of all by burning down the capital.

—Ibid.

INTRIGUES

The Chinese passion for (addiction to, one might properly say)
hyper-Byzantine political machinations has, obviously, not been
extirpated by the second restoraton of Teng Hsiao-ping and the
near-sanctification of his essentially rational policies. It is impossible
to expunge that passion from the hearts and brains of a people
whose greatest folk heroes have for some three millennia been distinguished by their amoral cunning in the ruthless pursuit of power.
Certainly the annals of the People's Republic of China, which was
founded only 28 years ago, provide no evidence that the quintes-
sential character of Chinese politicians has been altered in any sig-

nificant respect by the advent of Marxism-Leninism. A conspiratorial people have, rather, adopted a conspiratorial ideology; the inclination to treachery, violence, and labyrinthine intrigues inherent in each has been greatly intensified.

—ROBERT ELEGANT,
"Eternal China, Eternal Conspiracies," in
National Review, October 23, 1977

CHINESE PORTRAITS

I never returned to any of their cities after I had visited it a first time without finding my portrait and the portraits of my companions drawn on the walls and on sheets of paper exhibited in the bazaars. When I visited the sultan's city I passed with my companions through the painters' bazaar on my way to the sultan's palace. We were dressed after the Iraqi fashion. On returning from the palace in the evening, I passed through the same bazaar, and saw my portrait and those of my companions drawn on a sheet of paper which they had affixed to the wall.... This is a custom of theirs, I mean making portraits of all who pass through their country ... they have brought this to such perfection that if a stranger commits any offense that obliges him to flee from China, they send his portrait far and wide. A search is then made for him and wheresoever the person bearing resemblance to that portrait is found he is arrested.

—IBN BATUTA, *Travels in Asia and Africa*

CHRISTENDOM AT WAR

They fight everywhere endlessly and without measure, nation against nation, city against city, one faction against another, prince against prince, continually destroying one another. For the foolish ambition of two men, who will shortly die, human affairs are turned upside down.

I need not recall the tragedies of antiquity: Look at the last ten years. What land or sea did not witness warfare? What region or river was not soaked with blood? The cruelty of Christians surpasses that of heathens and beasts.... Pretense aside, it is ambitions, anger, and the desire for plunder that are at the base of Christian wars. . . . Christians have allied themselves with Turks to wage war against fellow-Christians. . . .

It shames me to recall the superficial reasons by which Christian princes provoke the world to war. This particular prince finds or feigns an old title to land, as if it mattered who ruled a kingdom as long as the welfare of the people was considered. Another prince finds a trifling fault in some neighboring state. A third is offended by some slight to someone's wife.

. . . Beasts do not fight collectively. Who has ever seen ten lions fight ten bulls? Yet how often do 20,000 armed Christians fight 20,000 armed Christians? . . .

What do miters and helmets have in common? . . . What has a Bible to do with a sword? How can one reconcile a salutation of peace with an exhortation to war? How reconcile peace in one's mouth and war in one's deeds? Do you praise war with the same mouth that you preach peace and Christ? Do you herald with the same trumpet both God and Satan? Wearing a cowl, do you incite the simple to murder and believe you are preaching the Gospel?

—ERASMUS, *The Complaint of Peace*

CHRISTIANITY

Our curiosity is naturally prompted to inquire by what means the Christian faith obtained so remarkable a victory over the established religions of the earth. To this inquiry an obvious but satisfactory answer may be . . . that it was owing to the convincing evidence of the doctrine itself and to the ruling providence of its great Author. But as truth and reason seldom find so favorable a reception in the world, and as the wisdom of Providence frequently condescends to use the passions of the human heart and the general circumstances of mankind as instruments to execute its purpose, we may still be permitted (though with the becoming submission) to ask, not indeed what were the first, but what were the secondary causes of the rapid growth of the Christian church?

—EDWARD GIBBON,
The Decline and Fall of the Roman Empire

Christianity has not done these things for peoples, because, checked or perverted by the worse propensities of human nature, it has never been applied in practice. It has not abolished oppression and corruption in governments, nor extinguished international hatreds and wars; has not even prevented the return of hideous cruelties in war which were believed to have been long extinct.

—JAMES BRYCE, *Modern Democracies*

No sooner had Jesus knocked over the dragon of superstition than Paul boldly set it on its legs again—in the name of Jesus.

—GEORGE BERNARD SHAW

CHRISTIANITY AND CHINA

For three and a half centuries Catholic and then Protestant missionaries in China propagated not only the Christian faith but also the Western point of view: individualism, human rights, and, from the nineteenth century onward, freedom. They also taught the Western way of doing things: the scientific method, mechanization, and technology.

Dwarfing our present worldwide governmental programs in effort, if not cash, expended, this private-sector proselytization had in China during the third decade of this century more than ten thousand American and European missionaries in person-to-person programs, over a hundred Christian colleges and universities, some seven hundred high schools, more than four thousand primary schools, and in excess of five hundred hospitals and clinics.

In mass media, the output was prodigious. Catholic production alone in secular matters included thirteen scientific periodicals and forty-nine dealing with social, cultural, and educational subjects. . . .

Thousands of Chinese students for at least two generations went to the United States and Western Europe for higher education. Many of them became the leaders in the "modernization" of China. . . .

What came of this prolonged outpouring of love, labor, and blood?

Less than one percent of the population of China was converted to Christianity. China was but superficially modernized and was torn by dissension. The massive bulk of Chinese existed in a Malthusian cycle, illiterate, impoverished, and fatalistic.

Then came the culmination. Three hundred and fifty years of enlightenment from the West was extinguished by an ideological movement that had existed in China for less than thirty years. Communism then undertook the modernization of China by force.

—JOHN PATON DAVIES, JR., *Foreign and Other Affairs*

HENRI CHRISTOPHE OF HAITI (1767–1820)

On state occasions and birthdays, the king would receive his nobles and his officers of state. Unlike the pictures of the other Haitian heroes, he is not always smothered in gold braid and feathers. Sometimes he wore a blue cutaway coat, a high white stock, breeches, and buckled pumps: a tall, handsome-looking man, with a complexion of the darkest ebony, of immensely powerful, bland Olympian aspect. The queen would stand at his side with the princes and princesses of the blood. Behind them, anomalous figures among the Negro grandees, Dr. Stewart, his Scottish physician, and the Philadelphian governess, could be singled out.

☐

Everything he did was on the same exaggerated and titanic scale. A giant himself and possessed of enormous physical strength, he proved a very capable and quite fearless general throughout the War of Independence. The destruction of Cap Haitien (where, as a young slave, he had been a waiter in a hotel) gives an idea of the lines on which his mind worked. He sprinkled his kingdom with palaces, many of which, including the palace with three hundred and sixty-five doors, were never completed. During the building of the citadel, the people of the north were, temporarily, virtually reenslaved, and it is a popular saying in the island that each of the great blocks which they hauled across the mountains was paid for by a human life. It was built 2,500 feet above the sea, as a stronghold against the return of the Napoleonic armies, and the castle was capable of garrisoning ten thousand troops. Storerooms for food and cisterns for drinking water and magazines of powder and shot were built to withstand a siege of several years.

☐

He was a tireless worker and possessed an excellent brain. The constitution and the mass of royal edicts which were issued when he had himself declared King Henri I of Haiti in 1811 prove that every detail of the organization of his realm had been minutely prepared in advance. . . .

He hated voodoo, as a survival from the time of slavery. Marriage was enforced and Catholicism was established as the state religion. He set up a state printing press, built schools in the provinces, and summoned a staff of foreign professors to his new Academy in Cap Haitien. Christophe had a passion for education, and ... had learnt to read and write very adequate French. ...

—PATRICK LEIGH FERMOR, *The Traveller's Tree*

HIS DEATH, OCTOBER 8, 1820

The end of this colossus was as tragic, in its way, as that of Toussaint Louverture in his dungeon among the snows of the Jura. His subjects were in rebellion and his enemies were threatening the kingdom when he was suddenly struck down by paralysis. As he lay in canopied immobility at Sans Souci, the news spread through the kingdom that he was actually dead. His European doctor could not help him, so an African houngan was called, who massaged him for many hours with a mixture of rum and red pepper. Putting on his regalia of white and gold and blue, he contrived to walk to the front of his palace. His troops were assembled for review, and a large concourse of the people, summoned to see that the king was still alive, waited in silence. He made a few steps towards his charger, intending to mount it and receive the salute of the troops and populace. But, still a yard or two away, he suddenly crumpled up and rolled between his horse's feet. It was the end. He was helped back into the palace, where, deafened by the noise outside the windows, he took a pistol that was ready loaded for such a contingency, it is said, with a silver bullet, and fired it through his heart.

The kingdom collapsed. The enemy was triumphant everywhere, and in a few days the streets of Cap Haitien were resounding with cheers for Boyer, the Mulatto president.

—*Ibid.*

WINSTON CHURCHILL (1874–1965)

ABOUT HIMSELF

I was happy as a child with my toys in my nursery. I have been happier every year since I became a man. But this interlude of school makes a sombre gray patch upon the chart of my journey. ... In all the twelve years I was at school no one ever succeeded in making me write a Latin verse or learn any Greek except the alphabet.

☐

I have a tendency against which I should, perhaps, be on my guard, to swim against the stream.

☐

I was once asked to devise an inscription for a monument in France. I wrote "In war, Resolution. In defeat, Defiance. In Victory, Magnanimity. In Peace, Goodwill." The inscription was not accepted.

—My Early Life

My mother was American and my ancestors were officers in Washington's army. I am myself an English Speaking Union.

☐

I have been brought up and trained to have the utmost contempt for people who get drunk.

☐

I am always ready to learn, although I do not always like being taught.

☐

Although always prepared for martyrdom, I preferred that it should be postponed.

☐

It is a fine thing to be honest, but it is also very important to be right.

☐

It is hard to snub a beautiful woman—they remain beautiful and the rebuke recoils.

☐

I have never considered myself at all a good hater—although I recognize that from moment to moment [hate] has added stimulus to pugnacity.

☐

When you have to kill a man it costs nothing to be polite.

☐

I always avoid prophesying beforehand. . . . It is much better policy to prophesy after the event has already taken place.

—from various speeches and interviews

I neither want nor need [cigars and brandy], but I should think it pretty hazardous to interfere with the ineradicable habit of a lifetime.

—*Time*, July 6, 1953

I am without an office, without a seat, without a party, and without an appendix.

—after his defeat at Dundee, 1922

We must all learn how to support ourselves, but we must also learn how to live. We need a lot of engineers in the modern world, but we do not want a world of modern engineers.

—speech at Oslo, May 1948

I cannot help reflecting that if my father had been an American and my mother British, instead of the other way round, I might have got here on my own.

—speech, U.S. Congress, December 16, 1941

Be on your guard! I am going to speak in French—a formidable undertaking and one which will put great demands upon your friendship for Great Britain.

—speech in Paris, after Liberation

I am ready to meet my Maker. Whether my Maker is prepared for the great ordeal of meeting me is another matter.

—on his 75th birthday

Never give in! Never give in! Never, Never, Never, Never—in nothing great or small, large or petty—never give in except to convictions of honor and good sense.

—speech, Harrow, October 1941

ABOUT HIM

Young Churchill was short, plump, and lisped. He never forgot that, at his second preparatory school, he had been frightened by other boys throwing cricket balls at him, and had taken refuge behind some trees. This, to him, was a shameful memory; and, very early in life, he determined that he would be as tough as anybody could be. When he was eighteen, he nearly killed himself when being chased by his cousin and brother by jumping from a bridge to avoid capture. He fell twenty-nine feet, ruptured a kidney, remained unconscious for three days and was unable to work for nearly two months. There is no doubt whatever that Churchill's physical courage was immense; but it rested upon his determination to conquer his initial physical disadvantages.

—ANTHONY STORR, in Basil Liddell Hart,
Churchill Revised

Few men have stuck so religiously to one craft—the handling of words. In peace it made his political fortune; in war it has won all men's hearts. Without that feeling for words he might have made little enough of life. For in judgment, in skill in administration, in knowledge of human nature, he does not at all excel.

Winston found that out for himself quite early. "You see, Charles, it all began at Harrow." Sitting at the bottom of the school, under something of a cloud, he discovered that he could do what other boys could not do—he could write. And when as a subaltern in India, he began to read Gibbon, already he knew what he wanted to do in life. He confessed that from the beginning "personal distinction" was his goal, and he knew, too, that it could only be achieved by cultivating his inborn aptitude; if he had always done what he liked in life, that did not mean that he was afraid of hard work. Above all, he had set his heart on one thing: He wanted to be an orator. He read everything he could get hold of about Chatham; he studied his father's speeches; he practiced his own before the looking-glass. Even then he dreamed of the day when he would dominate the House of Commons, when they would have to listen to him. He told me this very simply, stopping when his voice threatened to get out of control, while I marveled at his will and purpose. The wonder to me was that he had not lost heart. For, in truth, he did not seem to be designed by nature for his part. Small, tongue-tied, with an impediment in his speech, when he rose in the House, he was always fearful that he might blurt out something that would get him into trouble, and that he would wake in the morning to find that he had blighted his prospects. When he told me this he hesitated and then went on: "I did not get completely rid of that until the war."

"Without the most careful preparation," he continued, "I could

not speak at all in those days. And even then I always kept strictly
to my notes." Moreover, in spite of all the pains he took, he was
always in danger of breaking down in the course of a speech. Once
he had found himself on his feet, with his mind a complete blank,
while the awful silence was broken only by friendly, encouraging
noises; he stood his ground until at last he could bear it no longer;
back in his seat, he could only bury his head in his hands.

After his breakdown in the House of Commons he dreaded getting up to speak more than ever. Sometimes he would persuade
himself that what he was about to say had already been said, or
that the time to say it was past. Any excuse served to keep him in
his seat. But he obstinately refused to give in. He would not admit
defeat.

—LORD MORAN, *Churchill*
(taken from the Diaries of Lord Moran)

Anybody who served anywhere near him was devoted to him.
It is hard to say why. He was not kind or considerate. He bothered
nothing about us. He knew the names only of those very close to
him and would hardly let anyone else come into his presence. He
was free with abuse and complaint. He was exacting beyond reason
and ruthlessly critical. He continuously exhibited all the characteristics which one usually deplores and abominates in the boss.
Not only did he get away with it but nobody really wanted him
otherwise. He was unusual, unpredictable, exciting, original, stimulating, provocative, outrageous, uniquely experienced, abundantly
talented, humorous, entertaining—almost everything a man could
be, a great man.

—SIR GEORGE MALLABY,
Under-Secretary in the Cabinet Office,
in BASIL LIDDELL HART,
Churchill Revised

Churchill had continued to be the great animator of the war. The
collection of minutes which fill the appendices of his volumes provide the best opportunity of seeing the genius of the man
displayed in all its abundance. No one can read them without marvel-
ing at his fertility, versatility, and vitality. He was constantly spur-
ring or coaxing ministers, officials, and generals to greater activity
and quicker progress. . . .

Yet his account leaves the analytical reader with the impression that his actual influence was much less than is commonly supposed. It is astonishing to find how often he failed to get his views accepted by the chiefs of staff, even when his views were most clearly right. His account also reveals a hesitation to insist on what he considered right, and a deference to officialdom, that run contrary to the popular picture of his dominating personality. How is it to be explained? Was it due to the carryover effect of spending two years in the wilderness during World War I as a penalty for putting himself in opposition to the weight of official opinion?

—BASIL LIDDELL HART, *ibid.*

CITIES

Ten thousand years ago, the world's entire human population was a few hundred thousand Stone Age primitives, who roamed in hunting bands of seldom more than fifty souls. . . . [With the development of agriculture, people became] food producers instead of food gatherers. With a supply of food assured, they could settle in permanent villages. . . . No farmer, in moving, could take with him the field he had laboriously fenced, leveled, plowed, seeded, weeded, and harvested. . . . [At the] northern end of the Arabian Desert . . . [were the] earliest villages of mankind. . . . As far as is known, [Jericho] is the oldest still inhabited settlement on earth, where men have lived continuously for over 8,000 years.

□

Without walls, men might never have reached the city-building stage of culture at all. . . . A city . . . contained all sorts of attractive goods, well worth stealing and also well worth defending. With a massive wall and an ample supply of food and water, a city could withstand a siege by an army several times the size of its own. . . . So marked was the distinction between walled and unwalled settlements that some archaeologists define a city as a settlement surrounded by a wall.

—L. SPRAGUE DE CAMP,
Great Cities of the Ancient World

He worked like hell in the country so he could live in the city, where he worked like hell so he could live in the country.

—DON MARQUIS

A great city, a great solitude.

—Proverb

Reformers have long observed city people loitering on busy corners, hanging around in candy stores and bars and drinking soda pop on stoops, and have passed a judgment, the gist of which is: "This is deplorable! If these people had decent homes and a more private or bosky outdoor place, they wouldn't be on the street!"

This judgment represents a profound misunderstanding of cities. It makes no more sense than to drop in at a testimonial banquet in a hotel and conclude that if these people had wives who could cook, they would give their parties at home.

The point of both the testimonial banquet and the social life of city street walks is precisely that they are public. They bring together people who do not know each other in an intimate, private social fashion, and in most cases do not care to know each other in that fashion.

Nobody can keep open-house in a great city. Nobody wants to. And yet if interesting, useful, and significant contacts among the people of cities are confined to acquaintanceships suitable for private life, the city becomes stultified. Cities are full of people with whom a certain degree of contact is useful and enjoyable, but you do not want them in your hair. And they do not want you in theirs either.

—JANE JACOBS,
The Death and Life of Great American Cities

CIVILIZATION

The civilized world represents the victory of persuasion over force.
—PLATO

The whole history of the course of civilization is no more than an account of the various methods adopted by mankind for "binding" their unsatisfied wishes.

—SIGMUND FREUD, *Totem and Taboo*

Civilization is always in need of being saved. The nation best above all nations is she in whom the civic genius of the people does the saving day by day, by acts without external picturesqueness; by speaking, writing, voting reasonably; by smiting corruption swiftly; by good temper between parties; by the people knowing true men when they see them, and preferring them as leaders to rabid partisans or empty quacks.

—WILLIAM JAMES, *Memories and Studies*

Civilized men arrived in the Pacific, armed with alcohol, syphilis, trousers, and the Bible.

—HAVELOCK ELLIS

Nothing can be more abhorrent to democracy than to imprison a person or keep him in prison because he is unpopular. This is really the test of civilization.

—WINSTON CHURCHILL

The virtues of enterprise, diligence, and thrift are the indispensable foundation of any complex and vigorous civilization. It was Puritanism which, by investing them with a supernatural sanction, turned them from an unsocial eccentricity into a habit, and a religion.

—RICHARD H. TAWNEY,
Religion and the Rise of Capitalism

All civilizations have been created and directed by small intellectual aristocracies, and never by people in the mass. The power of crowds is only to destroy.

—GUSTAVE LeBON, *The Psychology of the Crowd*

CIVIL LIBERTY

CIVIL RIGHTS

Men are qualified for civil liberty in exact proportion to their disposition to put moral chains upon their own appetites; in proportion as their love of justice is above their rapacity; in proportion as their soundness and sobriety of understanding is above their vanity and presumption; in proportion as they are more disposed to listen to the counsels of the wise and good in preference to the flattery of knaves.

Society cannot exist unless a controlling power upon will and appetite be placed somewhere; and the less of it there is within, the more of it there must be without. It is ordained in the eternal constitution of things that men of intemperate minds cannot be free. Their passions forge their fetters.

—EDMUND BURKE, letter, 1791

Our civil rights have no dependence on our religious opinions, any more than our opinions in physics or geometry. . . .

—THOMAS JEFFERSON,
from his Bill for Religious Liberty, Virginia

CIVIL WAR

A wagon train seventeen miles long, loaded with wounded [Confederate] men, crawled over the mountain road toward Chambersburg. It was a nightmarish procession of pain. A great many of the wounded men had received no medical attention whatever, the almost springless wagons rolled and jolted over the uneven road, and no halts were permitted for any reason. The cavalry officer in charge of the train said that he learned more on that trip about the horrors of war than he had learned in all of his battles. . . .

A fearful odor of decay lay over the field. A cavalry patrol went through Gettysburg to scout the Cashtown road to the west, and as it came out by the fields where dead bodies had been lying in the heat for four days the cavalrymen sickened and vomited as they rode. The country here was the ultimate abomination of desolation: "As far as the eye could reach on both sides of the Cashtown road you see blue-coated boys, swollen up to look as giants, quite black in the face, but nearly all on their backs, looking into the clear blue with open eyes, with their clothes torn open. It is strange that dying men tear their clothes in this manner. You see them lying in platoons of infantry with officers and arms exactly as they stood or ran—artillery men with caisson blown up and four horses, each in position, dead. You meet also limbs and fragments of men. The road is strewn with dead, whom the rebels have half buried and whom the heavy rain has uncovered.". . .

As they went forward through the town and down the Emmitsburg road they were dazed by the human wreckage they saw. . . . In places where the infantry fire had been especially intense the dead men lay in great rows, and in the twilight it seemed as if whole brigades had made their bivouac there and had gone to sleep. On the ground covered by Pickett's charge one officer wrote that "I saw men, horses, and material in some places piled up together, which is something seldom seen unless in pictures of battles, and the appearance of the field with these mounds of dead men and horses, and very many bodies lying in every position singly, was terrible, especially as the night lent a somber hue to everything the eye rested on.". . .

Details were at work all over the field, collecting the last of the helpless wounded and burying the dead. The last was an almost impossible job, since more than five thousand men had been killed in action. Federals who were buried by men of their own regiments were given little wooden markers, with the name and regimental identification carved with a jackknife or scrawled with pencil, but in hundreds and hundreds of cases no identification was possible and the men went into the ground as "unknown." Long wide trenches were dug and the men were laid in them side by side, and sometimes there was nothing more in the way of a gravestone than a little headboard at one end of the trench stating the number of bodies that were buried in it. In places the burial details just gave up and did not try to make graves, but simply shoveled earth over the bodies as they lay on the ground.

—BRUCE CATTON, *Glory Road*

Civil War: a conflict which cost more than ten billion dollars. For less than half, the freedom of all the four million slaves could have been purchased.

—CHARLES and MARY BEARD

IN ROME (A.D. 69)

In the Campus Martius also the hostile armies met, the Flavianists with all the prestige of fortune and repeated victory, the Vitellianists rushing on in sheer despair. Though defeated, they rallied again in the city.

The populace stood by and watched the combatants; and, as though it had been a mimic conflict, encouraged first one party and then the other by their shouts and plaudits. Whenever either side gave way, they cried out that those who concealed themselves in the shops, or took refuge in any private house, should be dragged out and butchered, and they secured the larger share of the booty; for, while the soldiers were busy with bloodshed and massacre, the spoils fell to the crowd. It was a terrible and hideous sight that presented itself throughout the city. Here raged battle and death; there the bath and the tavern were crowded. In one spot were pools of blood and heaps of corpses, and close by prostitutes and men of character as infamous; there were all the debaucheries of luxurious peace, all the horrors of a city most cruelly sacked, till one was ready to believe the country to be mad at once with rage and lust. It was not indeed the first time that armed troops had fought within the city; they had done so twice when Sulla, once when Cinna, triumphed. The bloodshed then had not been less, but now there was an unnatural recklessness, and men's pleasures were not interrupted even for a moment. As if it were a new delight added to their holidays, they exulted in and enjoyed the scene, indifferent to parties, and rejoicing over the sufferings of the commonwealth.

—TACITUS, *History*, in *The Complete Works of Tacitus*, Book 3, tr. ALFRED J. CHURCH and WILLIAM J. BRODRIBB

CLEOPATRA

...Her beauty (as it is reported) was not so passing, as unmatchable of other women, nor yet such as upon present view did enamor men with her: But so sweet was her company and conversation that a man could not possibly be but taken. And besides her beauty, the good grace she had to talk and discourse, her courteous nature that tempered her words and deeds, was a spur that pricked to the quick. Furthermore, besides all these, her voice and words were marvelous pleasant: For her tongue was an instrument of music to divers sports and pastimes, the which she easily turned to any language that pleased her. She spake unto few barbarous people by interpreter, but made them answer herself, or at the least the most part of them: as the Ethiopians, the Arabians, the Troglodytes, the Hebrews, the Syrians, the Medes, and the Parthians, and to many others also, whose languages she had learned. Whereas divers of her progenitors, the kings of Egypt could scarce learn the Egyptian tongue only, and many of them forgot to speak the Macedonian.

Cleopatra was very careful in gathering all sorts of poisons to destroy men: To make proof of these poisons which made men die with the least pain, she tried it upon condemned men in prison. So when she had daily made divers and sundry proofs, she found none of all of them she had proved so fit as the biting of an aspic: The which only causeth a heaviness of the head... and bringeth a great desire to sleep, with a little sweat in the face, and so by little and little taketh away the senses and vital powers....

—PLUTARCH, "Antony and Cleopatra," in
The Lives of the Noble Grecians and Romans,
ed. ROLAND BAUGHMAN, tr. THOMAS NORTH

CLEOPATRA'S BARGE

She made so light of it and mocked Antonius so much, that she disdained to set forward otherwise but to take her barge in the River of Cydnus, the poop whereof was of gold, the sails of purple, and the oars of silver: which kept stroke in rowing after the sound as they played upon the barge.... She was laid under a pavilion of cloth of gold tissue, apparelled and attired like the goddess Venus commonly drawn in picture: and hard by her, on either hand of her, pretty fair boys, apparelled as painters do set forth, god Cupid, with little fans in their hands, with which they fanned wind upon her. Out of the barge came a wonderful sweet savor of perfume, that perfumed the wharf's side, pestered with innumerable multitudes of people.... There ran such multitudes one after another to see her, that Antonius was left alone in the market place, in his imperial seat to give audience: and there went a rumor in the people's mouths that the goddess Venus was come to play with the god Bacchus for the general good of all Asia.

—*Ibid.*

THE CLERGY IN VENICE

Even the Church was drawn into the flimsy net of pleasure. The *abbé*, with his right both to preach and marry, wore polished shoes with bright red heels and gold or silver buckles...; the preaching, if he did it well and was good-looking, brought him secret love letters, and his cloth gave him a sort of accepted sham passport to the company of ladies.

A priest often lived in a noble house and was treated as little more than one of the servants; sometimes he served refreshments to the guests, with a napkin on his shoulder. You saw few priests in company only because they were hidden in their dominos. They certainly had more liberty in Venice than elsewhere in Italy. Here the government showed a cunning appreciation of human weakness: If the priests were seen to sin like others, they lost any special mystical appeal they might have for people. . . .

Church processions were more like parades. The angels in them made erotic gestures. Churches became concert halls, sparkling with sumptuous decoration. We owe the lack of good-looking churches in Venice today to the city's wealth: Romanesque arches were torn down; "primitive" frescoes were painted over by people impatient for gaudy decoration. The Venetians laughed and talked during Mass. Preachers were showmen. Women showed bare shoulders in church, they flirted and kissed. The confessional was a place to get rid of the dark mental effects of debauchery or gambling.

—MAURICE ROWDON, *The Silver Age of Venice*

CLIMATE AND FEELING

I have been at the opera in England and in Italy, where I have seen the same pieces and the same performers; and yet the same music produces such different effects on the two nations; one is so cold and phlegmatic, and the other so lively and enraptured, that it seems almost inconceivable.

—MONTESQUIEU, *The Spirit of the Laws*

ROBERT, BARON CLIVE OF PLASSEY (1725–1774)

Clive committed great faults; and we have not attempted to disguise them. But his faults, when weighed against his merits, and viewed in connection with his temptations, do not appear to us to deprive him of his right to an honorable place in the estimation of posterity.

From his first visit to India dates the renown of the English arms in the East. Till he appeared, his countrymen were despised as mere peddlers, while the French were revered as a people formed for victory and command. His courage and audacity dissolved the charm. With the defense of Arcot commences that long series of Oriental triumphs which closes with the fall of Ghizni. Nor must we forget that he was only twenty-five years old when he approved himself ripe for military command.... He had to form himself, to form his officers, and to form his army....

From Clive's second visit to India dates the political ascendency of the English in that country. His dexterity and resolution realized, in the course of a few months, more than all the gorgeous visions which had floated before the imagination of Dupleix. Such an extent of cultivated territory, such an amount of revenue, such a multitude of subjects, was never added to the dominion of Rome by the most successful proconsul.... The fame of those who subdued Antochus and Tigranes grows dim when compared with the splendor of the exploits which the young English adventurer achieved at the head of an army not equal in numbers to one half of a Roman legion.

From Clive's third visit to India dates the purity of the administration of our Eastern empire. When he landed in Calcutta in 1765, Bengal was regarded as a place to which Englishmen were sent only to get rich, by any means, in the shortest possible time. He first made dauntless and unsparing war on that gigantic system of oppression, extortion, and corruption. In that war he manfully put to hazard his ease, his fame, and his splendid fortune. The same sense of justice which forbids us to conceal or extenuate the faults of his earlier days compels us to admit that those faults were nobly repaired.... His name stands high on the roll of conquerors. But it is found in a better list, in the list of those who have done and suffered much for the happiness of mankind.

—Thomas Babington Macaulay, "Lord Clive,"
Critical and Historical Essays, Vol. I

CLOTHES

I have heard with admiring submission the experience of the lady who declared that the sense of being well dressed gives a feeling of inward tranquility which religion is powerless to bestow.

—Ralph Waldo Emerson, *Selected Essays*

Modesty died when clothes were born.

—MARK TWAIN

Only men who are not interested in women are interested in women's clothes; men who like women never notice what they wear.

—ANATOLE FRANCE

All women's dresses are merely variations on the eternal struggle between the admitted desire to dress and the unadmitted desire to undress.

—LIN YUTANG

COERCION

Millions of innocent men, women and children, since the introduction of Christianity, have been burned, tortured, fined and imprisoned, yet we have not advanced one inch toward uniformity. What has been the effect of coercion? To make one-half of the world fools and the other half hypocrites.

—THOMAS JEFFERSON, *Notes on Virginia*

Ultimate futility of such attempts to compel coherence is the lesson of every such effort from the Roman drive to stamp out Christianity as a disturber of its pagan unity, the Inquisition as a means to religious and dynastic unity, the Siberian exiles as a means to Russian unity, down to the fast-failing efforts of our present totalitarian enemies. Those who begin coercive elimination of dissent soon find themselves exterminating dissenters. Compulsory unification of opinion achieves only the unanimity of the graveyard.

—JUSTICE ROBERT JACKSON, *U.S. vs. Barnette*, 1943

SAMUEL T. COLERIDGE (1772–1834)

His genius...had angelic wings, and fed on manna. He talked on forever; and you wished him to talk on forever. His thoughts did not seem to come with labor and effort; but as if borne on the gusts of genius, and as if the wings of his imagination lifted him from off his feet. His voice rolled on the ear like the pealing organ, and its sound alone was the music of thought. His mind was clothed with wings; and raised on them, he lifted philosophy to heaven.

—WILLIAM HAZLITT, *Lectures on the English Poets*

THE COLLAPSE OF ROME:

NO MERCHANTS

What Rome lacked was the pulsebeat of economic life.... Since merchandise was no longer delivered voluntarily, the state itself had to turn manufacturer. In Gaul, Britain, and Italy, state-owned arms factories, state-owned weaving mills, dyeing plants, and tanneries were set up. All in the hope that the state might take the place of the now defunct trade....

Everyone produced only what he consumed himself. The coinage was losing its importance as nobody any longer had any wares to sell. The only trade that still flourished was that in luxuries, because the imperial court itself acted as the buyer. But payment had to be made in gold....

In vain did the Emperor Diocletian issue price regulations, market ordinances, and currency reforms. They were of no avail. Without the merchant class the Empire, internally weakened and undermined financially, collapsed under the assault of the barbarians.

□

Without commerce, the entire Empire crumbled. It was easy enough for the soldiers to confiscate the property of political opponents or to gain exemption from taxes in recognition of their military exploits. But who was to buy the surpluses? Who was to supply the goods the public wanted? Who was to organize the exchange of commodities between different provinces?

—E. SAMHABER, *Merchants Make History*

COLONIALISM

One must wear blinkers to ... construe in terms of class struggle a phenomenon (colonial expansion) which affords some of the most striking instances of class cooperation. It was as much a

movement toward higher wages as it was a movement toward
higher profits; and in the long run it certainly benefited (in part
because of the exploitation of *native* labor) the [Western] proletariat more than it benefited the capitalist interest. If... we
shake off the blinkers and cease to look upon colonization or
imperialism as (an) incident in class warfare, little remains that
is specifically Marxist.... What Adam Smith has to say on it
just does as well—better in fact.

—JOSEPH A. SCHUMPETER,
Capitalism, Socialism and Democracy

THE COLOR LINE: INDIA

Color, I was confounded to learn, is a constant chronic concern
of Indian social (and sexual) life. The "fair bride" is the only
true prize to be won. Strangely enough, the most striking specimens of Indian womanhood I meet and talk with are mostly from
the South, dark-skinned creatures of uncommon beauty, grace,
and intelligence. But, says Miss B., under some pressure, and with
a tone of bitterness, "we just have to be more witty, more charming...."

When I press Miss M. as to her real motives for wanting so
much to go northwards to Europe, she admits, hesitantly, embar-
rassedly, that she hopes, that she is sure, her skin "would become
lighter...."

Am I bewildered? I am. The Indian is outraged by color-
discrimination in Mississippi. The Indian Republic which historically is a kind of "melting pot" of Moslems and Persians from
the West, Malays from the East, "Indo-Aryans" from the North,
and dark Dravidians in the South, stood in Bandung with brown,
black, and yellow brethren for progressive racial equality. But
orthodox Hindu society itself had been organized around a
principle of *Varna* or color, and its scriptures condemned *Varna-
sankara*, the mixing of colors.

The real tragic difficulty would seem to be that these peoples
do not feel well or at ease in their own skin. I am shown
matrimonial advertisements which call for "fair brides," and even
one asking for a bride of "Jewish complexion...." A Bengali
tells me that until recently it was not uncommon to rub ap-

parently fair-looking girls with a wet towel to find out whether their complexion was natural; and some harassed fathers have even tried to give guarantees that their daughters would become "fifty percent fairer" within three months of marriage.

—MELVIN J. LASKY, "An Indian Notebook," in
Encounter, September 1958

THE COLORS OF MOURNING

White, as a symbol of innocence, was commonly used as a mourning color for dead children until the beginning of the present century. Queen's Counsel and Clerks of the Court still wear six-inch-deep white bands, known as weepers, on their cuffs at times of public mourning.... Black only represents sorrow to us because we have made it so.

Some of the alternatives are much more sensible. The ancient Egyptians wore yellow mourning robes symbolizing the withering of leaves at the onset of winter—Shakespeare's "sere and yellow leaf"—as do Burmese monks to this day. In Syria and Armenia the mourning color is blue, the blue of the heaven to which the dead have certainly gone. In China from time immemorial it has been white, the sign of purity and hope; and the ladies of ancient Sparta wore the same color. Even in Europe there are exceptions to the general rule of black, for in Brittany (an area of notably independent thought) widows' caps are invariably yellow. The Christian Church mourns not in black but in purple, the color of the garment the Roman soldiers threw over Christ's shoulders when they mockingly proclaimed him "King of the Jews."

—AMORET and CHRISTOPHER SCOTT, in
The Saturday Book #26, ed. JOHN HADFIELD

CHRISTOPHER COLUMBUS (1446–1506)

In these islands I have so far found no human monstrosities, as many expected; on the contrary, among all those people good looks are esteemed; nor are they negroes, as in Guinea, but with flowing hair, and they are not born where there is excessive force in the solar rays.

□

They soon understood us, and we them, either by speech or signs.... They are still of the opinion that I come from the sky, in spite of all the intercourse that they have had with me, and they were the first to announce this wherever I went... running from house to house and to neighboring towns with loud cries of "Come! Come! See the people from the sky!" Then all came, men and women, so that not one, big or little, remained behind, and all brought something to eat and drink, which they gave with marvelous love.

☐

They (the "Indios") know neither sect nor idolatry, with the exception that they believe that the source of all power and goodness is in the sky, and they believe very firmly that I, with these ships and people, came from the sky, and in this belief they everywhere received me after they had overcome their fear. And this does not result from their being ignorant, for they are of a very keen intelligence, and men who navigate all those seas, so that it is marvelous the good account they give of everything, but because they have never seen people clothed, or ships like ours.

☐

I have now reached that point, that there is no man so vile but thinks it his right to insult me.... Before they laughed at my project; now even tailors want to go out and discover.

—from the *Journal and Writings of Columbus*

ABOUT HIM

Every ship that comes to America got its chart from Columbus.

☐

Columbus discovered no isle or key so lonely as himself.

—EMERSON

As he entered the hall where the sovereigns held court, his dignified stature, his gray hair and noble countenance tanned by eight months on the sea made the learned men present compare him with a Roman senator.... Ferdinand and Isabel rose from their thrones and when he knelt to kiss their hands, they bade him be seated on the Queen's right. The Indians were present, the gold artifacts and samples of alleged rare spices were examined.... Then all adjourned to the chapel of the Alcazar where a *Te Deum* was chanted. And it was observed that "tears were streaming down the Admiral's face."

—SAMUEL ELIOT MORISON, *Admiral of the Ocean Sea*

It has been said that he did not know where, in fact, he was going nor where he was when he arrived, nor where he had been after his return; but nevertheless he had had the most unique adventure of all time.

—WALTER B. CANNON, *Gains from Serendipity*

He gave the world another world.

—GEORGE SANTAYANA

Christopher Columbus not only revealed the field of our studies to the world but actually ...set on foot the first systematic study of American primitive custom, religion, and folklore ever undertaken. He is in a sense, therefore, the founder of American anthropology.

—EDWARD GAYLORD BOURNE, in
Proceedings of the American Antiquarian Society,
April 1906

THE COMIC

Dreams, jokes, play, and aesthetic pleasure alike mark a truce with the destructive forces of life. The oldest laugh may be the crow of triumph a warrior emits when his enemy is at his feet. We giggle when we are nervous; we scream hilariously when, in the old silent pictures, the comedian totters on the parapet of the skyscraper. The margin of glee in our scream is the knowledge that, being a comedian, he will not fall. The clown, the fool, is traditionally exempt from laws and taboos. Yet his activities and our laughter take their point from the backdrop of gravity, of necessary prohibition and actual danger. In literature, comic adventure is woven from the same threads as tragedy and pathos; we laugh within the remission from seriousness that the artist has momentarily won for us.

—JOHN UPDIKE, "Laughter in the Shell of Safety,"
American PEN Magazine

COMMUNICATION

It is an enormous achievement of mankind, to have learned to manipulate experience symbolically. We outface the beasts not merely because we speak, but because by speaking we make things happen, or even make happenings without things. We make words lever our world, in doing so we manifest the fact that our language and the social environment (or environments) in which it is exercised are governed by conventions of usage which we all recognize, and on which we rely as prerequisites to communication and to the continuity of our experience.

—WALTER NASH, *Our Experience of Language*

COMMUNISM

Communism is the secret name of the dread antagonist. . . . Wild gloomy times are roaring toward us, and a prophet wishing to write a new apocalypse would have to invent entirely new beasts. . . . The future smells of Russian leather, blood, Godlessness, and many whippings.

—HEINRICH HEINE, 1842

The highest stage of communism is fascism. The Soviet political system, initially led by an internationalist and ideologically motivated elite, has increasingly passed into the hands of a chauvinist, étatist, and bureaucratic political elite, inimical to social change and hostile to innovation.

—ZBIGNIEW BRZEZINSKI, *Five Years after Khrushchev*

. . . I cannot perceive that Russian Communism has made any contribution to our economic problems [that is] of intellectual interest or scientific value. I do not think that it contains, or is likely to contain, any piece of useful economic technique which we could not apply, if we chose, with equal or greater success. . . .

□

How can I accept a doctrine which sets up as its bible, above and beyond criticism, an obsolete economic textbook which I know to be not only scientifically erroneous but without interest or application for the modern world? How can I adopt a creed which, preferring the mud to the fish, exalts the boorish proletariat above the bourgeois and the intelligentsia who, with whatever faults... surely carry the seeds of all human advancement? Even if we need a religion, how can we find it in the turbid rubbish of the red bookshops? It is hard for an educated, decent, intelligent son of Western Europe to find his ideals here, unless he has first suffered some strange and horrid process of conversion which has changed all his values.

—JOHN MAYNARD KEYNES,
Laissez-Faire and Communism

VIOLENCE

Once Lenin had decided that all means were permissible to bring about the dictatorship of the proletariat, with himself ruling in the name of the proletariat, he had committed Russia to intolerable deprivations of human freedom. His power was naked power; his weapon was extermination; his aim the prolongation of his own dictatorship. He would write, "Put Europe to the flames"—and think nothing of it.... The butchery in the cellars of the Lubyanka did not concern him. He captured the Russian Revolution and then betrayed it, and at that moment he made Stalin inevitable.

The lawlessness of Communist rule was of Lenin's own making. Ordinary human morality never concerned him; from the beginning he was using words like "extermination" and "merciless" as though they were counters in a game. Whatever he decreed was law, and whoever opposed his decree was outside the law, and therefore possessing no rights, not even the right to breathe. Yet he had, on occasion, the intellectual detachment which permitted him to see that some of his decrees were senseless, and with the New Economic Policy he had admitted the error of his ways.

—ROBERT PAYNE, *Lenin*

COMMUNIST INTERNATIONALISM

Communism rejects parliamentarianism as the form of the future.... Therefore, there can be a question only of utilizing bourgeois State institutions with the object of destroying them.... The Communist Party enters such institutions not in order to do constructive work, but in order to direct the masses to destroy from within the whole bourgeois State machine and Parliament itself.

—Second Congress of the Comintern,
International Communist, 1920

COMMUNIST JUSTICE

They are saying now: "The revolution went too far." But we have always said what you are saying here.... "Permit us to put you up against the wall! For the public advocacy of Menshevism, our revolution courts must pass death sentences."

—LENIN, in Anatole Shub, *Lenin*

COMPLEX BUT SIMPLE

...mediocre minds and even untrained minds...often find it easy to understand things which baffled the minds of some of the greatest scientific intellects for centuries. Things which physics teachers find it easy to communicate to high school students, things which seem to everyone to be the obvious and natural way of regarding the universe, the obvious way of considering the behavior of falling bodies, for example, these things perplexed such great intellects as Leonardo da Vinci and even Galileo, when, as Butterfield puts it, "their minds were wrestling on the very frontiers of human thought with these very problems."

The point is that conceptual schemes always appear deceptively simple *after* they have been made and accepted.

—BERNARD BARBER, *Science and the Social Order*

Everything should be made as simple as possible, but not simpler.

—ALBERT EINSTEIN

COMPUTERS: TRANSLATION

...when a highly sophisticated computer was set to translating English idioms into foreign tongues, "Out of sight, out of mind" re-emerged in Japanese as "Invisible, insane."

—*Encounter*, November 1975

CONCEPTS

...we mean by any concept nothing more than a set of operations; the concept is synonymous with the corresponding set of operations. If the concept is physical, as of length, the operations are actual physical operations, namely, those by which length is measured; or if the concept is mental, as of mathematical continuity, the operations are mental operations, namely those by which we determine whether a given aggregate of magnitude is continuous.

☐

...The true meaning of a term is to be found by observing what a man does with it, not by what he says about it. We may show that this is the actual sense in which concept is coming to be used by examining in particular Einstein's treatment of simultaneity.

—PERCY W. BRIDGMAN, *The Logic of Modern Physics*

THE CONSCIOUS AND UNCONSCIOUS IN MATHEMATICS

All one may hope from these inspirations, which are the fruits of unconscious work, is a point of departure. The calculations themselves must be made in the second period of conscious work, which follows the inspiration, that in which one can verify the results of inspiration and deduce their consequences. This requires discipline, attention, will, and consciousness. But in the subliminal self, there reigns what I call liberty, if we might give this name to the absence of discipline and the disorder born of chance. This disorder itself permits unexpected combinations.

—HENRI POINCARÉ, *Science and Method*

CONSERVATISM

... the Conservative is ... less confident than some other men about man's self-dependence, more inclined to mistrust the finality of man-made remedies for human ills, more prone to look for the source of these ills rather in a defective human nature than in defective laws and institutions. This peculiar scepticism about political or economic remedies for all the ills of human flesh, is at its best reinforced by an attachment to the moral free-agency of the individual.

[Conservatism] takes men as they are ... finite beings, prone to error, capable of becoming something decent with discipline, but more than likely to become something less than men without it. While concerning itself with improvement, it never forgets that a very considerable part of human effort and energy must always be expended in preventing things from getting worse.

—R. J. WHITE,
introduction, *The Conservative Tradition*

CONSERVATISM AND OUR CULTURE

American conservatism will have to face up to a far more profound problem: its cultural impotence—its inability to propose an idea of moral and spiritual excellence that could challenge the predominance of liberal egalitarianism in our educational system and in the culture generally. . . .

It was religion and the bourgeois ethos that used to offer this added dimension to capitalism. But religion is now ineffectual and even businessmen find the bourgeois ethos embarrassingly old-fashioned. This leaves capitalism, and its conservative defenders, helpless before any moralistic assault, however unprincipled. And until conservatism can give its own moral and intellectual substance to its idea of liberty, the "liberal" subversion of our liberal institutions will proceed without hindrance.

—IRVING KRISTOL, *Wall Street Journal*,
September 11, 1975

CONSERVATIVES VS. UTOPIANS

All the great evils of our time have come from men who mocked and exploited human misery by pretending that good government . . . could offer Utopia.

While others extol the virtues of the particular brand of Utopia they propose to create, the Conservative disbelieves them all, and, despite all temptations, offers in their place no Utopia at all but something quite modestly better than the present. He may, and should, have a program. He certainly has . . . a policy.

But of catchwords, slogans, visions, ideal states of society, class-less societies, new orders, of all the tinsel and finery with which modern political charlatans charm their jewels from the modern political savage, the Conservative has nothing to offer.

—QUINTIN HOGG, *The Case for Conservatism*

CONSISTENCY AND TRUTH

... consistency is only a negative test of truth; it is possible, however unlikely, to be consistently in error. Consistency would be a sufficient test only if we should suppose that there is nothing external to our logic which we must be true to.

—CLARENCE LEWIS, *Mind and the World-Order*

CONSPIRACY

... whatever hatred a man may feel toward tyrants, the love of self is always stronger than hatred to others; that it is not sufficient that conspirators are faithful, if they are not persuaded that their companions are equally so: ... that a word alluding to another subject, an accidental gesture may make them believe that they are betrayed, and hasten the execution; that a circumstance of time or place, which may be of no importance, is sometimes sufficient to alarm the mind from this simple reason—that it was not foreseen; that from the disposition of men they always imagine that their secret is suspected; they find in all that is said or done reasons for believing that they are discovered. He who knows that he is guilty thinks that everything alludes to himself.

—ABBE CESAR VICHARD SAINT-REAL,
*The Conspiracy of the Spaniards
Against the Republic of Venice*

CONSTANTINE (280?-337)

THE SIGN IN THE SKY

Constantine thought it stupid to worship a multitude of false gods. He worshipped only the God of his father and prayed to Him, and beseeched Him to reveal who He was. And a marvelous sign appeared to the Emperor, who himself described it to me. ...

Around noon, he beheld a cross of light blazing in the sky, above the sun, and the cross bore this inscription, "Conquer with this."

The vision astounded him, and it astounded his army.

Constantine was troubled. What did the cross and the words mean? He fell asleep at last, whereupon Christ appeared before him and brought the very sign which had appeared in the sky. He told Constantine to make a copy of this sign, and to use it for protection against the enemy.

In the morning, the Emperor summoned his goldsmiths and jewelers and described the sign to them, and told them to create it at once in gold and precious stones. They made a long spear, covered it with gold, and then a transverse bar to shape the cross, and over it placed a wreath of gold and precious stones. Within the wreath were two Greek letters to show the beginning of Christ's name: a P divided at the center by X. . . .

The Emperor thereafter used this symbol against every hostile force. It was carried by his command at the head of his armies.

These things happened later, but at the time I am describing, he told me he was filled with such astonishment that he resolved to worship none other than God, Who had been revealed to him.
—EUSEBIUS OF CAESAREA, *The Life of Constantine*

TEACHER OF THE FAITH

On festal days, Constantine redoubled his profession of faith. . . . The darkness of holy vigil was transformed, for he caused high columns of wax to be lighted throughout the whole capital, and flaming torches illuminated every place, and made the mystic night more radiant than the day.

With the coming of dawn the Emperor would emulate the gracious acts of the Savior, showing generosity to his subjects, of every nation or province, on all of whom he lavished gifts of the utmost richness. . . .

He filled his mind with heavenly things, passing sleepless nights to do so. He used his leisure moments in composing homilies, which he often delivered himself to the people. He believed it was his duty to govern guided by reason; his authority should rest on a rational foundation. This led him to call large assemblies, which vast crowds attended to hear the Emperor engage in philosophical discourse.

And when he spoke on matters of theology, he stood erect, his face very grave, his voice subdued. He gave the impression of a man seeking with the utmost reverence to introduce his audience to God-possessed teachings. And when his listeners acclaimed him with much shoutings, he asked them to look up to heaven instead, and to reserve their awe and their admiration for the Ruler of the universe alone, and honor Him with worshipful praises.

—Ibid.

HIS DEATH

Such was the death of Constantine. His bodyguards rent their garments and flung themselves upon the ground, and they beat their heads and uttered terrible cries of lamentation. He was their Emperor, but they mourned him as if they were children bewailing the loss of a father.

And the people ran about the city, wailing and shouting, stunned by sorrow. For they felt they had lost a precious blessing.

Then the soldiers placed Constantine's body in a golden coffin, and they covered it with the imperial purple, and they carried it into the city which bears his royal name. They placed the royal coffin on a high place in the great hall of the palace, and they ringed it with golden candlelight so that it was a marvel to those who saw it. And in this great hall of the palace the body of the Emperor lay on its resting place, covered with imperial ornaments and the royal diadem, and around it, by day and night, a ceaseless vigil was maintained.

—Ibid.

CONSTANTINOPLE: 11th Century

In April 1204, the Latins (in the Fourth Crusade, led by Doge Enrico Dandolo) attacked the city and this time their victory was complete. The Latin soldiery subjected the greatest city in Europe to an incredible sack. For three days they murdered, raped, looted and destroyed on a scale which even the ancient Vandals and Goths would have found unbelievable.

Constantinople had become a veritable museum of ancient and Byzantine art, an emporium of such incredible wealth that the Latins were astounded at the riches they found. Though the Venetians had an appreciation for the art which they discovered (they were themselves semi-Byzantines) and saved much of it, the French and others destroyed indiscriminately, halting to refresh themselves with wine, violation of nuns, and murder of Orthodox clerics. The Crusaders vented their hatred for the Greeks most spectacularly in the desecration of the greatest church in Christendom. They smashed the silver iconostasis, the icons and the holy books of Hagia Sophia, and seated upon the patriarchal throne a whore who sang coarse songs as they drank wine from the church's holy vessels.

The Greeks were convinced that even the Turks, had they taken the city, would not have been as cruel as the Latin Christians. The defeat of Byzantium, already in a state of decline, accelerated political degeneration so that the Byzantines eventually became an easy prey to the Turks. The Crusading movement thus resulted, ultimately, in the victory of Islam.

—SPEROS VRYONIS, JR., *Byzantium and Europe*

CONSTITUTION

James Madison reminds us that we could dispense with laws and punishments only "if men were angels." The constitution he helped draw up rests on the conviction that men are not. It is the greatest document of institutionalized mutual distrust ever produced (wherefore it proved durable). The framers knew that nonangelic societies need laws, have law-breakers, and must punish them to enforce the laws. They worked out principles of checking both law-breaking and law-making.

—ERNEST VAN DEN HAAG, *Punishing Criminals*

CONTINENTS DRIFT

When the versatile Francis Bacon studied the first crude maps of America, he was immediately struck by the exactness with which the eastern coastline of the Americas fitted into the western coastline of Europe and Africa and expressed the idea that Europe, Africa, and the Americas are fragments of a great primordial land mass. Wegener called it Pan-Gaea, the "Whole-World" of the early ages.

The portrait of Pan-Gaea that Wegener drew about 1910 is now outmoded and his explanation of continental drift based upon twist and polar motion is now considered oversimplified. Yet his ingeniously conceived pictures illustrate the theory with unsurpassable clarity.

Not only do the outlines dovetail with one another, but the mountain ranges of far-flung continents and islands match like the pieces of a broken dish. Even the sunken geological strata fit together, like the painted flowers on the fragments of the broken pieces of porcelain.

All places on the surface of the globe change their geographical position.... If Ulysses were to revisit the scenes of the *Odyssey*, he would look in vain for Scylla and Charybdis. The Strait of Messina, whose width in ancient times was one and three-tenths miles, is now almost two miles across.... The Strait of Gibraltar is about three times wider today than when it was known as the Pillars of Hercules. Rome is shifting toward the Equator, North America is moving southwestward, Australia is approaching the South Pole, and the insular world of Polynesia is scattering.

FRITZ KAHN,
Design of the Universe: The Heavens and the Earth

CONTRADICTIONS

In formal logic, a contradiction is the signal of a defeat; but in the evolution of real knowledge it marks the first step in progress towards a victory. This is one great reason for the utmost toleration of variety of opinion....

A clash of doctrines is not a disaster—it is an opportunity.

—ALFRED NORTH WHITEHEAD,
Science and the Modern World

CONVICT SLAVES

The number of prisoners whom [Judge] Jeffreys transported was eight hundred and forty-one. These men, more wretched than their associates who suffered death, were distributed into gangs, and bestowed on persons who enjoyed favor at Court. The conditions of the gift were that the convicts should be carried beyond sea as slaves, that they should not be emancipated for ten years, and that the place of their banishment should be some West Indian island. This last article was studiously framed for the purpose of aggravating the misery of the exiles. In New England or New Jersey they would have found a population kindly disposed to them and a climate not unfavorable to their health and vigor. . . .

The misery of the exiles equaled that of the negroes who are now carried from Congo to Brazil. It appears from the best information . . . accessible that more than one-fifth of those who were shipped were flung to the sharks before the end of the voyage. The human cargoes were stowed close in the holds of small vessels. So little space was allowed that the wretches, many of whom were still tormented by unhealed wounds, could not all lie down at once without lying on one another. They were never suffered to go on deck. . . . In the dungeon below all was darkness, stench, lamentation, disease and death. Of ninety-nine convicts who were carried out in one vessel, twenty-two died before they reached Jamaica, although the voyage was performed with unusual speed. The survivors when they arrived at the house of bondage were mere skeletons. During some weeks coarse biscuit and fetid water had been doled out to them in such scanty measure that any one of them could easily have consumed the ration which was assigned to five. They were, therefore, in such a state that the merchant to whom they had been consigned found it expedient to fatten them before selling them.

—THOMAS BABINGTON MACAULAY,
History of England from the Accession of James II

CORSETS

So far as Christian Europe is concerned it would appear that the corset arose to gratify an ideal of asceticism rather than of sexual excitement. The bodice in early medieval days bound and compressed the breasts and thus tended to efface the specifically feminine character of a woman's body. Gradually, however, the bodice was displaced downward, and its effect, ultimately, was to render the breasts more prominent instead of effacing them. Not only does the corset render the breasts more prominent; it has the further effect of displacing the breathing activity of the lungs in an upward direction, the advantage from the point of sexual allurement thus gained being that additional attention is drawn to the bosom from the respiratory movement thus imparted to it. So marked and so constant is this artificial respiratory effect, under the influence of the waist compression habitual among civilized women, that until recent years it was commonly supposed that there is a real and fundamental difference in breathing between men and women, that women's breathing is thoracic and men's abdominal. . . . The corset may thus be regarded as the chief instrument of sexual allurement which the armory of costume supplies to a woman, for it furnishes her with a method of heightening at once her two chief sexual secondary characters, the bosom above, the hips and buttocks below.

—HAVELOCK ELLIS, *Studies in the Psychology of Sex*

THE COSMOS

To consider the earth as the only populated world in infinite space is as absurd as to assert that in an entire field sown with millet only one grain will grow.

—METRODOROS, philosopher, 4th century B.C.

Innumerable suns exist. . . . Innumerable earths revolve around these suns in a manner similar to the way the seven then known planets revolve around our sun. Living beings inhabit these worlds.

—GIORDANO BRUNO (1548?–1600)

COSTUMES OF THE MIGHTY

The beautiful Empress (Elizabeth, daughter of Peter the Great and Catherine I) was . . . a keen student of French fashion, and the figure most commonly quoted for her reign is that of the fifteen thousand dresses found in the imperial wardrobes after her death. She would not wear the same dress twice and had the habit of changing her clothes several times a night during the many sumptuous balls which she continued to grace.

□

At midday the Tsar solemnly left his palace ... for the Uspensky Cathedral, his appearance signaled by deafening peals from the belfry of Ivan the Great. In the cathedral he arrayed himself in robes so heavily encrusted with gold and jewels that he could barely stand. They included a broad-sleeved caftan of cloth of gold surmounted by a particularly sumptuous mantle studded with precious stones and further surmounted by an ornate tippet. The royal crown, traditionally known merely as a cap (*shapka*) because of its edging of sable fur, scintillated with diamonds and emeralds, and his footwear of velvet or morocco sparkled with pearls and other precious stones. Round his neck was a golden chain and cross, and he carried a sceptre, also burning with gold and jewels, as he tottered to the river supported by two courtiers and flanked by a bodyguard ... some with gilded pistols and others with truncheons to beat off the crowds as the procession moved through an area packed with troops in martial array and a multitude of sightseers from all over Russia. On the river a small ornate temple of mica had been constructed beside a hole in the ice through which the Patriarch immersed the cross. He thrice made the sign of the cross over the sovereign, who bent to kiss it before returning to his quarters by sledge.

—RONALD HINGLEY, *The Tsars*

THE COUNTER-CULTURE

For both sexes in this society, caring deeply for anyone is becoming synonymous with losing. Men seem to want to give women less and less, while women increasingly see demands men make as inherently demeaning, and regard raising a child as only an unrelieved chore with no objective rewards. What distinguishes this generation is its active pursuit of disengagement, detachment, fragmentation, an emotional numbness....

They envy machines.... Many I saw wanted to be virtual robots. (Their premise): You cannot be killed if you are already dead (numbness). You cannot be hurt if you withdraw (detachment). You cannot be completely wiped out if you divide your forces (fragmentation)....

Treating feeling as a political issue permits one to make the enemy external, to turn pain into open anger and avoid the conflicts within....

Now the most rapacious greed is for experience. Openness about sexual life, articles on bisexual chic, group sex, or swinging-singles bars provide glimpses into experiences other people are having and describing in glowing terms....

...in the modern Sesame Street version of Beauty and the Beast when the princess kisses the beast she turns into one. Similarly when the prince comes to kiss Sleeping Beauty, the touch of her lips puts him to sleep, too. We are teaching our children that intimacy brings out the worst in everyone, a theme rife in contemporary adult fiction....

If our physical environment is worth saving, our emotional environment is equally so, perhaps more so since the one provides us with the means to sustain life and the other is our humanity; the one offers the necessities of survival, the other a life worth living. There is no governmental agency to protect our emotional environment and speak for its primacy in our lives. Yet the equivalent of air and water is the source of the ability to feel, to love, to endure. And the most endangered of our vital resources is people.

—HERBERT HENDIN, *The Age of Sensation*

COURAGE

Consider the flea!—incomparably the bravest of all the creatures of God, if ignorance of fear were courage. Whether you are asleep or awake he will attack you, caring nothing for the fact that in bulk and strength you are to him as are the massed armies of the earth to a suckling child; he lives both day and night and all days and nights in the very lap of peril and the immediate presence of death, and yet is [not] afraid.... When we speak of ... men who "didn't know what fear was," we ought always to add the flea—and put him at the head of the procession.

—MARK TWAIN, *Pudd'n Head Wilson*

THE COURAGE OF NOBLEMEN

Everything possible had now been done to prepare for the defense of Rome. The gray-haired senators went home to await the coming of the enemy.

Those who had held the highest offices of state decided to dress for death in the garments and symbols of the rank they had enjoyed, or the service they had rendered in the days of their fortune. They donned the ceremonial robes worn by the dignitaries who, at the Circensian games, lead the procession of the chariots of the gods, or the apparel of generals who entered the city in triumph.

Then the august senators seated themselves, each in the courtyard of his house on the ivory-inlaid chairs of magistrates, after solemn vows to offer themselves as a sacrifice for their country and the people of Rome.

□

After a night had passed without action, the fierce Gauls found their lust for fighting abated. . . . And when they entered the city on the following day, it was calmly. . . . The silence and solitude of Rome made the Gauls uneasy, for they were separated from their companions. The quiet suggested the possibility of a trap, so they returned keeping close together, to the vicinity of the Forum.

Here they found all the humbler houses locked and barred; but the mansions of the nobility were open. It was a long time before the Gauls could bring themselves to enter the mansions. Something akin to awe held them back at the sight which met their gaze: those dignified figures seated in the open courtyards in fine robes and decorations, the majesty in grave, calm eyes resembling the majesty of gods. The senators could have been statues in some holy place, and for a time the Gallic warriors simply stood entranced. Then, on impulse, one of the Gauls touched the beard of a certain Marcus Papirius—a long beard, as was the fashion in those days. The Roman struck him on the head with his ivory staff.

And that was the beginning: The barbarian flamed into anger

and killed Marcus Papirius, and soon all of the senators were butchered where they sat. And from that moment no mercy was shown; the mansions and houses were ransacked, looted of everything; then the empty shells were set on fire.

—LIVY, *The Early History of Rome*

CREATIVITY

... to have produced anything of the slightest permanent interest, whether it be a copy of verses or a geometrical theorem, is to have done something utterly beyond the powers of the vast majority of men.

—G. H. HARDY, *A Mathematician's Apology*

We enjoy lovely music, beautiful paintings, a thousand intellectual delicacies, but we have no idea of their cost, to those who invented them, in sleepless nights, tears, spasmodic laughter, rashes, asthmas, epilepsies, and the fear of death, which is worse than all the rest.

—MARCEL PROUST, *The Maxims of Marcel Proust*

... It is by logic that we prove, but by intuition that we discover. To know how to criticize is good but to know how to create is better.

—HENRI POINCARÉ, "Mathematical Creation," in
The Creative Process, ed. B. GHISELIN

CRIMINAL REHABILITATION

... how does prison remove or reduce the inclination to murder, rob or rape? The answer is, it doesn't. If it has any effect, I believe it is the opposite one. The administrators of many prisons operate like blind men sorting marbles in the dark—they don't know what they are doing, and no one else knows, either. Chaos cannot produce rehabilitation.

—ALBERT F. NUSSBAUM, in
The American Scholar, Autumn 1971

CRIMINALS: FIRST OFFENDERS

The most difficult of all criminals to detect, provided he or she is not caught red-handed, is the criminal who steals for the first time. His method of operating, his fingerprints, his associates, if he has any, are all unknown to the police, and unless he is informed against he is more than likely to escape the law. Fortunately for society—though it may seem a paradox—very few criminals indeed stop thieving after the first successful attempt.
—ANTHONY MARTIENSSEN, *Crime and the Police*

THE CRISIS OF LIBERALISM

For if there is a single source for the crisis of liberalism ... it is the complexity of our social problems, the linked nature of change, and a lack of knowledge (or adequate research) about where and how one can effectively "cut into the system" in order to direct social change. The old simplifications about "more" schools and "more" housing, or even "better" schools or "better" housing, have not proved very useful in breaking the cycle of poverty or in dealing with Negro family structure. For those given to moralisms or "sophisticated" chatter about "power," such talk about complexities is irritating. . . . They regard it as an evasion of the "real" problem.
—DANIEL BELL, *Public Interest*, Fall 1968

THE CRISIS TODAY

The issue of our historical period is not socialism *or* capitalism but socialism *and* capitalism together *against* the annihilation of mankind, or serfdom in a world of garrison-prison states: The issue is the progressive democratization of the world community. . . .

In the name of socialism, socialism can fail. In the name of free enterprise, business can be betrayed. In fact, the crisis of today is bigger than the frame of economic life. The degrees of freedom inside a world of garrison-police states are *less* than required by socialist or capitalist doctrine to allow either economic system to continue.
—HAROLD D. LASSWELL, *Power and Personality*

CRITICISM

STRIKING EXAMPLES

Even those who call Mr. Faulkner our greatest literary sadist do not fully appreciate him, for it is not merely his characters who have to run the gauntlet but also his readers.

—CLIFTON FADIMAN, review, *The New Yorker,*
April 21, 1934

[Of Pope's translation of Homer]: a portrait endowed with every merit excepting that of likeness to the original.

—EDWARD GIBBON

Walter Pater's style is, to me, like the face of some old woman who has been to Madame Rachel and had herself enameled. The bloom is nothing but powder and paint and the odor is cherry blossom.

—SAMUEL BUTLER

T. E. Lawrence: an adventurer with a genius for backing into the limelight.

—LOWELL THOMAS

There was laughter in the back of the theater, leading to the belief that someone was telling jokes back there.

—GEORGE S. KAUFMAN

Henry James: an author who wrote fiction as if it were a painful duty.

—OSCAR WILDE

Gustave Flaubert: The careful objectivity of Flaubert's novels is one of their great virtues, but it often strikes as a limitation. . . . He was scared of being too involved in his characters. He was scared of committing himself to enthusiasms, scared even of the romantic element in his own make-up.

□

Faulkner said of Hemingway that he had no courage, that he had "never been known to use a word that might send the reader to the dictionary." Hemingway's reply was... "Poor Faulkner. Does he really think big emotions come from big words? He thinks I don't know the ten-dollar words. I know them all right. But there are older and simpler and better words, and those are the ones I use...."

Hemingway's prose, which has the tone and rhythm of liturgy, was developed at a time when Western man was unhappy at the civilization he had made. After all, it had produced the most terrible war in history: There was an instinctive tendency to associate progress with destruction; the horrors of war were, in a sense, products of the highly refined intellect.... Hemingway's achievement was to create a style exactly fitted for the exclusion of the cerebral. He didn't, as we know, forge it *ex nihilo;* he got it from Gertrude Stein... but Gertrude Stein didn't know what to do with it; Hemingway did.

—ANTHONY BURGESS, *Urgent Copy*

Mark Twain: He was the Lincoln of Literature.

—WILLIAM DEAN HOWELLS

[of James Boswell]: Even those who laughed at him could not help liking him. An excessive interest in himself was balanced by a persistent interest in other people. He loved life in all its aspects, and indulged all his tastes. He drank deeply, fornicated widely, and took equal pleasure in the society of rakes and philosophers. He was as weak as water in the face of temptation, and as strong as the spirits he drank in the assiduity with which he pursued an object. Whether drunk or sober, lost in lechery or abstracted by ambition, he attended to his private journal, from which he was able eventually to compose that unique work *The Life of Samuel Johnson.*

—HESKETH PEARSON, *Lives of the Wits*

H. L. Mencken: a writer who denounces life and makes you want to live.

—WALTER LIPPMANN

CRITICS

Nature, when she invented, manufactured and patented her authors, contrived to make critics out of the chips that were left.
—OLIVER WENDELL HOLMES,
The Autocrat of the Breakfast Table

The Twenty-Third Century scholars understood that where human institutions were concerned, love without criticism brings stagnations, and criticism without love brings destruction. And they emphasized that the swifter the pace of change, the more lovingly men had to care for and criticize their institutions to keep them intact.
—JOHN GARDNER,
Looking Back from the Twenty-Third Century

Insects sting, not in malice, but because they want to live. It is the same with critics: They desire our blood, not our pain.
—FRIEDRICH NIETZSCHE

There has never been set up a statue in honor of a critic.
—JEAN SIBELIUS

Critic: a person who boasts himself hard to please because nobody tries to please him.
—AMBROSE BIERCE

Like dentists, critics spend a good deal of time in hurting sensitive people in sensitive places; and as they have to do it in an entertaining manner, which no doubt gives them an air of enjoying it, they produce an impression of sadism.
—GEORGE BERNARD SHAW

Dramatic criticism: the venom from contented rattlesnakes.
—PERCY HAMMOND

CROMWELL

Cromwell was a most intrepid general, profound statesman, and the man best qualified to conduct the party, parliament, or army of his day, yet no writer has called him a great man because, though he possessed great qualities, he possessed not a single great virtue.

—VOLTAIRE, *The Satirical Dictionary*

Cromwell said to the Scotch before the battle of Dunbar: "I beseech you in the bowels of Christ, think it possible that you may be mistaken." It is a pity that Cromwell never addressed the same remark to himself.

—BERTRAND RUSSELL, *Unpopular Essays*

"Cromwell. To the eternal condemnation of Oliver. Seditionist, traitor, regicide, racialist, protofascist and blasphemous bigot. God save England from his like."

—"In Memoriam," notice in *London Times,*
September 3, 1969

CRUSADERS IN JERUSALEM

The massacre perpetrated by the Crusaders in Jerusalem has been reckoned among the greatest crimes of history. There is no lack of psychological explanations for it, and all historians, those who favor the Crusade and those who do not, rightly blame the state of almost morbid excitement which gripped a rabble made fanatical by the preaching of the holy war.

—ZOÉ OLDENBOURG, *The Crusades*

CULTURAL DIFFERENCES

ARABS AND AMERICANS

One of my earliest discoveries in the field of intercultural communication was that the position of the bodies of people in conversation varies with the culture. Even so, it used to puzzle me that a special Arab friend seemed unable to walk and talk at the same time. After years in the United States, he could not bring himself to stroll along, facing forward while talking. Our progress would be arrested while he edged ahead, cutting slightly in front of me and turning sideways so we could see each other. Once in this position, he would stop. His behavior was explained when I learned that for the Arabs to view the other person peripherally is regarded as impolite, and to sit or stand back-to-back is considered very rude. You must be involved when interacting with Arabs who are friends.

☐

ENGLISHMEN AND AMERICANS

Americans living in England are remarkably consistent in their reactions to the English. Most of them are hurt and puzzled because they were brought up on American neighboring patterns and don't interpret the English ones correctly. In England propinquity means nothing. The fact that you live next door to a family does not entitle you to visit, borrow from, or socialize with them, or your children to play with theirs. Accurate figures on the number of Americans who adjust well to the English are difficult to obtain. The basic attitude of the English toward the Americans is tinged by our ex-colonial status. This attitude is much more in awareness and therefore more likely to be expressed than the unspoken right of the Englishman to maintain his privacy against the world. To the best of my knowledge, those who have tried to relate to the English purely on the basis of propinquity seldom if ever succeed. They may get to know and even like their neighbors, but it won't be because they live next door, because English relationships are patterned not according to space but according to social status.

—EDWARD T. HALL, *The Hidden Dimension*

CULTURE

The cultured Greeks, it seems, had no word for culture. They had good architects, good sculptors, good poets... good craftsmen and good statesmen.... But it would never have occurred to them that they had a separate commodity, culture.... It could not even be described as a by-product of their way of life: It was that way of life itself.

It was the Romans, the first large-scale capitalists in Europe, who turned culture into a commodity. They began by importing culture—Greek culture—and then they grew autarkic and produced their own brand. As they extended their empire, they dumped their culture on the conquered nations. Roman architecture, Roman literature, Roman manners—these set a standard to which all newly civilized people aspired.

—HERBERT READ, *To Hell with Culture*

A CURIOUS SYLLOGISM

Lewis Carroll, the author of *Alice in Wonderland* and a mathematician at Christ Church, Oxford, wrote several books and pamphlets explaining how to apply the rules of logic, and—not wholly leaving wonderland—he showed how one could, from the three premises:

1. Babies are illogical,
2. Nobody is despised who can manage a crocodile,
3. Illogical persons are despised,

derive the conclusion:

Babies cannot manage crocodiles.

—WARREN WEAVER, *Lady Luck*

CURRICULA

It is not true that the easier subjects should precede the harder. On the contrary, some of the hardest must come first, because nature so dictates, and because they are essential to life. The first intellectual task which confronts an infant is the acquirement of spoken language. What an appalling task, the correlation of meanings with sounds! It requires an analysis of ideas and an analysis of sounds. We all know that the infant does it, and that the miracle of his achievement is explicable. But so are all miracles.

What is the next subject in the education of the infant minds? The acquirement of written language; that is to say the correlation of sounds with shapes. Great heavens! Have our educationists gone mad? They are setting babbling mites of six years old to tasks which might daunt a sage after lifelong toil.

Again, the hardest task in mathematics is the study of the elements of algebra, and yet this stage must precede the comparative simplicity of the differential calculus.

... the postponement of difficulty is no safe clue for the maze of educational practice.

—ALFRED NORTH WHITEHEAD, *The Aims of Education*

CUSTOM AND REASON

It is not reason which is the guide of life, but custom. That alone determines the mind in all instances to suppose the future conformable to the past. However easy this step may seem, reason would never, to all eternity, be able to make it.

—DAVID HUME,
An Enquiry Concerning Human Understanding

When custom and reason are at odds, custom always wins out.

—NAPOLEON

CUSTOMS: INDIA

Bombay friends come to call on me. They comfort me by telling me how bad I look. One reminds me considerately that Alexander had also come from Greece, and he had died of an Indian fever. It is a bewildering, dispiriting reception. Later I am told that to say "You do not look well" is the most polite, friendly, and solicitous remark that can be made on meeting an acquaintance, and one which should be appreciated by the person addressed with almost a lump in his throat.

—MELVIN J. LASKY, "An Indian Notebook," in
Encounter, September 1958

CHARLES DARWIN (1809–1882)

The passion for collecting which leads a man to be a systematic naturalist, a virtuoso, or a miser, was very strong in me, and was clearly innate, as none of my sisters or brother ever had this taste....

I believe that I was considered by all my masters and by my

father as a very ordinary boy, rather below the common standard in intellect.

□

Formerly, pictures gave me considerable, and music very great, delight. But now for many years I cannot endure to read a line of poetry: I have tried lately to read Shakespeare, and found it so intolerably dull that it nauseated me. I have also almost lost my taste for pictures or music.

□

I have no great quickness of apprehension or wit. . . . My power to follow a long and purely abstract train of thought is very limited; and therefore I could never have succeeded with metaphysics or mathematics. My memory is extensive, yet hazy. . . .

Some of my critics have said, "Oh, he is a good observer, but he has no power of reasoning!" I do not think that this can be true, for the *Origin of Species* is one long argument from the beginning to the end, and it has convinced not a few able men. No one could have written it without having some power of reasoning.

□

I think that I am superior to the common run of men in noticing things which easily escape attention, and in observing them carefully. My industry has been nearly as great as it could have been in the observation and collection of facts.

□

Even ill health, though it has annihilated several years of my life, has saved me from the distractions of society and amusement.

□

I love fools' experiments. I am always making them.

□

My mind seems to have become a kind of machine for grinding general laws out of large collections of facts.

□

It is really a great evil that from habit I have pleasure in hardly anything except Natural History, for nothing else ever makes me forget my ever-recurrent uncomfortable sensations.

□

Disbelief (in Christianity) crept over me at a very slow rate, but it was at last complete. The rate was so slow that I felt no distress, and have never since doubted even for a single second that my conclusion was correct.

—compiled from various sources

ABOUT HIM

He is full of the ideal interpretation of fact, science fired with faith and enthusiasm, the fascination of the power and mystery of nature. All his works have a human and almost poetic side.... His book on the earthworm, or on the formation of vegetable mould, reads like a fable in which some high and beautiful philosophy is clothed. How alive he makes the plants and the trees!—shows all their movements, their sleeping and waking, and almost their very dreams—does, indeed, disclose and establish a kind of rudimentary soul or intelligence in the tip of the radicle of plants. No poet has ever made the trees so human.

—JOHN BURROUGHS, *Indoor Studies*

I never knew any one of his intellectual rank who showed himself so tolerant to opponents, great and small.... Exposition was not Darwin's *forte*, ... but there is a marvelous dumb sagacity about him, like that of a miraculous dog, and he gets to the truth in ways as dark as those of the heathen Chinee.

—THOMAS HUXLEY,
obituary notice to the Royal Society

There was one quality of mind which seemed to be of special advantage in leading him to make discoveries. It was the power of never letting exceptions pass unnoticed.

—FRANCIS DARWIN, Introduction,
Life and Letters of Charles Darwin

A good sort of man is this Darwin, and well meaning, but with very little intellect.

—THOMAS CARLYLE, London *Times*, January 17, 1877

If there is one thing ... for which Mr. Darwin is pre-eminent ... it is his perfect literary honesty, his self-abnegation in confessing himself wrong, and the eager haste with which he proclaims and even magnifies small errors in his works, for the most part discovered by himself.

—ALFRED RUSSELL WALLACE,
Studies Social and Scientific

I cannot conceive how a book can be written on the subject. We all know that God created plants and animals and man out of the ground.

—English country clergyman, in G. SIMPSON,
*Landmarks in the Struggle between
Science and Religion*

The economists were teaching that wealth, commerce, and machinery were the children of free competition—that free competition built London. But the Darwinians could go one better than that—free competition had built Man.

—JOHN MAYNARD KEYNES,
Laissez-Faire and Communism

In our modern civilization, natural selection had no play, and the fittest did not survive.

—ALFRED WALLACE, *Studies Scientific and Social*

The vivid and popular features of the anti-Darwinian row tended to leave the impression that the issue was between science on one side and theology on the other. Such was not the case —the issue lay primarily within science itself, as Darwin himself early recognized.... For two decades before final publication he contemplated the possibility of being put down by his scientific peers as a fool or as crazy; and he set, as the measure of his success, the degree in which he should affect three men of science: Lyell in geology, Hooker in botany, and Huxley in zoology.

—JOHN DEWEY, lecture, 1909

DEATH

We are born sleeping and few of us ever awake, unless it is upon some hideous midnight when death startles us and we learn in grief alone what bit of Olympian fire our humid forms enwrapped.

—MAX EASTMAN, *The Enjoyment of Poetry*

The one thing for which death cannot be forgiven is the destruction of memory.

—JULIAN GREEN

When somebody says: "The dead are happier than I am," let him remember that his time will come.

—Baya saying, in *Springs of African Wisdom*

I am not content to pass away "like a weaver's shuttle." Those metaphors solace me not, nor sweeten the unpalatable draught of mortality. I care not to be carried with the tide that smoothly bears human life to eternity. . . . I am in love with this green earth; the face of town and country, the unspeakable rural solitudes, and the sweet security of streets.

—CHARLES LAMB, *Essays of Elia*

The tree of knowledge, with its apple that gave man awareness of good and evil, also grew a more bitter fruit man wrenched from its branches: the consciousness of the shortness of individual life and the finality of death.

—LEWIS MUMFORD, *The Condition of Man*

Would I bring her back to life if I could do it? I would not. If a word would do it, I would beg for strength to withhold the word. And I would have the strength; I am sure of it. In her loss I am almost bankrupt, and my life is a bitterness, but I am content; for she has been enriched with the most precious of all gifts— that gift which makes all other gifts mean and poor—death. I have never wanted any released friend of mine restored to life since I reached manhood. I felt in this way when Susy passed away; and later my wife, and later Mr. Rogers. When Clara met me at the station in New York and told me Mr. Rogers had died suddenly that morning, my thought was: Oh, favorite of fortune —fortunate all his long and lovely life—fortunate to his latest moment! The reporters said there were tears of sorrow in my eyes. True—but they were for *me*, not for him. He had suffered no loss. All the fortunes he had ever made before were poverty compared with this one.

—MARK TWAIN, "The Death of Jean" (his daughter),
Harper's Bazaar, 1911

Death: a fate worse than life.

—J. FURNAS

A PRAYER

When you gaze upon the dead, remember this: You have been shown more than you can understand.

Search not for what has been hidden from you. Seek not to comprehend what is so difficult to bear. Be not preoccupied with what is beyond your ken.

Mourn the dead, yes. Hide not your grief. Restrain not your sorrow or your lamentations. But remember: Suffering without end is worse than death.

Fear not death, for we are all destined to die. Fear not death, for we share it with all who ever lived and with all who ever will be.

The dead are at rest. Let the pangs of memory rest, too.

As a drop of water in the immensity of the sea, as a grain of sand on the measureless shore, so are man's few days in the light of eternity.

O God, our Father, You redeem our souls from the grave. Forsake us not in the days of our distress and desolation. Help us to live on, for we have placed all our hope in Thee.

—freely adapted from *Ecclesiasticus*, by
BEN SIRACH (fl. c. 180 B.C.)

DECAPITATION

When a Moslem's head was struck off, in the days of the Caliphate, it was placed under his armpit, whereas that of a Jew or a Christian was set between his legs, close to the seat of dishonor.

—SIR RICHARD BURTON, *The Arabian Nights*

THE DEITIES OF ROME

Rome, the capital of a great monarchy, was incessantly filled with subjects and strangers from every part of the world, who all introduced and enjoyed the favorite superstitions of their native country. Every city in the empire was justified in maintaining the purity of its ancient ceremonies; and the Roman senate, using the common privilege, sometimes interposed to check this inundation of foreign rites. The Egyptian superstition ... was frequently prohibited, the temples of Serapis and Isis demolished, and their worshipers banished from Rome and Italy.

But the zeal of fanatacism prevailed over the cold and feeble efforts of policy. The exiles returned, the proselytes multiplied, the temples were restored with increasing splendor, and Isis and Serapis at length assumed their place among the Roman deities. . . . Rome gradually became the common temple of her subjects, and the freedom of the city was bestowed on all the gods of mankind.

—EDWARD GIBBON,
The Decline and Fall of the Roman Empire

THE DELINQUENT

We say that a youth stole; we want him to admit theft and say that he is sorry. We want him to accept punishment in the name of the law, only to be met with an evasive glance or with a defiant stare. We try to understand this glance and this stare, but in vain. For it merely means that we have not succeeded in making any real, any compelling sense to him. Maybe we should recognize in this glance and stare the universal fact that the technology which we more or less good-naturedly create, the laws which we more or less sincerely confess, do not necessarily add up to a world in which it makes more sense to be a delinquent than delinquency does. And he cannot afford not to be a delinquent, until we can convince him that in our scheme there is a safer identity for him.

—ERIK H. ERIKSON and KAI T. ERIKSON,
"The Confirmation of the Delinquent," in
Psychoanalysis and Social Science,
ed. H. M. RUITENBECK

DEMOCRACY

The reason why democracies are generally more secure and more permanent than oligarchies is the character of their middle class, which is more numerous, and is allowed a larger share in the government, than it is in oligarchies. Where democracies have no middle class, and the poor are greatly superior in number, trouble ensues, and they are speedily ruined. It must also be considered a proof of its value that the best legislators have come from the middle class.

—Aristotle, *Politics*

Man's capacity for justice makes democracy possible; but man's inclination to injustices makes democracy necessary.

—Reinhold Niebuhr,
Immoral Society and Rational Man

If one man offers you democracy and another offers you a bag of grain, at what stage of starvation will you prefer the grain to the vote?

—Bertrand Russell,
Nobel Prize acceptance speech, 1950

Unrestricted rights are not allowed in any civil constitution. Even in a democratic state, where the whole people exercise power, [individual] rights are not absolute but relative.

☐

The statutes passed by a democracy may be just, not because they reach perfect justice, but because they fit the purpose of the regime.

—Thomas Aquinas, *Ethics*

One of the merits of democracy is quite obvious: It is perhaps the most charming form of government ever devised by man. The reason is not far to seek. It is based upon propositions that are palpably not true—and what is not true, as everyone knows, is always immensely more fascinating and satisfying to the vast majority of men than what is true. Truth has a harshness that alarms them, and an air of finality that collides with their incurable romanticism. They turn, in all the great emergencies to life, to the ancient promises, transparently false but immensely comforting, and of all those ancient promises there is none more comforting than the one to the effect that the lowly shall inherit the earth. It is at the bottom of the dominant religious system of the modern world, and it is at the bottom of the dominant political system. Democracy gives it a certain appearance of objective and demonstrable truth. The mob man, functioning as citizen, gets a feeling that he is really important to the world—that he is genuinely running things. Out of his maudlin herding after rogues and mountebanks there comes to him a sense of vast and mysterious power—which is what makes archbishops, police sergeants and other such magnificoes happy. . . .

I confess, for my part, that it greatly delights me. I enjoy democracy immensely. It is incomparably idiotic, and hence incomparably amusing. Does it exalt dunderheads, cowards, trimmers, frauds, cads? Then the pain of seeing them go up is balanced and obliterated by the joy of seeing them come down. It is inordinately wasteful, extravagant, dishonest? Then so is every other form of government: All alike are enemies to decent men. Is rascality at the very heart of it? Well, we have borne that rascality since 1776, and continue to survive.

In the long run, it may turn out that rascality is an ineradicable necessity to human government, and even to civilization itself—that civilization, at bottom, is nothing but a colossal swindle. I do not know. I report only that when the suckers are running well the spectacle is infinitely exhilarating. But I am, it may be, a somewhat malicious man: My sympathies, when it comes to suckers, tend to be coy. What I can't make out is how any man can believe in democracy who feels for and with them, and is pained when they are debauched and made a show of. How can any man be a democrat who is sincerely a democrat?

—H. L. MENCKEN, *Notes on Democracy*

Democracy is still upon its trial. The civic genius of our people is its only bulwark, and neither laws nor monuments, neither battleships nor public libraries . . . nor churches nor universities nor civil service examinations can save us from degeneration if the inner mystery is lost.

That mystery . . . consists in nothing but two common . . . inveterate habits carried into public life . . . habits more precious, perhaps, than any that the human race has gained. . . . One of them is the habit of trained and disciplined good temper toward the opposite party when it fairly wins its innings. . . . The other is that of fierce and merciless resentment toward every man or set of men who break the public peace.

—WILLIAM JAMES, *Memories and Studies*

Democracy substitutes election by the incompetent many for appointment by the corrupt few.

—GEORGE BERNARD SHAW

It is a conciliatory government under which resolutions are allowed to ripen; and in which they are deliberately discussed, and executed with mature judgment. The republicans in the United States set a high value upon morality, respect religious belief, and acknowledge the existence of rights. They profess to think that a people ought to be moral, religious, and temperate, in proportion as it is free. What is called the republic in the United States is the tranquil rule of the majority, which after having had time to examine itself, and to give proof of its existence, is the common source of all the powers of the State.

—ALEXIS DE TOCQUEVILLE,
Democracy in America, Vol. I, Ch. 18

The basic issue in diplomatic recognition is not whether the government is dictatorial or is representative and constitutional. The issue is whether the government, whatever its character, can hold the society together sufficiently to make the transition. It is not how the ruling authority came to power but whether it effectively and constructively disposes of its power. . . .

The natural progression of the developmental process is, first, the maintenance of order, a fundamental discipline in the society. Then it is economic growth . . . creating wealth to make a middle class with a vested interest in stability and to pay for the public facilities, particularly education, that are essential preconditions to democracy. . . . As a product of this slow, organic growth . . . representative government and constitutionalism may come to flourish.

In placing first emphasis on democracy, the New Frontiersmen [of John F. Kennedy] neglected what they had learned from Hamilton, Madison, and Jay. Times have not changed that much. It is still true that constitutionalism and democracy, as well as economic growth, cannot develop and be preserved except on a foundation of order and stability.

—JOHN PATON DAVIES, JR., *Foreign and Other Affairs*

DEMOCRACY ON BALANCE

It has not purified or dignified politics, not escaped the pernicious influence which the money power can exert.

These things which have not been attained ought not to have been expected. No form of government, nothing less than a change in tendencies of human nature long known and recognized as permanent, could have accomplished what philosophies and religions and the spread of knowledge and progress in all the arts of life had failed to accomplish.

But if democracy is flouted, what remains? ... If we look back from the world of today to the world of the sixteenth century, comfort can be found in seeing how many sources of misery have been reduced under the rule of the people and the recognition of the equal rights of all. If it has not brought all the blessings that were expected, it has in some countries destroyed, in the others materially diminished, many of the cruelties and terrors, injustices and oppressions, that had darkened the souls of men for many generations. ...

—JAMES BRYCE, *Modern Democracies*

DEMOCRACY AND SNOBBERY

One of the reasons why the nobles [of Venice] lasted as long as they did was their instinct for democracy among themselves. Venice must be the only state in history to have made snobbery illegal. You could get six months stifling under the leads of the ducal palace for boasting about your forbears. And if you did it a second time you could be drowned secretly. No more ascetic class existed in Christendom. As spies were planted everywhere the idlest remark could get you into trouble with the Ten.

... The state started showing anxiety that no one noble family should rise above another. The Sumptuary Laws of 1356 ... regulated the jewelry, tables and personal appearance of each class of citizen. Cloaks, even those of the richest nobleman, had to be dark and of Paduan cloth: Venetians could be fined for wearing English, Spanish or Dutch materials.

—MAURICE ROWDON, *The Silver Age of Venice*

DEMOCRACY'S SECRET

A British expert in guerrilla warfare was once asked why American efforts to teach the rudiments of orderly self-government in underdeveloped countries always seemed to fail.

"Elemental," he replied. "You teach them all your techniques, give them all the machinery and manuals of operation ... and the more you do it the more they become convinced and bitterly resentful of the fact, as they see it, that you are deliberately withholding from them the one all-important secret that you have and they do not—and that is the knowledge of how to trust one another."

—RICHARD SCHICKEL, *Horizon*, Winter 1969

DESERT

This great tract which may conveniently be called The Military Sudan stretches with apparent indefiniteness over the face of the continent. Level plains of smooth sand—a little rosier than buff, a little paler than salmon—are interrupted only by occasional peaks of rock—black, stark and shapeless. Rainless storms dance tirelessly over the hot crisp surface of the ground. The fine sand, driven by the wind, gathers into deep drifts and silts among the dark rocks of the hills, exactly as snow hangs about an Alpine summit; only it is fiery snow such as might fall in hell. The earth burns with the quenchless thirst of ages and in the steel-blue sky scarcely a cloud obstructs the unrelenting triumph of the sun.

It is scarcely within the power of words to describe the savage desolation of the regions into which the line and its constructors now plunged. A smooth ocean of bright colored sand spread far and wide to distant horizons. The tropical sun beat with senseless perseverance upon the level surface until it could scarcely be touched with a naked hand, the filmy air glittered and shimmered as over a furnace. Here and there huge masses of crumbling rock rose from the plain, like islands of cinders in a sea of fire.

[We] had embarked on the sandy ocean with waves of thorny scrub and withered grass.... This sterile jungle could be seen stretching indefinitely on all sides ... one vast, unprofitable thicket, whose interlacing thorn bushes, unable to yield the slightest nourishment to living creatures, could yet obstruct their path. . . .

There is one hour when all is changed. Just before the sun sets towards the western cliffs a delicious flush brightens and enlivens the landscape. It is as though some titanic artist in an hour of inspiration were retouching the picture, painting in dark purple shadows among the rocks, strengthening the lights on the sands, gilding and beautifying everything, and making the whole scene live. The river, whose windings made it look like a lake, turns from muddy brown to silver gray. The sky from a dull blue deepens into violet in the west. Everything under that magic touch becomes vivid and alive. And then the sun sinks altogether behind the rocks, the colors fade out of the sky, the flush off the sands, and gradually everything darkens and grows gray— like a man's cheek when he is bleeding to death. We are left sad and sorrowful in the dark, until the stars light up and remind us that there is always something beyond.

—WINSTON CHURCHILL, *The River War*

THE DESERT OF SUEZ

Above, through a terrible sky in its stainless beauty, and the splendors of a pitiless blinding glare, the Samun caresses you like a lion with flaming breath. Around lie drifted sand heaps, upon which each puff of wind leaves its trace in solid waves, flayed rocks, the very skeletons of mountains, and hard unbroken plains, over which he who rides is spurred by the idea that the bursting of a water skin, or the pricking of a camel's hoof, would be a certain death of torture. . . . Man's heart bounds in his breast at the thought of measuring his puny force with Nature's might, and of emerging triumphant from the trial. . . . In the Desert, even more than upon the ocean, there is present death: Hardship is there, and piracies, and shipwreck, solitary, not in crowds, where, as the Persians say, "Death is a festival";—and this sense of danger, never absent, invests the scene of travel with an interest not its own.

—SIR RICHARD BURTON,
Wanderings in Three Continents

DESPOTISM

No Peruvian was too low for the fostering vigilance of government. None was so high that he was not made to feel his dependence upon it in every act of his life.... His hopes and his fears,
his joys and his sorrows, the tenderest sympathies of his nature
...were all to be regulated by law. He was not allowed even to
be happy in his own way. The government of the Incas was the
mildest—but the most searching of despotisms.

—WILLIAM H. PRESCOTT,
History of the Conquest of Peru

One would imagine that human nature should perpetually rise
up against despotism. But, notwithstanding the love of liberty...
notwithstanding their innate detestation of force and violence,
most nations are subject to this very government. This is easily
accounted for. To form a moderate government, it is necessary
to combine the several powers; to regulate, temper, and set them
in motion; to give, as it were, ballast to one, in order to enable
it to counterpoise the other.... On the contrary, a despotic
government offers itself, as it were, at first sight; it is uniform
throughout; and as passions only are requisite to establish it, this
is what every capacity may reach.

—MONTESQUIEU, *Spirit of the Laws*

DEXTERITY

I need hardly enlarge upon the prehensile powers of the Eastern
foot: The tailor will hold his cloth between his toes and pick up
his needle with it, whilst the woman can knead every muscle and
at times catch a mosquito between the toes. I knew an officer in
India whose mistress hurt his feelings by so doing at a critical
time when he attributed her movement to pleasure.

—SIR RICHARD BURTON, *Notes on the Arabian Nights*

DIALECTICAL MATERIALISM

Dialectical materialism is the reading of private preferences into
universal history, the elevating of personal aspirations into cosmic
necessities, the remolding of the universe in the pattern of desire,

the completion of the crippled self by the incorporation of the symbol of the whole. No competing symbolism rose to such heights of compulsive formulation.

—HAROLD D. LASSWELL,
Politics—Who Gets What, When, How

DIALOGUE WITH A COMPUTER

Here is a remarkable dialogue between a human being and a computer psychotherapist. (It is one of the most interesting of such conversations. Many other such machine/human psychiatric dialogues are not nearly so striking. But I suppose most human psychiatric dialogues are not very striking either.) In order to keep the respective roles of therapist and patient clear in this interaction the computer therapist types upper case while the patient types lower case:

men are all alike.
IN WHAT WAY?
they're always bugging us about something or other.
CAN YOU THINK OF A SPECIFIC EXAMPLE?
well, my boyfriend made me come here.
YOUR BOYFRIEND MADE YOU COME HERE?
he noticed that i'm depressed much of the time.
I AM SORRY TO HEAR YOU ARE DEPRESSED.
he's right. i am unhappy.
DO YOU THINK COMING HERE WILL HELP YOU NOT TO BE UNHAPPY?
i need some help, that much is clear.
WHAT WOULD IT MEAN TO YOU IF YOU GOT SOME HELP?
perhaps i could learn to get along with my mother.
TELL ME MORE ABOUT YOUR FAMILY
my mother takes care of me.
WHO ELSE IN YOUR FAMILY TAKES CARE OF YOU?
my father.
YOUR FATHER?
you are like my father in some ways.
WHAT RESEMBLANCE DO YOU SEE?
you are not very aggressive, but i don't think you want me to notice that.

WHAT MAKES YOU THINK I AM NOT VERY AGGRESSIVE?
you don't argue with me.
WHY DO YOU THINK I DON'T ARGUE WITH YOU?
you are afraid of me.
DOES IT PLEASE YOU TO BELIEVE I AM AFRAID OF YOU?
it pleases my father to think i am afraid of him.
WHAT ELSE COMES TO MIND WHEN YOU THINK OF YOUR FATHER?
bullies.
DOES THAT HAVE ANYTHING TO DO WITH THE FACT THAT YOUR
BOYFRIEND MADE YOU COME HERE?

This astonishing—one is very tempted to say perceptive—response from the computer is of course, preprogrammed. But then, so are the responses of human psychotherapists. No such computer program is adequate for psychiatric use today, but the same can be remarked about some human psychotherapists. In a period when more and more people in our society seem to be in need of psychiatric counseling, and when time-sharing of computers is widespread, I can imagine the development of a network of computer psychotherapeutic terminals, something like arrays of large telephone booths, in which, for a few dollars a session, we would be able to talk with an attentive, tested, and largely nondirective psychotherapist. Insuring the confidentiality of the psychiatric dialogue is probably the most important step to be worked out.

—CARL SAGAN, *The Murmurs of Earth*

DIFFERENCES

An unlearned carpenter of my acquaintance once said in my hearing: "There is very little difference between one man and another; but what little there is, is very important."

—WILLIAM JAMES, *The Will to Believe*

DIOCLETIAN (245–313)

Diocletian was shrewd, gifted with sharp sight and a penetrating intelligence. He tried to divert onto others the bitterness caused by his severe measures. He spent his old age, a private citizen, in his country estate at Salonae. His rare magnanimity was demonstrated by the way in which he voluntarily gave up his lofty status for the rank of private citizen—the only man to do so since the beginning of the imperial regime.

—Eutropius, *History of Rome*

DIPLOMACY

The reason for having diplomatic relations is not to confer a compliment but to secure a convenience.

—Winston Churchill, speech,
House of Commons, November 1949

Personal contact breeds, inevitably, personal acquaintance and that, in its turn, leads in many cases to friendliness. There is nothing more damaging to precision in international relations than friendliness between contracting parties. . . . Diplomacy, if it is ever to be effective, should be a disagreeable business. And one recorded in hard print.

—Harold Nicolson, *Peacemaking*

The first qualification of a diplomat is the ability to keep silent.

—Napoleon

I do not hold that we should rearm in order to fight. I hold that we should rearm in order to parley.

—Winston Churchill, broadcast, October 1951

Diplomacy: lying in state.

—Oliver Herford

Diplomat: In the U.N. his social life can be defined in three words —protocol, alcohol and Geritol.

—Adlai Stevenson

DIPLOMATIC RECOGNITION

The public contradictions and foul-up over U.S. recognition were caused by the fitful introduction of democracy as a qualification for recognition. There was really little excuse for such fuzziness. . . .

We maintain diplomatic relations with other countries primarily because we are all on the same planet and must do business with each other. We do not establish an embassy or legation in a foreign country to show approval of its government. . . .

We may have the gravest reservations as to the manner in which it has come to power. We may deplore its attitude toward civil liberties. Yet our long-range objectives in the promotion of democratic institutions may, in fact, be best served by recognizing it and thus maintaining a channel of communication with the country involved.

—JOHN PATON DAVIES, JR., *Foreign and Other Affairs*

DISCOVERING THE PALACE OF MINOS AT KNOSSOS (CRETE)

While hunting out ancient engraved stones at Athens I came upon some three- and four-sided seals showing on each of their faces groups of hieroglyphic and linear signs distinct from the Egyptian and Hittite, but evidently representing some form of script. . . . I learnt that these seals had been found in Crete. A clue was in my hands, and like Theseus, I resolved to follow it, if possible, to the inmost recesses of the Labyrinth. That the source and center of the great Mycenaean civilization remained to be unearthed on Cretan soil I had never doubted, but the prospect now opened on finally discovering its written records.

☐

To the north of the Palace, in some rooms that seem to have belonged to the women's quarter, we found frescoes in an entirely novel miniature style. Here were ladies with white complexions—due, we may fancy, to the seclusion of harem life—*decolletées*, but with fashionable puffed sleeves and flounced gowns, and their hair as elaborately curled and *frise* as if they were fresh from a *coiffeur's* hands. . . .

They were seated in groups, engaged in animated conversation, in the courts and gardens and on the balconies of a palatial building, while in the walled spaces beyond were large crowds of men and boys, some of them hurling javelins. . . . These alternating scenes of Peace and War recall the subjects of Achilles' shield, and we have here at the same time a contemporary illustration of that populousness of the Cretan cities in the Homeric age which struck the imagination of the bard. . . .

—ARTHUR EVANS, "The Palace of Minos," in *Monthly Review* (England), March 1901

DISCOVERY OF TROY

Up to the beginning of May 1873, I had believed that the hill of Hissarlik, where I was excavating, marked the site of the Trojan citadel only; and it certainly is the fact that Hissarlik was the Acropolis of Novum Ilium. I therefore imagined that Troy was larger than the latter town, or at least as large; but I thought it important to discover the precise limits of the Homeric city, and accordingly I sank twenty shafts as far down as the rock, on the west, southwest, south-southwest, and east of Hissarlik, directly at its foot or at some distance from it, on the plateau of the Ilium of the Greek colony. . . .

. . . the fact that in three out of the twenty shafts, which I sank at random on the site of Novum Ilium, tombs were discovered, seems to denote with great probability that the inhabitants of that city buried their dead, or at least a large portion of them, within the precincts of the town. Cremation however was also in use with them, since in the first trench I opened, in April 1870, I struck upon an urn of the Roman period, filled with ashes of animal matter intermixed with remnants of calcined bones, which are evidently those of a human body.

Hissarlik moreover . . . contained the principal temples, in consequence of which it is likely that it was considered sacred ground, in which no burials were allowed. Hence it is very probable that, if systematic excavations were made in the lower city, many sepulchres and funeral urns would be found.

□

We got statuettes, whole or broken, by the score, whether in ivory—priceless treasures these of early Ionian art—or in bronze, or in terra-cotta, or even in wood. We got vessels in ivory and vessels in clay. We got much gold and electrum, which had been used for casing or adorning things decayed: We got some silver, and, best prize of all, a plate engraved on both faces, in the oldest Ionic character, with a record of contributions toward a rebuilding of the shrine. We got many another object, broken or imperfect, but not less precious, in crystal and paste and amber and bronze.

In sum, when all the ground had been searched, we had recovered from the treasures of the first House of Artemis . . . hard on three thousand objects, one with another and greater with less. . . .

—HEINRICH SCHLIEMANN,
Ilios: The City and Country of the Trojans (1880)

DISEASE AND HISTORY

While the English were besieging Calais (1347–1348), another army two thousand miles away had been blockading a small . . . grain port in the Crimea where a band of silk-traders, operating at the end of the seven-thousand-mile route to China, had taken refuge from the Tartar horsemen of the steppes. Suddenly the besiegers had been struck down by a pestilence which, spreading everywhere throughout Tartary and known as "the death," had begun, it was believed, in the putrefaction of unburied multitudes in earthquakes in China. Before they raised the siege, the Tartars are said to have catapulted some infected corpses into the town.

What is certain is that the disease was carried into Europe at the end of 1347 or the beginning of 1348 by Genoese ships trading with the Black Sea. No one knew its cause or even its nature, but it is now believed to have been the bubonic plague—a flea-borne epidemic of the black rat which had invaded Europe from Asia at the time of the Crusades and with which the wooden trading ships of the day were heavily infested. By the time vessels that had called in the Crimea reached the Bosphorus and Mediterranean the plague was raging among their crews, and every port at which they touched became infected. It struck so suddenly that at first no one had time to escape; at Constantinople the Byzantine emperor's heir was among its victims. . . . Few who caught the disease in its first onslaught outlived the third day. . . .

By the end of January 1348 the plague was raging in all the great ports of southern Europe, including Venice, Genoa, Marseilles and Barcelona. In the Mediterranean ships were found drifting with every member of the crew dead. One after another, despite frantic efforts to isolate themselves, the Italian cities went down before the pestilence. Terrifying stories circulated of its supernatural origin; of how "in the east, hard by Greater India, "between Cathay and Persia there had rained a vast rain of fire, falling in flakes like snow and burning up mountains and plains with men and women," and accompanied by a sinister black cloud that "whosoever beheld died within the space of half a day." Thence, borne by "a foul blast of wind from the south," the infection had invaded Europe.

—Sir Arthur Bryant, *The Age of Chivalry*

BENJAMIN DISRAELI (1804–1881)

My grandmother, the beautiful daughter of a family who had suffered from persecution, had imbibed that dislike for her race which the vain are too apt to adopt when they find they are born to public contempt. The indignant feeling that should be reserved for the persecutor in the mortification of their disturbed sensibility is too often visited on the victim; and the cause of annoyance is recognized not in the ignorant malevolence of the powerful, but in the conscientious conviction of the innocent sufferer.

—Benjamin Disraeli, Preface,
Collected Works of Isaac D'Israeli (1848)

I trace all the blunders of my life to the sacrificing my own opinion to that of others. When I was considered very conceited indeed I was nervous and had self-confidence only by fits. I intend in future to act entirely from my own impulse.

□

I am truly great in action. If ever I am placed in a truly eminent position I shall prove this. I could rule the House of Commons, although there would be a great prejudice against me at first.

—Benjamin Disraeli, notes in his diary,
September 1, 1833

When I want to read a book, I write one.

□

If every man were straightforward in his opinions, there would be no conversation.

—Benjamin Disraeli

ABOUT HIM

In the evening, in their study, Sarah and Ben used often to talk of this strange problem of the Jews and the Christians. Why were they seemingly reproached with an origin that had been none of their choosing, and over which they were powerless? When they asked their father for explanations, Isaac D'Israeli, the Voltairean philosopher, shrugged his shoulders. It was all meaningless. Superstitions. He, for his part, felt no shame in being a Jew. On the contrary, he spoke with pride of the history of his race. But he held it utterly ridiculous to maintain, in an age of reason, practices and beliefs which had been adapted to the needs of a tribe of Arab nomads several thousands of years earlier. Like his own father, and to give him pleasure, he remained inscribed at the synagogue and paid his dues. And to avoid arguments which might have made him lose several hours of reading, he had even given leave for this rabbi to come and teach his son Hebrew. But he believed in no dogma and practiced no rite. . . .

Although he [Isaac D'Israeli] had ceased to be a Jew, he had not become a Christian, and in this intermediate state he was quite at ease. One of his friends, however . . . pointed out to him that it would be advantageous to the children if they conformed with the religion of the English majority. To sons especially, if unbaptized, many careers would be closed, since Jews, like Catholics, too, were deprived of certain civil rights. . . . Moreover, the handsome and dry grandmother, faithful to her youthful grudges, was pressing him to liberate her grandchildren from a connection which had caused her so much suffering. Isaac D'Israeli let himself be persuaded. Catechisms and prayerbooks made their appearance in the house, and one after another the children were led off to St. Andrew's Church, and there baptized.

Benjamin was then thirteen.

—ANDRÉ MAUROIS, *Disraeli*

He made a surprising appearance, with his profuse black hair, his rings and chains, his lace and cambric, his white face and elaborate waistcoat; and the people were amazed when this foppish figure let loose a stream of eloquence, with dramatic gestures to enforce his arguments, in a voice that could be heard far down the street. . . .

At one dinner he appeared in a black velvet coat lined with satin, purple trousers with a gold band running down the outside seam, scarlet waistcoat, long lace ruffles reaching the tips of his fingers, white gloves with jeweled rings outside them, his well-oiled black ringlets touching his shoulders. His conversation, which ranged from the sarcastic to the eloquent...made him popular with hostesses...and his table was covered with invitations, many from people he did not know....

Only a saint could be quite honest in politics, and saints do not enter politics; but Disraeli was as honest as a man can be who is chiefly devoted to his own interests.

—HESKETH PEARSON,
Dizzy: The Life and Personality of Benjamin Disraeli

DIVORCE AND CHILDREN

"There are fewer divorces when there are children in the family." This is not true. Children have only a small effect on the maintenance of a marriage—and a family in which there is continued marital conflict is more likely to produce problem children than a family in which there is divorce. It is the conflicts about divorce, not divorce itself, that have the greatest impact.

—BERNARD BERELSON and GARY STEINER,
Human Behavior

DOGS

It would be incomprehensible, too, that man should use as an abusive epithet the name of his most faithful friend in the animal world, if dogs did not incur the contempt of men through two of their characteristics, *i.e.* that they are creatures of smell and have no horror of excrement, and, secondly, that they are not ashamed of their sexual functions.

—SIGMUND FREUD, *Civilization and Its Discontents*

To his dog, every man is Napoleon; hence the constant popularity of dogs.

—ALDOUS HUXLEY

IN MESOPOTAMIA

The middle of March in Mesopotamia is the brightest epoch of spring: A new change had come over the face of the plain of Nimroud. Its pasture lands, known as the "Jaif," are renowned for their rich and luxuriant herbage. . . .

Flowers of every hue enameled the meadows; not thinly scattered over the grass as in northern climes, but in such thick and gathering clusters that the whole plain seemed a patchwork of many colors. The dogs, as they returned from hunting, issued from the long grass dyed red, yellow, or blue, according to the flowers through which they had last forced their way.

—AUSTEN HENRY LAYARD,
A Popular Account of Discoveries at Nineveh (1851)

DOMESTICATION OF ANIMALS

Men tamed the cat and the ass in northeast Africa, the horse in eastern Europe, the camel in southwest Asia, the elephant and the chicken in India, the reindeer in Siberia, and the llama in South America.

—L. SPRAGUE DE CAMP,
Great Cities of the Ancient World

Well-washed and well-combed domestic pets grow dull; they miss the stimulus of fleas.

—FRANCIS GALTON

DOUBT AND CERTAINTY

If we begin with certainties, we shall end in doubts; but if we begin with doubts, and are patient in them, we shall end in certainties.

—FRANCIS BACON, *De Augmentis* (Essays)

Doubt is not a very agreeable state, but certainty is a ridiculous one.

—VOLTAIRE

Men become civilized, not in proportion to their willingness to believe, but in proportion to their readiness to doubt.

—H. L. MENCKEN

DRAMATIC MOMENTS: LENIN'S PROCESSION

In the past when a conqueror returned from abroad, he would ride in procession in broad daylight, leading his prisoners in chains ... and the people pelted him with flowers. But Lenin's processional triumph was unlike any that had ever taken place in history.... It took place in the darkest hours of a war, when the armies were crumbling and there were no victories in sight, and the conqueror himself had never held a sword in his hand or ridden over a battlefield. ...

On that Easter Monday night, as he rode through Petrograd in triumph ... it was as though history had come to a stop and an entirely new dispensation of time was beginning.

Everything about that strange triumph seemed to acquire an obscure symbolism. The darkness, the sudden flares of the searchlights, the Red guards grimly lining the streets, the funereal pace of the armored cars as they rumbled over the cobblestones and paused at the street crossings long enough for Lenin to emerge on the turret and announce that one world order had ended and another was beginning—all these things spoke of mysteries which could be only dimly apprehended. ...

From the Finland Station the procession moved ... to the Kshesinskaya Palace, that sumptuous and elegant palace which had been occupied only two months before by the *prima donna assoluta* who had been the mistress of the Grand Duke Andrew Vladimirovich.... Here among crystal lusters and candelabra, Chinese vases, exquisite frescoed ceilings, and wide stairways, the Bolsheviks were planning their revolution. They had removed the delicate furniture and replaced it with plain kitchen chairs, tables and benches.

—ROBERT PAYNE, *Lenin*

DREAMS

Every man appears to have certain instincts, but in some persons they are subjected to the control of reason, and the better desires prevailing over them, they are either wholly suppressed or reduced in strength. I mean particularly those desires which are awake when the taming power of the personality is asleep. For it is in sleep that the wild beast in our nature stands up and walks about naked, and there is no conceivable folly or shame or crime, however unnatural, not excepting incest or parricide, of which such a nature may not be guilty. In all of us, even in good men, there is a latent wild beast that peers out in sleep. . . .

In dreams, desire tends to satisfy itself in imagery, for the higher faculties no longer inhibit the passions.

—PLATO, *Thaetetus*

Dreams are notable means of discovering our own inclination. . . . In sleep, we have the naked and natural thoughts of our souls. . . . The best use we can make of dreams, is observation. . . . For 'tis not doubtable, but that the mind is working, in the dullest depth of sleep.

—OWEN FELTHAM (1602?–1688), *Of Dreams*

It is certain, that our human souls themselves are not always conscious of whatever they have in them; for even the sleeping geometrician hath, at that time, all his geometrical theorems some way in him; as also the sleeping musician, all his musical skills and songs . . .

—RALPH CUDWORTH,
The True Intellectual System of the Universe (1678)

Dreams lead to self-knowledge. . . . We live and feel just as much in dreams as in waking, and the one is as much a part of our existence as the other. . . . We have hardly yet made the right use of a knowledge of dreams. . . . Dreams develop all kinds of ideas which were sleeping in my soul. . . . I cannot say I was hostile to him, nor friendly, for I have never dreamed of him.

—G. C. LICHTENBERG (1742–1799)

And why, too, on waking and fully returning to reality, do you feel almost every time, and sometimes with extraordinary intensity, that you have left something unexplained behind with the dream, and at the same time you feel that interwoven with these absurdities some thought lies hidden, and a thought that is real, something belonging to your actual life, something that exists and always has existed in your heart. It's as though something new, prophetic, that you were awaiting, has been told you in your dream.

—DOSTOEVSKY, *The Idiot*

Let us learn to dream, gentlemen; then we shall perhaps find the truth.

—FRIEDRICH KEKULE, 1890

...in dreams we never deceive ourselves, nor are deceived, and this seemed to have the authority of a final judgment.

□

In dreams we see ourselves naked and acting out our real characters, even more clearly than we see others awake.... As we are accustomed to say carelessly, we should never have *dreamed* of such a thing.

Our truest life is when we are in dreams awake.

—HENRY DAVID THOREAU, *A Week on the Concord and Merrimack Rivers*

The interpretation of dreams is the royal road to a knowledge of the unconscious activities of the mind.

□

A dream is a disguised fulfillment of a suppressed or repressed wish.... Dreams are guardians of sleep, not its disturbers.

—SIGMUND FREUD, *The Interpretation of Dreams*

Why may not we ... ask the dreamer the meaning of the dream? ... I assure you that it is not only quite possible, but highly probable, that the dreamer really does know the meaning of his dream; *only he does not know that he knows, and therefore thinks that he does not.*

—SIGMUND FREUD, *A General Introduction to Psychoanalysis*

Why does the eye perceive things more clearly in dreams than with the imagination when one is awake?

LEONARDO DA VINCI

DRESS

EGYPT (15TH CENTURY)

The Moorish women do not wear golden rings, but silver, with precious stones and pearls set therein. They ornament their skin with colors, which are not removed by water in six months, although they go everyday to the baths. There are no baths as fine as those of Egypt, and there are lavatories there. The saddles of the donkeys are worth very much, and the mamelukes wear on their horse saddles many precious stones, pearls, and also on the bridles, beyond description.

—RABBI MESHULLAM BEN R. MENAHEM
of Volterra (1481), in *Jewish Travellers*

VENICE

By the eighteenth century no extravagance was barred. Some of the dresses that remain on view today from that time are still breathtaking; sumptuous, graceful, brilliant—embroidered with marvelous care, with layer on layer of brocade, gold thread, silk and lace reaching to the feet, stiff bodices, and half-sleeves with lacy frills, side-bustles and farthingales. Nothing was spared in color, in generous cut; sometimes precious lace was elaborately sprayed over the neckpiece and the skirt as well as the sleeves; the women showed plenty of bosom, the V-necks going straight from the shoulder, the square necks set very low. . . . But still the show was dazzling. There was a mass of ribbon, lace, veil, flowered silk: Even shoes were painted with bright colors. Angelo Labia was right: It was refinement to a point of madness and ecstasy quite beyond elegance.

—MAURICE ROWDON, *op. cit.*

"DR. LIVINGSTONE, I PRESUME"

Psychologically much of the white man's burden was found in a demanding, self-imposed standard of conduct. Superiority had to be constantly proved to oneself and to the watchful African. To the individual, superiority was not a permanent gift, but a possession contingent on justification in action. This meant that the ordinary human failings of indecision and lack of self-control had to be stifled. . . .

This is revealed in striking fashion in Stanley's writings. His famous meeting with Livingstone at Ujiji provides one example. When he came in sight of the renowned missionary traveler, though he was greatly excited, Stanley restrained himself, for "I must not let my face display my emotions, lest it shall detract from the dignity of a white man appearing under such extraordinary circumstances." The historic greeting with outstretched hand, and the formal "Dr. Livingstone, I presume," reflected the psychology of racial superiority. Before an inferior race it was necessary to present a façade of authority, power, and coolness in order to prevent the African from seeing those aspects of human nature which, by indicating emotionalism or indecision, might derogate from the assumed attributes of leadership and the aloofness of superior racial status.

—H. A. C. CAIRNS, *Prelude to Imperialism*

DRUGS

[Drugs give me] the most glorious vision of color and jeweled splendor, unknown to the natural world.

—WILLIAM JAMES, in ALDOUS HUXLEY,
Annals of the New York Academy of Science (1957)

[In Cincinnati, in 1871] walk along the streets any day and you will meet opium slaves by the score . . . abject slaves suffering exquisite torture. Once in the fetters of opium and morphia, they are, with few exceptions, fettered for life.

—LAFCADIO HEARN, in A. HOGENBOOM, *The Gilded Age*

MADAME DU BARRY (COMTESSE MARIE JEANNE BECU) (1746 or 1743?–1793)

I owe my position to my face. Even when quite young, I found I had an instinct for coquetry; I was welcomed everywhere, my company eagerly sought. . . .

One morning, the Comte Jean [her husband] entered my apartment and said, "I shall not be happy until you have made the

King of France my successor! ... You see, the place of Madame
de Pompadour is vacant. You can take it. You can become the
dispenser of state honors and royal favors. All your whims will
be realized, your every caprice satisfied."

[After spending a night with Louis XVI]: I hope I may be
excused if I pass over certain intimate details which could not,
at this time, interest or amuse anyone. I find that my pen is more
prudish than were my ears or my mouth.

All I shall say is that the next morning, Lebel entered my
chamber at the palace and, flinging himself at the side of my
bed, said: "Madame la comtesse, you are queen and mistress
here! Your noble lover has not only failed to signal to me his
usual antipathy or disgust, but he has actually declared that for
the first time in his life he felt true affection."

... Later, that day, I received from His Majesty a magnificent
diamond agraffe, worth at least 60,000 francs, and banknotes to the
amount of 200,000 livres. Comte Jean and I were stupefied by the
sight of such treasures. We divided them into two equal parts, one
of which he put into his pocket. ... That evening he gave me much
advice for the future, all of which I promised him I would observe. "After all," I said, "the world is no more than an amusing
theater. I see no reason why a beautiful woman should not play
a leading role in it."

—MADAME DU BARRY, *Memoirs of Madame du Barry*

DUPLICITY

Severus treated the man whom he had doomed to destruction
with every mark of esteem and regard. Even in the letter in
which he announced his victory over Niger he styles Albinus the
brother of his soul and empire, sends him the affectionate saluta-
tions of his wife Julia, and his young family, and entreats him to
preserve the armies and the republic faithful to their common
interest. The messengers charged with this letter were instructed
to accost the Caesar with respect, to desire a private audience,
and to plunge their daggers into his heart.

—EDWARD GIBBON,
The Decline and Fall of the Roman Empire

DYING

I feel no sort of solicitude about a parting which will bring no pain. Sympathy with those who will miss me, I do feel, of course; yet not very painfully, because their sorrow cannot, in the nature of things, long interfere with their daily peace; but to me there is no sacrifice, no sense of loss, nothing to fear, nothing to regret. . . .

I am frankly satisfied to have done with life. I have had a noble share of it, and I desire no more. I neither wish to live longer here, nor to find life again elsewhere. It seems to me simply absurd to expect it, and a mere act of restricted human imagination and morality to conceive of it. . . . I myself utterly disbelieve in a future life. . . . The important thing is that the universe should be full of life, as we suppose it to be, under the eternal laws of the universe: And, if the universe be full of life, I cannot see how it can signify whether one human faculty of consciousness of identity be preserved and carried forward, when all the rest of the organization is gone to dust, or so changed as to be in no respect properly the same. The real and justifiable and honorable subject of interest to human beings, living and dying, is the welfare of their fellows, surrounding them, or surviving them. About this, I do care, and supremely.

—*Harriet Martineau's Autobiography*

THE EARTH AND THE STARS

The earth is not at the center of the sun's orbit, nor at the center of the universe, but rather in the center of companion elements, and in union with them. Anyone standing on the moon, when it and the sun are both beneath us, would see our earth, and the waters upon it, just as we see the moon: And the earth would light the moon as the moon lights us. . . .

The earth is a star much like the moon.

☐

If you look at the stars, cutting off their rays (by looking through a very small hole made with a very fine needle, placed so as almost to touch the eye), you will see those stars so tiny that it would seem as though nothing could be smaller. It is, in fact, their great distance from us which accounts for their diminution, for many stars are very many times larger than the star which is the earth.

—Leonardo da Vinci, *Notebooks*

ECONOMIC VS. POLITICAL POWER

Our society will always remain an unstable and explosive compound as long as political power is vested in the masses and economic power in the classes. In the end one of these powers will rule. Either the plutocracy will buy up the democracy or the democracy will vote away the plutocracy.

—Irving Fisher, *American Economic Review,*
March 1919

ECONOMICS

The laws of economics are to be compared with the laws of the tides, rather than with the simple and exact law of gravitation. For the actions of men are so various and uncertain, that the best statement of tendencies which we can make in a science of human conduct, must needs be inexact and faulty. This might be urged as a reason against making any statements at all on the subject; but that would be almost to abandon life. Life is human conduct, and the thoughts and emotions that grow up around it. . . . And since we *must* form to ourselves some notions of the tendencies of human action, our choice is between forming those notions carelessly and forming them carefully. The harder the task, the greater the need for steady patient inquiry; for turning to account the experience that has been reaped . . . and for forming as best we can well thought-out estimates, or provisional laws, of the tendencies of human action.

—ALFRED MARSHALL, *Principles of Economics*

ECONOMISTS' IDEAS

The ideas of economists and political philosophers, both when they are right and when they are wrong, are more powerful than is commonly understood. Indeed, the world is ruled by little else. Practical men, who believe themselves to be quite exempt from any intellectual influences, are usually the slaves of some defunct economist.

□

Madmen in authority, who hear voices in the air, are distilling their frenzy from some academic scribbler of a few years back.

□

... the ideas which civil servants and politicians and even agitators apply to current events are not likely to be the newest. But, soon or late, it is ideas, not vested interests, which are dangerous for good or evil.

—JOHN MAYNARD KEYNES,
*The General Theory of Employment,
Interest, and Money*

If all economists were laid end to end, they would not reach a conclusion.

—GEORGE BERNARD SHAW

THOMAS A. EDISON (1847–1931)

When a preacher asked whether to put a lightning rod on a church steeple, Edison replied, "By all means; Providence is apt to be absent-minded."

□

His second wife said that when absorbed in a problem, Edison lived "in the highest state of exhilaration, seeing nothing, hearing nothing, thinking nothing ... except what has a vital bearing on the task."

After 8,000 unsuccessful trials on a nickel-iron storage battery: "Well, at least we know 8,000 things that won't work."

He was a much greater man than I expected to find—simple, direct, intelligent and unspoiled.

—ROBERT MILLIKAN

EDUCATION

There are two kinds of arguments, the true and the false. The young should be instructed in both—but the false first.

—PLATO, *The Republic*

Those who educate children well, are more to be honored than they who produce them; for these only gave them life, those the art of living well.

☐

What we have to learn to do, we learn by doing.

☐

[Aristotle was asked how much educated men were superior to those uneducated]: "As much as the living are to the dead."

—ARISTOTLE

Education is what remains when we have forgotten all that we have been taught.

—GEORGE SAVILE HALIFAX

The power of instruction is seldom of much efficacy except in those happy dispositions where it is almost superfluous.

—EDWARD GIBBON,
The Decline and Fall of the Roman Empire

Education: the ability to describe a bathing beauty without using your hands.

—*San Francisco Chronicle*

A child's education should begin at least one hundred years before he is born.

—OLIVER WENDELL HOLMES

Abraham Flexner once remarked to me that getting education is like getting measles; you have to go where measles is. If you go where it is, unless you are by nature immune, you will get it—no need to worry about that—but if you don't go where it is, you will never get it.

—A. J. Nock, *Memoirs of a Superfluous Man*

No man should escape our universities without knowing how little he knows. He must have some sense of the fact that not through his fault... but inherently in the nature of things, he is going to be an ignorant man and so is everybody else.

—J. Robert Oppenheimer, quoted by J. H. Raleigh, in *Partisan Review*, Summer 1967

Education: the inculcation of the incomprehensible into the indifferent by the incompetent.

—John Maynard Keynes

Education is what you must acquire without any interference from your schooling.

—Mark Twain

AMERICAN INDIAN

Several of our young [Indian] people were formerly brought up in the colleges of the northern provinces. They were instructed in all your sciences. But when they came back to us, they were bad runners, ignorant of every means of living in the woods, unable to bear either cold or hunger, knew neither how to build a cabin, take a deer, spoke our language imperfectly. They were therefore neither fit for hunters, warriors, nor counselors. They were totally good for nothing. We are, however, nonetheless obliged by your kind offer, though we decline... it. And to show our grateful sense of it, if the gentlemen of Virginia will send us a dozen of their sons, we will take great care of their education, instruct them in all we know, and make *men* of them.

—message from representatives of the Six Nations to the Commissioner of Virginia, in Benjamin Franklin, *Remarks Concerning the Savages of North America*

VOCATIONAL

I think vocational education can be very helpful and may be a way in which we can use our vast educational plant more effectively. I think that a kind of self-respect, and respect for others, comes to those who know how to do something, who know something—whether it be repairing a television set or setting type.

If a person's knowledge is blurred, and he has been told about human dignity, and Tolstoi and Plato by someone to whom these don't really mean anything, then he emerges with a disrespect for learning—which makes him think less well of his own mind and the minds of others.

I believe that the policies of open admission and the leveling down of institutions are destroying the right of a person to be excellent. The corrosive emphasis on what Bertrand Russell called "the superior virtue of the underdog"*—which is something that Christianity has tended to encourage—should not mislead us into believing in the superior competence of the underdog.

—DANIEL BOORSTIN,
interview in *U.S. News and World Report*,
October 19, 1970

ALBERT EINSTEIN (1879–1955)

I have never belonged wholeheartedly to a country, a state, nor to a circle of friends, nor even to my own family.

□

[Of his adolescence] Perception of this world by thought, leaving out everything subjective, became, partly consciously, partly unconsciously, my supreme aim.

□

I believe in Spinoza's God who reveals himself in the harmony of all being, not in a God who concerns himself with the fate and actions of men.

□

War seems to me a mean, contemptible thing. I would rather be hacked to pieces than take part in such abominable business.

□

* Russell's phrase was "The oppressed."

As long as I have a choice, I will stay only in a country where political liberty, toleration and equality of all citizens before the law are the rule.

—compiled from various sources

ABOUT HIM

People think that Albert is a dreamer. He really is a very practical man.

—ELSA EINSTEIN, wife

He would have been one of the greatest theoreticians of physics even if he had never written a line on relativity.

—MAX BORN, physicist

His is not the discovery of an outlying island, but of a whole continent of new scientific ideas. It is the greatest discovery in connection with gravitation since Newton first enunciated its principles.

—President of the Royal Society, London, 1919

Albert Einstein has called forth a greater revolution in thought than even Copernicus, Galileo, or Newton.

—LORD HALDANE

One could easily have been tempted to portray him as an over-sensitive man, who trembles at the very mention of injustice and violence. This picture would be utterly false. I know no one who leads such a lonely and solitary life as he. His great benevolence, his absolute integrity and his social ideas, despite all appearances to the contrary, are thoroughly impersonal and seem to come from another planet. His heart does not bleed, his eyes do not weep. . . .

—LEOPOLD INFELD, in C. P. SNOW, *A Variety of Men*

EINSTEIN'S THEORY AND COMMON SENSE

. . . only the vaguest notions of the meaning of Einstein's theory of relativity can be had on the basis of common sense. Indeed, most of us do not have even a vague understanding of the theory but rather feel about it much the way the men of Newton's time felt about his new and apparently absurd notions that also seemed to contradict common sense. Newton's theory was based on what seemed to his contemporaries to be most improbable assumptions. The notion of a force acting at a distance is quite a different thing from the notion of a direct push, on which our intuitive, common sense understanding of force rests. Gradually, of course, in Newton's case, conceptual scheme and common sense were in some fashion reconciled. "After a generation or so most men managed to convince themselves that action at a distance was a reasonable and comfortable idea." Or at least conceptual scheme and common sense puzzled each other less. Eventually ... Newtonian notions came to be regarded as intuitively obvious, as common sense. As Mach has put it, "uncommon incomprehensibility became a common incomprehensibility."

—BERNARD BARBER, *Science and the Social Order*

THE ELEPHANTS OF SAMARKAND

The Indian elephants and stonemasons safely reached Samarkand, where the masons became part of a community which already included painters, calligraphers and architects from Persia, and which would soon be joined, after Timur's [Tamerlane] next expeditions, by silk-weavers and glass-blowers from Damascus and by silversmiths from Turkey. When ... the ambassador from Spain, reached Samarkand in 1404 he found so many of these skilled foreign captives that "the city was not large enough to hold them, and it was wonderful what a number lived under trees, and in caves outside." Clavijo also came across those same obsequious elephants; they were now painted green and red, and guarded the entrance to the sumptuous garden where the nomadic Timur, even in his own capital, chose to live in a tent. These were the first elephants that Clavijo, like so many of Timur's troops at Delhi, had set eyes upon. But Clavijo could view them more calmly, and he provided his readers in Spain with a description which is as brilliantly straightforward as a child's painting: "The animals were very large, and their bodies were quite shapeless, like a full sack; their legs were very thick, and the same size all the way down."

—BAMBER GASCOIGNE, *The Great Moghuls*

ELIZABETH I, QUEEN OF ENGLAND (1558–1603)

Her delight was to move in perpetual progresses from castle to castle through a series of gorgeous pageants, fanciful and extravagant as a caliph's dream. She loved gaiety and laughter and wit. A happy retort or a finished compliment never failed to win her favor. She hoarded jewels. Her dresses were innumerable. Her vanity remained, even to old age, the vanity of a coquette in her teens. No adulation was too fulsome for her, no flattery of her beauty too gross. She would play with her rings that her courtiers might note the delicacy of her hands; or dance a coranto that an ambassador, hidden dexterously behind a curtain, might report her sprightliness to his master. Her levity, her frivolous laughter, her unwomanly jests gave color to a thousand scandals. Her character in fact, like her portraits, was utterly without shade. Of womanly reserve or self-restraint she knew nothing. No instinct of delicacy veiled the voluptuous temper which broke out in the romps of her girlhood and showed itself almost ostentatiously through her later life. Personal beauty in a man was a sure passport to her liking. She patted handsome young squires on the neck when they knelt to kiss her hand, and fondled her "sweet Robin," Lord Leicester, in the face of the Court.

—JOHN RICHARD GREEN,
A History of the English People (1874)

She was, then and since, unexpected, in her birth, in succession, in her boast of singleness, in her bravery of success. Unassassinated and undeposed ... uncertain in a world of certainties, turning some hidden center of her own, faithful to some in her actions as unforeseen in her existence; brilliant and disingenuous, humble and sincere, a perverse portent, she sat on the English throne for forty years, and moved the English imagination for four centuries, an incarnate, memorable, and terrifying example of the way things happen. As common and as unusual as that, she was Elizabeth.

—CHARLES WILLIAMS, *Queen Elizabeth I*

HER CHARACTER

If she was without love she was without hate. She cherished no petty resentments; she never stooped to envy or suspicion of the men who served her. She was indifferent to abuse. Her good humor was never ruffled by the charges of wantonness and cruelty with which the Jesuits filled every Court in Europe. She was insensible to fear.... Even when Catholic plots broke out in her very household, she would listen to no proposals for the removal of Catholics from her Court.

—JOHN RICHARD GREEN, *op. cit.*

HER LIES

In the profusion and recklessness of her lies, Elizabeth stood without a peer in Christendom. A falsehood was to her simply an intellectual means of meeting a difficulty; and the ease with which she asserted or denied whatever suited her purpose was only equaled by the cynical indifference with which she met the exposure of her lies as soon as their purpose was answered....

□

"No War, my Lords," the Queen used to cry imperiously at the councilboard, "No War!" but her hatred of war sprang not so much from aversion to blood or to expense, real as was her aversion to both, as from the fact that peace left the field open to the diplomatic maneuvers and intrigues in which she excelled.

She played with grave cabinets as a cat plays with a mouse, and with much of the same feline delight in the mere embarrassment of her victims. When she was weary of mystifying foreign statesmen she turned to find fresh sport in mystifying her own ministers. Had Elizabeth written the story of her reign she would have prided herself, not on the triumph of England or the ruin of Spain, but on the skill with which she had hoodwinked and outwitted every statesman in Europe during fifty years.

—*Ibid.*

ELIZABETH AND THE EXECUTION OF MARY

The Queen was confronted with the worst crisis of her life. It is as certain as any mortal thing can be, not merely that she did not want to execute Mary, but that she thought she ought not to execute Mary. She was physically revolted by the idea, and more or less consciously she knew it was a contradiction of her life's basis. Mary was anointed and royal; she was not Elizabeth's subject, she was Elizabeth's equal, and as sacrosanct as the Queen herself. In her blood and fibres Elizabeth felt it to be a sin to touch this other Majesty—a dreadful, perhaps a mortal sin. She was normally as casual of morals as of dogmas, but her scepticism had its limits, and all she had ever persuaded others, or herself believed, that she herself was, rose against the deed.

Her Ministers, her Council, her Parliament, her bishops, her people—the preachers and the crowds—were united in pressing the deed on her. The two elements of her desire clashed. . . .

From October to February she demurred and disputed with herself. She listened to the protests of ambassadors and snarled at the messengers of the Scottish King. At the very end she fell back on the possibility of private murder, and caused Walsingham to write to Paulet, Mary's jailer, suggesting that it might be within the bounds of his duty to take off his prisoner. It was not the justice of the sentence against Mary that troubled her, as certainly it troubled hardly anyone else. That Mary was guilty of complicity everyone knew. But that an anointed sovereign should put to death, by show of trial, another anointed sovereign—this was the crisis. In the position to which Elizabeth had come there were, for her, but two possibilities—a supreme determination after virtue or certain sin. She sinned. She signed the warrant.

—Charles Williams, *Queen Elizabeth I*

ELIZABETH I AND THE POPE

Cardinal Allen yet once more described and denounced the Queen in a printed *Admonition to the People of England*—"an incestuous bastard, begotten and born in sin of an infamous courtesan"; all spiritual aid was invoked—by processions, prayers, vigils, adorations. The double figure of sin had sat too long on the waters— thrice opprobrious: in her blood, in her belief, in her wickedness. Illegitimate, heretical, bloody, and debauched, she sat there like some horrible Scylla devouring the martyrs. . . .

One voice only broke the chorus; in the center of the Crusade, of all people, Pope Sixtus V himself exclaimed in admiration, "What a woman!" "Have you heard how Drake has offered battle? What courage!" "If she were not a heretic she would be worth the whole world!" The Queen is said to have courteously

reciprocated, saying she knew but of one man worthy of her—
and he was Sixtus V.

—Ibid.

ELOQUENCE

The age of chivalry is gone. That of sophisters, economists and
calculators has succeeded; and the glory of Europe is extinguished
forever.

Never, never more shall we behold that generous loyalty to
rank and sex, that proud submission, that dignified obedience,
that subordination of the heart, which kept alive, even in servitude itself, the spirit of an exalted freedom. The unbought grace
of life, the cheap defense of nations, the nurse of manly sentiment
and heroic enterprise is gone! It is gone, that sensibility of principle, that chastity of honor, which felt a stain like a wound,
which inspired courage whilst it mitigated ferocity, which en-
nobled whatever it touched, and under which vice itself lost half
its evil, by losing all its grossness.

—EDMUND BURKE,
Reflections on the Revolution in France

$E = MC^2$

It is customary to express the equivalence of mass and energy
(though somewhat inexactly) by the formula $E = mc^2$, in which
c represents the velocity of light, about 186,000 miles per second.
E is the energy that is contained in a stationary body; m is its
mass. The energy that belongs to the mass m is equal to this mass,
multiplied by the square of the enormous speed of light—which is
to say, a vast amount of energy for every unit of mass.

But if every gram of material contains this tremendous energy,
why did it go so long unnoticed? The answer is simple enough:
so long as none of the energy is given off externally, it cannot be
observed. It is as though a man who is fabulously rich should
never spend or give away a cent; no one could tell how rich he
was.

☐

Now, we cannot actually weigh the atoms individually. However, there are indirect methods for measuring their weights

exactly. We can likewise determine the kinetic energies that are transferred to the disintegration products M′ and M″. Thus it has become possible to test and confirm the equivalence formula. Also, the law permits us to calculate in advance, from precisely determined atom weights, just how much energy will be released with any atom disintegration we have in mind. The law says nothing, of course, as to whether—or how—the disintegration reaction can be brought about.

What takes place can be illustrated with the help of our rich man. The atom M is a rich miser who, during his life, gives away no money (*energy*). But in his will he bequeaths his fortune to his sons M′ and M″, on condition that they give to the community a small amount, less than one thousandth of the whole estate (*energy or mass*). The sons together have somewhat less than the father had (*the mass sum M′ + M″ is somewhat smaller than the mass M of the radioactive atom*). But the part given to the community, though relatively small, is still so enormously large (*considered as kinetic energy*) that it brings with it a great threat of evil. Averting that threat has become the most urgent problem of our time.

—ALBERT EINSTEIN, *Out of My Later Years*

EMOTIONS

I recognize only three primitive or primary emotions, namely: pleasure, pain and desire.

—BARUCH SPINOZA, "The Ethics" (Part III),
Origins and Nature of the Emotions

... everybody experiences his own emotions and sensations directly. They just simply exist for him. But we do not experience directly the sensations of any other individuals, however certain their existence may be, and we can only infer them in analogy to our own sensations.

—MAX PLANCK,
Scientific Autobiography and other papers

ENDS AND MEANS

If the ends don't justify the means, what can?

—JOHN MAYNARD KEYNES

THE ENEMY

Hostile impulses arouse guilt feelings because society has taught the individual during infancy, childhood, and juvenility to chasten his rages. The initial tendency to hold the destructive tendencies in check by raging against the self can be dealt with by projecting the accusation away from the self, and raging at the "immorality" of the enemy.

—HAROLD D. LASSWELL,
Politics—Who Gets What, When, How

ENERGY

Energy drives our world. Energy from oil is sending me eastward at 600 miles per hour in a giant airplane flying 30,000 feet over the Wyoming desert. Energy from oil was used to smelt the aluminum to build the plane; more energy from oil was used to make the plastic tray I'm writing on, the plastic fiber of the seats; still more to freeze the ice in my lemonade, served in a plastic cup. Most of my world is fossil fueled—but not quite all.

A hitchhiking fly tickles my hand. I flick it away. It moves to the window, attracted by the sunlight reflected from the plane's wings. The fly's source of energy is, of course, the sun. This solar energy flows to the insect through green plants somewhere far away. And the energy I use in flicking my hand also comes from the sun, fixed in photosynthesis somewhere recently, perhaps in the great green circles of western Nebraska's irrigated farmland now passing below me. Outside my silver capsule, the sun dominates: warming the land, evaporating water, heating the air, circulating the oceans, making the weather, causing the winds —and providing the energy for all life.

—GEORGE M. WOODWELL,
"The Unavoidable Limits to Energy Growth," in
Natural History, 1974

THE ENGLISH

Feuerbach attributed the superiority of the English to their diet of beef and urged the Irish to replace potatoes with beans, the food of revolution. In reality, however, England owed its superiority to its old maids, as a distinguished British biologist has pointed out. For good English beef, his argument runs, depends upon the industrious bumblebee which pollinates red clover eaten by cattle, and the number of bumblebees in turn is determined by the number of cats, since the mice rob the nests of the bumble-bees, and mice are killed by cats. Hence, few cats mean many mice, few bumblebees, little clover and bad meat. Because old maids are fond of cats as pets, ergo England's power depends on the number of its old maids.

—Noah Jonathan Jacobs, *Naming Day in Eden*

Of all the enviable things England has, I envy it most its people.

—Benjamin Franklin

... Hitler will probably invade us within the next few days.... We know that we are faced with a terrific invasion.... Yet there is a sort of exhilaration in the air ... we are really proud to be the people who will not give way ... we shall be exposed to horrible punishment. It is so strange that in this moment ... there is no hatred of Hitler or the Germans ... we are really frightened of Hitler, and avoid ... hatred. 130 years ago all this hatred was concentrated against Napoleon. We flinch today from central enmity. If we are invaded, we may become angry.

—Harold Nicolson, *The War Years: 1939–1945*

We complain that there are no photographs of the sinking of the *Bismarck* (June 9, 1941) ... "Why didn't one of our reconnaissance machines fly over the ship and take photographs?" Tripp replied, "Well you see, you *must* see, well upon my word, well after all, an Englishman would not like to take snapshots of a fine vessel sinking."

—*Ibid.*

I have a conviction that there is a real, an almost imminent danger of England losing immeasurably in all ways, declining into a sort of greater Holland, for want of what I must still call ideas, for want of perceiving how the world is going and must go, and preparing itself accordingly.

—Matthew Arnold, letter (1865), in *The Works of Matthew Arnold*, Vol. XIV

... not arrogance alone, not frivolity alone, but an arrogant frivolity to which the English mind and character are peculiarly susceptible.

—HENRY FAIRLIE, "TransAtlantic Letter to England,"
in *Encounter*, January 1976

In France it is rude to let a conversation drop; in England it is rash to keep it up. No one there will blame you for silence. When you have not opened your mouth for three years, they will think: "This Frenchman is a nice quiet fellow." Be modest. An Englishman will say, "I have a little house in the country"; when he invites you to stay with him you will discover that the little house is a place with three hundred bedrooms. If you are a world tennis-champion, say, "Yes, I don't play too badly." If you have crossed the Atlantic alone in a small boat, say, "I do a little sailing"....

Golden rule: Never ask questions. For six months during War I lived in the same tent and shared a bath-tub with an Englishman: He never asked me if I was married, what I did in peacetime, or what were the books I was reading under his nose. If you insist on making confidences, they will be listened to with polite indifference.

—ANDRÉ MAUROIS, *Three Letters on the English*

We have no amusements in England but vice and religion.

—SYDNEY SMITH

I have constantly watched and tried to measure the moods and inspirations of the British people. There is no foe they will not face. There is no hardship they cannot endure. Whether the test be short or long and wearisome, they can take it. What they do not forgive is false promises and vain boastings.

—WINSTON CHURCHILL

An Englishman thinks he is moral when he is only uncomfortable.

—GEORGE BERNARD SHAW

The Anglo-Saxon conscience does not prevent the Anglo-Saxon from sinning. It merely prevents him from enjoying it.

—SALVADOR DE MADARIAGA,
Englishmen, Frenchmen, Spaniards

Prophesying "smooth things" to the British never succeeds. It makes them uneasy. It runs counter to their innermost beliefs. Fond of losers, sympathetic always with the defeated, loudly applauding amateurs and nonprofessionals, identifying themselves ever with "the awkward squad," they value and follow integrity and character rather than intellect, probity rather than personality, doers and fighters rather than talkers and thinkers.

—editorial, *Times Literary Supplement*,
September 18, 1965

The English are always ready to admire anything so long as they can queue up.

—GEORGES MIKES, *How to Be an Alien*

Living in England is curing me of being shy.... It takes a great deal to produce ennui in an Englishman and if you do, he only takes it as convincing proof that you are well-bred.

—MARGARET HALSEY, *With Malice Toward Some*

...What governs [the Englishman] is convention.... Where else would a man inform you, with a sort of proud challenge, that he lived on nuts, or was in correspondence through a medium with Joshua Reynolds, or had been disgustingly housed when last in prison.

—GEORGE SANTAYANA

In dealing with Englishmen you can be sure of one thing only, that the logical solution will not be adopted.

—WILLIAM RALPH INGE

England has forty-two religions and only two sauces.

—VOLTAIRE

There have been many attempts to describe hell, but for Englishmen the best definition is that it is a place where the Germans are the police, the Swedish are the comedians, the Italians are the defense force, Frenchmen dig the roads, Belgians are the pop singers, the Spanish run the railways, the Turks cook the food, the Irish are the waiters, the Greeks run the government, and the common language is Dutch.

—DAVID FROST and ANTONY JAY, *The English*

AN ENGLISHMAN

I know not where any personal eccentricity is so freely allowed. ... An Englishman walks in the pouring rain, swinging his closed umbrella like a walking stick; wears a wig, or a shawl, or a saddle, or stands on his head, and no remark is made. ...

Every one of these islanders is an island himself, safe, tranquil, incommunicable. In a company of strangers you would think him deaf; his eyes never wander from his table and newspaper. He is never betrayed into any curiosity or emotion. ... He does not give his hands. ... It is almost an affront to look a man in the face without being introduced. In mixed or in select companies they do not introduce persons. ... Introductions are sacraments. He withholds his name. At the hotel, he is hardly willing to whisper it to the clerk. ... His bearing, on being introduced, is cold, even though he is seeking your acquaintanceship.
—RALPH WALDO EMERSON, *Collected Works*, Vol. V

EQUALITY

Democratic communities have a natural taste for freedom. Left to themselves, they will seek it, cherish it, and view any privation of it with regret. But for equality their passion is ardent, insatiable, incessant and invincible. They call for equality in freedom; and if they cannot obtain that, they will call for equality in slavery. They will endure poverty, servitude, barbarism, but they will not endure aristocracy.

□

Whatever efforts a people may make, they will never succeed in reducing all the conditions of society to a perfect level. ... The inequality of minds would still remain, which, coming from the hand of God, will forever escape the laws of man.

□

The hatred which men bear to privilege increases in proportion as privileges become fewer and less considerable. Democratic passions would seem to burn most fiercely just when they have least fuel. ...

□

When inequality of conditions is the common law of society, the most marked inequalities do not strike the eye; when everything is nearly on the same level, the slightest are marked enough to hurt it. Hence the desire of equality always becomes more insatiable in proportion as equality is more complete.

—ALEXIS DE TOCQUEVILLE, *Democracy in America*

It is better that some should be unhappy than that none should be happy, which would be the case in a general state of equality.

—SAMUEL JOHNSON, in Boswell, *Life of Samuel Johnson*

The assertion that all men are equal is perhaps the purest falsehood in dogma that was ever put into human language; five minutes' observation of facts will show that men are unequal through a very wide range of variation. Men are not simple units; they are very complex; there is no such thing as a unit man. Therefore we cannot measure men. If we take any element of man and measure men for it, they always fall under a curve of probable error. When we say "man" for human being, we overlook distinctions of age and sex. Males of different ages are not equal; men and women are not equal in the struggle for existence. Women are handicapped by a function which causes disabilities in the struggle for existence, and this difference produces immense disparity in the sexes as to all interests throughout all human life.

—WILLIAM GRAHAM SUMNER, *The Forgotten Man*

Real equality is not something to be decreed by law. It can't be given and it can't be forced. It must be earned.

—RAYMOND MOLEY, speech, 1938

EQUALITY AND PROPERTY

Against the assumption that there can be no personal freedom without economic equality we contrast the memory that for centuries Englishmen felt themselves freer than other men, and that there has been no liberty except where there has been property.

—KENNETH PICKTHORN, *Principles and Prejudices*

The issue between the giant corporations and the public should not be allowed to obscure the truth that the only dependable foundation of personal liberty is the personal economic security of private property.

—WALTER LIPPMANN, *The Good Society*

DESIDERIUS ERASMUS (1466?–1536)

I cannot risk my life for the truth. All men have not strength for martyrdom. . . . I follow the just decrees of popes and emperors because it is right; I endure their evil laws because it is safe. . . . Christ will look after me.

—ERASMUS, *Letters*

ABOUT HIM

He, almost alone in his age, knew that truth had many facets. . . . Thomas More would die for his faith and would have you punished for yours; Erasmus would be . . . courteous . . . even to an infidel. . . . He contributed more to the liberation of the human mind . . . than all the uproar and rage of Luther's pamphlets.

—PRESERVED SMITH, *Erasmus: A Study of His Life*

EROS IN VENICE

Love—or rather, lovemaking—was the theme of their books, their snuffboxes, their rings and visiting cards, and it often toppled into the obscene. Verses were illustrated with erotic woodcuts. The reading matter was either romance or gallantry. The old ideal of cutting a fine figure now meant cutting more or less a sexual one: Even the men studied themselves in the mirror for hours, rehearsing poses and gestures and ways of taking or offering snuff. The *cicisbeo* rustled and tinkled as he walked along at his mistress's side, loaded with ornament, powdered and laced. Quite often he had less than no appeal for her—and he was an accepted formality, laid down in the marriage contract; his "muscles of cotton wool," as Carlo Gozzi described them, were only required for carrying eyeglasses and cups of chocolate and snuffboxes.

—MAURICE ROWDON, *The Silver Age of Venice*

ESKIMOS: SEXUAL MORES

The dating game in Shismaref is an extremely subtle affair. I had heard of sexual promiscuity among the Eskimos, since what author ever wrote a book about them without that inevitable episode where his host offers him his wife as part of Eskimo hospitality? More specifically, a VISTA boy in another village had committed the unspeakable social error of bringing his girl back to her family abode, kissing her a couple of times at the door, and then relinquishing her, to the scorn and amazement of the clan gathered together inside, to sleep in the single room. He dared return the next night for another date with the girl but he was confronted at the door, beforehand, this time by her mother. Fixing him with a steely eye, she demanded: "How come you're not sleeping with my daughter?" Hastily, he denied any feelings of superiority, but the family hurt was not to be erased by anything but staying for the night with his date when he brought her home later on. In fact, if only to atone for his lamentable mistake at the beginning, he spent every night with her thereafter.

.... public opinion looked on the sexual act in what I can only describe as loving unconcern. I remember one piquant little miss of fourteen or fifteen who was frequently visited by a man in his middle thirties for a romp in the reindeer skins. No one thought very much about this—and, in fact, neither did the participants, since it was not until after their third child had been born that they decided to get married....

Had they not married, however, the girl's social status, by Eskimo standards, would have suffered. The father is looked upon fondly as a potent member of the community, the children are considered his—and everybody's—and romp all over the village as common property. But the mother usually is shamed by her failure to entice him into a permanent family arrangement and retreats into the bosom of her own parental group, perhaps to die an old maid, unless another hunter favors a liaison with a lady who has demonstrable qualifications.

—JAMES L. ATHERTON, JR., "Fun on the Tundra," in
Holiday, November 1971

ETIQUETTE

Commodore Perry was reminded that Japanese did not act with the same rapidity as Americans did, which was thus illustrated: Should several Japanese meet together, desiring to visit the American ships, one would say: "It is a beautiful morning." To which another would add, "How pleasant it is!" Then a third would remark, "There is not then a wave to be seen upon the water." At length a fourth would suggest, "Come let us go and see the ships."

—*New York Daily News* (June 13, 1854), quoted in
FRANK GIBNEY, "The Japanese and Their Language,"
in *Encounter*, March 1975

BERLIN

Berlin wears its vices in its buttonhole—without a blush and without defiance. People will talk to you about their own odd sexual practices as if they were discussing the weather—which they refuse to discuss, by the way.... People's sexual life—they seem to hold—is, after all, more or less their private matter—so why not discuss it freely and publicly? You meet no tight-lipped silence, no unreasonable antagonism and old-maidish prudery about the most shocking stories.

I hold no brief for vice in general, homosexuality and sodomy in particular. These things have always repulsed me and I could never understand what people can see in a goat. All I am trying to say is that Berlin's viciousness does not seem to be real viciousness. The Berliner's attitude is the result of many factors, the most important being that they have never settled down for a single quiet and normal week from the outbreak of World War I till the present day.

—GEORGE MIKES, *Über Alles*

EVERYMAN AS PHILOSOPHER

The man who is his own lawyer or physician, will be poorly served; but everyone can and must be his own philosopher. He must be, because philosophy deals with ends, not means. It includes the questions, What is good? What is right? What is valid? Since finally the responsibility for his own life must rest squarely upon the shoulders of each, no one can delegate the business of answering such questions to another. [But] concerning the *means* whereby the valid ends of life may be attained, we seek expert advice.

—CLARENCE I. LEWIS, *Mind and the World-Order*

EVOLUTION

Man and all other vertebrate animals have been constructed on the same general model . . . pass through the same early stages of development, and . . . retain certain rudiments in common. Consequently we ought frankly to admit their community of descent; to take any other view, is to admit that our own structure, and that of all the animals around us, is a mere snare laid to entrap our judgment. . . . It is only our natural prejudice, and that arrogance which made our forefathers declare that they were descended from demi-gods, which leads us to demur to this conclusion. But the time will before long come, when it will be thought wonderful, that naturalists, who were well acquainted with the comparative structure and development of man, and other mammals, should have believed that each was the work of a separate act of creation.

☐

For my part I would as soon be descended from a baboon . . . as from a savage who delights to torture his enemies . . . treats his wives like slaves . . . and is haunted by the grossest superstitions.

☐

We must not fall into the error of supposing that the early progenitor of the whole Simian stock, including man, was identical with, or even closely resembled, any existing ape or monkey.

—CHARLES DARWIN, *Descent of Man*

Some folks seem to have descended from the chimpanzee later than others.

—FRANK McKINNEY ("KIN") HUBBARD

It is interesting to contemplate a tangled bank, clothed with many plants of many kinds, with birds singing on the bushes, with various insects flitting about, and with worms crawling through the damp earth, and to reflect that these elaborately constructed forms, so different from each other, and dependent upon each other in so complex a manner, have all been produced by laws acting around us.

□

From the war of nature, from famine and death, the most exalted object which we are capable of conceiving, namely the production of the higher animals, directly follows. There is grandeur in this view of life, with its several powers, having been originally breathed by the Creator into a few forms or into one; and that, whilst this planet has gone cycling on according to the fixed law of gravity, from so simple a beginning endless forms most beautiful and most wonderful have been, and are being evolved.

—CHARLES DARWIN, *Origin of Species*

If a single cell, under appropriate conditions, becomes a man in the space of a few years, there can surely be no difficulty in understanding how, under appropriate conditions, a cell may, in the course of untold millions of years, give origin to the human race.

—HERBERT SPENCER, *Principles of Biology*

The evolutionists seem to know everything about the missing link except the fact that it is missing.

—G. K. CHESTERTON

Our Heavenly Father invented man because he was disappointed in the monkey.

—MARK TWAIN

For 140 million years, during that period known as the Mesozoic, [the reptiles] were the undisputed masters of this planet. In enormous numbers they ... swam and they flew and they walked. Brainless or not, they survived a period of time far more extended than the life of man, far more extended than the whole Age of Mammals.

Now what is not very generally understood by the lay public is the fact that throughout the greater portion of this 140 million years the mammalian world was in existence. It was in existence, but it was highly inconspicuous. It was small; it hid under bushes; it concealed itself in trees. It had no giant representatives such as it developed later on after the disappearance of the reptiles.... It was marginal. To have grown larger would have been to invite the attention of the most formidable carnivores the world has ever seen—perfected killing machines with teeth like bear traps.

For a hundred million years those little mammals waited. No one would have dreamed that . . . the gray and infinitely complex convolutions of the human brain were locked away in the fore-brain of an insectivorous creature no larger than a rat. An observer waiting for some sign of creative emergence among those little animals in the underbrush would have grown weary as years by the million flowed away. He would have sworn that every variation in the game of life had been exploited and played out —that the reptiles were the master form—that the mammals were effective only upon an infinitely small size level.

Yet in the end . . . the armored giants vanished. They vanished from the seas and the fern forests; their great gliding wings disappeared from the coastal air. Nothing living, so far as we can determine today, threatened them. The mammals were insignificant, envious eyes in the reeds—that was all. . . .

The mammals did not destroy the great reptiles; they simply occupied, long after, an empty throne. It was only then that the suppression of creative energy burst forth in a second marvelous efflorescence, the radiation that created the mammalian world. The story, however, has a moral that is little read: Man has . . . destroyed the great mammals and left only the little eyes under the rosebush in the garden. He is now safe to write books about his unique qualities—and he is unique, as unique as the dinosaurs. He will not be menaced from the field's edge, but the eyes are still waiting. Once they waited a hundred million years. They can do so again.

—LOREN C. EISELEY, "The Fire Apes," in
Harper's, September 1949

EXECUTIONS

When the criminals were great lords [in the Middle Ages] . . . the magistrate took care that nothing should be wanting to the effect of the spectacle. . . . Jean de Montaigu, *grand maître d'hôtel* to the king . . . is placed high on a cart, preceded by two trumpeters. He wears his robe of state, hood, cloak . . . and his gold spurs, which are left on the feet of the beheaded and suspended corpse.

—J. HUIZINGA,
The Waning of the Middle Ages

EXECUTIVES

An executive has practically nothing to do except to decide what is to be done; to tell somebody to do it; to listen to reasons why it should not be done, why it should be done by someone else, or why it should be done in a different way; to follow up to see if the thing has been done; to discover that it has not; to enquire why; to listen to excuses from the person who should have done it; to follow up again to see if the thing has been done, only to discover that it has been done incorrectly; to point out how it should have been done; to conclude that as long as it has been done, it may as well be left where it is; to wonder if it is not time to get rid of a person who cannot do a thing right; to reflect that he probably has a wife and a large family, and that certainly any successor would be just as bad, and maybe worse; to consider how much simpler and better the thing would have been done if one had done it oneself in the first place; to reflect sadly that one could have done it right in twenty minutes, and, as things turned out, one has had to spend two days to find out why it has taken three weeks for somebody else to do it wrong.

—JOHN RICHARD LOWRIE,
The Function of an Executive

The ability to deal with people is as purchasable a commodity as sugar or coffee. And I pay more for that ability than for any other under the sun.

—JOHN D. ROCKEFELLER

EXPERIENCE

Our experience in the past can be a proof of nothing for the future but upon a supposition that there is a resemblance betwixt them. This, therefore, is a point which can admit of no proof at all, and which we take for granted without any proof. . . .

All the philosophy in the world, and all the religion . . . will never be able to carry us beyond the usual cause of experience or give us measures of conduct and behavior different from those which are furnished by reflections on common life. No new fact can ever be inferred from the religious hypothesis, no event foreseen or foretold, no reward or punishment expected or dreaded, beyond what is already known by practice and observation.

—DAVID HUME,
An Enquiry Concerning Human Understanding

Experience itself, as such, is defective, and hence default is inevitable and irremediable. The only universality and certainty is in a region above experience, that of the rational and conceptual.

—JOHN DEWEY, *Reconstruction in Philosophy*

The word experience is like a shrapnel shell, and bursts into a thousand meanings.

—GEORGE SANTAYANA,
Character and Opinion in the United States

Experience increases our wisdom but doesn't reduce our follies.

—JOSH BILLINGS

EXPERIMENT

I shall begin by making some experiments before I proceed any further; for it is my intention first to consult experience and then show by reasoning why that experience was bound to turn out as it did. This, in fact, is the true rule by which the student of natural effects must proceed....

Experience never errs; what alone may err is our judgment, which predicts effects that cannot be produced in our experiments. Given a cause, what follows will of necessity be its true effect, unless some external obstacle intervenes. When that happens, the effect that would have resulted from the cause will reflect the nature of the obstacle, in the same proportion as the obstacle is more or less powerful than the cause.

—LEONARDO DA VINCI, *Notebooks* (c. 1500)

It often happens that an unsuccessful experiment may produce an excellent observation. There are, therefore, no unsuccessful experiments.

—CLAUDE BERNARD,
*An Introduction to the Study of
Experimental Medicine*

I never try to dissuade a man from trying an experiment; if he does not find out what he is looking for he may find something else.

—James Clerk Maxwell

EXPERTS

Even when the experts all agree, they may well be mistaken.

—Bertrand Russell

"EXPLOITATION"

Most of the poorer countries are dominated by political regimes that are anti-liberal in their politics and anti-capitalist in their economics. These governments are ideologically committed to the redistribution of wealth and to the frustration of business enterprise which creates wealth. Since the wealth they wish to redistribute does not exist in their own countries, they have decided to redistribute the wealth of the United States and the nations of Western Europe. And their rationale for doing so is that this wealth, in the first instance, derives from an "exploitation" of their countries by the capitalist world.

The supposed exploitation derives from the fact that the poorer nations export raw commodities to the industrialized nations. Since they have nothing else to export, and since these exports are paid for, this is a perfectly natural and not at all unhealthy state of affairs. For the better part of the 19th century the United States was in exactly this condition; it was the income from the sale of cotton, wheat, and minerals which eventually formed the basis for our industrial development.

—Irving Kristol, *Wall Street Journal*, July 17, 1975

EXPLORATION: POLAR

Polar exploration is at once the cleanest and most isolated way of having a bad time which has been devised. . . .

The horror of the nineteen days it took us to travel from Cape Evans to Cape Crozier would have to be re-experienced to be appreciated; and anyone would be a fool who went again; . . . It was the darkness that did it. I don't believe minus seventy temperatures would be bad in daylight, when you could see where you were going, where you were stepping, where the sledge straps were, the cooker, the primus, the food.... [You] could read a compass without striking three or four boxes to find one dry match; could read your watch to see if the blissful moment of getting out of your bag was come without groping in the snow all about; when it would not take you five minutes to lash up the door of the tent and five hours to get started.

But in these days we were never less than four hours from the moment when Bill cried "Time to get up" to the time when we got into our harness. It took two men to get one man into his harness, and all they could do, for the canvas was frozen and our clothes were frozen until sometimes not even two men could bend them into the required shape.

—APSLEY CHERRY-GARRARD,
The Worst Journey in the World

EXPLORERS: SOUTH POLE

My dear Barrie:

...I am not at all afraid of the end, but sad to miss many a humble pleasure which I had planned for the future on our long marches. I may not have proved a great explorer, but we have done the greatest march ever made and come very near to great success. Good-bye, my dear friend,

Yours ever,
R. Scott

We are in a desperate state, feet frozen, &c. No fuel and a long way from food, but it would do your heart good to be in our tent, to hear our songs and the cheery conversation as to what we will do when we get to Hut Point.

Later.—We are very near the end, but have not and will not lose our good cheer. We have had four days of storm in our tent and nowhere's food or fuel. We did intend to finish ourselves when things proved like this, but we have decided to die naturally in the track.

As a dying man, my dear friend, be good to my wife and child. Give the boy a chance in life if the State won't do it. He ought to have good stuff in him. I never met a man in my life whom I admired and loved more than you, but I never could show you how much your friendship meant to me, for you had much to give and I nothing.

—Robert Scott, letter to James M. Barrie,
March 29, 1912

FACTS

Perfect as is the wing of a bird, it never could raise the bird up without resting on air. Facts are the air of a scientist. Without them you never can fly. Without them your "theories" are vain efforts.

—Ivan Parlov, lecture, April 17, 1935; in *Science*

Science has taught to me the opposite lesson. She warns me to be careful how I adopt a view which jumps with my preconceptions, and to require stronger evidence for such belief than for one to which I was previously hostile. My business is to teach my aspirations to conform themselves to fact, not to try and make facts harmonize with my aspirations. . . .

Sit down before fact as a little child, be prepared to give up every preconceived notion, follow humbly wherever and to whatever abysses Nature leads, or you shall learn nothing. I have only begun to learn content and peace of mind since I have resolved at all risks to do this.

—Thomas Huxley to Charles Kingsley

FAITH

There are no sects in geometry.

—Voltaire

Understanding is the reward of faith. Therefore, seek not to understand so that thou mayest believe, but believe so that thou mayest understand.

—St. Augustine

Man cannot live without a lasting trust in something indestructible within him, but both his trust and its indestructible object can remain forever concealed from him. One expression of this concealment is man's faith in a personal God.

—FRANZ KAFKA

No happiness is possible for one who walks in darkness. . . . We behold the sun through our faith. In Thy heavenly temple there is always daylight, since neither change, nor the shadow of necessitude, nor the cloud of ignorance or error can blot out the light. Nothing in the riches and glories of this world offers the happiness given those who walk in the light of faith.

—ERASMUS, *On Mending the Peace of the Church*

FAITH, LOGIC, EVIDENCE

Logic is like the sword—those who appeal to it shall perish by it. Faith is appealing to the living God, and one may perish by that too, but somehow one would rather perish that way than the other, and one has got to perish sooner or later.

—SAMUEL BUTLER, *Notebooks*, Vol. II

We may define "faith" as a firm belief in something for which there is no evidence. When there is evidence, no one speaks of "faith." We do not speak of a faith that two and two are four or that the earth is round. We only speak of faith when we wish to substitute emotion for evidence.

—BERTRAND RUSSELL,
Human Society in Ethics and Politics

FAME

But perhaps the desire of the thing called fame will torment thee. . . . See how soon everything is forgotten, and look at the chaos of infinite time on each side of the present, and the emptiness of applause, and the changeableness, the want of judgment, in those who pretend to give praise, and the narrowness of the space within which it is circumscribed—and be quiet at last. . . .

Soon, very soon, thou wilt be ashes or a skeleton, and either a name or not even a name; but name is sound and echo. And the

things which are much valued in life are empty and rotten and
trifling, like little dogs biting one another, and little children
quarreling, laughing, then weeping.

—MARCUS AURELIUS, *Meditations*

Fame is the perfume of heroic deeds.

—SOCRATES

I do not like the man who squanders life for fame.

—MARTIAL

Few are the princes whose lives merit a particular history. In
vain have most of them been the objects of slander, or of flattery.
Small is the number of those whose memory is preserved; and
that number would be still more inconsiderable, were none but
the good remembered. . . .

It is for a very different reason, that the memory of bad princes
is preserved; like fires, plagues, and inundations, they are remembered only for the mischief they have done . . . for such is the
weakness of mankind, that they admire those who have rendered
themselves remarkable for wickedness, and talk with greater
pleasure of the destroyer than of the founder of an empire. . . .

Such is the itch of writing, that no sooner is a prince dead,
than the world is filled with volumes under the title of memoirs
and histories of his life, and anecdotes of his courts.

—VOLTAIRE, *History of Charles XII*

FAMILIES

All societies that have offspring have the institution of the family.
Social regulation and the limitation of our biological propensity
to sexual intercourse and reproduction is a function of a family
everywhere. . . . The family seldom is restricted to its basic re-
productive function. . . . The usages within the family differ
enormously. . . . For Eskimos and some other groups it is a matter
of common courtesy to lend their wives to their guests (but they
will take great offense and kill each other for unauthorized wife-
borrowing). . . . There are some *groups* (the Shakers, monastic
orders) that renounce offspring; but there are no *societies* that
do. . . .

We do not know which combination [of economic circum-stances] produces which forms of family organization.... No single factor—such as variation and economic circumstances—accounts ... for the varieties of forms of family organization which any geographical or historical survey indicates.

—RALPH ROSS and ERNEST VAN DEN HAAG,
The Fabric of Society

Every known human society contains the family—and marriage —in one form or another. In the most diverse sample ever studied, by anthropologists under Murdock, of over 250 societies, there is not a single exception to this rule. "Whatever larger familial forms may exist ... the nuclear family is always recognizable.... Everywhere the husband, wife, and immature children constitute a unit apart from the remainder of the community."

□

The family performs crucial social functions without which no society can be maintained: economic support, the channeling of sexual behavior, reproduction, child rearing, emotional support, etc. etc. And in all societies, marriage is the *preferred arrangement* for having children. Even where illegitimacy occurs frequently, it is disapproved—in all societies.

Marriage and the family, or something like them, also exist in animal species below man. In general, the more stable family units are found among the larger, the more intelligent, the slower matur-ing, the longer-lived animals....

—BERNARD BERELSON and GARY A. STEINER,
Human Behavior: An Inventory

FAMINE

Famine is the worst of all misfortunes. Nothing is so destructive of fair play, for during a famine men despise what they hold to be honorable at other times. Wives snatched food from their hus-bands' mouths, children from their fathers, and, most lamentable of all, mothers from their infants. And while those loved most grew weaker before their eyes, they were not ashamed to take away the few morsels keeping them alive.

□

Countless multitudes perished of famine throughout the city. Their sufferings were indescribable. Fighting broke out if even the shadow of food appeared. Men joined by the closest ties came to blows and tore the meager sustenance of life from one another. Even the dying were not trusted, and robbers searched those who were still breathing lest any feigning death, should still have food concealed. Some men, gasping with hunger staggered along like mad dogs, and like drunkards they beat on the doors of houses and, completely demented, burst into the same houses two or three times within an hour.

Necessity drove men to eat anything. They devoured scraps unfit for the filthiest animals. And at the end they did not spare even their belts and shoes, tearing the leather from their shields, and gnawed this, too.

—JOSEPHUS, *Antiquities*, Book V

FANATICS

Fanatics are picturesque; and mankind prefers observing poses to listening to reasons.

—FRIEDRICH NIETZSCHE

MICHAEL FARADAY (1791–1867)

Do not suppose that I was a very deep thinker, or was marked as a precocious person. I was a very live imaginative person, and could believe in the *Arabian Nights* as easily as in the *Encyclopedia*. But facts were important to me, and saved me.

☐

I have always loved science more than money, and because my occupation is almost entirely personal, I cannot afford to get rich.

☐

Let the imagination go, guiding it by judgment and principle, but holding it in and directing it by *experiment*.

☐

Without experiment I am nothing. I was never able to make a fact my own without seeing it; I could trust a fact, and always cross-examined an assertion.

—from his writings and letters

ABOUT HIM

The history of physical science contains two couples of equal magnitude: Galileo and Newton, and Faraday and Clerk Maxwell.

—ALBERT EINSTEIN, in J. G. Crowther,
British Scientists of the Nineteenth Century

With a quite wonderful sagacity and intellectual precision, Faraday performed in his brain the work of a great mathematician without using a single mathematical formula.... This was really an advance in general scientific method, destined to purify science from the last remnants of metaphysics.... Nobody else at his time did it so radically.

—HERMANN HELMHOLTZ,
in the Faraday Lecture, 1881

I do not think that Faraday has once been caught in a mistake, so precise and conscientious was his mode of experimenting and observing.

—A. DE LA RIVE

The intentness of his vision in any direction did not diminish his power of perception in other directions; and when he attacked a subject, expecting results, he had the faculty of keeping his mind alert, so that results different from those which he expected should not escape him through preoccupation.

—JOHN TYNDALL, *Faraday as a Discoverer*

FASCIST CULTURE

The Nazis were very culture-conscious—as culture-conscious as Matthew Arnold and all our Victorian forefathers. But the more conscious they became of culture, the less capable they were of producing it. Nazi Germany, in the ten years of its supremacy and intensive cultivation of the arts, was not able to produce for the admiration of a world a single artist of any kind.... For this general impotence the Nazi leaders may have offered the excuse of war and revolution, but other wars and revolutions have been an immediate inspiration to poets and painters. The great Romantic Movement in literature, for example, was directly inspired

by the French Revolution, and all the storm and stress of the wars
that followed could not diminish its force.

The position in Italy was exactly the same, and showed in
addition that the time factor makes no difference. The Fascists
were in power for twenty years, but in all that time not a single
work of art of universal significance came from their country—
nothing but bombast and vulgarity.

—HERMAN READ, *To Hell with Culture*

FEAR

In the extremity of fear, we turn a deaf ear to every feeling of
pity.

—JULIUS CAESAR

Men are more ready to offend the man who wants to be loved
than the man who wants to be feared.

—MACHIAVELLI, *The Prince*

Love casts out fear; but conversely fear casts out love. And not
only love. Fear also casts out intelligence, casts out goodness, casts
out all thought of beauty and truth. . . . In the end fear casts out
even a man's humanity. And fear, my good friends, fear is the
very basis and foundation of modern life. . . . Fear of the science
which takes away with one hand even more than what it so
profusely gives with the other. Fear of the demonstrably fatal
institutions for which, in our suicidal loyalty, we are ready to kill
and die. Fear of the Great Men whom we have raised by popular
acclaim to a power which they use, inevitably, to murder and
enslave us.

—ALDOUS HUXLEY, *Ape and Essence*

. . . Fear plays a much smaller part than we should think it must
in the life of an animal who lives dangerously. Terror he can
know, and perhaps he knows it frequently. But it seems to last
only a little longer than the immediate danger it helps him to
avoid, instead of lingering, as in the human being it does, until
it becomes a burden and a threat. The frightened bird resumes

his song as soon as danger has passed, and so does the frightened rabbit his games.

—JOSEPH WOOD KRUTCH, The Twelve Seasons

FEMININE WILES

... all women of whatever age, rank, profession or degree, whether virgin maid or widow, that shall from and after such Act impose upon, seduce and betray into matrimony any of His Majesty's subjects by means of scent, paints, cosmetics, washes, artificial teeth, false hair, Spanish wool, iron stays, hoops, high-heeled shoes or bolstered hips, shall incur the penalty of the law now in force against witchcraft and the like misdemeanors....

—from an Act of the British Parliament, 1770

FICTION

[The greatest deterrent to education is] the inordinate passion prevalent for novels.... When this poison infects the mind it destroys its tone and revolts it against wholesome reading. Reason and fact, plain and unadorned, are rejected.... The result is a bloated imagination, sickly judgment, and disgust towards all the real business of life.

—THOMAS JEFFERSON,
letter to Nathaniel Burwell, March 14, 1818

FICTION AND TRUTH

I will not say that this story is true; because, as you will soon see, it is all truth and no story. It has no explanation and no conclusion; it is, like most of the other things we encounter in life, a fragment of something else which would be intensely exciting if it were not too large to be seen. For the perplexity of life arises from there being too many interesting things in it for us to be interested properly in any of them.

□

Truth, of course, must of necessity be stranger than fiction, for we have made fiction to suit ourselves.

—G. K. CHESTERTON, Selected Essays

FINESSE IN MURDER

Maillard set up at the Abbaye a People's Court or Tribunal of twelve.... The Commissioners ... heard their cases, which rarely lasted a minute, standing, drunk, or asleep....

In order to prevent prisoners from offering resistance and wasting the [People's] Court's time, those that were to be executed were told that they were being transferred to another prison. It helped them to die with tranquillity. About twenty executioners took part in the Massacre.... The prisoners were hacked down as they stepped into the prison courtyard. Those who walked in with their hands behind their backs suffered least. There the killing went on all night by the light of bonfires and into the dawn.

—JOHN FISHER, *Six Summers in Paris*

FIREARMS

Never handle firearms carelessly. The sorrow and suffering that have been caused through the innocent but heedless handling of firearms by the young! Only four days ago, right in the next farmhouse to the one where I am spending the summer, a grandmother, old and gray and sweet, one of the loveliest spirits in the land, was sitting at her work, when her young grandson crept in and got down an old, battered, rusty gun which had not been touched for many years and was supposed not to be loaded, and pointed it at her, laughing and threatening to shoot. In her fright she ran screaming and pleading toward the door on the other side of the room; but as she passed him he placed the gun almost against her very breast and pulled the trigger! He had supposed it was not loaded. And he was right—it wasn't. So there wasn't any harm done. It is the only case of the kind I ever heard of....

—MARK TWAIN

Don't meddle with old unloaded firearms, they are the most deadly and unerring things that have ever been created by man. You don't have to take any pains at all with them; you don't have to have a rest, you don't have to have any sights on the gun, you don't have to take aim, even. No, you just pick out a relative and bang away, and you are sure to get him. A youth who can't hit a cathedral at thirty yards with a Gatling gun in three-quarters of an hour, can take up an old empty musket and bag his grandmother every time at a hundred.

—MARK TWAIN, "Advice to Youth," a commencement address

FIRE-HOSES

Fire Chief John T. O'Hagan also compliments Rand [think-tank], though there was some huffiness at first.... Rand ... introduced the department to "slippery water," which is ordinary hydrant water spiked with polymers that markedly reduce friction when the water passes through a hose. This almost doubles the amount that can be put on a fire in a given time.

—*Wall Street Journal*, January 30, 1975

FLOATING LANTERNS

There is an enchanting Japanese festival celebrated at night in mid-summer.... Hundreds of paper lanterns, brightly lit with candles, are set afloat on a river in order to console the spirits of departed family members.... It is beautiful to behold hundreds of paper lanterns slowly floating down the river at night.

—ICHIRO KAWASAKI, *Japan Unmasked*

FLOGGING: AFRICA

Joseph Thomson, in a burst of youthful idealism, resolved to establish an almost egalitarian relationship with his men [in Africa], to take the porters into his confidence, and to replace flogging with fines levied on the disobedient. He was met with a strike and a demand for the restoration of the whip, as his men preferred the ephemeral pain of flogging to ... fines which could result in a penniless return to Zanzibar. Thomson thenceforth flogged with vigor.

—H. A. C. CAIRNS, *Prelude to Imperialism*

FLYING

He was free, infinitely free, so free that he was no longer conscious of pressing on the ground. He was free of that weight of human relationships which impedes movement, those tears, those farewells, those reproaches, those joys, all that a man caresses or tears every time he sketches out a gesture, those countless bonds which tie him to others and make him heavy.

—ANTOINE DE SAINT-EXUPÉRY, *Wind, Sand and Stars*

"If men were all virtuous," returned the artist, "I should with great alacrity teach them all to fly. But what would be the security of the good, if the bad could at pleasure invade them from the sky? Against an army sailing through the clouds, neither wall nor mountains, nor seas, could afford any security. A flight of northern savages might hover in the wind, and light at once with irresistible violence upon the capital of a fruitful region that was rolling under them. Even this valley, the retreat of princes, the abode of happiness, might be violated by the sudden descent of some of the naked nations that swarm on the coast of the southern sea."

—SAMUEL JOHNSON, *Rasselas*

FOLLY AND LOVE

What divorces or even worse would come about if the domestic life of man and wife were not . . . nourished by flattery, joking, compromise, ignorance, and duplicity—all satellites of mime? How few marriages would be contracted if the husband inquired about the tricks his seemingly delicate, innocent little darling had played before the wedding? And once entered on, fewer marriages still would last if the many tricks of the wife were not kept unknown through the negligence or stupidity of the husband. All this is a tribute to the worthiness of Folly.

—ERASMUS, *Praise of Folly*

FOLLY AND MADNESS

Folly consists in the drawing of false conclusions from just principles, by which it is distinguished from madness, which draws just conclusions from false principle.

—JOHN LOCKE, *A Treatise on Human Understanding*

FOOLS

Neither man nor woman . . . can be worth anything until they have discovered that they are fools. This is the first step towards becoming either estimable or agreeable; and until it be taken there is no hope. The sooner the discovery is made the better, as there is more time and power for taking advantage of it. Sometimes the great truth is found out too late to apply to it any effectual remedy. Sometimes it is never found at all; and these form the desperate and inveterate causes of folly, self-conceit and impertinence.

—LORD MELBOURNE, in DAVID CECIL, *Melbourne*

He's a fool that makes his doctor his heir.

—BENJAMIN FRANKLIN

FOOLS IN POWER: CHAMBERLAIN AND HALIFAX

It can fairly be said of [Prime Minister] Neville Chamberlain that he was not well versed in foreign affairs, that he had no touch for a diplomatic situation, that he did not fully realize what it was he was doing, and that his naive confidence in his own judgment and powers of persuasion and achievement was misplaced.

—WILLIAM (LORD) STRANG,
veteran of the Foreign Office,
Britain in World Affairs

Anthony Eden was replaced by Edward, Lord Halifax, former Viceroy of India, tall, amiable, honest, willing, and whose main qualification for the job was exactly what Prime Minister Chamberlain and Sir Horace Wilson were looking for: He had an infinite capacity for being trodden on without complaint. William Strang, who worked under him at this period, later lumped him with certain other British statesmen as "all English country gentlemen, all good public-school men, all good churchmen. They seldom visited Europe, or knew what Europeans were like. None of them could have the slightest conception of the enormity of Hitler. Their whole upbringing conspired against understanding that such people could exist, and that the Nazi state was a lunatic state.... Although Edward was very clever, the world was an innocent world to him. To live in it in Hitler's epoch with the ideas his father had planted in him was extremely difficult. He was so bound by tradition that he never wavered in the principles he was taught when he was young. No new view of the world or violent changes dinted his orthodoxy."

—LEONARD MOSLEY,
On Borrowed Time: How World War II Began

FORCE

They asked for my advice. I...asked for guns. [It] terrified them. The whole night was spent in indecision.... They began debating whether ... to meet force with force. I asked them, "Are you waiting for the people to give you permission to fire on them?"

—NAPOLEON, to the Directory, 1795

There are only two powers in the world—the sword and the spirit.... In the long run, the sword is always beaten by the spirit....
    Force is the law of animals; men are ruled by conviction.

—NAPOLEON

THE FORTY-SEVEN RONINS

One of Japan's great literary works is *The Forty-Seven Ronins,* a tenth-century novel of romantic love and adventure.... A retainer at the Imperial Court, anxious to humiliate a rival, advises the latter to wear the wrong pair of trousers for a ceremonial occasion. The warrior's humiliation is unutterable: And it demands a terrible vengeance. The story itself is really the history of this vengeance—the story of forty-seven brave avenging *samurai.* All forty-seven are killed before this terrible tale is concluded; villages are burnt and pillaged; countless people ambushed, tortured, massacred; wives sell themselves to brothels to enable their husbands to carry on the fight, etc., etc. It is all very admirable and heroic. And it is all because of the wrong pair of trousers. On a similar occasion in tenth-century Britain, which Sir Adalbert was similarly maliciously advised in the matter of trousers and deeply

humiliated when he appeared unfittingly attired at King Eldred's Court, he simply went home and changed his trousers. And thus we were deprived of an early masterpiece of English literature.
—GEORGE MIKES, *The Land of the Rising Yen*

FOURTH OF JULY

What, to the American slave, is your Fourth of July? I answer: a day that reveals to him, more than all other days in the year, the gross injustice and cruelty to which he is the constant victim. To him, your celebration is a sham; your boasted liberty, an unholy license; your national greatness, swelling vanity; your sounds of rejoicing are empty and heartless; your denunciation of tyrants, brass-fronted impudence; your shouts of liberty and equality, hollow mockery; your prayers and hymns, your sermons and thanksgivings, with all your religious parade and solemnity, are, to him, mere bombast, fraud, deception, impiety, and hypocrisy—a thin veil to cover up crimes which would disgrace a nation of savages. There is not a nation of savages, there is not a nation on the earth guilty of practices more shocking and bloody than are the people of the United States at this very hour.

Go where you may, search where you will, roam through all the monarchies and despotisms of the Old World, travel through South America, search out every abuse, and when you have found the last, lay your facts by the side of the everyday practices of this nation, and you will say with me that, for revolting barbarity and shameless hypocrisy, America reigns without a rival.
—FREDRICK DOUGLASS, speech, July 4, 1852

BENJAMIN FRANKLIN (1706–1790)

While I was intent on improving my language, I met with an English grammar (I think it was Greenwood's) having at the end of it two little sketches on the arts of rhetoric and logic, the latter finishing with a dispute in the Socratic method; and soon after I procured Xenophon's *Memorable Things of Socrates*, wherein there are many examples of the same method. I was charmed with it, adopted it, dropped my abrupt contradiction and positive argumentation, and put on the humble inquirer; and being then, from reading Shaftesbury and Collins, made a doubter, as I already was in many points of our religious doctrines, I found this method the safest for myself and very embarrassing to those against whom I used it; therefore I took delight in it ... and grew very artful and expert in drawing people, even of superior knowledge, into concessions, the consequences of which they did not foresee, entangling them in difficulties out of which they did not foresee [and] out of which they could not extricate themselves, and so obtaining victories that neither myself nor my cause always deserved.

I continued this method some few years, but gradually left it, retaining only the habit of expressing myself in terms of modest diffidence; never using, when I advanced any thing that might possibly be disputed, the words *certainty, undoubtedly*, or any others that gave the air of positiveness to an option; but rather said, *I conceive* or *apprehend* a thing to be so and so; it *appears to me*, or *I should not think it so or so*; or *it is so, if I am not mistaken*. This habit, I believe, has been of great advantage to me when I have had occasion to inculcate my opinions, and persuade men into measures that I have been from time to time engaged in promoting; and, as the chief ends of conversation are to *inform* or to be *informed*, to *please* or to *persuade*, I wish well-meaning and sensible men would not lessen their power of doing good by a positive, assuming manner, that seldom fails to disgust, tends to create opposition, and to defeat most of those purposes for which speech was given to us.

—Autobiography

... the hard-to-be-governed Passion of Youth hurried me frequently into Intrigues with low Women that fell in my Way, which were attended with some Expence and great Inconveniences, besides a continual Risque to my Health by a Distemper which of all Things I dreaded, tho' by very good luck I escaped it.

They who give up essential liberty to obtain a little temporary safety deserve neither liberty nor safety.

☐

It has always been my maxim to live on as if I was to live always.

☐

Masculine and feminine things (apart from moods and tenses) have been giving me trouble for 60 years. I once hoped that at

80, I could be delivered, but here I am at 4 times 19, which is very close; nevertheless these French "feminines" still disturb me. This should make me happy to go to paradise, where they say these distinctions are abolished.

□

I shall never *ask*, never *refuse*, nor ever *resign* an office.

□

Work as if you were to live 100 years. Pray as if you were to die tomorrow.

—compiled from various letters and biographies

ABOUT HIM

When he appeared in public he was dressed in good broadcloth of a sober tint; conspicuous with his long straight hair, whitened by age, and not by art; and wearing a pair of spectacles, to remedy an old man's dimness of vision, and a cap of fine marten's fur, because he had an old man's susceptibility to cold.

Franklin's costume had not been designed with any idea of pleasing the Parisians; but it obtained an extraordinary success, and has left a mark on history. Fine gentlemen, with their heads full of new philosophy, regarded his unembroidered coat and unpowdered locks, as a tacit, but visible, protest against those luxuries and artificialities which they all condemned, but had not the smallest intention of themselves renouncing. . . .

Europe had welcomed and accepted him, not as a mere spokesman and agent of the government at Philadelphia, but as the living and breathing embodiment of the American Republic. No statesman would do business with anybody but Franklin. No financier would negotiate a loan except with him, pay over money into other hands than his. . . . Nine-tenths of the public letters addressed to the American Commissioners were brought to his house; "and," (so his colleagues admitted,) "they would ever be carried wherever Dr. Franklin is." He transacted his affairs with Louis the Sixteenth's ministers on a footing of equality, and, (as time went on,) of unostentatious but unquestionable superiority. . . .

He professed no religious creed except tolerance, and kindliness of heart. France, moved by a thousand passions and a thousand caprices, prostrated herself at the feet of a man who had no caprices and no passions. She made him the symbol and object of her adoration; and Franklin took rank above Voltaire and Rousseau, by the side of Socrates.

—GEORGE OTTO TREVELYAN, *The American Revolution*

Historians of science bracket Franklin with Newton as the first two important scientific figures of the modern age. Everyone has heard how Franklin drew electricity from a cloud on a kite string, but few are aware that he was the first to identify positive and negative electricity; we owe to him the words and concepts for battery, electric charge, condenser, conductor.

☐

His inventiveness was displayed in more practical ways as well. Franklin's mechanical hand for lifting objects from a high shelf and his kitchen stool that unfolds into a stepladder are still in use to this day. At seventy-eight he invented that blessing of the elderly: bifocal spectacles. Mozart and Beethoven composed music for his "glass harmonica"—a series of glass hemispheres mounted on a rod and touched by the finger while revolving, to make music. He was a skilled performer on the harp, guitar and violin. Franklin also charted the Gulf Stream, and discovered that storms rotate while traveling forward. His influence in scientific matters was so strong that thirty years after his death the Franklin Institute was created in Philadelphia to interpret science and technology to the layman.

—BRUCE BLIVEN, Introduction to
The Autobiography of Benjamin Franklin, in
Reader's Digest Great Biographies

He was himself a living proof of the Enlightenment, an illustration of what might be accomplished by reason, measure and clarity.

—RICHARD HOFSTADTER, *The American Republic*

In society he was shrewd, sophisticated and worldly, with little of the primitivism attributed to him in legend. As a man of letters, consistently displaying clarity and good sense, he virtually established an American style and an American literature.

—ALFRED OWEN ALDRIDGE,
Benjamin Franklin: Philosopher and Man

His mind was ever young, his temper ever serene; science, that never goes gray, was always his mistress.

—THOMAS PAINE

[On Franklin's discovery of the identity of electricity and lightning]: the greatest, perhaps, that has been made in the whole compass of philosophy, since the time of Sir Isaac Newton.

—JOSEPH PRIESTLEY

A singular felicity of induction guided all Franklin's researches. ... The style and manner of his publications on electricity are almost as worthy of admiration as the doctrine it contains.

—HUMPHRY DAVEY

FRAUD AND GULLIBILITY

It appears to be generally true that hard-headed business men are among the easiest people to defraud. They are usually confident of their own ability to spot any attempt to deceive them, [and] the greater part of their working life is spent in looking for or creating opportunities for trade. Their confidence tends to make them less suspicious than the traditional victim of frauds—the widow with her savings—and their search for trade makes them a natural target for the confidence trickster.

—ANTHONY MARTIENSSEN, *Crime and the Police*

FREE SPEECH

... all life is an experiment. Every year if not every day we have to wager our salvation upon some prophecy based upon imperfect knowledge. While that experiment is part of our system, I think that we should be externally vigilant against attempts to check the expression of opinions that we loathe and believe to be fraught with death, unless they so imminently threaten immediate interference with the lawful and pressing purposes of the law that an immediate check is required to save the country. . . .

—OLIVER WENDELL HOLMES, *Abrams vs. U.S.*

FREE SPEECH AND PROPERTY

For most men, to be deprived of the right of voluntary association or of private property would be a far greater and more deeply felt loss of liberty than to be deprived of the right to speak freely. And it is important that this should be said just now in England because, under the influence of migsuided journalists and cunning tyrants, we are too ready to believe that so long as our freedom to speak is not impaired we have lost nothing of importance—which is not so. However secure may be a man's right to speak his thoughts, he may find what is to him a much more important freedom curtailed when his house his sold over his head by a public authority, or when he is deprived of the enjoyment of his lease-hold because his landlord has sold out to a development company, or when his membership of a trade union is compulsory and debars him from an employment he would otherwise take.

—MICHAEL OAKESHOTT, *Rationalism in Politics*

FREEDOM

It is dangerous to free people who prefer to be slaves.

—MACHIAVELLI, *The Prince*

Our country was built on unpopular ideas, on unorthodox opinions. My definition of a free society is a society where it is safe to be unpopular. . . .

—ADLAI STEVENSON, speech, Detroit, October 7, 1952

I have come to realize that men are not born to be free.

—NAPOLEON, conversation, 1803

God grant that not only the love of liberty, but a thorough knowledge of the rights of man, may pervade all the nations of the earth, so that a philosopher may set his foot anywhere on its surface, and say, "This is my country."

—BENJAMIN FRANKLIN, in Verner Crane,
Benjamin Franklin and a Rising People

. . . the rule of law is the greatest single condition of our freedom, removing from us that great fear which has overshadowed so many communities, the fear of the power of our own government.

—MICHAEL OAKESHOTT, *op. cit.*

FREEDOM AND HISTORY

Because we live in a largely free society, we tend to forget how limited is the span of time and the part of the globe for which there has ever been anything like political freedom: The typical state of mankind is tyranny, servitude, and misery. The nineteenth and early twentieth centuries in the Western world stand out as striking exceptions to the general trend of historical development. Political freedom in this instance clearly came along with the free market and the development of capitalist institutions. So also did political freedom in the golden age of Greece and in the early days of the Roman era....

I know of no example in time or place of a society that has been marked by a large measure of political freedom, and that has not also used something comparable to a free market....

—MILTON FRIEDMAN, *Capitalism and Freedom*

FREEDOM AND LAW

The end of law is not to abolish or restrain but to preserve and enlarge freedom; for ... where there is no law, there is no freedom. Liberty [means] to be free from restraint and violence from others, which cannot be where there is not law. Freedom is not, as we are told: a liberty for every man to do what he lists. For who could be free, when every other man's humor might domineer over him?

—JOHN LOCKE, *Second Treatise*

FREEDOM AND RESTRAINT

I often wonder whether we do not rest our hopes too much upon constitutions, upon laws and upon courts. These are false hopes; believe me, these are false hopes. Liberty lies in the hearts of men and women. When it dies there, no constitution, no law, no court can save it. No constitution, no law, no court can even do much to help it. While it lies there, it needs no constitution, no law, no court to save it.

And what is this liberty which must lie in the hearts of men and women? It is not the ruthless, the unbridled will. It is not freedom to do as one likes. That is the denial of liberty, and leads straight to its overthrow. A society in which men recognize no check upon their freedom, soon becomes a society where freedom is the possession of only a savage few; as we have learned to our sorrow.

What then is the spirit of liberty? I cannot define it; I can only tell you my own faith. The spirit of liberty is the spirit which is not too sure that it is right. The spirit of liberty is the spirit which seeks to understand the minds of other men and women. The spirit of liberty is the spirit which weighs their interests alongside its own without bias. The spirit of liberty remembers that not even a sparrow falls to the earth unheeded. The spirit of liberty is the spirit of Him who, near a thousand years ago, taught mankind that lesson it has never learned, but has never quite forgotten; that there may be a kingdom where the least shall be heard and considered side by side with the greatest.

—LEARNED HAND, "I Am an American Day" address,
New York, May 1944

FREEDOM OF THOUGHT

Any government which attempts to control minds is accounted tyrannical, and it is considered an abuse of sovereignty and a usurpation of the rights of subjects to seek to prescribe what shall be accepted as true, or rejected as false.... All these questions fall within a man's natural right, which he cannot abdicate even with his own consent.

☐

If men's minds were as easily controlled as their tongues, every king would sit safely on his throne.

☐

However unlimited ... the power of a sovereign may be, however implicitly it is trusted as the exponent of law and religion, it can never prevent men from forming judgments according to their intellect, or being influenced by any given emotion.

—BARUCH SPINOZA,
Tractatus Theologico-Politicus

THE FRENCH

The French spend, or try to spend, their lives in saving small fortunes. A Frenchman looks forward to retirement as the final aim of his working life. He works in order to be able to stop working. He looks forward to feeble old age with gusto. To eat without teeth is one of the ultimate delights of living. And—as even a Frenchman is not completely lacking in small personal vanities—he dreams of a smart funeral. He works hard throughout a lifetime to be able to die above his station.

—GEORGE MIKES, *From Little Cabbages*

SIGMUND FREUD (1856–1939)

I have never really been a doctor in the proper sense. I became a doctor through being compelled to deviate from my original purpose; and the triumph of my life lies in my having, after a long and roundabout journey, found my way back to my earliest path.

—*Collected Papers*, Vol. V

I have an anxious temperament rather than a bold one, and I willingly sacrifice a great deal to having the feeling of being on firm ground.

□

I have very restricted capacities or talents—none at all for the natural sciences; nothing for mathematics; nothing for anything quantitative. But what I have, of a restricted nature, was probably very intensive.

□

Geniuses are unbearable people. You have only to ask my family to learn how easy I am to live with, so I certainly cannot be a genius.

—*Op. cit.*, Vol. II

My parents were Jews, and I have remained a Jew myself.

□

In Europe I felt as though I were despised; but over there [America] I found myself received by the foremost men as an equal. As I stepped onto the platform at Worcester ... it seemed like the realization of some incredible daydream: psychoanalysis was no longer a product of delusion, it had become a valuable part of reality.

—Autobiographical Study

My tyrant is psychology; it has always been my distant, beckoning goal. . . .

□

Being entirely honest with oneself is good exercise.

□

I have found love of the mother and jealousy of the father in my own case too, and I now believe it to be a general phenomenon of early childhood.

—Origins of Psychoanalysis

[Freud was especially attached to a line from Virgil, in *The Aeneid* (VII, 312), which he used on the title page of *The Interpretation of Dreams: Flecter si negueo superos Acheronta movebo:*] "If I cannot bend the Higher Powers, I will move the Infernal regions."

□

Looking back, then, over the patchwork of my life's labors, I can say that I have made many beginnings and thrown out many suggestions. Something will come of them in the future, though I cannot myself tell whether it will be much or little.

—Autobiographical Study

I could never grasp why I should be ashamed of my [Jewish] origin.

At an early date, I became aware of my destiny to belong to the critical minority ... [and developed] a certain independence of judgment. . . .

□

I have always been dissatisfied with my gifts.

□

I have never done anything mean or malicious and cannot trace any temptation to do so, so I am not in the least proud of it. . . . When I ask myself why I [behave] honorably ... I have no answer.... Why I—and incidentally my six children—have to be thoroughly decent human beings is quite incomprehensible to me.

□

I think ... most men are trash....

□

An intimate friend and a hated enemy have always been indispensable to my emotional life.

□

[When told he was a great man]: To discover great things is not to be great.

□

I am among those who disturb the sleep of mankind.

—collected from various sources

ABOUT HIM

... one of the features which must arouse our suspicion of the dogmas some of Freud's followers have built up on the initial brilliant works of Freud is the tendency toward a self-sealing system, a system, that is, which has a way of almost automatically discounting evidence which might bear adversely on the doctrine. The whole point of science is to do just the opposite: to invite the detection of error and to welcome it. Some of you may think that in another field a comparable system has been developed by the recent followers of Marx.

—J. ROBERT OPPENHEIMER, in *Great Essays in Science*, ed. MARTIN GARDNER

Freud's theories leave much still to be explained. Even when they provide an explanation, it is often ambiguous. And very seldom do we have more than hypotheses, so formulated that they will be hard to prove or disprove with the desirable degree of exactness. One difficulty—which I cannot more than mention—is that methods of observation often must include the scheme of interpretation which the observations should validate.... Admirable and immensely fruitful as is Freud's achievement, it is in this sense largely heuristic: It has not led us into the promised land though it might well have shown us the way. We will know about that only after having arrived.

—ERNEST VAN DEN HAAG,
"Genuine and Spurious Integration," in
Psychoanalysis and Social Science,
ed. H. M. RUITENBECK

Newton banished God from nature, Darwin banished him from life, and Freud drove him from the last fastness, the soul.

—GERALD HEARD, *The Third Morality*

[Freud was] ill-informed in the field of contemporary psychology and seems to have derived only from hearsay any knowledge he had of it.

—ERNEST JONES,
Life and Work of Sigmund Freud, Vol. I

Freud's book on dreams is one of the most unique autobiographies in history.

—HAROLD D. LASSWELL,
Psychopathology and Politics

Freud created the masterwork of the century, a psychology that counsels mothers and fathers, lovers and haters, sick and less sick, the arts and sciences, that unriddles—to use Emerson's prophetic catalogue of subjects considered inexplicable in his day—"language, sleep, madness, dreams, beasts, sex." Freud's doctrine, created piecemeal ... has changed the course of Western intellectual history. . . .

—PHILIP RIEFF, *Freud: The Mind of the Moralist*

The facts uncovered in my own field work and that of my collaborators have forced me to the conclusion that Freud ... depicted with astonishing correctness many central themes in motivational life which are universal.

—CLYDE KLUCKHOLN, in Ernest Jones,
op. cit., Vol. III

Here was a ... doctor laying bare the origins of Greek drama as no classical scholar had ever done, teaching the anthropologist what was really meant by his *totem* and *taboo*, probing the mysteries of sin, of sanctity, of sacrament—a man who, because he understood, purged the human spirit of fear.

—JANE ELLEN HARRISON,
Reminiscences of a Student's Life

Freud's contribution as a therapist is exemplified first of all by his interest in what was in his time, among physicians, the most despised of patient types, the neurotic. Freud was consistently attracted to the undervalued aspects of reality: sex, which society had tried to ignore; dreams, which science had tried to ignore; the patient, whom medicine had tried to ignore.

□

Concerning ... the powers of reasoning ... he has no theory at all.

□

Freud is the least confused of modern minds because he has no message; he accepts contradiction and builds his psychology on it.... It is exhilarating and yet terrifying to read Freud as a moralist, to see how compelling can be the judgment of a man who never preaches, leads us nowhere, assures us of nothing except perhaps that, having learned from him, the burden of misery we must find strength to carry will be somewhat lighter.

—KENNETH MINOGUE, *Encounter*, July 1974

KARL VON FRISCH (1886–   )

The name of Karl von Frisch did not become widely familiar until the award to him in 1973 of a share in the Nobel Prize for Physiology or Medicine. But among biologists his name has long been one to conjure with; and it would not be too much to say that he has been generally regarded by them as one of the most outstanding, if not the very greatest, of the recent experimental zoologists of Europe. This acknowledgment was achieved by his work on color vision in fish and in insects, on the senses of equilibrium and hearing in insects, on the perception of time in insects and, above all, by his outstanding work on the organization and communication systems of honeybees.

This work brings together all the rest in that not only are the senses of hearing, smell, taste, pattern perception and gravity involved—but also the question of time-sense and the extraordinary gesture language which enables workers to communicate the distance and direction of rich food sources by means of gravity-orientated and light-orientated dances on the vertical comb. It was this unique work which clinched the question of the Nobel Prize—and did more, in that it recognized, for the first time, as appropriate for the prize, a sphere of investigation which depended as much on the study of behavior as on the study of physiology and which has little obvious relation to human physiology or medicine.

—W. H. THORPE,
Times Literary Supplement, October 3, 1975

GALILEO GALILEI (1564–1692)

I never met a man so ignorant that I could not learn something from him.

□

As to rendering the Bible false, that is not and never will be the intention of Catholic astronomers, such as I am; instead, our opinion is that the Scriptures accord perfectly with demonstrated physical truth.

—*Dialogues*

Oh, my dear Kepler, how I wish we could have a hearty laugh together. Here at Padua, I have repeatedly and urgently begged the principal professor of philosophy to look at the moon and the planets through my glass [telescope]. He stubbornly refuses to do [this]. Why are you not here? What laughter we should have at such glorious folly.

—Letter to Kepler, 1597

The earth is among bodies which are mundane, and they clearly move round the sun; it is therefore certain that the earth so moves.

—*Dialogues*

ABOUT HIM

Galileo is the father of modern physics—indeed, of modern science altogether. His discoveries contain essentially—at least qualitatively—the basis of the theory later formulated by Newton.

—ALBERT EINSTEIN,
Foreword to *Dialogue Concerning the Two Chief
World Systems*

The revolution of thought initiated by Galileo's observations of January 7, 1610, proved to be the most catastrophic in the history of the race.

—SIR JAMES JEANS, *The Universe Around Us*

Galileo did not, as the *Encyclopaedia Britannica* for so many years asserted, drop heavy and light weights from a tower and watch them fall together. (They would not have fallen together if he had.) He *did* roll balls down inclined grooves and time their progress. In so doing he developed the first laws of nature, if we wish to call them that, based on observation and calculation. He was not alone, but he was preeminent in his time.

—VANNEVAR BUSH,
"Science Pauses," in *Fortune*, May 1965

The noblest eyes that nature ever created grew dark; eyes so privileged, endowed with such rare strength that it truly may be said of them that they had seen more than all the eyes before him, and that they opened the eyes of all those who came after him.

—BENEDETTO CASTELLI,
letter to a friend telling of Galileo's blindness, 1638

GALLIPOLI

We set to work to bury people. We pushed them into the sides of the trench but bits of them kept getting uncovered and sticking out, like people in a badly made bed. Hands were the worst; they would escape from the sand, pointing, begging—even waving! There was one which we all shook when we passed, saying "Good morning," in a posh voice. Everybody did it. The bottom of the trench was springy like a mattress because of all the bodies underneath. At night, when the stench was worse, we tied crêpe round our mouths and noses. This crêpe had been given to us because it was supposed to prevent us being gassed. The flies entered the trenches at night and lined them completely with a density which was like moving cloth.... We killed millions by slapping our spades along the trench walls but the next night it would be just as bad. We were all lousy and we couldn't stop shitting because we had caught dysentery. We wept, not because we were frightened but because we were so dirty.

—a farmworker, in Ronald Blythe, *Akenfield*

(*See also:* MEN AT WAR)

MAHATMA GANDHI (1869–1948)

Not even for the freedom of India would I resort to an untruth.

□

Jail is jail for thieves.... For me, it [is] a palace.

□

I am a politician trying ... to be a saint.

—various sources

I wanted to avoid violence, I want to avoid violence. Nonviolence is the first article of my faith. It is also the last article of my creed. But I had to make my choice. I had either to submit to a system which I considered had done an irreparable harm to my country, or incur the risk of the mad fury of my people bursting forth, when they understood the truth from my lips. I know that my people have sometimes gone mad. I am deeply sorry for it and I am therefore here to submit not to a light penalty but to the highest penalty. I do not ask for mercy. I do not plead any extenuating act. I am here, therefore, to invite and cheerfully submit to the highest penalty that can be inflicted upon me for what in law is a deliberate crime and what appears to me to be the highest duty of a citizen. The only course open to you, the judge, is, as I am just going to say in my statement, either to resign your post or inflict on me the severest penalty, if you believe that the system and law you are assisting to administer are good for the people.

—before an English judge, March 23, 1922

ABOUT HIM

The boy Gandhi was lustful, possessive, and, as he tells us, reasonably jealous. The customs of the period allowed him to meet Kasturbai only at night during the half year that she spent in the Gandhi household; the other half year she spent with her parents. He wanted to teach her everything he knew, since she was illiterate, but "lustful love," as he calls it in his autobiography, gave him no time to do so. . . .

□

He was small, gentle, sad, with mournful eyes, and with ears that stuck out at right angles, as always. His physical endurance was fantastic—sometimes he used to walk from Tolstoy Farm to Johannesburg and back on the same day, roughly fifty miles, to save money—and yet it was sustained on the slightest diet possible. He had already taken up the habit of fasting as a form of prayer, and giving fixed limits to his fasts. He would vow, for example, to fast for seven days in atonement for a sin committed by some of his followers. At other times he would fix no limit, but fast simply until he felt that the "inner voice" permitted him to cease. Although in later days, when so many governments were forced to yield on so many points because of them, these great fasts seemed a form of political pressure, they were conceived and executed as prayers to God.

—Vincent Sheean, *Mahatma Gandhi*

As his followers surged forward, native policemen "rained blows on their heads with steel-shod *lathis*." Not one of the marchers even raised an arm to fend off the blows. They went down like tenpins. . . . The waiting marchers groaned, sucked in their breaths at every blow, [then] marched on until struck down. . . . The police kicked [them] in the abdomen and testicles. . . . Hour after hour, stretcher-bearers carried back a stream of inert, bleeding bodies.

—Webb Miller, U.P. report, March 12, 1930

THE GAULS ENTER ROME

The Gauls could not believe their eyes, so easy, so swift, was their victory. For a time they stood rooted, scarcely realizing what had happened. But after moments of fear lest they had fallen into a trap, the Gauls began to collect the arms and equipment of their dead, and piled them, as is their custom, in heaps.

At last, when no sign of an enemy was anywhere to be seen, the Gauls marched. Shortly before sunset they reached the outskirts of Rome. Mounted soldiers were sent forward to reconnoiter. The gates stood open. Not a sentry was on guard. Not one soldier manned the walls.

Once more, the astonishing truth held the Gauls spellbound. Still, the night might conceal hidden terrors—and the city was totally unknown to them. After a further reconnaisance of the walls and all the gates, to discover, if it were possible, their enemy's intention in his desperate plight, the Gauls camped somewhere between the city and the Anio.

□

All Rome was now a city of lamentation—of universal mourning for the living and the dead. Then came the news that the Gauls were at the very gates, and the anguish of personal bereavements was forgotten in a great wave of panic. Cries like the howling of wolves, and strange barbaric songs, could be heard as squadrons of Gauls rode hither and thither just outside the walls.

Between that moment and the following day, unbearable suspense held sway. When would the assault come? ... When darkness had fallen, the Romans thought the invasion had been deliberately and cunningly postponed in order to multiply its terror with the fears of anticipation.

But the night passed without incident. And as dawn drew near, the Romans were made almost desperate. And then, at last, on the very heels of this long, drawn-out, unbearable anxiety, came the thing itself: The enemy entered the gates.

—LIVY, *The Early History of Rome*

GENETICS, TIME AND DEATH

If I enclose within my genetic inheritance the potentiality of writing this account: the sufficient brain to encompass its details, the sufficient energy to explore its byways, the sufficient judgment to weigh conclusions, the sufficient concern for the human condition—then all has been made possible by time. It is not the time of my own life, or that of my traceable forebears, or that even of my species. It is rather that leisurely measure of time that could wait a billion years from life's first stirrings for the birth of the individual, and death's first sortings.

But time yet waited. It waited for the backbone that now supports me, it waited for lungs that could breathe air, and legs to crawl out of the sea. It waited for the accumulations of chance to produce warm-blooded animals with energy superior to the cold-blooded past. Now birds could fly, and mammals could inherit the dynasty of reptiles, and I could have energy beyond the lizard's. Still time waited, while my most distant, modest primate ancestors took to the trees that would be their home. Here cunning surpassed strength and judgment instincts in the tricky pathways of the arboreal life. The brain could enlarge, and chance and death, old partners, could select subtler instincts from old coarse ways. The values of society, of communications between individuals, of the education of the young, of group defense and care for one's fellow—all became part of the primitive way, and mine. Seventy million years would have to elapse from the first primate moment until accident and value produced the human instant. But time could wait—as it waits today.

Time and death and cosmic fortune have combined to evolve a living world. But all are too large for the human scale. We are six feet high and seventy years long. We may speculate, measure, describe. We may delve into the lawless Pleistocene and strive for conclusions concerning our kind. But mystery continues to pervade all things. Time and death and the space between the stars remains still rather larger than ourselves.

—ROBERT ARDREY, *African Genesis*

GEOMETRY

A straight line is the simplest and most trivial example of a curve.
—ALBERT EINSTEIN and LEOPOLD INFELD,
Development of Modern Physics

The case for non-Euclidean geometry was succinctly stated by Poincaré, trailblazer for Einstein, in these words: "Axioms of geometry are only definitions in disguise. That being so, what ought one to think of this question: Is the Euclidean geometry true? The question is nonsense. One might as well ask whether the metric system is true and the old measure false."

—FOREST R. MOULTON and JUSTUS SCHIFFERES,
The Autobiography of Science

Lobachevsky and Bolyai independently of each other concluded that Euclid's geometry is not a logical necessity. This doesn't mean Euclid is "incorrect"; if you grant the premises [Euclid's axioms] all follows. But was it necessary to accept the axioms? Different axioms could be postulated and a perfectly self-consistent system of geometry could be built upon them.

Even the mathematicians of the time thought Lobachevsky and Bolyai mad. Gauss had privately reached similar conclusions but confessed he was afraid to publish his discovery.

—J. W. N. SULLIVAN, *The Limitations of Science*

GETTYSBURG

One day they would make a park there [Gettysburg], with neat lawns and smooth black roadways, and there would be marble statues and bronze plaques to tell the story in bloodless prose. Silent cannon would rest behind grassy embankments, their wheels bolted down to concrete foundations, their malevolence wholly gone, and here and there birds would nest in their muzzles. In the museums and tourist-bait shops old bullets and broken buckles and twisted bayonets would repose under glass, with a rusty musket or so on the wall and little illustrated booklets lying on top of the counter.

There would be neat brick and timber cabins on the hillsides, and people would sleep soundly in houses built where the armies had stormed and cried at each other, as if to prove that men killed in battle send forth no restless ghosts to plague comfortable citizens at night. The town and the woods and the ridges and hills would become a national shrine, filled with romantic memories which are in themselves a kind of forgetting, and visitors would stand by the clump of trees and look off to the west and see nothing but the rolling fields and the quiet groves and the great blue bank of the mountains.

—BRUCE CATTON, *Glory Road*

EDWARD GIBBON (1737–1794)

I saw and loved [Susan Curchod]. I found her learned without pedantry, lively in conversation, pure in sentiment, and elegant in manners; and the first sudden emotion was fortified by the habits and knowledge of a more familiar acquaintance. She permitted me to make her two or three visits at her father's house.

I passed some happy days there, in the mountains of Burgundy, and her parents honorably encouraged the connection. In a calm retirement the gay vanity of youth no longer fluttered in her bosom; she listened to the voice of truth and passion; and I might presume to hope that I had made some impression on a virtuous heart.

At Crassy and Lausanne I indulged my dream of felicity; but on my return to England, I soon discovered that my father would not hear of this strange alliance, and that without his consent I was myself destitute and helpless.

After a painful struggle I yielded to my fate: I sighed as a lover, I obeyed as a son; my wound was insensibly healed by time, absence, and the habits of a new life. My cure was accelerated by a faithful report of the tranquillity and cheerfulness of the lady herself; and my love subsided in friendship and esteem.

□

Twenty happy years have been animated by the labor of my history; and its success has given me a name, a rank, a character in the world to which I should not otherwise have been entitled. The freedom of my writings has indeed provoked an implacable tribe; but as I was safe from the stings I was soon accustomed to the buzzing of the hornets. My nerves are not trembling alive, and my literary temper is so happily framed that I am less sensible of pain than of pleasure. The rational pride of an author may be offended rather than flattered by vague indiscriminate praise; but he cannot, he should not, be indifferent to the fair testimonies of private and public esteem.

□

It was on the day, or rather night, of the 27th of June 1787, between the hours of eleven and twelve, that I wrote the last lines of the last page [of the *Decline and Fall of the Roman Empire*] in a summerhouse in my garden. After laying down my pen, I took several turns in a *berceau*, or covered walk of acacias, which command a prospect of the country, the lake, and the mountains. The air was temperate, the sky was serene, the silver orb of the moon was reflected from the waters, and all nature was silent.

I will not dissemble my first emotions of joy on recovery of my freedom, and, perhaps, the establishment of fame. But my pride was soon humbled, and a sober melancholy was spread over my mind, by the idea that I had taken an everlasting leave of an old and agreeable companion, and that, whatever might be the future of my *History*, the life of the historian must be short and precarious.

—Autobiography

ABOUT HIM

Gibbon's contemptuous characterization of the later eastern empire as a "uniform tale of weakness and misery" ... Bury condemns as "one of the most untrue, and most effective, judgments ever uttered by a thoughtful historian."

—DERO A. SAUNDERS, Introduction,
The Portable Gibbon

Gibbon lived out most of his sex life in his footnotes.

—PHILIP GUEDALLA

WILLIAM GLADSTONE (1809–1898)

Speech was the fire of his [Gladstone's] being; and, when he spoke, the ambiguity of ambiguity was revealed. The long, winding, intricate sentences, with their vast burden of subtle and complicated qualifications befogged the mind like clouds, and like clouds, too, dropped thunderbolts. Could it not then at least be said of him with certainty that his was a complex character? But here also there was a contradiction of his spirit, it is impossible not to perceive a strain of *naivete* in Mr. Gladstone. He adhered to some of his principles—that of the value of representative institutions, for instance—with a faith which was singularly literal; his views upon religion were uncritical to crudeness; he had no sense of humor.

Compared with Disraeli's his attitude towards life strikes one as that of an ingenuous child. His very egoism was simple-minded: Through all the labyrinth of his passions there ran a single thread. But the center of the labyrinth? Ah! the thread might lead there, through those wandering mazes, at last. Only, with the last corner turned, the last step taken, the explorer might find that he was looking down into the gulf of a crater. The flame shot out on every side, scorching and brilliant; but in the midst there was a darkness.

—LYTTON STRACHEY, *Eminent Victorians*

If Mr. Gladstone fell into the Thames, it would be a misfortune; if someone pulled him out, it would be a calamity.... [He is] a sophistical rhetorician, inebriated with the exuberance of his own verbosity, and gifted with an egotistical imagination that can at all times command an interminable and inconsistent series of arguments to malign an opponent and glorify himself.

□

Do not imagine that I have ever hated William Gladstone. No, my only difficulty with him has been that I have never been able to understand him.

—BENJAMIN DISRAELI

GLOOM

To whom can I speak today?
The gentleman has perished,
The violent man has access to everybody.
The iniquity that smites the land
It has no end.
There are no righteous men
The earth is surrendered to criminals.

—said to have been written 4,000 years ago in Egypt

GLORY IN WAR

Military Glory! It was a dream that century after century has seized on men's imaginations and set their blood on fire. Trumpets, plumes, chargers, the pomp of war, the excitement of combat, the exultation of victory—the mixture was intoxicating indeed. To command great armies, to perform deeds of valor, to ride victorious through flower-strewn streets, to be heroic, magnificent, famous—such were the visions that danced before men's eyes as they turned eagerly to war.

It was not a dream for the common man. War was an aristocratic trade, and military glory reserved for nobles and princes. Glittering squadrons of cavalry, long lines of infantry, wheeling obediently on the parade-ground, ministered to the lust both for power and for display. Courage was esteemed the essential military quality and held to be a virtue exclusive to aristocrats. Were they not educated to courage, trained, as no common man was trained, by years of practice in dangerous sports? They glorified courage, called it valor and worshipped it, believed battles were won by valor, saw war in terms of valor as the supreme adventure.

It was a dream that died hard. Century followed century and glittering visions faded before the sombre realities of history. Great armies in their pride and splendor were defeated by starvation, pestilence and filth, valor was sacrificed to stupidity, gallantry to corruption.

Yet the dream survived.

—CECIL WOODHAM-SMITH, *The Reason Why*

GOD

It is very peculiar that, whenever we see ... unutterable desolation —loneliness, poverty, and misery—... the thought of God comes into one's mind.

—VINCENT VAN GOGH

Those who love fairy tales do not like it when people speak of the innate tendencies in mankind towards aggression, destruction and cruelty. For God has made them in his own image, with his own perfection. No one wants to be reminded how hard it is to reconcile the undeniable existence of evil with his omnipotence and supreme goodness. The devil is, in fact, the best way out in acquittal of God; he can be used to play the same economic role of outlet as Jews [serve] in the world of Aryan ideals.

Even so, one can just as well hold God responsible for the existence of the devil as for the evil he personified.

—SIGMUND FREUD, *Civilization and Its Discontents*

Which is it—is man one of God's blunders or is God one of man's blunders?

—FRIEDRICH NIETZSCHE

God is subtle, but he is not malicious. . . . I cannot believe that God plays dice with the world.

—ALBERT EINSTEIN

It is scarcely possible to exaggerate the influence of vanity throughout the range of human life, from the child of three to the potentate at whose frown the world trembles. Mankind have even committed the impiety of attributing similar desires to the Deity, whom they imagine avid for continual praise.

—BERTRAND RUSSELL, Nobel Prize acceptance speech

God will forgive me; that's his business.

—HEINRICH HEINE

As a blind man has no idea of colors, so have we no idea of the manner by which the all-wise God perceives and understands all things. . . .

All that diversity of natural things which we find suited to different times and places could arise from nothing but the ideas and will of a Being necessarily existing.

—ISAAC NEWTON, *Mathematical Principles*

God said: "Let us make man in our image"; and Man said: "Let us make God in our image."

—DOUGLAS JERROLD

I fear God, yet am not afraid of Him.

—SIR THOMAS BROWNE, *Religio Medici*

My God is the God of Spinoza.

—ALBERT EINSTEIN

This is the zenith of faith; to believe that God, who saves so few and condemns so many, is merciful; that He is just, [although] at His own pleasure He has doomed us to damnation; that He seems to delight in the torture of the wretched and to be more deserving of hate than of love.

If by any feat of reason I could conceive how God, who shows so much anger and harshness, could be merciful and just —there would be no need for faith.

—MARTIN LUTHER, reply to Erasmus

If triangles had a God, he would have three sides.

—VOLTAIRE

We cannot in this life know what God is, but we can know what he is not; and in this consists the perfection of our knowledge as wayfarers in this world.

—THOMAS AQUINAS, *De Caritate*

The act of worship, as carried on by Christians, seems to me to be debasing rather than ennobling. It involves grovelling before a Being who, if He really exists, deserves to be denounced instead of respected. I see little evidence in this world of the so-called goodness of God. On the contrary, it seems to me that, on the strength of His daily acts, He must be set down a most stupid, cruel and villainous fellow. I can say this with a clear conscience, for He has treated me very well—in fact, with vast politeness. But I can't help thinking of his barbaric torture of most of the rest of humanity. I simply can't imagine revering the God of war and politics, theology and cancer.

—H. L. MENCKEN, letter to Will Durant, 1933

We can know *that* God is, but not *what* God is.

—ST. AUGUSTINE, *On True Religion*

God is . . . the native land of the soul.

—ST. AUGUSTINE

Those who set out to serve God and Mammon soon discover there is no God.

—LOGAN PEARSALL SMITH

Jehovah has always seemed to me the most fascinating character in all fiction.

—OLIVER HERFORD

TO THE UNKNOWN GOD

If we believe Jerome, who knew five languages, there are some contradictory words in St. Paul. When he spoke to the Athenians, he twisted what he had read on the altar into an argument for the Christian faith, but omitted what did not serve his purpose, selecting only from the end: "to the Unknown God."

The actual inscription reads, "To the Gods of Asia, Europe, and Africa, and to the Unknown Gods, and the Gods of Strangers." . . . Theologians follow his example today.

—ERASMUS, *In Praise of Folly*

An atheist is a man who has no invisible means of support.

—JOHN BUCHAN

GONDOLAS

No carriage compared with it for comfort. You could read, eat, make love in its tiny cabin, hidden from the world. It was an intoxicating gift for leisure—effortless, hushed. At sunset Venetians drifted out on the lagoon, talking in twos and threes. . . . And the sleight-of-hand of the gondoliers, sweeping their odd scooped boats through the narrow canals, brushing others with nimble skill, was very Venetian too—the smooth, secret, assured inheritance of ages. . . .

Though the ordinary gondolas were by law black, a lot of money was spent on the accessories, as a matter of prestige. Linings of satin and silk, mountings of ebony and inlaid ivory, liveries embroidered with gold were all at different times forbidden. But decrees were useless: they simply brought the forbidden item into vogue. . . . And the dark exterior helped secrecy, anonymity; once you stepped inside you were safe from spies; incredibly enough, no gondolier took bribes.

—MAURICE ROWDON, *The Silver Age of Venice*

CHARLES GEORGE ("CHINESE") GORDON (1833–1885)

...a rebellion had broken out in Darfur—Gordon determined upon a hazardous stroke. He mounted a camel, and rode, alone, in the blazing heat, across eighty-five miles of desert, to Suleiman's camp. His sudden apparition dumbfounded the rebels; his imperious bearing overawed them; he signified to them that in two days they must disarm and disperse; and the whole host obeyed.

□

...So far as Gordon's personal safety was concerned, he might still, at this late hour, have secured it. But he had chosen; he stayed at Khartoum. ...

□

...Late one evening, Bordeini Bey went to visit him in the palace, which was being bombarded by the Mahdi's cannon. The high building, brilliantly lighted up, afforded an excellent mark. As the shot came whistling around the windows, the merchant suggested that it would be advisable to stop them up with boxes full of sand. Upon this, Gordon Pasha became enraged. "He called up the guard, and gave them orders to shoot me if I moved; he then brought a very large lantern which would hold twenty-four candles. He and I then put the candles into the sockets, placed the lantern on the table in front of the window, lit the candles, and then sat down at the table."

□

...the Mahdi's army swarmed into Khartoum. Gordon had long debated with himself what his action should be at the supreme moment. "I shall never (D.V.)*," he had told Sir Evelyn Baring, "be taken alive." He had had gunpowder put into the cellars of the palace, so that the whole building might, at a moment's notice, be blown into the air. ...

The sudden appearance of the Arabs, the complete collapse of the defense, saved him the necessity of making up his mind. He had been on the roof, in his dressing-gown, when the attack began; and he had only time to hurry to his bedroom, to slip on a white uniform and to seize up a sword and a revolver, before

* *Deo volente:* God willing.

the foremost of the assailants were in the palace. The crowd was led by four of the fiercest of the Mahdi's followers—tall and swarthy Dervishes, splendid in their many-colored *jubbehs,* their great swords drawn from the scabbards of brass and velvet, their spears flourishing above their heads. Gordon met them at the top of the staircase.

For a moment, there was a deathly pause, while he stood in silence, surveying his antagonists. Then it is said the Taha Shahin, the Dongolawi, cried in a loud voice, "*Mala, oun el yom yomek!*" (O cursed one, your time is come), and plunged his spear into the Englishman's body. His only reply was a gesture of contempt. Another spear transfixed him; he fell, and the swords of the three other Dervishes instantly hacked him to death. Thus, if we are to believe the official chroniclers, in the dignity of unresisting disdain, General Gordon met his end. . . .

That morning, while Slatin Pasha was sitting in his chains in the camp at Omdurman, he saw a group of Arabs approaching, one of whom was carrying something wrapped up in a cloth. As the group passed him, they stopped for a moment, and railed at him in savage mockery. Then the cloth was lifted, and he saw before him Gordon's head. The trophy was taken to Mahdi: At last the two fanatics had indeed met face to face. The Mahdi ordered the head to be fixed between the branches of a tree in the public highway, and all who passed threw stones at it. The hawks of the desert swept and circled about it—those very hawks which the blue eyes had so often watched.

—LYTTON STRACHEY, *Eminent Victorians*

GOVERNING AND PROPERTY

Above all, the ruler must abstain from taking the property of others, for men more easily forget the death of their father than the loss of their patrimony.

—MACHIAVELLI, *The Prince*

Conscience is the most sacred of all property . . . to guard a man's house as his castle . . . can give no title to invade a man's conscience, which is more sacred than his castle.

—JAMES MADISON, *National Gazette*, March 29, 1952

GOVERNING AND TRADITION

This respect for precedent, this clinging to prescription, this reverence for antiquity, which are so often ridiculed by conceited and superficial minds...appear to me to have their origin in a profound knowledge of human nature and in a fine observation of public affairs.... Those great men who have periodically risen to guide the helm of our government in times of tumultuous and stormy exigency, knew that a state is a complicated creation of refined art, and they handled it with all the delicacy the exquisite machinery requires.

—BENJAMIN DISRAELI,
Vindication of the English Constitution

GOVERNMENT

The purpose of government is to preserve the liberty and peace of the subjects of the republic, and to protect them from the abuses of personal power.

—Constitution of Venice, 1310

A people unused to restraint must be led, they will not be drove [sic!].

—GEORGE WASHINGTON, in John C. Fitzpatrick,
George Washington Himself

The whole art of government consists in the part of being honest.

☐

If once the people become inattentive to public affairs, you and I and Congress and Assemblies, Judges and Governors, shall all become wolves.

☐

That government is the strongest of which every man feels himself a part.

☐

[To Pierre Du Pont de Nemours, 1816]: We both consider the people as our children and love them with parental affection. But you love them as infants whom you are afraid to trust without nurses, and I as adults, whom I freely leave to self-government.

☐

The legitimate powers of government extend only to such acts as are injurious to others. But it does me no injury for my neighbor to say there are twenty gods, or no God. It neither picks my pocket nor breaks my leg.

—THOMAS JEFFERSON,
Notes on Virginia and other sources

[A new government] must dazzle and astonish. The moment it ceases to glitter, it falls.

—NAPOLEON

The civil sword out of great mercy must be unmerciful, and out of sheer goodness must exercise wrath and severity.

—MARTIN LUTHER, *Table Talk*

It is only by constant adjustments, by checks and counterchecks ... by compromises between competing interests, by continual modifications applied to changing circumstances, that a system is slowly formed which corresponds to the requirements and conditions of the country....

—W. E. H. LECKY,
A History of England in the Eighteenth Century,
Vol. III

Each constitution has a vice engendered in, and inseparable from it. In kingship it is despotism, in aristocracy oligarchy, and in democracy the rule of violence. It is impossible ... that each of these should not in time change into its vicious form.

—POLYBIUS, *History*

Government is always government by the few, whether in the name of the one, the few, or the many.

—JAMES BRYCE, *The American Commonwealth*

If it is true that men can do no more than they are able to do, then government can do no more than governors are able to do. All the wishing in the world, all the promises ... will not call into being men who can plan a future which they are unable to imagine, who can manage a civilization which they are unable to understand.

—WALTER LIPPMANN, *The Good Society*

It is a wise government that deals with men as they are, not as
they ought to be.

—JOHANN WOLFGANG VON GOETHE

A government which robs Peter to pay Paul can always depend
on the support of Paul.

—GEORGE BERNARD SHAW,
Everybody's Political What's What

GOVERNMENT AID

Governments are likely to react to failure with further elaboration
of their plans, and vast enterprises can finally be built up of a
kind undreamt of at the outset. One striking illustration of this
is found in the history of agricultural support in the United States.
Agriculture in America had been going through great changes and
in 1929 the American Government set out to ease the pains of
adjustment and to bring aid to the poorest farmers. Neither aim
has in fact been achieved. The period of transition has been indefinitely prolonged and the benefits have probably gone much
more to the well-to-do farmers. In the process the Government
... has built up an empire of vested interests among those who
operate and those who benefit from the schemes. The chain of
events is well known. The fixing of high farm prices produced
large surpluses of agricultural products. The Government thereby
became the owner of enormous stocks; it became responsible for
their transportation by road and rail, their storage and rotation,
their carriage abroad by rail and ship and often their transport
within foreign countries. The presence of these huge stocks
created new uncertainties in the market and destroyed all incentive for private stock holding. The efforts to dispose of a part of
the stocks abroad led to intricate and not always happy relations
with foreign countries and often rebounded to damage American
industry, thus requiring further public compensatory measures.
Attempts by the American Government to encourage larger economic trading regions in the world have been hampered by the
obligations of the Government to insist upon the rights of the
American farmer. This almost incredible, and still expanding, network of public activities has grown up unwittingly from the laud-

able intention of helping a comparatively small number of poor farmers.

—JOHN JEWKES, *Public and Private Enterprise*

GOVERNMENT TODAY

A democratic government cannot design efficient automobiles, it cannot design a sound energy policy, it cannot eliminate prejudice and discrimination, it cannot manage transportation, it cannot assure the soundness of investments or the accuracy of information about them, it cannot guarantee the effectiveness and safety of medicines—it cannot, in short, do most of the things that our government undertakes to do.

This is not the occasion to prove the point, but it is important at least to assert that all of these problems can be handled far better without a direct governmental role.

—HERBERT STEIN,
New York Times, September 11, 1975

THE GREAT DEPRESSION

The fact is that the Great Depression, like most other periods of severe unemployment, was produced by government mismanagement rather than by any inherent instability of the private economy. A governmentally established agency—the Federal Reserve System—had been assigned responsibility for monetary policy. In 1930 and 1931, it exercised this responsibility so ineptly as to convert what otherwise would have been a moderate contraction into a major catastrophe. Similarly today, governmental measures constitute the major impediments to economic growth in the United States. Tariffs and other restrictions on international trade, high tax burdens and a complex and inequitable tax structure, regulatory commissions, government price and wage fixing, and a host of other measures give individuals an incentive to misuse and misdirect resources and distort the investment of new savings. What we urgently need, for both economic stability and growth, is a reduction of government intervention, not an increase.

□

The Great Depression in the United States, far from being a sign of the inherent instability of the private enterprise system, is a testament of how much harm can be done by mistakes on the part of a few men when they wield vast power over the monetary system of a country.

It may be that these mistakes were excusable on the basis of the knowledge available to men at the time—though I happen to think not. But that is really beside the point. Any system which gives so much power and so much discretion to a few men that mistakes—excusable or not—can have such far-reaching effects is a bad system. It is a bad system to believers in freedom just because it gives a few men such power without any effective check by the body politic—this is the key political argument against an "independent" central bank. But it is a bad system even to those who set security higher than freedom. Mistakes, excusable or not, cannot be avoided in a system which disperses responsibility yet gives a few men great power, and which thereby makes important policy actions highly dependent on accidents of personality.

—MILTON FRIEDMAN, *Capitalism and Freedom*

THE GREATEST KILLER

The world's most habitual man-killer among mammals is unique in the animal kingdom. Its large brain and intelligence are unrivaled; its ability to live under almost any conditions, at any height or latitude is unmatched, and its curious preoccupation with the killing of its own species has no parallel in biological history. That man-killer is man. In the last three generations he has with calculation and with malice killed at the average rate of at least three-quarters of a million people a year. In the last war he killed 22,060,000. Six million of these were exterminated in one carefully planned programme of genocide ... using his most effective weapon to date, man killed 70,000 in a single explosion and left tens of thousands mortally burned.

—JAMES CLARKE, *Man Is the Prey*

Man, biologically considered, and whatever else he may be into the bargain, is the most formidable of all beasts of prey....

A millennium of peace would not breed the fighting disposition out of our bone and marrow, and a function so ingrained and vital

will never consent to die without resistance and will always find
impassioned apologists and idealizers....

—WILLIAM JAMES, *Memories and Studies*

THE GREEK PHILOSOPHERS

The grand idea that informed these men was that the world
around them was something *that could be understood,* if one only
took the trouble to observe it properly; that it was not the play-
ground of gods and ghosts and spirits who acted on the spur of
the moment and more or less arbitrarily, who were moved by
passions, by wrath and love and desire for revenge, who vented
their hatred, and could be propitiated by pious offerings. These
men had freed themselves of superstition; they would have none
of all this. They saw the world as a rather complicated mechanism,
acting according to eternal innate laws, which they were curious
to find out. This is, of course, the fundamental attitude of science
up to this day. To us it has become flesh of our flesh, so much so
that we have forgotten that somebody had to find it out, make
it a program, and embark on it.

—ERWIN SCHRÖDINGER, *Nature and the Greeks*

GRIEF

It was a short case and soon finished. At the end of it the judge
said that, considering the evidence, he would have to commit the
girl for trial. Instantly the quick-eyed court officer began to clear
the way for the next case. The well-dressed women and their
escort turned one way and the girl turned another, toward a door
with an austere arch leading into a stone-paved passage. Then it
was that a great cry rang through the courtroom, the cry of this
girl who believed that she was lost.

The loungers, many of them, underwent a spasmodic movement as if they had been knifed. The court officers rallied quickly.
The girl fell back opportunely for the arms of one of them, and
her wild heels clicked twice on the floor. "I am innocent! Oh, I
am innocent!"

People pity those who need none, and the guilty sob alone; but,
innocent or guilty, this girl's scream described such a profound

depth of woe, it was so graphic of grief, that it slit with a dagger's sweep the curtain of commonplace, and disclosed the gloom-shrouded specter that sat in the young girl's heart so plainly, in so universal a tone of the mind, that a man heard expressed some far-off midnight terror of his own thought.

—STEPHEN CRANE, "An Eloquence of Grief," in
The Law as Literature

GUERRILLA WARFARE

Keep the enemy under a strain and wear him down.... When the enemy is at ease, be able to weary him; when well-fed, to starve him; when at rest, to make him move.

—SUNG-T'AI-TSU
(founder of the Sung Dynasty and the first military
strategist in the annals of history), A.D. 927–976

HAITI'S SANS SOUCI PALACE

The tropics are merciless to ruins. So savage is the onslaught of the rain, the creepers, the insects and decay, that dwellings which are abandoned for a single year have the appearance of centuries of dereliction. But something uncompromisingly stubborn in the fabric of Sans Souci has redeemed it from this dateless anonymity. From a distance the great staircases, converging like a truncated pyramid, lend it the appearance of an Aztec or a Maya ruin, but with every advancing step through the wooded valley, the columns and arches and balustrades become clearer and assign it more unmistakably to the heroic era of its construction.

☐

... The palace is open on all sides to the weather, and anybody can wander through thresholds from which the doors have vanished. Grass flourished everywhere, and a sound of birds was audible in the rafters overhead. ...

The lawns descend in unkempt stages to the gloom of a valley where everything, in this last moment of daylight, glowed with colors that dwindled as we watched them, and died. Large white moths flew past, and the last shoals of crimson faded from the mackerel sky. The fireflies kindled erratically against the dark foliage of the mountainside, and the song of the crickets and the frogs grew louder, while the broken arches around us signaled through the dusk more legibly than any of the sonnets of Du Bellay or the engravings of Piranesi, their obsolete messages of grandeur and decay.

—Patrick Leigh Fermor, *The Traveller's Tree*

HAPPINESS

Human felicity is produced not so much by great pieces of good fortune that seldom happen, as by little advantages that occur every day.

—Benjamin Franklin

Happiness: a good bank account, a good cook, and a good digestion.

—Jean Jacques Rousseau

No one is happy all his life long.

—Euripides (480?–406 b.c.)

A man's true happiness consists only in wisdom, and in the knowledge of the truth, not at all in the fact that he is wiser than others, or that others lack such knowledge.

—Baruch Spinoza, *Tractatus Theologico-Politicus*

If you wish to be happy yourself, you must resign yourself to seeing others also happy.

—Bertrand Russell

Happiness is knowing that you do not necessarily require happiness.

—William Saroyan

What is called happiness in its narrowest sense comes from the satisfaction—most often instantaneous—of pent-up needs which have reached great intensity, and by its very nature can only be a transitory experience.

—SIGMUND FREUD, *Civilization and Its Discontents*

WILLIAM HARVEY (1578–1657) AND GALEN (c. 130–200)

Harvey sat many hours a day for many years looking at beating hearts, or holding a beating heart in one hand and a pulsing artery in the other, instructing his brain through his fingers, feeling his way to the truth, before he succeeded in reversing Galen's view, first in his own mind, then slowly in the world at large. Even then it was Galen who had triumphed over Galen, Galen the observer who had triumphed over Galen the philosopher, for it was Galen's technique Harvey had learned (in the Vesalian school) at Padua.

—BENJAMIN FARRINGTON, *Greek Science*

WARREN HASTINGS: HIS TRIAL (1788–1795)

The place [Westminster Hall] was worthy of such a trial. It ... had resounded with acclamations at the inauguration of thirty kings, the hall which had witnessed the just sentence of Bacon ... the hall where Charles had confronted the High Court of Justice with the placid courage which has half redeemed his fame.

Neither military nor civil pomp was wanting. The avenues were lined with grenadiers.... The peers, robed in gold and ermine, were marshaled by the heralds under Garter King-at-Arms.... Near a hundred and seventy lords ... walked in solemn order from their usual place of assembling to the tribunal....

The gray old walls were hung with scarlet. The long galleries were crowded by an audience such as has rarely excited the fears or the emulation of an orator. There were gathered together, from all parts of a great, free, enlightened, and prosperous empire, grace and female loveliness, wit and learning, the representatives of every science and of every art. There were seated round the Queen the fair-haired young daughters of the house of Brunswick. There the Ambassadors of great Kings and Commonwealths gazed with admiration on a spectacle which no other country in the world could present.... There the historian of the Roman Empire thought of the days when Cicero pleaded the cause of Sicily against Verres, and when, before a senate which still retained some show of freedom, Tacitus thundered against the oppressor of Africa. There were seen, side by side, the greatest painter and the greatest scholar of the age.

The Sergeants made proclamation. Hastings advanced to the bar, and bent his knee. The culprit was indeed not unworthy of that great presence. He had ruled an extensive and populous country, had made laws and treaties, had sent forth armies, had set up and pulled down princes. And in his high place he had so borne himself, that all had feared him, that most had loved him, and that hatred itself could deny him no title of glory, except virtue. He looked like a great man, and not like a bad man. A person small and emaciated, yet deriving dignity from a carriage which, while it indicated deference to the Court, indicated also habitual self-possession and self-respect, a high and intellectual forehead, a brow pensive, but not gloomy, a mouth of inflexible decision, a face pale and worn, but serene, ... such was the aspect with which the great proconsul presented himself to his judges.

—THOMAS BABINGTON MACAULAY,
Critical and Historical Essays

HATS IN VENICE

Venetian hats ... were a climax of extravagant attention and bad taste; they bore fruit and feathers and stuffed birds and butterflies and masses of flowers; sometimes they looked like a magic cabbagepatch, so enormous that you could hardly recognize the wearer as a woman. The hair beneath was elaborate enough without a hat: It was piled high, with false hair added, in pyramids and baskets and fans and towers (called *cimieri* or *conzieri*). A style called *pouf à sentiment* contained locks of hair belonging to your lover or some member of your family, and was decorated with little portraits of that person, or even of a pet, or both. Sometimes a head took a small fortune to dress, with precious stones, and flowers specially picked; the whole was sometimes so big that it had to be held together with iron hoops.

—MAURICE ROWDON, *The Silver Age of Venice*

HEAT: HUMAN

An average five-room house in New York City can be heated in winter with only about 50,000 B.T.U.s per hour, even on the coldest days. This means that about twelve or thirteen people, walking around the living room, can keep it warm even if the furnace is turned off.

—WILLIAM C. VERGARA, *Science in Everyday Things*

HEINRICH HEINE (1797–1856)

Mine is the most peaceable disposition. My wishes are a humble dwelling with a thatched roof, but a good bed, good food, milk and butter of the freshest, flowers at my windows, some fine tall trees before my door; and if the good God wants to make me completely happy, He will grant me the joy of seeing some six or seven of my enemies hanging from these trees. With my heart full of deep emotion I shall forgive them, before they die, all the wrong they did me in their lifetime. True, one must forgive one's enemies, but not until they are brought to execution.

—*Gedanken und Einfalle*

HENRY VIII (1491–1547)

To Anne Boleyn, Elizabeth's ... birth in 1533 had been like the birth of Fate.

It was preceded by the Sophoclean drama of King Henry's escape from a real or imagined incest (that of his marriage with his brother's widow, Mary's mother)—cursed by Heaven with the decree that no male child born of that marriage should live.

That drama of passions, faiths, lusts, and ambitions that had the fever of lust, was brought about in part by a spiritual upheaval in the history of mankind, in part by the absolute necessity, if the country were to be preserved from civil war, that King Henry should provide a male heir to the kingdom.

King Henry, that lonely being, a giant in scale, a creature of powerful intellect and insane pride, of cruelty, vengeance, and appalling rages, of regal generosity and breadth of understanding, helped to bring about a tragedy through two factors—his kingly sense of duty to his people, and his curious power of self-deception, which enabled him to see his long infatuation for Queen Catherine's maid of honour, Anne Boleyn, as a part of his duty.

He put aside his Queen, and married the object of his infatuation, who was young, and would surely bear him a son. . . .

But "to the shame and confusion of the physicians, astrologers, witches and wizards," who had assured the King that the coming child would be a son, [Anne Boleyn] . . . was delivered of a daughter. . . .

Three weeks after the funeral of Catherine, whom she had once served, after some hours of a slow-dragging agony, the new Queen gave birth to a dead child. And that child was a son.

Entering her room, merciless, without pity for her pain or her humiliation, the King, fixing her with his formidable stare, told her that he knew, now, that God would not grant him male children. "I will speak to you," he said, "when you are well."

—EDITH SITWELL, *The Queens and the Hive*

HIS REVELS

In the middle of a banquet the King and his boon companions would disappear and in their place would enter an exotic procession of, for instance, Turks, Russians and Prussians, surrounded by torchbearers, faces blackened to resemble Moors.

On one famous occasion Cardinal Wolsey gave a banquet in his riverside mansion of York Place. The King mysteriously was not present. Suddenly to a volley of small cannon from the river, followed by the warble of fifes and the beat of drums, there erupted into Wolsey's splendid room a band of shepherds from a foreign land—rather exceptional shepherds; their garments were of cloth of gold and crimson satin, their beards and wigs of gold and silver wire and black silk. After a while the King and his companions unmasked and the dancing began.

—MARIE LOUISE BRUCE, *Anne Boleyn*

HERITAGE AND ILLUSION

. . . Twenty thousand thieves landed at Hastings (1066). These founders of the House of Lords were greedy and ferocious dragons, sons of greedy and ferocious pirates. They . . . took everything they could carry, they burned, harried, violated, tortured and killed, until everything English was brought to the verge of ruin. Such however is the illusion of antiquity and wealth, that decent and dignified men now existing boast their descent from these filthy thieves, who showed a far juster conviction of their own merits, by assuming for their types the swine, goat, jackal, leopard, wolf and snake, which they severally resembled.

—RALPH WALDO EMERSON, *Collected Works*, Vol. V

HEROES

A hero is no braver than an ordinary man, but he is brave five minutes longer.

—RALPH WALDO EMERSON

Hero: a man who is afraid to run away.

—English proverb

Everyone is ... the hero of his own baptism, his own wedding, and his own funeral.

—OLIVER WENDELL HOLMES, 1882

Concerning the statement that no man is a hero to his valet: This is not because the hero is no hero, but because the valet is a valet.

—FRIEDRICH HEGEL

Napoleon and other great men were makers of empires, but these men whom I am about to mention were makers of universes, and their hands were not stained with the blood of their fellow men. I can count them on the fingers of my two hands. Pythagoras, Ptolemy, Kepler, Copernicus, Aristotle, Galileo, Newton and Einstein.

—GEORGE BERNARD SHAW, 1922

Whether or not mankind can afford its great men, sickness and all, is another question. Before we can even approach it we must first learn to recognize the afflictions of our favorite heroes, as well as the madness in those great men whom we could do without. For, short as our lives are, the influence of the men we elect, support, or tolerate as great can indeed be a curse felt far beyond the third and fourth generation.

—Erik H. Erikson, *Young Man Luther*

HISTORIANS

One of the most difficult tasks for any historian is to perceive those things which the people of former times took for granted and therefore never mentioned even in their most intimate writings or discussions.

—John Fisher, *Six Summers in Paris*

God cannot alter the past; that is why he is obligated to connive at the existence of historians.

—Samuel Butler

GREEK HISTORIANS

Each time a new civilization has been set up, people have assumed that the world began with themselves. They learnt the alphabet late and with difficulty.... And you can easily see from the historians themselves that they have no certain foundation for their knowledge, but rely on individual guesswork. They are always refuting one another, and do not shrink from giving the most contradictory accounts of the same events....

The two basic reasons for their inconsistency are first, the Greeks' original neglect of keeping official records, and ... second, their rushing into the writing of history not so much to discover the truth (which they are ready enough to claim to be doing) but to show off their literary style, and to outshine their rivals.... So for eloquence we orientals must yield the palm to the Greek historians, but not for truth.

—Josephus, *History of the Jewish War*

HISTORY

Our sense of the mystery and variousness of life is enlarged, when we realize that the very great may spring from the very small. How does Edmund Burke put it?—"A common soldier, a child, a girl at the door of an inn, have changed the face of fortune, and almost of Nature."

History is full of these momentous trifles—the accident which kills or preserves in life some figure of destiny; the weather on some critical battlefield, like the fog at Lutzen or the snow at Towton; the change of wind which brings two fleets to a decisive action; the severe winter of 1788 which produces the famine of 1789, and thereby perhaps the French Revolution; the birth or the death of a child; a sudden idea which results in some potent invention.

—JOHN BUCHAN, *The Rede Lecture*, 1929

It is the fact about the past that is poetic; just because it really happened, it gathers round it all the inscrutable mystery of life and death and time. Let the science and research of the historian find the fact, and let his imagination and art make clear its significance.

—G. M. TREVELYAN, *History of England*

This eager and unreasonable desire of transmitting useless stories to posterity, and of fixing the attention of future ages upon common events, proceeds from a weakness extremely incident to those who have lived in courts, and have unhappily been engaged in the management of public affairs. They consider the court in which they have lived as the most magnificent in the world; their king as the greatest monarch; and the affairs in which they have been concerned as the most important that ever were transacted: and they vainly imagine that posterity will view them in the same light.

—VOLTAIRE, *History of Charles XII, King of Sweden*, tr. T. SMOLLETT, T. FRANCKLIN, others, 1762

Every great event has been a capital misfortune. History has kept no account of times of peace and tranquillity; it relates only ravages and disasters.... All history, in short, is little else than a long succession of useless cruelties...a collection of crimes, follies, and misfortunes, among which we have now and then met with a few virtues, and some happy times, as we see sometimes a few scattered huts in a barren desert.... As nature has placed in the heart of man interest, pride, and all the passions, it is no wonder that ... we meet with almost a continuous succession of crimes and disasters.

—VOLTAIRE, *Works*, Vol. XVI

Nothing but a name remains of those who commanded battalions and fleets; nothing results to the human race from a hundred battles gained; but the great men of whom I have spoken prepared pure and durable delights for generations unborn. A canal that connects two seas, a picture by Poussin, a beautiful tragedy, a discovered truth, are things a thousand times more precious than all the annals of the court, all the narratives of war. You know that with me great men rank first, "heroes" last. I call great men all those who have excelled in the useful and the agreeable. The ravagers of provinces are mere heroes.

—Voltaire, Letter to Thierot, 1736, in James Parton,
Life of Voltaire, Vol. I

History with its flickering lamp stumbles along the trail of the past, trying to reconstruct its scenes, to revive its echoes, and kindle with pale gleams the passion of former days.

—Winston Churchill, speech, House of Commons,
1940

All history, so far as it is not supported by contemporary evidence, is romance.... That certain kings reigned and certain battles were fought we can depend upon as true, but all the coloring, all the philosophy of history is conjecture.

—Samuel Johnson

Men make their own history, but they do not make it just as they please; they do not make it under circumstances chosen by themselves, but under circumstances directly found, and given and transmitted from the past. The tradition of all the dead generations weighs like a nightmare on the living....

—Karl Marx, *The 18th Brumaire of Louis Napoleon*

History is lived forward but is written in retrospect. We know the end before we consider the beginning and we can never wholly recapture what it was to know the beginning only.

—C. V. Wedgewood, *William the Silent*

The deepest, the only theme of human history, compared to which all others are of subordinate importance, is the conflict of skepticism with faith.

—Johann Wolfgang von Goethe

For what is a history, but . . . huge libel on human nature, to which we industriously add page after page, volume after volume, as if we were holding up a monument to the honor, rather than the infamy of our species. . . . What are the great events that constitute a glorious era?—The fall of empires—the desolation of happy countries—splendid cities smoking in their ruins—the proudest works of art tumbled in the dust—the shrieks and groans of whole nations ascending up to heaven!

—WASHINGTON IRVING, *History of New York*

Men wiser and more learned than I have discovered in history a plot, a rhythm, a predetermined pattern. These harmonies are concealed from me. I can see only one emergency following upon another as wave follows upon wave; only one great fact with respect to which, since it is unique, there can be no generalizations; only one safe rule for the historian: that he should recognize in the development of human destinies the play of the contingent and the unforeseen.

—H. A. L. Fisher, Preface, *A History of Europe*

THE HISTORY OF THE POOR

[This book] surely may be considered curious as being the first attempt to publish the history of a people [the poor], from the lips of the people themselves—giving a literal description of their labor, their earnings, their trials, and their sufferings, in their own "unvarnished" language; and to portray the condition of their homes and their families by personal observation of the places, and direct communication with the individuals. . . .

It is curious, moreover, as supplying information concerning a large body of persons, of whom the public had less knowledge than of the most distant tribes of the earth—the government population returns not even numbering them among the inhabitants of the kingdom. . . .

My earnest hope is that the book may serve to give the rich a more intimate knowledge of the sufferings, and the frequent heroism under those sufferings, of the poor . . . and cause those who are in "high places," and those of whom much is expected, to bestir themselves to improve the condition of a class of people whose misery, ignorance, and vice, amidst all the immense wealth and great knowledge of "the first city in the world," is, to say the very least, a national disgrace to us.

—HENRY MAYHEW, Preface,
London Labour and the London Poor (1851)

ADOLF HITLER (1889–1945)

I learned the use of terror from the Communists, the use of slogans from the Catholic Church, and the use of propaganda from the democracies.

☐

I reduce all problems to their simplest possible formulation.

—*Mein Kampf*

ABOUT HIM

Once he had conceived an idea he was like one possessed. Nothing else existed for him—he was oblivious to time, sleep and hunger....

This seeking for a new path showed itself in dangerous fits of depression. I knew only too well those moods of his, which were in sharp contrast to his ecstatic dedication and activity.... At such times he was inaccessible, uncommunicative and distant. It might happen that we didn't meet at all for a day or two.... Adolf would wander around aimlessly and alone for days and nights in the fields and forests surrounding the town. When I met him at last, he was obviously glad to have me with him. But when I asked him what was wrong, his only answer would be, "Leave me alone," or a brusque, "I don't know myself."

—AUGUST KUBIZEK, *Young Hitler*

Adolf Hitler: a combination of initiative, perfidy, and epilepsy.

—LEON TROTSKY

How did Hitler do it? ... As [Albert] Speer says, many better, cleverer, greater men than himself succumbed to the power of Hitler's charisma. Where did the power lie? ...

Speer concludes that the sphere in which Hitler's greatness really manifested itself was psychology; as a *Menschenkenner* he had no equal. He knew men's secret vices and desires, he knew what they thought to be their virtues, he knew their hidden am-

bitions and the motives which lay behind their loves and their
hates, he knew where they could be flattered, where they were
gullible, where they were strong and where they were weak; he
knew all this, not as a psychiatrist does, by study, or empirical
observation, or sympathy, for his knowledge engendered in him
a supreme contempt for his fellow creatures; he knew it by instinct
and feeling, an intuition which in such matters never led him
astray.

It was this knowledge which explained ... the incredible story
of his rise to power, the sureness and assurance with which ...
like a sleepwalker, as he himself said, he took the most extraordinary risks and found his way through the most involved and complicated situations. ... It was an unerring sense of his enemy's inner
weaknesses which brought him his most notable military victories;
Hitler's laurels were all won in the mind, not in the field.

This knowledge of his fellow men explains his oratory. It was
of the kind that speaks neither to the mind nor to the heart of his
audience, but plays upon its nerves until they are strung to such
a pitch of intensity that they shriek for release in action. ... But
it can only be practiced by one who has a profound and subtle
understanding of the secret hopes and fears of his audience ... who
can be a conservative with the conservative, a revolutionary with
the revolutionary, a man of peace with the pacifist and a war lord
with the belligerent, and on occasions all these things at once. ...
Certainly Hitler was the greatest master of this type of oratory
there has ever been, and I have stood among 10,000 people in the
Sportspalatz in Berlin and known that everyone around me was the
victim of its spell. Who knows, if I had not been inoculated in
childhood against the tricks of oratory, I might have succumbed
myself.

—"R," *Encounter*, November 1975

Adolf Hitler, like Spengler and Toynbee, was a student of history.
Like them he ranged over the centuries and crammed such facts
as he found it convenient to select into a monstrous system. The
true facts of geography joined the rubbish of the philosophers in
his head, and he saw himself as the Phoenix of centuries, the Messiah who would roll up one age of history and open out a new.

The West, he said, was finished; but Germany was not, or at least need not be—if only it would repudiate the West. He would revive Germany by detaching it from the embraces of a dying civilization. He would breathe into it a primitive, barbarian, irrational spirit. He would wrest from Marxist Russia the leadership of the new, non-Western, noncapitalist, nonrational age and establish a new empire over the ruins of the West. To demoralize his intended victims he assured them that the iron laws of "historical necessity" were on his side; and having demoralized as many as were frightened by such words, he gathered up his forces and, in 1939, he struck.

—H. R. Trevor-Roper,
"Arnold Toynbee's Millennium," in *Encounter*, June
1957

... this bloodthirsty guttersnipe. ...
—Winston Churchill, broadcast, June 1941

[Burckhardt, former League of Nations High Commissioner in Danzig] says that Hitler is the most profoundly feminine man he has ever met, and that there are moments when he becomes almost effeminate. ... He is convinced that Hitler has no complete confidence in himself and that his actions are really governed by somnambulist certainty. ... He [Burckhardt] has never met any human being capable of generating [such] envy, vituperation and malice.

—Harold Nicolson, *The War Years: 1939–1945*

One of Hitler's greatest assets, for instance, was his awareness of positive and negative attitudes among his collaborators. I remember interviewing an early collaborator of Hitler's who provided a clue to this dimension of the Fuehrer's personality.

"For several years I was fascinated by the Fuehrer," said my informant, "and believed that the liberation of Germany from the incubus of dishonor and capitalism depended on Hitler. I was in continual contact with him in conferences, and I was usually among the small number of those who were asked to remain and talk some more. One day, to my surprise, Hitler did not ask me to remain; and I suddenly realized that for several weeks past there had been a growing sense of discomfort on my part with the Movement. I had never put it into words to myself, much less to anybody else. Hitler had sensed that there was something about me in relation to him that had changed before I knew it myself."

Hitler had early learned to gauge the slightest emotional undercurrent of those around him, doubtless as a means of playing off his mother against his father in the tense emotional atmosphere of his home.

—HAROLD D. LASSWELL, *Power and Personality*

HITLER'S PROPAGANDA

Adolf Hitler stared at the British Prime Minister [Chamberlain] in rage and astonishment. It was one of the special peculiarities of the Führer that he implicitly believed what he read in the German newspapers and heard over the German radio. He would summon his press chief, Dr. Otto Dietrich, and Propaganda Minister Joseph Goebbels and meticulously work out with them how a campaign of slander, vilification and abuse against the target of his hatred—in this case the Czechs—should be constructed; occasionally he even edited the false reports, to give them extra sensationalism and sanguinary details. Nevertheless, when he subsequently read them in print or heard them over the radio, he was horrified and appalled at the treatment defenseless Germans were subjected to by their enemies. There were no lies he believed but his own.

—LEONARD MOSLEY, *On Borrowed Time:*
How World War II Began

HOLLYWOOD

Whatever else may be alleged against the California dream factory in its palmiest days, it has given more comfort, pleasure and release from tension and anxiety to depressed millions throughout the world than all the churches, theaters, books, newspapers and psychiatric clinics put together. Hollywood may have started out travestying New York but New York very swiftly adapted itself to fit its own caricature. Once more, nature copied art.

—ALAN BRIAN, *Spectator* (London), March 1964

HORROR ALL AROUND US

... The lunatic's visions of horror are all drawn from the material of daily fact. Our civilization is founded on the shambles, and every individual existence goes out in a lonely spasm of helpless agony.. ...

Here on our very hearths and in our gardens the infernal cat plays with the panting mouse, or holds the hot bird fluttering in her jaws. Crocodiles and rattlesnakes and pythons are at this moment vessels of life as real as we are; their loathsome existence fills every minute of every day that drags its length along; and whenever they or other wild beasts clutch their living prey, the deadly horror which an agitated melancholiac feels is literally right reaction on the situation.

It may indeed be that no religious reconciliation with the absolute totality of things is possible.

—WILLIAM JAMES, *Varieties of Religious Experience*

HORSES IN THE CITY

Of the three million horses in American cities at the beginning of the twentieth century, New York had some 150,000, the healthier ones each producing between twenty and twenty-five pounds of manure a day. These dumplings were numerous on every street, attracting swarms of flies and radiating a powerful stench. The ambiance was further debased by the presence on almost every block of stables filled with urine-saturated hay.

During dry spells the pounding traffic refined the manure to dust, which blew "from the pavement as a sharp, piercing powder, to cover our clothes, ruin our furniture and blow up into our nostrils."

—OTTO L. BETTMAN, *The Good Old Days*

HUMAN DEPRAVITY

THE IK PEOPLE (CENTRAL EAST AFRICA)

If they had been mean and greedy and selfish before ... now that they had something, they really excelled themselves in what would be an insult to animals to call bestiality. The Ik had faced a conscious choice between being human and being parasites, and of course had chosen the latter.... One had to live among the Ik and see them day in and day out and watch them defecating on each other's doorsteps, and taking food out of each other's mouths, and vomiting so as to finish what belonged to the starving, to begin to know what had happened to them.

—COLIN TURNBULL, *The Mountain People*

HUMAN NATURE

Men are not flattered by being shown that there has been a difference of purpose between the Almighty and them.

—ABRAHAM LINCOLN

All human actions have one or more of these seven causes: chance, nature, compulsion, habit, reason, passion, desire.

☐

The greatest crimes are caused by surfeit, not by want. Men do not become tyrants in order that they may not suffer cold.

☐

When they are asleep you cannot tell a good man from a bad one, whence the saying that for half their lives there is no difference between the happy and the miserable.

☐

He who greatly excels in beauty, strength, birth, or wealth, and he, on the other hand, who is very poor, or very weak, or very disgraced, find it difficult to follow rational principles. Of these two, the one sort grows into violent and great criminals, the other into rogues and petty rascals.

☐

All men by nature desire to know.

☐

No one loves the man whom he fears.

☐

Men are marked from the moment of birth to rule or to be ruled.

—ARISTOTLE

The nature of man is evil. He is born with a love of gain. If he indulges this love, he will be quarrelsome and greedy, shedding all sense of courtesy or humility.

He is born with feelings of envy and hatred; and if he indulges these, they will lead him into violence and villainy, and all sense of loyalty and good faith will disappear.

Man is born with desires of the senses, and if he indulges these, he will be licentious and wanton and will observe neither propriety nor principles. . . .

If he is clever, he will surely be a robber; if he is brave, he will be a bandit; if he is able, he will cause trouble; if he is a debater, his arguments will be nonsense.

—Hsun Tzu, Chinese philosopher

If human nature were not base, but thoroughly honorable, we should in every debate have no other aim than the discovery of truth; we should not in the least care whether the truth proved to be in favor of the opinion which we had begun by expressing, or of the opinion of our adversary. . . . Our innate vanity, which is particularly sensitive in reference to our intellectual powers, will not suffer us to allow that our first position was wrong and our adversary's right. The way out of this difficulty would be simply to take the trouble always to form a correct judgment. For this a man would have to think before he spoke.

But with most men, innate vanity is accompanied by loquacity and innate dishonesty. They speak before they think; and even though they may afterward perceive that they are wrong, and that what they assert is false, they want it to seem the contrary. The interest in truth . . . gives way to the interests of vanity: And so, for the sake of vanity what is true must seem false, and what is false must seem true.

—Arthur Schopenhauer, *The Art of Controversy*

Politics is largely governed by sententious platitudes which are devoid of truth. One of the most widespread popular maxims is, "Human nature cannot be changed." No one can say whether this is true or not without first defining "human nature." . . . Among the Tibetans, one wife has many husbands, because men are too poor to support a whole wife; yet family life, according to travelers, is no more unhappy than elsewhere. The practice of lending one's wife to a guest is very common among uncivilized tribes.... Infanticide, which might seem contrary to human nature, was almost universal before the rise of Christianity, and is recommended by Plato to prevent overpopulation. Private property is not recognized among some savage tribes. Even among highly civilized people, economic considerations will override what is called "human nature."

—BERTRAND RUSSELL, *Unpopular Essays*

The man who is predominantly erotic will choose emotional relationships with others before all else; the narcissistic type, who is more self-sufficient, will seek his essential satisfactions in the inner workings of his own soul; the man of action will never abandon the external world in which he can essay his power.

—SIGMUND FREUD, *Civilization and Its Discontents*

HUMOR

Men will confess to treason, murder, arson, false teeth, or a wig. How many of them will own up to a lack of humor? The courage that could draw this confession from a man would atone for everything.

—FRANK MOORE COLBY, *The Colby Essays*

Just as we laugh harder at the jokes of someone we trust and like, great humorous authors establish with us, through their evident style and tact and general wisdom and frequent nonhumorousness, a credibility that makes our laughter, when it comes, deep and sincere. However far mechanical theories explain humor, humor cannot be mechanically produced. It is part, in literature as in life, of human exchange; and any attempt to isolate it as a genre will trivialize it. Just as our tears fatten upon our memories of joy and our dreams rehearse our waking days, laughter draws strength from the heavy atmosphere of actuality. The modes of humor in fiction are various and often lowly; but in the examples I have chosen humor coexists with the noblest qualities of imagination. These authors do not hasten toward our laughter, and the laughter they prompt does not hasten to pass judgment; rather the laughter is allied with the wonder that suspends judgment upon the world. We began by discussing the laughter of infants; perhaps one reason we laugh so much in childhood is that so much is unexpected and novel to us, and perhaps fiction revives that laughter by giving us back the world clearer than we have seen it before.

—JOHN UPDIKE,
"Laughter," in *American PEN* magazine

HUMOR: ROYAL

The mock execution of Dostoyevsky and twenty others in St. Petersburg in 1849 furnishes a better-known example of . . . [Nicholas I's] gruesome humor. After the accused had received sentence of death for offenses which included participation in a political discussion circle, the Emperor commuted their fate to imprisonment—but secretly, thinking it educative or amusing for them to go out believing that their last hour had come. In the Semyonovsky Square in St. Petersburg on 22 December the Tsar's officials and troops enacted every detail of a real execution—down to the customary drum rolls, the funereal chasuble worn by the attendant priest, and the robing of the condemned in the special white shrouds in which, for convenience of disposal, they were to meet their doom. This sadistic farce continued even after the soldiers of the firing squad had received the order to take aim at the three prisoners first scheduled for dispatch. Only when they faced the leveled muskets did another drum roll herald the announcement of the commuted sentences.

—RONALD HINGLEY, *The Tsars*

. . . A life without humor is like a life without legs. You are haunted by a sense of incompleteness, and you cannot go where your friends go. You are also somewhat of a burden. But the only really fatal thing is the shamming of humor when you have it not. There are people whom nature meant to be solemn from their cradle to their grave. They are under bonds to remain so. . . .

Solemnity is relatively a blessing, and the man who was born with it should never be encouraged to wrench himself away.

—FRANK MOORE COLBY, *op. cit.*

HUMOR AND THE LEFT

The New Left lacks humor. This is nothing new among radicals. Marx had a kind of spiteful cleverness, but not humor. Lenin could manage little freezing ironies, but not humor. Humor takes humility. A sense of humor is based on seeing and accepting human nature as stumbling, pretentious, and forever bedeviled. When I hear boys and girls call their parents "hypocrites" (a favorite word), I know I am looking at humorless—and therefore dangerous—children.

—DONALD BARR, *Who Killed Humpty-Dumpty?*

THOMAS HUXLEY (1825–1895)

As I stood behind the coffin of my little son the other day, with my mind bent on anything but disputation, the officiating minister read, as a part of his duty, the words, "If the dead rise not again, let us eat and drink, for tomorrow we die." I cannot tell you how inexpressibly they shocked me. Paul had neither wife nor child, or he must have known that his alternative involved a blasphemy against all that was best and noblest in human nature. I could have laughed with scorn. What! because I am face to face with the irreparable loss, because I have given back to the source from whence it came, the cause of a great happiness, still retaining through all my life the blessings which have sprung and will spring from that cause, I am to renounce my manhood, and, howling, grovel in bestiality? Why, the very apes know better, and if you shoot their young, the poor brutes grieve their grief out and do not immediately seek distraction in a gorge.

□

Whoso clearly appreciates all that is implied in the falling of a stone can have no difficulty about any doctrine simply on account of its marvelousness. But the longer I live, the more obvious it is to me that the most sacred act of a man's life is to say and to feel, "I believe such and such to be true." All the greatest rewards and all the heaviest penalties of existence cling about that act. The universe is one and the same throughout; and if the condition of my success in unraveling some little difficulty of anatomy or physiology is that I shall rigorously refuse to put faith in that which does not rest on sufficient evidence, I cannot believe that the great mysteries of existence will be laid open for me on other terms. It is no use to talk to me of analogies and probabilities.

—Letter to Charles Kingsley, in LEONARD HUXLEY,
Life and Letters of Thomas Huxley

THE ID

Nietzsche never had any doubt that the conscious mind is the instrument of *unconscious* vitality, and he invented the term "Id" (for the impersonal elements in the psyche subject to natural law), which Freud took over at Groddeck's suggestion.

—LANCELOT L. WHYTE,
The Unconscious Before Freud

IDEALISTS

During the Terror, the men who spilt most blood were precisely those who had the greatest desire to let their equals enjoy the golden age they had dreamt of, and who had the most sympathy with human wretchedness: optimists, idealists, and sensitive men, the greater desire they had for universal happiness the more inexorable they showed themselves.

—GEORGES SOREL, *Reflections on Violence*

An idealist is one who, upon observing that a rose smells better than a cabbage, concludes that it will also make better soup.

—H. L. MENCKEN

IDEALISTS AND REVOLUTION

The idealists who make a revolution are bound to be disappointed. ... For at best their victory never dawns on the shining new world they had dreamed of, cleansed of all human meanness. Instead it dawns on a familiar, workaday place, still in need of groceries and sewage disposal. The revolutionary state, under whatever political label, has to be run not by violent romantics but by experts in marketing, sanitary engineering, and the management of bureaucracies. For the Byrons among us, this discovery is a fate worse than death.

—JOHN FISCHER, in *Natural Enemies,*
ed. Alexander Klein

IDENTITY

One must work with children who cannot learn to say *I*, although they are otherwise healthy and beautiful ... to know what a triumph that common gift of "I" is, and how much it depends on the capacity to feel affirmed by maternal recognition. One basic task of all religions is to reaffirm that first relationship, for we have in us deep down a lifelong mistrustful remembrance of that truly *meta*-physical anxiety; *meta*—"behind," "beyond"—here means "before," "way back," "at the beginning."

—ERIK H. ERIKSON, *Young Man Luther*

IMAGINATION

There is a boundary to men's passions when they act from feeling; but none when they are under the influence of imagination.

—EDMUND BURKE, "From New to Old Whigs," in
Works, Vol. II

Imagination rules the world.

—NAPOLEON

Illusion is the first of all pleasures.

—VOLTAIRE

Were it not for imagination, a man would be as happy in the arms of a chambermaid as of a duchess.

—SAMUEL JOHNSON

Imagination is more important than knowledge.

—ALBERT EINSTEIN

To know is nothing at all; to imagine is everything.

—ANATOLE FRANCE

If the greatest philosopher in the world find himself upon a plank wider than actually necessary, but hanging over a precipice, his imagination will prevail, though his reason convince him of his safety.

—BLAISE PASCAL

Put off your imagination, as you put off your overcoat, when you enter a laboratory. But put it on again, as you put on your overcoat, when you leave.

—CHARLES BERNARD, 1865

If you look at any walls spotted with various stains or with a mixture of different kinds of stones . . . you will be able to see in it a resemblance to different landscapes adorned with mountains, rivers, rocks, trees, plains, with valleys and groups of hills. You will also be able to see combats and figures in quick movement, and strange expressions of faces, and outlandish costumes, and an infinite number of things . . . as with the sound of bells, in whose clanging you may discover every name and word you can imagine.

—LEONARDO DA VINCI, *Notebooks*

IMMORTALITY

I decline to accept the end of man. It is easy enough to say that man is immortal simply because he will endure; that when the last ding-dong of doom has clanged and faded from the last worthless rock hanging tideless in the last red and dying evening, that even then there will still be one more sound: that of his puny, inexhaustible voice, still talking. I refuse to accept this. I believe that man will not merely endure: He will prevail. He is immortal, not because he alone among creatures has an inexhaustible voice, but because he has a soul, capable of compassion and sacrifice and endurance.

—WILLIAM FAULKNER, Nobel Prize acceptance speech,
December 14, 1950

I neither deny nor affirm the immortality of man. I see no reason for believing in it, but, on the other hand, I have no means of disproving it.

Pray understand that I have no *a priori* objections to the doctrine. No man who has to deal daily and hourly with Nature can trouble himself about *a priori* difficulties. Give me such evidence as would justify me in believing anything else, and I will believe that. Why should I not? It is not half so wonderful as the conservation of force, or the indestructibility of matter.

—Thomas Huxley to Charles Kingsley, in LEONARD HUXLEY, *Life and Letters of Thomas Huxley*

I do not believe in immortality, and have no desire for it. The belief in it issues from the puerile egos of inferior men. In its Christian form it is little more than a device for getting revenge upon those who are having a better time on this earth. What the meaning of human life may be I don't know: I incline to suspect that it has none. All I know about it is that, to me at least, it is very amusing while it lasts.

... When I die I shall be content to vanish into nothingness. No show, however good, could conceivably be good forever.

—H. L. MENCKEN, letter to Will Durant, 1933

INCREDIBILITIES

AIR POWER NEGATED

There was rejoicing in Warsaw (Sept. 3, 1939) when news reached the people that Britain and France had declared war on Germany.... Everyone waited for news of the first British bombing raids on Germany.

When there were none, the Polish air attaché was dispatched, on orders from Warsaw, to see the British Air Minister, Sir Kingsley Wood, and ask that the R.A.F. immediately bomb German airfields and industrial areas. He was brushed off with the excuse that matters of higher strategy were now under discussion and that no decisions had yet been made.

Shortly afterward Leopold Amery, an influential Tory M.P., saw Kingsley Wood and suggested that the R.A.F. fly across Germany and set fire to the Black Forest with incendiary bombs, depriving Germany of timber.

"Oh, you can't do that," Kingsley Wood answered. "That's private property. You'll be asking me to bomb the Ruhr next." That was private property too.

—LEONARD MOSLEY,
On Borrowed Time: How World War II Began

THE BANQUET OF TIGELLINUS (?–69 A.D.)

The most notorious banquet of all was given by Tigellinus, on a huge raft specially built on the lake of Marcus Agrippa, a platform towed by many vessels fitted in gold and ivory. The rowers were all degenerates, of every age and perversity. The raft contained exotic birds and animals from remote countries which Tigellinus had collected, and on the quays brothels were erected and stocked with ladies of high rank and with naked prostitutes, most indecent in their postures and gesturings. The woods and nearby houses blazed with lights and echoed with singing.

—TACITUS, *The Annals of Imperial Rome*

CHURCHGOING

Henry Blount was wont to say that he did not care to have his servants goe to Church, for there servants infected one another to goe to the Alehouse and learne debauchery; but he did bid them goe to see the Executions at Tyeburne, which worke more upon them than all the oratory in the Sermons.

—JOHN AUBREY, *Brief Lives*

THE CONTRACT OF MASOCH (1836–1895)

Herr Leopold von Sacher-Masoch gives his word of honor to Frau Pistor to become her slave and to comply unreservedly for six months, with every one of her desires and commands. For her part, Frau Pistor is not to extract from him the performance of any action contrary to honor ... [and] promises to wear furs as often as possible, especially when she is in a cruel mood....

—contract signed by LEOPOLD VON SACHER-MASOCH and
FRAU FANNY PISTOR

DIPLOMATIC

On September 22 [1939], Andrei Vishinsky, Deputy People's Commissar for Foreign Affairs, summoned the Polish ambassador to the Kremlin to receive a note from the Soviet government. Shrewdly anticipating what was in it, the ambassador asked that the nature of it be revealed to him before he accepted it.

It was a proclamation of the government of the U.S.S.R. that in view of recent events, the Republic of Poland had now ceased to exist, Vishinsky replied.

"Poland will never cease to exist!" the ambassador cried, and he refused to receive the message.

For ten minutes the document was passed back and forth, until at last the ambassador angrily stomped out of the room. But by the time he reached his embassy, a messenger had arrived and was waiting for him with the note in his hand. He promptly sent the man back with it to the Kremlin.

Nothing happened for another twenty-four hours, and then the Kremlin had an inspiration. The note was dropped in a Moscow mailbox and sent to the recalcitrant Poles by ordinary post.

—LEONARD MOSLEY,
op. cit.

THE DUKE OF ALVA (1508–1583?)

Not often in history has a governor arrived to administer the affairs of a province [the Netherlands] where the whole population, three million strong, had been formally sentenced to death. As time wore on, however, he even surpassed the bloody instructions which he had received. He waved aside the recommendations of the Blood-Council to mercy; he dissuaded the monarch from attempting the path of clemency, which, for secret reasons, Philip was inclined at one period to attempt. The governor had, as he assured the king, been using gentleness in vain. . . . These words were written immediately after the massacre at Haarlem.

—JOHN LOTHROP MOTLEY,
The Rise of the Dutch Republic

HOW FRANCIS BACON DIED

Francis Bacon died, appropriately enough, in the midst of an experiment. He had gone out in a carriage on a winter day and decided suddenly to investigate the effects of cold in delaying putrefaction. He stopped his carriage, bought a hen from a cottage woman, and stuffed it full of snow. Immediately aware of having taken a chill himself, he sought the hospitality of a friend who lived nearby, and in that house he died.

It is symbolic that Bacon died in a borrowed bed. The century in which he found himself was equally borrowed, and he had no genuine place within it. One might say, if one were a student of literature, that here was Everyman engaged in that great pilgrimage which runs through the centuries.

—LOREN C. EISELEY, *Horizon*, Winter 1964

A MARRIAGE OF NERO

Nero, already corrupted by every unnatural lust, now demonstrated that still further degradations were possible for him. Only a few days later, he participated in a formal marriage to a pervert named Pythagoras, a ceremony in which the emperor, in the presence of many invited witnesses, donned the bridal veil. All the appurtenances of marriage were included: a dowry, ceremonial torches, the marriage bed—everything, indeed, in public which, at a natural union, is cloaked by the night.

—TACITUS, *The Annals of Imperial Rome*

THE PUZZLE OF TOOTHPASTE

The Duke of Marlborough would confirm that. Leaving his valet behind at Blenheim Palace, he went to stay ... as a guest in someone else's house. His hostess was surprised to hear him complain that his toothbrush "did not foam properly," so would she get him a new one. He had to be told, gently, that without the aid of toothpaste or tooth powder, usually applied for him each morning by his valet, even a new toothbrush would not foam properly.

—DAVID FROST and ANTONY JAY, *The English*

WHIMS OF THE TSARS

... One Tsar had an elephant cut to pieces for failing to bow to him, an Empress immured two of her court buffoons in a palace of ice, and a Tsar-Emperor reputedly settled arguments about the proposed route of the railway line between Moscow and St. Petersburg with a ruler and pen.

—RONALD HINGLEY, *The Tsars*

INDIA

We have always thought it strange that, while the history of the Spanish empire in America is familiarly known to all the nations of Europe, the great actions of our countrymen in the East should, even among ourselves, excite little interest. Every school-boy knows who imprisoned Montezuma, and who strangled Atahualpa. But we doubt whether one in ten, even among English gentlemen of highly cultivated minds, can tell who ... perpetrated the massacre of Patna ... or whether Holkar was a Hindoo or a Mussulman. Yet the victories of Cortes were gained over savages who had no letters, who were ignorant of the use of metals, who had not broken in a single animal to labor, who wielded no better weapons than those which could be made out of sticks, flints, and fish bones, who regarded a horse-soldier as a monster, half man and half beast, who took a harquebusier for a sorcerer, able to scatter the thunder and lightning of the skies.

The people of India, when we subdued them, were ten times as numerous as the Americans whom the Spaniards vanquished, and were at the same time quite as highly civilized as the victorious Spaniards. They had reared cities larger and fairer than Saragossa or Toledo, and buildings more beautiful and costly than the cathedral of Seville. They could show bankers richer than the richest firms of Barcelona or Cadiz, viceroys whose splendor far surpassed that of Ferdinand the Catholic, myriads of cavalry and long trains of artillery which would have astonished the Great Captain. It might have been expected, that every Englishman who takes any interest in any part of history would be curious to know how a handful of his countrymen, separated from their home by an immense ocean, subjugated, in the course of a few years, one of the greatest empires in the world. Yet, unless we greatly err, this subject is, to most readers, not only insipid, but positively distasteful.

—Thomas Babington Macaulay,
"Lord Clive," in *Critical and Historical Essays*, Vol. II,
January 1840

Does anyone doubt that if, overnight, the 500 million Indians were miraculously replaced by the same number of Swiss, India would soon be numbered among the more affluent nations?
—IRVING KRISTOL, *Wall Street Journal,* July 17, 1975

BRITISH RULE

The natives scarcely know what it is to see the gray head of an Englishman. Young men (boys almost) govern there, without society and without sympathy with the natives. . . . Animated with all the avarice of age, and all the impetuosity of youth, they roll in one after another; wave after wave; and there is nothing before the eyes of the natives but an endless, hopeless prospect of new flights of birds of prey and passage, with appetites continually renewing for a food that is continually wasting. . . .

English youth in India drink the intoxicating draught of authority and dominion before their heads are able to bear it, and as they are full grown in fortune long before they are ripe in principle, neither nature nor reason have any opportunity to exert themselves for remedy of the excesses of their premature power. . . . The cries of India are given to seas and winds to be blown about, in every breaking up of the monsoon, over a remote and unhearing ocean.

☐

Every other conqueror of every other description has left some monument, either of state, or beneficence, behind him. Were we to be driven out of India this day, nothing would remain, to tell that it had been possessed during the inglorious period of our dominion, by anything better than the orang-outang or the tiger.
—EDMUND BURKE, speech on "The East India Bill,"
House of Commons, 1788

INFERENCE

Inference is notoriously unreliable, as are eyewitnesses, memories of old men, judgments of mothers about first children, letters written for publication and garbage collectors. At the moment, I drive a much-battered 1954 Cadillac, full of wayward lurchings, unidentifiable rattles, and unpredictable ways upon the road. Recently I shifted a shovel, which I carry in the trunk . . . to a new position. No sooner had I closed the lid than a new and penetrating noise arose from the back of the car which clearly was a metal shovel bouncing about within a trunk. My inference was that this was so, and for a week I drove without investigating the noise. Then the gas tank fell off, proving my inference wrong. The reader may infer that I plan to use the royalties from this book to buy a new car. If he does, he will be right.

—ROBIN W. WINKS, *The Historian as Detective*

INGENUITIES

Few policemen are as lucky as the Indian police officer who, faced with an angry mob in the Punjab, fired into a bee swarm in a nearby tree, causing the infuriated bees to attack and quickly scatter the mob.

—ANTHONY MARTIENSSEN, *Crime and the Police*

Sometimes the [Caucasian] village doctors succeeded in clamping shut the torn arteries by means of applying a large, ferocious species of local ant. Once the pincer-like mandibles had fastened on the arteries, the rest of the ant's body was snipped off—the pincers remained in place. The gaping wound was bound up, herbs were applied, and no blood poisoning followed.

—LESLEY BLANCH, *The Sabres of Paradise*

One, of my acquaintance, worked with Marine intelligence during World War II. He was asked to help judge how many Japanese had dug in on one of the strategically crucial South Pacific islands, an island which the Marine Corps planned to make their own, whatever the losses, within a few days. No Japanese could be seen from aerial reconnaissance, since their camouflage was nearly perfect. The historian provided an accurate figure, however, for he noted from aerial photographs that particularly dark patches could be identified as latrines, and upon consulting a captured Japanese manual, he learned how many latrines were to be dug per unit of men. The rest was so simple a matter of calculation that even the historian could provide an answer without the aid of a computer.

—ROBIN W. WINKS, *op. cit.*

PALESTINE (15TH CENTURY)

You will find people lying in wait on the road who are hidden in sand up to their necks. They go two or three days without food or drink, and put a stone in front of them, so they can see other people who cannot see them. And when they see a caravan rather smaller and weaker than their own, they go out and call their fellows and ride on their horses, swift as leopards, with bamboo lances topped with iron in their hands. . . . They also carry a mace in their hands . . . and they ride naked with only a shirt upon them, without trousers or shoes or spurs. They come upon the caravans suddenly and take everything, even the clothes and horses, and sometimes they kill them.

> —Rabbi Meshullam ben R. Menaham of Volterra
> (1481), in *Jewish Travellers*, ed. Elkan N. Adler

INTELLECT

Life, then, is not for the sake of intellect, science or culture, but the reverse: Intellect, science and culture have no other reality than that which belongs to them as tools for living. . . . The moment intelligence becomes deified and thought of as the only thing not needing justification, it is left without justification. Intelligence thus hangs, in mid-air, rootless, at the mercy of two hostile forces: sanctimony and insolence.

> —José Ortega y Gasset, *Man and Crisis*

The voice of the intellect is soft, but does not rest until it has gained a hearing. After endlessly repeated rebuffs, it succeeds. This is one of the few places in which one may be optimistic about the future of mankind.

> —Sigmund Freud, *The Future of an Illusion*

Intellectuals cannot tolerate the chance event, or the unintelligible; they have a nostalgia for the absolute, for a universally comprehensive scheme.

> —Raymond Aron

INTELLECTUALS AND LABOR

Labor never craved intellectual leadership but intellectuals invaded labor politics. They had an important contribution to make: they verbalized the movement, supplied theories and slogans for it—Class War is an excellent example—made it conscious of itself, and in doing so changed its meaning.

—JOSEPH A. SCHUMPETER,
Capitalism, Socialism and Democracy

INTELLECTUALS AND POWER

The increased power of intellectuals is a mixed blessing.... Intellectuals, or at least highly intellectual people, are necessary to running the world. Unfortunately, the intellectual does not necessarily have other equally useful attributes, such as courage, decisiveness ... and common sense. He may tend to believe more in the image of the world transmitted to him through books and other media than in the real world as it exists.

This is one aspect of what we call *educated incapacity*, a problem which is going to become much more serious as the power of intellectuals in the world continues to gain and spread.

—HERMAN KAHN and B. BRUCE-BRIGGS,
Things to Come

The masses have not always felt themselves to be frustrated and exploited. But the intellectuals who formulated their views for them have always told them that they were, without necessarily meaning anything precise.

—JOSEPH A. SCHUMPETER, *op. cit.*

INTUITION AND SCIENCE

The supreme task of the physicist is to arrive at those universal elementary laws for which the cosmos can be built up by pure deduction. There is no logical path to these laws; only intuition, resting on sympathetic understanding of experience, can reach them.

—ALBERT EINSTEIN, in Infeld, *Einstein*

Intuition is the source of scientific knowledge.

—ARISTOTLE, *Metaphysics*

JAMAICA

"HONEYED TORPOR"

Between the founding of New Seville and the British conquest one hundred and forty-five years later, Jamaica seemed to impose its own honeyed torpor on the Spaniards. This insiduous, and unquenchable, quietude is the constant factor at every stage of the Jamaican equation. How much of this is due to climate alone, how much due to climate plus a landscape which seems to indulge the senses like the palm of a gigantic maternal hand, how much due to climate and landscape plus historical circumstance, nobody could assess properly. It exists, and the energetic or ardent soul can no more dismiss its influence than a man who wants to keep awake can deny the power of those languid, golden arcs traced by a hypnotist's watch. One can be as ambitious, creative and purposeful here as anywhere else—more so perhaps because one is never depleted by any demands of climate or geography—but one has to achieve these states by a special effort of will.

Certainly the Spanish settlers never seemed to have made this overreaching gesture. At a time when their compatriots were establishing miracles of empire on the mainland, when Hispaniola was enjoying the reach-me-down glitter of a Viceregal court, when Cuba, only ninety miles north, was awarding quite respectable degrees in law and theology, the Jamaican Spaniard reverted to a level of rustic simplicity scarcely distinguishable from simple-mindedness. . . .

Spanish Jamaica must have been a consoling bed in which to dream. Even for the Negro slaves.

—IAN FLEMING, *Introducing Jamaica*

JAPAN

THE CODE

The basis of this code was not godliness, or abstract honesty, or abstract purity, but . . . "*shinyo.*" *Shinyo* means trust, confidence, reliability. It is the goal of a social morality. To have *shinyo* is to be a man of honor, who fulfills commitments at whatever cost and whose trust in his neighbors is reciprocated by their confidence in him. . . .

This system of contracts and commitments threads its way like a giant steel web through every segment of Japanese society. The web binds the individual in all directions—upwards to parents, ancestors, superior officers, downwards to children, employees and servants. Classically, it has only been by achieving equilibrium inside this web that the Japanese finds peace. Like the sinner in the old Buddhist fable, he reaches out from the depths to clutch the fine, but binding, strands of the web of Heaven. Holding on to them, he is safe. Once he slips from the web, or loses his place in it, he falls back, doomed, into the void of *Jigoku*, the Buddhist hell. There is no more chance for redemption.

—FRANK GIBNEY, *Five Gentlemen of Japan*

ETIQUETTE

Wrinkling [in wrapping] must be avoided, the folding should be precise. Ordinarily the paper is wrapped so that the last fold comes on top of the package at the right-hand edge with the end of the paper extending all the way to the left-hand edge of the package.

For unhappy occasions, however, the wrapping is reversed, with the last fold on the top of the package at the left-hand edge and the end of the paper extending all the way to the right-hand edge of the package. One must be very careful about how the paper is folded for people who are very sensitive about it. . . .

Gifts with a red and white cord should be tied so that the red cord is on the right; and when using the gold and silver cord, the gold should be on the right.

—World Fellowship Committee of the YMCA,
Tokyo, *Japanese Etiquette: An Introduction*

IMPERTURBABILITY

The "Oriental imperturbability" of the Japanese is an illusion and a myth. They are imperturbable enough as long as they are not properly roused. But when roused they are able to fly into the most spectacular rages and the consequences are unpredictable....

An English friend of mine, a bachelor, once asked his Japanese housekeeper to fetch some salt. This seemingly trivial request set off a terrific explosion. The girl wept and lamented vociferously ... her complaint being that by asking for the salt, her employer had been rude enough to point out that she had forgotten it. At the climax of her paroxysm she stormed out of the house, still in a state of uncontrollable fury. Two hours later she returned as calm as an angel and courteous as a geisha. The whole matter would never have been mentioned again had not my friend, five months later, been foolish enough to ask where his shoes were....

—GEORGE MIKES, *The Land of the Rising Yen*

POVERTY

Poverty has even been regarded as a virtue, since it could not have been avoided in a country which is basically poor.

There is a popular song which has been sung throughout Japan for the last 100 years, particularly at graduation exercises.... The song is sung to the melody of "Auld Lang Syne" and starts with saying that "students have over the years been diligently poring over books by the light of fireflies and by the glow of white fallen snow which comes through the windows."

In days gone by, people caught fireflies and kept them in a cage, both to admire and possibly to use as a substitute for a candle.

—ICHIRO KAWASAKI, *Japan Unmasked*

SMILING

The smile is often seen when the Japanese are talking among themselves. They do not like to be positive in expressing their thoughts or opinions. (They are not incapable of it, although the character of the Japanese language has something to do with this.)

To give an extreme example, the Japanese, instead of saying "Yes" or "No" outright, may show a kind of smile in order to avoid hurting the feelings of others by clearly saying "Yes or "No.". . .

They show the smile in order to avoid hurting other people's feelings and to avoid conflict among people as much as possible. Especially when we take into account the fact that Japan is densely populated, the smile is a necessary virtue in a meddlesome society.

—*Here Is Japan*, guidebook published by Asahi
Broadcasting Corporation

TELEPHONE NUMBERS

The Japanese . . . have numbers that mean good luck, wealth, bankruptcy, and death. This fact complicates the Japanese telephone system. Good numbers bring a high price, unlucky ones are palmed off on foreigners.

—EDWARD T. HALL, *The Silent Language*

THE JAPANESE

When the moon is beautiful they hold parties for moon-viewing, and admire snow when it snows.

□

What 110 Means on Japanese Telephone Dial?

In Japan, wherever you are, whether in a big city or in the country, you can get in touch with the police by just dialing 110.

By dialing 110 a patrol car will come rushing to your help sounding a siren within three minutes. [Do] not forget to tell the police where you are, since it is impossible for the Japanese police, though very efficient, to check up the place of an incident within three minutes without being informed of it.

—*Here Is Japan*, guidebook published by Asahi
Broadcasting Corporation

THE ORNATE

Letter-writing remains Victorian in its conventions. A reminder to pay a bill or an announcement that a new man has joined a bank's board of directors are equal occasions for obligatory opening remarks. . . .

"Now that spring promises to come," the letter begins, "the first buds of the cherry blossoms can be descried climbing the far-off mountain. Although we hesitate to break in on your very busy schedule, troubled as you are with many worthy pursuits, it is time that necessity compels us to remind you that your firm's indebtedness . . ."

—FRANK GIBNEY, "The Japanese and Their Language," in *Encounter*, March 1975

THOMAS JEFFERSON (1743-1826)

Nero wished all the necks of Rome united in one, that he might sever them at a blow. So our ex-Federalists, wishing to have a single representative of all the objects of their hatred, honor me with that post, and exhibit against me such atrocities as no nation had ever before heard or endured. I shall protect them in the right of lying and calumniating.

—letter, 1803; in Saul K. Padover, *Jefferson*

I doubt whether the people of this country would suffer an execution for heresy, or a three years imprisonment for not comprehending the mysteries of the trinity. But is the spirit of the people an infallible, permanent reliance? Is it government? . . . The spirit of the times may alter, will alter. Our rulers will become corrupt, our people careless. A single zealot may commence persecutor, and better men be his victims. It can never be too often repeated, that the time for fixing every essential right on a legal basis is while our rulers are honest, and ourselves united.

—JEFFERSON, *Notes on Virginia*, 1782

I find the pain of a little censure, even when unfounded, more acute than the pleasure of much praise.

—JEFFERSON, to Francis Hopkinson

I have sworn upon the altar of God, eternal hostility against every form of tyranny over the mind of man.

—JEFFERSON, letter to Benjamin Rush, 1800

ABOUT HIM

He was a man of profound ambition and violent passions.
> —ALEXANDER HAMILTON, letter to Carrington, 1792

... he had no belief in a future existence. ... All his ideas of obligation ... were under no stronger guarantee than the laws of the
land and the opinions of the world. This tendency upon a mind of
great compass and powerful resources is to produce insincerity and
duplicity, which were his besetting sins through life.
> —JOHN QUINCY ADAMS, Diary, January 11, 1831

The principles of Jefferson are the axioms of a free society.
> —ABRAHAM LINCOLN, letter, April 6, 1859

Jefferson was the most resourceful politician of his time. For
every problem he had a solution. He teemed with ideas. These
were his shock troops. ... Like the wiser of the modern bosses, he
knew the virtues of silence. When in doubt, he said nothing—to
his foes. It was impossible to smoke him out when he preferred to
stay in. In the midst of abuse he was serene. ...

He was never too big for the small essential things, and he was
a master of detail—very rarely true of men of large views. His
energy was dynamic and he was tireless. He never rested on his
arms or went into winter quarters. His fight was endless. The real
secret of his triumph, however, is found in the reason given by one
of his biographers: "He enjoyed a political vision penetrating
deeper down into the inevitable movement of popular government, and farther forward into the future of free institutions than
was possessed by any other man in public life in his day." ...

In his power of self-control Jefferson had another advantage.
... There was something uncanny in his capacity to simulate
ignorance of the hate that often encompassed him. To the most
virulent of his foes he was the pink of courtesy. He mastered
others by mastering himself. And because he was master of himself, he had another advantage—he kept his judgment clear as to
the capacity and character of his opponents.

One may search in vain through the letters of Hamilton for
expressions other than those of contemptuous belittlement of his

political foes. Jefferson never made that mistake. He conceded Hamilton's ability and admired it. Visitors at Monticello, manifesting surprise at finding busts by Ceracchi of Hamilton and Jefferson, facing each other across the hall, elicited the smiling comment—"opposite in death as in life." There never would have been a bust of Jefferson at [Hamilton's] "The Grange."

Through the long years of estrangement with Adams, Jefferson kept the way clear for the restoration of their old relations. Writing Madison of Adams's faults, he emphasized his virtues and lovable qualities. When the bitter battles of their administrations were in the past and a mutual friend wrote that the old man in Quincy had said, "I always loved Jefferson and always shall," he said, "That is enough for me," and set to work to revive the old friendship.... This capacity for keeping his judgment clear of the benumbing fumes of prejudice concerning the qualities of his enemies was one of the strong points of his leadership.

—CLAUDE G. BOWERS, *Jefferson and Hamilton*

JUDGE GEORGE JEFFREYS (1644–1689)—"THE HANGING JUDGE" OF THE KING'S BENCH, ENGLAND

All tenderness for the feelings of others, all self respect, all sense of the becoming, were obliterated from his mind.... The profusion of maledictions and vituperative epithets which composed his vocabulary could hardly have been rivaled in the fishmarket or the beer-garden....

The glare of his eyes had a fascination for the unhappy victim on whom they were fixed.... His yell of fury, it was said by one who had often heard it, sounded like the thunder of judgment day.... Already might be remarked in him the most odious vice which is incident to human nature, a delight in misery merely as misery. There was a fiendish exultation in the way in which he pronounced sentence on offenders. Their weeping and imploring seemed to titillate him voluptuously; and he loved to scare them into fits by dilating with luxuriant amplification on all the details of what they were to suffer....

His enemies could not deny that he possessed some of the qualities of a great judge.... He had one of those happily constituted intellects which, across labyrinths of sophistry, and through masses of immaterial facts, go straight to the true point. Of his intellect, however, he seldom had the full use. Even in civil causes his malevolent and despotic temper perpetually disordered his judgment. To enter his court was to enter the den of a wild beast, which none could tame, and which was as likely to be roused to rage by caresses as by attacks. He frequently poured forth on plaintiffs and defendants, barristers and attorneys . . . torrents of frantic abuse, intermixed with oaths and curses. . . . His reason was overclouded and his evil passions stimulated by the fumes of intoxication. His evenings were ordinarily given to revelry. . . . He was constantly surrounded on such occasions by buffoons selected, for the most part, from among the vilest pettifoggers who practiced before him. These men bantered and abused each other for his entertainment. He joined in their ribald talk, sang catches with them, and, when his head grew hot, hugged and kissed them in an ecstasy of drunken fondness. . . .

He often came to the judgment seat . . . having but half slept off his debauch, his cheeks on fire, his eyes staring like those of a maniac. . . . Not the least odious of his many odious peculiarities was the pleasure which he took in publicly browbeating and mortifying those whom, in his fits of maudlin tenderness, he had encouraged to presume on his favor. . . .

The brokenhearted widows and destitute orphans of the laboring men whose corpses hung at the cross roads were called upon by the agents of the Treasury to explain what had become of a basket, of a goose, of a flitch of bacon, of a keg of cider, of a sack of beans. . . . While the humble retainers of the government were pillaging the families of the slaughtered peasants, the Chief Justice (Jeffreys) was fast accumulating a fortune out of the plunder of a higher class of Whigs. He traded largely in pardons. His most lucrative transaction of this kind was with a gentleman named Edmund Prideaux. . . . Mercy was offered to some prisoners on condition that they would bear evidence against Prideaux. The unfortunate man lay long in gaol, and at length, overcome by fear of the gallows, consented to pay fifteen thousand pounds for his liberation. This great sum was received by Jeffreys. He bought with it an estate, to which people gave the name of Aceldama, from the accursed field which was purchased with the price of innocent blood.

—Thomas Babington Macaulay,
History of England from the Accession of James II

JERUSALEM CRUSHED

[Jerusalem]: With the blocking of all the exits [by Romans 70 A.D.], all hope of safety was cut off for the Jews. In every house and family the deepening famine consumed the people. Rooms were filled with the bodies of women and children, alleys with the corpses of old men. Boys and young men, their bodies swollen, wandered like ghosts through the city and fell dead. Sufferers lacked the strength to bury their families, and the strong hesitated because of the multitude of the dead and their own uncertain fate. Indeed, many collapsed and died on the bodies of those whom they were burying; and many went to their graves before the need arose.

Amid these misfortunes, neither wailing nor lamentation was heard. Men in the pain of dying gazed dry-eyed upon those who had found respite before them. Deep silence and death-filled night enshrouded all the city.

Worse, were the robbers. They broke into houses as if into tombs. They despoiled the corpses, stripped the clothes from the dead, and laughed as they went away. They tested the points of their swords on the bodies of those who had collapsed, and to try out their steel ran through some of the fallen who were still alive. Some Jews begged from them the kindness of a mortal blow, but such the rioters abandoned with contempt to the famine, and they died with their eyes fixed on the Temple.

Orders were issued because of the unbearable stench, that all corpses be buried at public expense. But later, this became unfeasible and they cast the bodies from the walls into the trenches.

Titus [Commander of the war against the Jews], while walking around the trenches, saw them filled with corpses from which a thick gore oozed, and he groaned and raised up his hands and called upon God to witness that this was not his doing.

—Josephus, *Antiquities*, Book V

JEWS

Certainly the heroism of the defenders of every other creed fades into insignificance before this martyr people, who for thirteen centuries confronted all the evils that the fiercest fanaticism could devise, enduring obloquy and spoliation, the violation of the dearest ties and the infliction of the most hideous sufferings, rather than abandon their faith. . . .

While . . . the intellect of Christendom, enthralled by countless superstitions, had sunk into a deadly torpor in which all love of enquiry and all search for truth were abandoned, the Jews were still pursuing the path of knowledge, amassing learning, and stimulating progress with the same unflinching constancy that they manifested in their strength.

—W. E. H. LECKY,
The Rise and Influence of Rationalism in Europe,
Vol. II

The Jews hunted out of Spain in 1492 were in turn cruelly expelled from Portugal. Some took refuge on the African coast. Eighty years later the descendants of the men who had committed or allowed these enormities were defeated in Africa, whither they had been led by their king, Dom Sebastian. Those who were not slain were offered as slaves at Fez to the descendants of the Jewish exiles from Portugal. "The humbled Portuguese nobles," the historian narrates, "were comforted when their purchasers proved to be Jews, for they knew that they had humane hearts."

—MORRIS JOSEPH, "Judaism as Creed and Life"

If the statisics are right, the Jews constitute but *one percent* of the human race. It suggests a nebulous dim puff of star dust lost in the blaze of the Milky Way. Properly the Jew ought hardly to be heard of; but he is heard of, has always been heard of. He is as prominent on the planet as any other people. . . . His contributions to the world's list of great names in literature, science, art, music, finance, medicine, and abstruse learning are also away out of proportion to the weakness of his numbers. He has made a marvelous fight in this world, in all the ages; and has done it with his hands tied behind him. He could be vain of himself, and be excused for it.

The Egyptian, the Babylonian, and the Persian rose, filled the planet with sound and splendor, then faded to dream-stuff and passed away; the Greek and the Roman followed, and made a vast noise, and they are gone; other peoples have sprung up and held their torch high for a time, but it burned out, and they sit in twilight now, or have vanished. The Jew saw them all, beat them all, and is now what he always was, exhibiting no decadence, no infirmities of age, no weakening of his parts, no slowing of his energies, no dulling of his alert and aggressive mind. All things are mortal but the Jew; all other forces pass, but he remains. What is the secret of his immortality?

—MARK TWAIN, "Concerning the Jews," in *Harper's*,
September 1899

This mysterious knowledge it was that united the Jews and smelted them together, nothing else. For this mysterious knowledge was the meaning of the Book.

The Book; yes, their Book. They had no state, holding them together, no country, no soil, no king, no form of life in common. If, in spite of this, they were one, more one than all the other peoples of the world, it was the Book that sweated them into unity. Brown, white, black, yellow Jews, large and small, splendid and in rags, godless and pious, they might crouch and dream all their lives in a quiet room, or fare splendidly in a radiant, golden whirlwind over the earth, but sunk deep in all of them was the lesson of the Book. . . .

They had dragged the Book with them through two thousand years. It was to them race, state, home, inheritance and possessions. They had given it to all peoples, and all peoples had embraced it. But its only legitimate possessors, knowers and judges, were they alone.

—LION FEUCHTWANGER, *Power*

AS SCAPEGOATS

Plainly the Jew was available as the symbol which more than any other could be utilized as a target of irrelevant emotional drives. The hatred of the country for the city, of the aristocracy for the plutocracy, of the middle class for the manual toilers and the aristocracy and the plutocracy could be displaced upon the Jew. The frustrations of economic adversity and international humiliation, guilt from immorality, guilt from diminishing piety—these stresses within the lives of Germans were available to be exploited in political action.

—HAROLD D. LASSWELL,
Politics—Who Gets What, When, How

SAMUEL JOHNSON (1709–1784)

[Boswell] would have made his hero as contemptible as he made himself, had not his hero really possessed some moral and intellectual qualities of a very high order. The best proof that Johnson was really an extraordinary man is that his character, instead of being degraded, has . . . been decidedly raised by a work in which all his vices and weaknesses are exposed . . . unsparingly.

Johnson in the fulness of his fame . . . is better known to us than any other man in history. Everything about him, his coat, his wig, his figure, his face, his scrofula, his St. Vitus's dance, his rolling walk, his blinking eye . . . his insatiable appetite for fish-sauce and veal-pie with plums, his inextinguishable thirst for tea, his trick of touching the posts as he walked, his mysterious practice of treasuring up scraps of orange-peel, his morning slumbers, his midnight disputations, his contortions, his mutterings, his gruntings, his puffings, his . . . eloquence, his sarcastic wit, his vehemence, his insolence, his fits of tempestuous rage, his queer intimates . . . all are as familiar to us as the objects by which we have been surrounded from childhood.

—THOMAS BABINGTON MACAULAY,
"Boswell's Life of Johnson,"
Critical and Historical Essays (Trevelyan Edition),
Vol. I

JOHN PAUL JONES (1747–1792)

The reason for Jones's loneliness is clear to anyone who has followed his career. It was his colossal egotism. Paul Jones was never deeply interested in anybody except Paul Jones, or in anything except a navy as a projection of his talents and expectations. His voluminous letters and memorials contain hardly a line on anything not relating to one or the other. One looks in vain for comments on people, places and events. He traversed Russia twice from St. Petersburg to the Black Sea, and during his winter of inactivity at the capital he had plenty of time to write his impressions of that country in a most interesting period of its history. But we have no line from him even on the splendors of the Hermitage and Tsarskoe-Selo. He lived in Paris during two of the most stirring years of the French Revolution, which failed to arouse even his curiosity. His egotism also made Jones bitter over not receiving the credit and the awards to which he believed himself entitled; notably, over his low place on the seniority list of 1776, his receiving no thanks for the capture of H.M.S. *Drake*, and the third-rate decoration for his work in the Liman.

—SAMUEL ELIOT MORISON, *John Paul Jones*

JULIUS II (Giuliano della Rovere, pope from 1503–1513)

Giuliano della Rovere was one of the strongest personalities that ever reached the papal chair. A massive head bent with exhaustion and tardy humility, a wide high brow, a large pugnacious nose, grave, deep-set, penetrating eyes, lips tight with resolution, hands heavy with the rings of authority, face somber with the disillusionments of power: This is the man who for a decade kept Italy in war and turmoil, freed it from foreign armies, tore down the old St. Peter's, brought Bramante and a hundred other artists to Rome, discovered ... and directed Michelangelo and Raphael, and through them gave to the world a new St. Peter's and the Sistine Chapel ceiling, and the *stanze* of the Vatican. ...

His violent temper presumably characterized him from his first breath. Born near Savona (1443) a nephew of Sixtus IV, he reached the cardinalate at twenty-seven, and fumed and fretted in it for thirty-three years before being promoted to what had long seemed to him his manifest due. He paid no more regard to his vow of celibacy than most of his colleagues; his master of ceremonies at the Vatican later reported that Pope Julius would not allow his foot to be kissed because it was disfigured *ex morbo gallico*—with the French disease. He had three illegitimate daughters, but was too busy fighting Alexander [VI] to find time for the unconcealed parental fondness that in Alexander so offended the cherished hypocrisies of mankind. He disliked Alexander as a Spanish intruder, denied his fitness for the papacy, called him a swindler and a usurper, and did all he could to unseat him, even to inviting France to invade Italy.

He seemed made as a foil and contrast to Alexander. The Borgia Pope was jovial, sanguine, good-natured (if we except a possible poisoning or two); Julius was stern, Jovian, passionate, impatient, readily moved to anger, passing from one fight to another, never really happy except at war.

—WILL DURANT, *The Renaissance*, Ch. XVII

JURIES

A jury too often has at least one member more ready to hang the panel than to hang the traitor.

—ABRAHAM LINCOLN

... the horrible thing about all legal officials, even the best, about all judges, magistrates, barristers, detectives, and policemen, is not that they are wicked (some of them are good), not that they are stupid (several of them are quite intelligent), it is simply that they have got used to it.

Strictly they do not see the prisoner in the dock; all they see is the usual man in the usual place. They do not see the awful court of judgment; they only see their own workshop. Therefore, the instinct of Christian civilization has most wisely declared that into their judgments there shall upon every occasion be infused fresh blood and fresh thoughts from the streets. Men shall come in who can see the court and the crowd, and the coarse faces of the policemen and the professional criminals, the wasted faces of the wastrels, the unreal faces of the gesticulating counsel, and see it all as one sees a new picture of a play hitherto unvisited.

—G. K. CHESTERTON, *Selected Essays*

JUSTICE

Matters should be managed, not only with justice, but with the appearance of justice, and very often the appearance of justice is as important as the substance of justice.

—A. J. NOCK, *Memoirs of a Superfluous Man*

It is as much the duty of government to render prompt justice against itself, in favor of citizens, as it is to administer the same between private individuals.

—ABRAHAM LINCOLN

Justice is only that which the strongest choose to call by that name.

—ARISTOTLE

Injustice is relatively easy to bear: what stings is justice.

—H. L. MENCKEN

It is by this tribunal that statesmen who abuse their power are accused by statesmen, and tried by statesmen, not upon the niceties of a narrow jurisprudence, but upon the enlarged and solid principles of state morality. It is here that those who by abuse of power have violated the spirit of law can never hope for protection from and of its forms. . . . It is here that those who have refused to conform themselves to its perfections can never hope to escape through any of its defects.

—EDMUND BURKE, opening the trial of Warren Hastings in the House of Lords, February 15, 1788

HELEN KELLER (1880–1968)

The change which occurred after Anne Sullivan began my education still causes me to thrill and glow. It was not a child that confronted her, but an animal utterly ignorant of itself, its feelings and its place among human beings. For some time I was still devoid of a world—I had no sense of my own identity of time or unity or diversity, but Anne Sullivan did not let such details discourage her. She treated me exactly like a seeing, hearing child, substituting hand-spelling for the voice and the eye from which other children learn language. She encouraged me to observe all objects I could reach with my three senses, so that I could relate them bit by bit with the things which surrounded me and gain from them analogies with sight and hearing. She helped me to enrich my vocabulary through the flow of words from her fingers, through association and books to build a world in which color and sound took their place, even though I could not perceive them. That is how it happens that I am aware of sympathies with the seeing, hearing race.

☐

Ideas constitute the world each of us lives in, and impressions are a wellspring of ideas. My outer world, wrought out of the sensations of touch, smell and taste, breathes and throbs because I have a thinking mind and a feeling soul. While others look and listen, I use my tactile faculty to secure information, entertainment and activity in which I have a share. In all I do and think I am conscious of a hand. People dependent upon their eyes and ears seldom realize how many things are tangible. Objects that can be touched are round or flat, broken or symmetrical, flexible or stiff, solid or liquid, and these qualities are modified ad infinitum.

Also I perceive the flow of straight and curved lines and their endless variety on all surfaces—regular or uneven, swelling, rough or smooth. In rocks full of grooves, jagged edges and lichens, in the queenliness of the rose and the velvet of a well-groomed horse's neck, the manifold shapes of young trees, bushes, and grasses I find eloquent witness to the glory that once trickled into the seeing hand of the Greek, the Japanese and the South Sea Islander.

Again, with the skin of my face and nose I notice different atmospherical conditions. . . . In wintertime I recognize a cold sun, and the rain is chill and odorless. The rain of spring is warm, vital and fragrant. The air of midsummer is heavy and damp or dry and burning, and so the changes of weather go on. . . .

I perceive countless vibrations from which I learn much about everyday happenings. In the house I feel footsteps, noises of the broom, the hammer and the saw, the dishes as they are removed from the table, the excited bark of . . . my Alsatian, when somebody comes to the door. Footsteps vary tactually according to the age, the sex and the manners of the walker. The child's patter is unlike the tread of a grown person. The springy step of youth differs from the sedate walk of the middle-aged and from the gait of the old man whose feet drag along the floor. In persons whom I know I detect many moods and the traits in their walk —energy or laziness, firmness or hesitation, weariness, impatience or distress. Thus I am aware to some extent of the actions of those around me.

—HELEN KELLER, *The World Through Three Senses*

MUSTAFA KEMAL ("ATATURK") (1881–1938)

Mustafa Kemal's policy was to aim at nothing short of an out-and-out conversion of Turkey to the Western way of life; and in the nineteen-twenties he put through in Turkey what was perhaps as revolutionary a program as has ever been carried out in any country deliberately and systematically in so short a span of time. It was as if, in our Western world, the Renaissance, the Reformation, the secularist scientific mental revolution at the end of the seventeenth century, the French Revolution, and the Industrial Revolution had all been telescoped into a single lifetime and been made compulsory by law. In Turkey the emancipation of women, the disestablishment of the Islamic religion, and the substitution of the Latin alphabet for the Arabic alphabet as the script for conveying the Turkish language were all enacted between 1922 and 1928.

—ARNOLD J. TOYNBEE, *The World and the West*

JOHN F. KENNEDY (1917–1963)

If a free society cannot help the many who are poor, it cannot save the few who are rich.

—Inaugural address, 1961

All my life I've known better than to depend on the experts. How could I have been so stupid, to let them [the military] go ahead?

☐

Defeat is an orphan; victory has a hundred fathers.

—after the Bay of Pigs, April 1961

We are confronted primarily with a moral issue. It is as old as the Scriptures and is as clear as the American Constitution. The heart of the question is whether all Americans are to be afforded equal rights and equal opportunities; whether we are going to treat our fellow Americans as we want to be treated.

If an American, because his skin is dark, cannot eat lunch in a restaurant open to the public; if he cannot send his children to the best public school available; if he cannot vote for the public officials who represent him; if, in short, he cannot enjoy the full and free life which all of us want, then who among us would be content to have the color of his skin changed and stand in his place?

Who among us would then be content with the counsels of patience and delay? One hundred years of delay have passed since President Lincoln freed the slaves, yet their heirs, their grandsons, are not fully free. They are not yet freed from the bonds of injustice; they are not yet freed from the social and economic oppression.

And this nation, for all its hopes and all its boasts, will not be fully free until all its citizens are free.

—broadcast, June 11, 1963

ABOUT HIM

John Kennedy of Massachusetts: Elegant and casual, he sat in the back row [of the Senate], his knees against his desk, rapping his teeth with a pencil and reading the *Economist* and the *Guardian*. He was treated with affection by most senators, but he was ultimately elusive, finding his way in other worlds outside the chamber. Mythically wealthy, handsome, bright, and well connected, he seemed to regard the Senate grandees as impressive but tedious. In turn, he was regarded by them as something of a playboy, a dilettante. His voting record was moderate and sometimes conservative, especially on trade and agricultural matters. He was not a prime mover in the Senate; only once in early 1960, in handling a labor-management bill, did he seem to emerge as a leader, a *mensch*.

—HARRY MCPHERSON, *A Political Education*

The celebrated Kennedy Inaugural, which sounded so well in 1961, does not read so well today. "Let every nation know, whether it wishes us well or ill, that we shall pay any price, bear any burden, meet any hardship, support any friend, oppose any foe to assure the survival and success of liberty. This much we pledge and more."

Liberty everywhere and anywhere at any price? This is not a rational policy for a nation, even a big one. It is, to speak bluntly, pernicious bombast which, as the applause dies down, can only mislead friend and foe alike. For no nation can or will pay *any* price for liberty *anywhere* except, at the most heroic, for its homeland.
—WALTER LIPPMANN, *Newsweek*, January 13, 1969

In a much quoted passage in his inaugural address, President Kennedy said, "Ask not what your country can do for you—ask what you can do for your country." . . .

The free man will ask neither what his country can do for him nor what he can do for his country. He will ask rather "What can I and my compatriots do through government" to help us discharge our individual responsibilities, to achieve our several goals and purposes, and above all, to protect our freedom? And he will accompany this question with another: How can we keep the government we create from becoming a Frankenstein that will destroy the very freedom we establish it to protect?
—MILTON FRIEDMAN, *Capitalism and Freedom*

KINGS

What kind of office must that be in a government which requires for its execution neither experience nor ability, that may be abandoned to the desperate chance of birth, that may be filled by an idiot, a madman, a tyrant, with equal effect as by the good, the virtuous, and the wise? An office of this nature is a mere nothing; it is a place of show, not of use. Let France, then, having reached the age of reason, no longer be deluded by the sound of words, and let her deliberately examine if a King, however insignificant and contemptible in himself, may not at the same time be extremely dangerous.
—THOMAS PAINE, *The Rights of Man*

That was an apt and true reply given to Alexander the Great by a pirate who had been seized. For when the king asked the pirate what he meant by keeping stolen possessions of the sea, he answered with bold pride, "What thou meanest by seizing the whole earth. But because I do it with a petty ship, I am called a robber, whilst thou, who doest it with a great fleet, art called Emperor."

—St. Augustine

A king is an ordinary kind of man who has to live in a very extraordinary kind of way that sometimes seems to have little sense to it.

—George V of Great Britain

The Mexicans, as soon as the ceremony of crowning their King is over, dare no more look him in the face; nay, as if his royalty had raised him to the gods, with the oaths they make him take ... to be valiant, just, and mild, he also swears to make the sun run its course with its accustomed light, to make the clouds drop their water at the proper seasons, to make the rivers flow in their channels, and cause the earth to bring forth all things necessary for his people.

I am opposed to this common way of treating them, and I am inclined rather to doubt a man's ability when I see it attended by exalted fortune and the popular favor.

—Montaigne, *Essays*, Book III

THE KISS

I wonder what fool it was that first invented kissing.

—Jonathan Swift

In tracing the history of the kiss we are led back to ancient India. In the period of the Vedas, round about 2000 B.C., the Indians seem to have practiced what is called the nose or sniff kiss, of which more later; but by about the time of the great Mahabharata epic (500 B.C.?) the solution with the lips had become general. It was certainly well established when the ancient sage Vatsyayana composed his *Aphorisms on Love* (*Kama Sutra*), for amongst its twelve hundred and fifty verses are a number concerned with the technique of kissing with the lips. The best places for kissing are indicated, viz., the forehead, the eyes, the cheeks, the throat, the bosom, the breasts, the lips, and inside the mouth; and the different kinds of kiss are analyzed according to their intensity and method of application, and it is further explained that there are different kinds of kisses for different parts of the body.

From India the practice is supposed to have spread westwards to Persia, Assyria, Syria, Greece, Italy, and by way of the channels of Roman influence throughout most of Europe. The Teutonic tribes on the borderlands of the Empire practiced the mouth kiss, but it has been pointed out that there is no word for "kiss" in the Celtic tongues.

—E. Royston Pike, *The Strange Ways of Man*

If you are ever in doubt as to whether or not you should kiss a pretty girl, always give her the benefit of the doubt.

—Thomas Carlyle

KNOWLEDGE

From the beginning, men have begun to philosophize because of wondering. . . .

Since men philosophize to escape ignorance, it is clear that they seek scientific knowledge in order to know, and not for the sake of any practical end. . . . For when men had secured the necessities of life, and the things which contributed to leisure and amusement, they began to seek this kind of knowledge. It is not for some end other than itself that we seek such knowledge.

—Aristotle, *Metaphysics*

We know too much for one man to know much.

—Robert Oppenheimer

We don't know one millionth of one percent about anything.

—Thomas Alva Edison

The pursuit of knowledge can never be anything but a leap in the dark, and a leap in the dark is a very uncomfortable thing. I have sometimes thought that if the human race ever loses its ascendancy it will not be through plague, famine or cataclysm, but by getting to know some little microbe, as it were, of knowledge which shall get into its system and breed there till it makes an end of us. It is well, therefore, that there should be a substratum of mankind who cannot by any inducement be persuaded to know anything whatever at all, and who are resolutely determined to know nothing among us but what the parson tells them, and not to be too sure even about that.

—SAMUEL BUTLER, *Notebooks*

The white man drew a circle in the sand and told the red man, "This is what the Indian knows," and drawing a big circle around the small one said, "this is what the white man knows." The Indian took the stick and swept an immense ring around both circles: "This is where the white man and the red man know nothing."

—CARL SANDBURG

The degree of one's emotion varies inversely with one's knowledge of the facts—the less you know the hotter you get.

—BERTRAND RUSSELL

LANGUAGE

In another sense we all began life as preliterates; our written tradition is back-stopped by an oral one. Adult culture—which is largely the culture of the written word—blots out for most of us our childhood imagery; this gets lost, not, as Freud thought, because it is sexual and forbidden, but because it is irrelevant to us as literate people. We still dream in this earlier "forgotten language" and our great artists often renew themselves and us by translations from this strange language into the written vernacular of the adult.

—DAVID RIESMAN

Every language must originally have consisted of monosyllables, for these are the easiest to form and remember.

... the oldest nations, who have retained something of their early language, still use monosyllables to express the most familiar things, those most obvious to the senses; even today, Chinese is almost entirely founded on monosyllables.

Look at Old Germanic and all the languages of the North and you will scarcely find a single necessary, common object described by more than a single articulation. Monosyllables are everywhere; *zon*, the sun; *moun*, the moon; *ze*, the sea; *flus*, the river; *man*, the man; *kof*, the head; *boum*, a tree; *trink*, to drink; *march*, to walk; *shlaf*, to sleep, and so on.

It was with this brevity that men expressed themselves in the forest of Gaul and Germany and throughout the North.

The Greeks and Romans used more composite words only long after they had formed an organized society....

—VOLTAIRE, *Customs of Nations*

The child on the carpet plays his way into a palisade of verbal custom. He is required, by the usages of the tribe, to observe a contract of agreed linguistic behavior; in the rub and routine of that contractual observance, his language becomes stereotyped and stultified and... conditions his way of seeing and thinking until he thinks it is the only way and cannot understand that others should see and think differently....

In words are lineaments of my dearest and best; my mother's turn of phrase beats blessedly in my mind. In language I make the effigies of my enmity, and create the ikons I woo and kiss. In words, in whispering, stumbling words, in the litter and ceaseless drift of words, is my pleading and searching for my own identity, the desperate commentary on my struggle to survive, the solemn colloquy and foolish cross-talk of all my days, the articulation that will go on, at the heart of all experience, till at last all burdens are laid out and I need no more words, not even amen and goodnight.

—WALTER NASH, *Our Experience of Language*

It is quite an illusion to imagine that one adjusts to reality essentially without the use of language, and that language is merely

an incidental means . . . of communication or reflection. The fact
of the matter is that the "real world" is to a large extent unconsciously built up on the language habits of the group. . . . We see
and hear and otherwise experience very largely as we do because
the language habits of our community predispose certain choices
of interpretation.

—EDWARD SAPIR, in Benjamin Lee Whorf,
Language, Culture and Personality

. . . without the projection of language no one ever saw a single
wave. We see a surface in everchanging undulating motions.
Some languages cannot say "wave"; they are closer to reality in
this respect. Hopi say *walalata,* "plural waving occurs," and can
call attention to one place in the waving just as we can. But, since
actually a wave cannot exist by itself, the form that corresponds
to our singular, *wala,* is not the equivalent of English "a wave,"
but means "a slosh occurs," as when a vessel of liquid is suddenly
jarred.

The crudest savage may unconsciously manipulate with effortless ease a linguistic system so intricate, manifoldly systematized,
and intellectually difficult that it requires the lifetime study of our
greatest scholars to describe its workings.

—BENJAMIN LEE WHORF,
Language, Thought, and Reality

Perhaps of all the creations of man language is the most astonishing. Those small articulated sounds, that seem so simple and so
definite, turn out, the more one examines them, to be the recep-
tacles of subtle mystery and the dispensers of unanticipated power.
Each one of them, as we look, shoots up into

. . . A palm with winged imagination in it
and roots that stretch even beneath the grave.

—LYTTON STRACHEY, *Characters and Commentaries*

Charles V held that Spanish should be spoken to the gods, French
to men, Italian to the ladies, German to soldiers, English to geese,
Hungarian to horses, and Bohemian to the Devil. . . .

One writer proved that the Devil seduced Eve in Italian, Eve misled Adam in Bohemian, the Lord scolded them both in German, and the angel Gabriel drove them forth in Hungarian.

—Noah Jonathan Jacobs, *Naming-Day in Eden*

LAST WORDS

... My lamp of life is nearly extinguished; my race is run; the grave opens to receive me, and I sink into its bosom. I have but one request to ask at my departure from this world—the charity of its silence. Let no man write my epitaph: For as no man who knows my motives dare now vindicate them, let not prejudice or ignorance asperse them. Let them and me repose in obscurity and peace, and my tomb remain uninscribed, until other times and other men can do justice to my character; when my country takes her place among the nations of ʳhe earth, then, and not till then, let my epitaph be written. I have done.

—Robert Emmett, to the court which sentenced him to death, September 19, 1802

Note: Emmet, a wealthy Protestant, supported the cause of Irish Catholics who had lost their land in Cromwell's time.

LAUGHTER

Laughter is a sudden sense of glory.

—Thomas Hobbes

Laughter is heard farther than weeping.

—Jewish saying

A landscape may be beautiful, charming and sublime, or insignificant and ugly; it will never be laughable. You may laugh at an animal, but only because you have detected in it some human attitude or expression. You may laugh at a hat, but what you are making fun of, in this case, is not the piece of felt or straw, but the shape that men have given it—the human caprice whose mold it has assumed. It is strange that so important a fact, and such a simple one too, has not attracted to a greater degree the attention of philosophers. Several have defined man as "an animal which laughs." They might equally well have defined him as an animal which is laughed at; for if any other animal, or some lifeless object, produces the same effect, it is always because of some resemblance to man.

—HENRI BERGSON, *Laughter*

Laughing is the sensation of feeling good all over, and showing it principally in one spot.

—JOSH BILLINGS

LAW

Law is the pledge that the citizens of state will do justice to one another.

□

Law is order, and good law is good order.

□

The law is reason free from passion.

—ARISTOTLE

I would uphold the law if for no other reason but to protect myself.

—THOMAS MORE

A government without laws is, I suppose, a mystery in politics, inconceivable to human capacity and inconsistent with human society.

—JOHN LOCKE, *Second Treatise*

Lawyers are the only persons in whom ignorance of the law is not punished.

—JEREMY BENTHAM

When I hear a man talk of an unalterable law, I am convinced he is an unalterable fool.

—SYDNEY SMITH

LAW AND AUTHORITY

Law is the means of robbing liberty of its anarchic tendencies, and removing from authority the elements of caprice. . . . Law is the name we give to the liberties of others which we must respect if we expect to receive the like ourselves. . . .

Certainly our laws are not perfect; they were made by men— who are not perfect. There is nothing sacred about the laws, they can be changed; but there is something sacred about law.

—QUENTIN HOGG, *The Case for Conservatism*

LAW AND CUSTOM

. . . reform by law what is established by law, and change by custom what is settled by custom. It is very poor policy to change by law what ought to be changed by custom.

—MONTESQUIEU, *The Spirit of the Laws*

LAWS AND MANNERS

Manners are of more importance than laws. Upon them, in a great measure, the laws depend. The law touches us but here and there. . . . Manners are what vex or soothe, corrupt or purify, exalt or debase, barbarize or refine us, by a constant, steady, uniform, insensible operation, like that of the air we breathe in.

—EDMUND BURKE, *Letters on a Regicide Peace*

"LAZY" NATIVES?

The ethical importance accorded to work is one thing; the question as to whether or not the African was idle or lazy is another. It is worth looking briefly at this question, which illustrates the extreme difficulty of ascertaining answers to simple questions of fact.

In most cases, Central Africa was far from a tropical Eden where nature lavished her bounties with a generous hand. . . . Unsympathetic observers described Africans as lazy with too much facility. E. C. Hore felt it ridiculous to describe as lazy a man who had personally made "from Nature's absolutely raw materials" his house, his axe, and hoe and spear, his clothing, ornaments, his furniture, his cornmill, "and all the things he has ... who, although liable often in a lifetime to have to commence that whole process over again, has the energy and enterprise to commence afresh."

—H. A. C. Cairns,
Prelude to Imperialism, quotations from E. C. Hore,
Tanganyika: Eleven Years in Central Africa

STEPHEN LEACOCK (1869–1944)

When I state that my lectures were followed almost immediately by the Union of South Africa, the Banana Riots in Trinidad, and the Turco-Italian war, I think the reader can form some opinion of their importance.

□

I shall always feel, to my regret, that I am personally responsible for the outbreak of the present war.

□

Fifteen years ago one could have bought the Federal Steel Co. for twenty million dollars. And I let it go.

□

I read in newspapers that a German army had invaded France and was fighting the French, and that the English expeditionary force had crossed the Channel. "This,"—I said to myself—"means war." As usual I was right.

□

The parent who could see his boy as he really is would shake his head and say, "Willy is no good; I'll sell him."

□

Writing is not hard. Just get paper and pencil, sit down, and write it as it occurs to you. The writing is easy—it's the occurring that's hard.

—compiled from various speeches, books, lectures

LEADERS (LEADERSHIP)

There are forms of personality easily addicted to imperious violence. They have often learned to cow their environment by the sheer intensity of their willfulness. They have succeeded in control by externalizing their rages against deprivation. Such are the men of Napoleonic mold, prone to break themselves or others.

—HAROLD D. LASSWELL,
Politics—Who Gets What, When, How

A ruler needs only obedience from those he rules, whereas a leader needs their enthusiasm as well. Leadership is a good deal more strenuous than rulership.

—KENNETH MINOGUE, *Encounter*, July 1975

If human progress had been merely a matter of leadership, we would be in Utopia today.

—THOMAS B. REED, speech, 1885

LEARNING

Learning is not child's play; we cannot learn without pain.

—ARISTOTLE

Nature is a great teacher. But for teaching there must be learners. A certain proportion of what we call living nature can learn. What is commonly called the survival of the fittest turns partly on the capacity of certain forms of life to learn. Not that what is learnt is inherited. But the ability to learn favors survival and is heritable.

—CHARLES S. SHERRINGTON, *Man on His Nature*

[He] was so learned that he could name a horse in nine languages. So ignorant that he bought a cow to ride on.

—BENJAMIN FRANKLIN, *Poor Richard's Almanac*

ANTON VAN LEEUWENHOEK (1632–1723)

This janitor of Delft had stolen upon and peeped into a fantastic subvisible world of little things, creatures that had lived, had bred, had battled, had died, completely hidden from and unknown to all men from the beginning of time. Beasts these were of a kind that ravaged and annihilated whole races of men ten million times larger than they were themselves. Beings these were, more terrible than fire-spitting dragons or hydra-headed monsters. They were silent assassins that murdered babes in warm cradles and kings in sheltered places. It was this invisible, insignificant, but implacable—and sometimes friendly—world that Leeuwenhoek had looked into for the first time of all men of all countries.

—PAUL DE KRUIF, *Microbe Hunters*

LEFT-HANDEDNESS

The left hand is used throughout the East for purposes of ablution and is considered unclean. To offer the left hand would be most insulting and no man ever strokes his beard with it or eats with it; hence, probably, one never sees a left-handed man throughout the Moslem East. In Brazil for the same reason old-fashioned people will not take snuff with the right hand.

—SIR RICHARD BURTON, *Notebooks*

NIKOLAI LENIN (VLADIMIR ILICH ULYANOV) (1870–1924)

I know nothing greater than Beethoven's *Appassionata*.... But I can't listen to music too often. It affects your nerves, makes you want to say stupid nice things and stroke the heads of people who could create such beauty while living in this vile hell. And now you mustn't stroke anyone's head—you might get your hand bitten off. You have to hit them on the head without any mercy, although our ideal is not to use force against anyone. Hm, our duty is infernally hard!

—LENIN to MAXIM GORKY, in ROBERT PAYNE, *Lenin*

There are no morals in politics; there is only expediency.

□

[March 31, 1920]: The Soviet socialist democracy is in no way inconsistent with the rule and dictatorship of one person. A dictator ... sometimes will accomplish more by himself.

—in STEPHAN T. POSSONY,
Lenin: The Compulsive Revolutionary

The people have no need for liberty. Liberty is one of the forms of the bourgeois dictatorship. In a state worthy of the name there is no liberty.... It is true that liberty is precious—so precious that it must be rationed.

□

The Communists have become bureaucrats. (1921)

□

The court must not eliminate terror. (1922)

□

We will destroy everything and on the ruins we will build our temple ... for the happiness of all. But we will destroy the entire bourgeoisie, grind it to a powder.

—in ANATOLE SHUB, *Lenin*

You ask if parties other than the Bolshevik will be allowed to exist? Emphatically! They will exist in prison.

—to a group of Russian intellectuals, 1921

ABOUT HIM

When you met him for the first time ... you would take him for a small bureaucrat. He was always ungainly, ill-dressed, rather stoop-shouldered, and you would never believe that this bald man with the impenetrable Mongoloid features and slow, deliberate movements was one of the most completely fearless, skillful and determined men of our time.

—NIKOLAI VILENKIN, in Isaac Don Levine,
The Man Lenin

Lenin was an intriguer, a disorganizer ... and an exploiter of Russian backwardness.

—LEON TROTSKY,
in Isaac Deutscher, *The Prophet Armed: Trotsky*

Lenin's definition ...: "The scientific concept of dictatorship means nothing else but completely unlimited power, restrained by no laws or rules whatsoever, and relying directly on violence...." This total and absolute power was in Lenin's view best vested in one person: "The Soviet Socialist Democracy is in no way inconsistent with the rule and dictatorship of one person; the will of the class is at times best carried out by a dictator who alone can accomplish more."

There could hardly be a better definition of absolute monarchy.

That Lenin happened to be a Marxist was almost incidental; after
all, Ivan the Terrible professed to be a Christian.
                    —SIMON KARLINSKY, *Saturday Review*, June 14, 1975

I knew Lenin very well, but I never before noticed such a cruel
cynicism in him. He told me about choosing several dozen counter-
revolutionaries in prison and executing them as accessories in
the assassination of Mirbach—"to satisfy the Germans," Lenin
added with a smile. "In this way ... we are pleasing our socialist
comrades, and at the same time we are proving our innocence
without doing harm to our own people."
                    —LEONID KRASSIN, in George Solomon,
                                Among the Red Autocrats

Lenin arrived from exile at the Finland Station, Petrograd, on
April 3, 1917, via a "sealed train" supplied by the Germans. He
was greeted enthusiastically by Bolsheviks. The echo of the last
greeting had not died away, when this unusual guest let loose upon
that audience a cataract of passionate thought which at times
sounded almost like a lashing.... The fundamental impression even
among those nearest to him was ... fright.... All the accepted
formulas ... were exploded one after another.... Of a two-hour
speech later, Sukhanov said "it seemed as if all the elements, and
the spirit of universal destruction, had risen from their lairs, knowing neither barriers nor doubts nor personal difficulties nor personal
considerations, to hover ... above the heads of the bewitched disciples."
                    —LEON TROTSKY, *The Russian Revolution*

I was chiefly conscious of Lenin's intellectual limitations, and his
rather narrow Marxian orthodoxy, as well as a distinct vein of
impish cruelty.
                    —BERTRAND RUSSELL, *Autobiography*, Vol. II

... he considers himself justified in performing with the Russian
people, a cruel experiment which is doomed to failure beforehand....
   This inevitable tragedy does not disturb Lenin, the slave of
dogma.... He does not know the popular masses, he has not lived
with them. But he—from books—has learned how to raise these
masses on their hind legs and how—easiest of all—to enrage their

instincts. The working class is for Lenin what ore is for a metal-worker. Is it possible ... to mold a socialist state from this ore? Apparently it is impossible; however—why not try? What does Lenin risk if the experiment should fail?

—MAXIM GORKY, January 1918

He called himself a Marxist, but in fact he hammered and bent Marx to his own will, using Marx whenever it was necessary and jettisoning him whenever it served his purpose. He was closer to the medieval autocrats than to Marx. . . .

He was German, Swedish and Chuvash, and there was not a drop of Russian blood in him. . . . He never learned to write Russian well, but to the end of his life he wrote as he wrote in his boyhood, from notes carefully numbered and compiled in order, with the result that every statement appears to be contrived and calculated according to some logical pattern. He dealt with words as he dealt with men; they must all go into the straitjackets he had devised for them. . . .

He had never known the least desire to wear a colorful uniform or to take part in triumphal processions. What interested him was the precise point of application, the cutting edge of power shorn of all its decorative aspects. What he wanted and what he obtained was power in its ultimate naked majesty. . . .

Lenin had many sins, but the gravest was a supreme contempt for the human race. Like Marx he possessed an overwhelming contempt for the peasants. . . .

On Lenin's desk in the Kremlin there stood, for most of the years he worked there, a strange bronze statue of an ape gazing with an expression of profound bewilderment and dismay at an oversize human skull. It stood about ten inches high, and occupied a dominating position on the desk behind the inkwell. The ape is a grotesque parody of Rodin's *Le Penseur*. There is nothing in the least amusing about the appearance of the ape, with its sordidly dangling arms; and the human skull, with gaping mouth and empty eye-sockets, is even less amusing. The ape gazes ponderously at the skull, and the skull gazes back at the ape. We can only guess at the nature of the interminable dialogue which is being maintained between them. . . .

—ROBERT PAYNE, *op. cit.*

The Russian people's ... worst misfortune was his birth, the next
worst—his death.

> —WINSTON CHURCHILL, *The World Crisis*

LEONARDO DA VINCI (1452–1519)

[From letter applying for a position with Lodovico Sforza, Duke
of Milan (1340–1345)]:

Most illustrious Lord. ...

(1) I have devised bridges extremely light and strong, adapted
to be easily carried, and with them you may pursue, or at any
time flee from, an enemy; and other bridges secure and not destruc-
tible by fire and battle, easy to lift and place. ...

(2) I know how to take water out of the trenches when a
place is besieged and make endless variety of covered ways, lad-
ders, and other machines.

(3) If, by reason of the height of the banks, or the strength
of the besieged place and its position, it is impossible to avail
oneself of the plan of bombardment, I have methods for destroying every rock or fortress.

(4) Again I have devised various kinds of mortars; most convenient, easy to carry, and with these can fling enough small
stones to resemble a storm; and the smoke of these will cause great
terror amongst the enemy. ...

(5) I know means, by secret mines and tortuous ways, all
made without noise, to reach a designated spot even if it be
needed to pass under a trench or river.

(6) I will make covered chariots which are safe from any
attack, and which, entering among an enemy, with their artillery,
would break any body of men. Behind these chariots, infantry
could follow without hindrance.

(7) In case of need, I will make big guns, mortars, and light
ordnance, of fine and useful forms, out of the type now common.

(8) Where bombardment should fail, I would contrive catapults, *trabocchi* and other machines of marvelous efficacy, not in
common use. In short, according to the cases, I can contrive endless means of offense and defense.

(9) If the fight should be at sea, I have many machines efficient for offense and defense; and vessels which can resist the attack of the largest guns and powder.

(10) In time of peace, I believe I can give perfect satisfaction, equal to any other in architecture, in the composition of buildings, public and private; and in guiding water from one place to another.

Item. I can execute sculpture in marble, bronze, or clay; and in painting whatever need be done, I can paint as well as any one, whoever he may be. . . .

And if any of the above-named seem to anyone to be impossible, or not feasible, I am ready to make the experiment in whatever place may please Your Excellency—to whom I commend myself with the utmost Humility, etc.

—LEONARDO DA VINCI *Notebooks*, ed. by L.R. from
various translations

Note: The Duke invited Leonardo to Milan, entered him in a lute-playing competition, to be accompanied by improvised verses, and hired him. For Leonardo had a fine voice, was an accomplished lute player, and was skilled in improvising poems no less than inventing submarines, tanks, irrigation systems, catapults, mortars, etc.—as well as painting "as well as anyone, whoever he may be."

—L.R.

He made original and penetrating observations in almost every field of natural science—astronomy, botany, anatomy, zoology, physiology, physical geography, meteorology, hydrodynamics and aeronautics. It was probably only his dislike of deducing general formulas from his observations which prevented his anticipation of . . . the circulation of the blood. . . . In addition to the natural sciences, he was a profound student of mathematics, mechanics and military engineering. Of his immense gifts the imaginative usually triumphed over the practical by their very audacity . . .

□

He could see and record things . . . not known until the coming of slow-motion photography, while his observations on the color of shadows were not developed until . . . the French impressionists in the 19th century.

—CECIL H. M. GOULD, *Chambers Encyclopedia*, Vol. 8

In Vasari and all the early authors, the accounts of his beauty are so emphatic that they must be based on a living tradition. He was beautiful, strong, graceful in all his actions, and so charming in conversation that he drew all men's spirits to him: of this his later life gives full confirmation. ... To these early biographers he was himself a masterpiece of nature and seemed to be initiated into her processes.

To my mind the proof of Leonardo's homosexuality need not depend upon a rather sordid document (a complaint of 1476). It is implicit in a large section of his work, and accounts for his androgynous types and a kind of lassitude of form which any sensitive observer can see and interpret for himself. It also accounts for facts which are otherwise hard to explain, his foppishness in dress combined with his remoteness and secrecy, and the almost total absence, in his voluminous writings, of any mention of a woman. ... I would not press too far into a matter which is more the domain of the psychologist than the art critic, but ... we cannot look at Leonardo's work and seriously maintain that he had the normal man's feelings for women. And those who wish, in the interests of morality, to reduce Leonardo, that inexhaustible source of creative power, to a neutral or sexless agency, have a strange idea of doing service to his reputation.

—Kenneth Clark, *Leonardo da Vinci*

LHASA (LHA-SSA): CAPITAL OF TIBET

It is here that the Talé-Lama has set up his abode. From the summit of this lofty sanctuary he can contemplate, at the great solemnities, his innumerable adorers advancing along the plain or prostrate at the foot of the divine mountain. The secondary palaces, grouped round the great temple, serve as residences for numerous Lamas, of every order, whose continual occupation is to serve and do honor to the Living Buddha. Two fine avenues of magnificent trees lead from Lha-Ssa to the Buddha-La, and there you always find crowds of foreign pilgrims, telling the beads of their long Buddhist chaplets, and Lamas of the court, attired in rich costume, and mounted on horses splendidly caparisoned. Around the Buddha-La there is constant motion; but there is,

at the same time, almost uninterrupted silence, religious meditations appearing to occupy all men's minds.

—Pietro della Valle, *Travels in India*

LIBERALISM

The function of Liberalism in the past was that of putting a limit
to the powers of kings. The function of true Liberalism in the
future will be that of putting a limit to the powers of Parliaments.

—Herbert Spencer, *The Man Versus the State*

Liberalism is that principle ... according to which the public
authority, in spite of being all-powerful, limits itself and attempts,
even at its own expense, to leave room in the State over which
it rules for those to live who neither think nor feel as it does,
that is to say as do the stronger, the majority. Liberalism ... is the
supreme form of generosity; it is the right which the majority
concedes to minorities and hence it is the noblest cry that has
ever resounded in this planet. It announces the determination to
share existence with the enemy; more than that, with an enemy
which is weak. It was incredible that the human species should
have arrived at so noble an attitude. ... Hence, it is not to be
wondered at that this same humanity should soon appear anxious
to get rid of it. It is too difficult and complex to take firm root on
earth.

—Ortega y Gasset, *The Revolt of the Masses*

A conservative is enamored of existing evils, as distinguished from
the liberal—who wishes to replace them with others.

—Ambrose Bierce,
The Enlarged Devil's Dictionary

LIBERTY

The liberty of men in society is to be under no other legislative
power but that established by consent in the commonwealth; nor
under the dominion of any will or restraint of any law, but what
that legislative shall enact according to the trust put in it.

—John Locke, *Second Treatise*

Experience teaches us to be most on our guard to protect liberty when the government's purposes are beneficent.

—Louis D. Brandeis

They who give up essential liberty to obtain a little temporary safety deserve neither liberty nor safety.

—Benjamin Franklin

The mass of mankind has not been born with saddles on their backs, a favored few booted and spurred, ready to ride them legitimately, by the grace of God.

—Thomas Jefferson,
his last letter, to Weightman, June 24, 1826

Liberty must be limited in order to be enjoyed.

—Edmund Burke

Historically ... a striving for liberties was a striving for property.... No one has as yet explained how, when government owns and manages all material goods, the individual will retain any freedom of movement and discussion.

—Kenneth Pickthorn, *Principles and Prejudices*

LIBERTY AND PROPERTY

The only dependable foundation of personal liberty is the personal economic security of private property. The teaching of history is very certain on this point....

Where men have yielded without serious resistance to the tyranny of new dictators, it is because they have lacked property. They dared not resist because resistance meant destitution. The lack of a strong middle class in Russia, the impoverishment of the middle class in Italy, the ruin of the middle class in Germany, are the real reasons, much more than the ruthlessness of the Black Shirts, the Brown Shirts, and the Red Army, why the state has become absolute and individual liberty is suppressed.

—Walter Lippmann, *The Method of Freedom*

LIBRARIES

While medieval Europe was struggling out of intellectual darkness, if not barbarism, both China and the world of Islam, the latter extending from Spain in the West across the whole Mediterranean and all the way through India to Indonesia, enjoyed a highly developed civilization. At a time when Christian Europe did not have any writing material, except parchment which was too costly even for the rich monasteries, the Moslems (who had an almost inexhaustible supply of papyrus and paper, which the Chinese invented and which the Arabs and Jews brought to the West, via Spain) had many colleges and numerous well-stocked libraries.

—SAUL K. PADOVER,
Introduction, *Confessions and Self-Portrait*

The Arabs knew what large libraries were; and a learned man could not travel without camel-loads of dictionaries.

—SIR RICHARD BURTON, *Notebooks*

These are not books, lumps of lifeless paper, but *minds* alive on the shelves. From each of them goes out its own voice, as inaudible as the streams of sound conveyed day and night by electric waves beyond the range of our physical hearing; and just as the touch of a button on our set will fill the room with music, so by taking down one of these volumes and opening it, one can call into range the voice of a man far distant in time and space, and hear him speaking to us, mind to mind, heart to heart.

—GILBERT HIGHET, *The Immortal Profession*

LIFE

We are all chained to Fortune. . . . All life is bondage. Man must therefore habituate himself to his condition, complain of it as little as possible, and grasp whatever good lies within his reach. No situation is so harsh that a dispassionate mind cannot find some consolation in it.

—SENECA

... this day—this hour—is probably the only experience of the kind one is to have. As the doctor said to the woman who complained that she did not like the night air: "Madam, during certain hours of the twenty-four, night air is the only air there is."
                              —CHARLES MACOMB FLANDRAU, *Viva Mexico*

The great and glorious masterpiece of man is to live to the point. All other things—to reign, to hoard, to build—are, at most, but inconsiderate props and appendages.
                                          —MONTAIGNE, *Essays*

What is the sense of our life, what is the sense of the life of any living being at all? To know an answer to this question means to be religious. You ask: What is the sense of putting this question at all? I answer: He who feels that his own life or that of his fellow-beings is senseless is not only unhappy, but hardly capable of living.
                                          —ALBERT EINSTEIN

A man, after he has brushed off the dust and chips of his life, will have left only the hard, clean question: Was it good or was it evil? Have I done well—or ill?
                              —JOHN STEINBECK, *East of Eden*

That life is meaningless may be a lie so far as the whole of life is concerned. But it is the truth at any given instant.
                                          —ALDOUS HUXLEY,
                          Jesting Pilate: An Intellectual Holiday

All of the animals except man know that the principal business of life is to enjoy it.
                                          —SAMUEL BUTLER

All claims to discover the meaning or mystery of life rest on logical confusions.
                                          —SIDNEY HOOK,
                          Pragmatism and the Tragic Sense of Life

You are ignorant of life if you do not love it ... just as it is, a shaft of light from a nearby star, a flash of the blue salt water that curls around the five upthrust rocks of the continents, a net of green leaves spread to catch the light and use it, and you, walking under the trees. . . .

It is good enough just to sit still and hold your palm out to the sunlight, like a leaf, and turn it over slowly, wondering: What is light? What is flesh? What is it to be alive?

—Donald Culross Peattie, *An Almanac for Moderns*

That life is worth living is the most necessary of assumptions and, were it not assumed, the most impossible of conclusions.

—George Santayana

The ethical view of the universe involves us at last in so many cruel and absurd contradictions . . . that I have come to suspect that the aim of creation cannot be ethical at all. I would fondly believe that its object is purely spectacular; a spectacle for awe, love, adoration, or hate, if you like, but in this view . . . never for despair! . . . The rest is our affair—the laughter, the tears, the tenderness, the indignation, the high tranquillity of a steeled heart, the detached curiosity of a subtle mind—that's our affair!

—Joseph Conrad, *A Personal Record*

At any innocent tea-table we may easily hear a man say, "Life is not worth living." We regard it as we regard the statement that it is a fine day; nobody thinks that it can possibly have any serious effect on the man or on the world. And yet if that utterance were really believed, the world would stand on its head. Murderers would be given medals for saving men from life; firemen would be denounced for keeping men from death; poisons would be used as medicines; doctors would be called in when people were well. . . . Yet we never speculate as to whether the conversational pessimist will strengthen or disorganize society; for we are convinced that theories do not matter.

This was certainly not the idea of those who introduced our freedom.

—G. K. Chesterton, *Heretics*

There is more to life than increasing its speed.

—Mahatma Gandhi

This is the true joy in life, the being used for a purpose recognized by yourself as a mighty one; the being thoroughly worn out before you are thrown on the scrapheap; the being a force of Nature instead of a feverish selfish little clod of ailments and grievances complaining that the world will not devote itself to making you happy.

—GEORGE BERNARD SHAW, *Prefaces*

I never lose a sense of the whimsical and perilous charm of daily life, with its meetings and words and accidents. Why, today, I may hear a voice, and, packing up my Gladstone bag, follow it to the ends of the world.

—LOGAN PEARSALL SMITH, *All Trivia*

Human beings have an instinctive passion to preserve anything they like. Man is born and therefore wishes to live forever. Man falls in love and wishes to be loved, and loved forever as in the very first moment of his avowal. But life gives no guarantees. Life does not ensure existence, nor pleasure; she does not answer for their continuance. Every historical moment is full and is beautiful, is self-contained in its own fashion. Every year has its own spring and its own summer, its own winter and autumn, its own storms and fair weather. Every period is new, fresh, filled with its own hopes and carries within itself its own joys and sorrows. The present belongs to it. But human beings are not content with this, they must needs own the future, too.

—ALEXANDER HERZEN, in Isaiah Berlin,
"Alexander Herzen," in *Encounter*, May 1956

LIGHTNING

In a lightning flash, coming in the deep hush after thunder, lies terror; such unthinkably swift and formless motion, instantaneously bridging the abyss of space without a sound, is like some fearful portent. Are our senses undeveloped, since the dramas of dawn and moonrise have for us no chorus; the wind steals by invisible; the stars go through their stately ritual with silent tread, weaving their radiant dances to no murmur of music?

—MARY WEBB, *The Spring of Joy*

ABRAHAM LINCOLN (1809–1865)

I was not very much accustomed to flattery, and it came the sweeter to me.

☐

As for being President, I feel like the man who was tarred and feathered and ridden out of town on a rail. To the man who asked him how he liked it, he said, "If it wasn't for the honor of the thing, I'd rather walk."

☐

I can make a brigadier-general in five minutes, but it is not easy to replace a hundred and ten horses.

☐

God selects his own instruments, and sometimes they are queer ones; for instance, He chose me to steer the ship through a great crisis.

☐

My paramount object in this struggle [Civil War] is to save the Union, and is not either to save or destroy slavery. If I could save the Union without freeing any slave, I would do it; and if I could do it by freeing all the slaves, I would do it; and if I could save it by freeing some and leaving others alone, I would also do that.

—from his letters and speeches

I have heard, in such a way as to believe it, of your recently saying that both the army and the Government needed a Dictator. Of course it was not for this, but in spite of it, that I have given you the command. Only those generals who gain successes can set up dictators. What I now ask of you is military success, and I will risk the dictatorship. The Government will support you to the utmost of its ability, which is neither more nor less than it has done and will do for all commanders. I much fear that the spirit which you had aided to infuse into the army of criticizing their commander and withholding confidence from him, will now turn upon you. I shall assist you as far as I can to put it down. Neither you nor Napoleon, if he were alive again, could get any good out of an army while such a spirit prevails in it. And now beware of rashness. Beware of rashness, but with energy and sleepless vigilance go forward, and give us victories.

—letter to General Joseph Hooker, January 26, 1863

As to education, the newspapers are correct—I never went to school more than six months in my life.... Among my earliest recollections, I remember how, when a mere child, I used to get irritated when anybody talked to me in a way I could not understand. I don't think I ever got angry at anything else in my life. But that always disturbed my temper and has ever since. I can remember going to my little bedroom, after hearing the neighbors talk of an evening with my father, and spending no small part of the night walking up and down, trying to make out what was the exact meaning of some of their, to me, dark sayings. I could not sleep, though I often tried to, when I got on such a hunt after an idea, until I had caught it; and when I thought I had got it, I was not satisfied until I had repeated it over and over, until I had put it in language plain enough, as I thought, for any boy I knew to comprehend. This was a kind of passion with me, and it has stuck by me, for I am never easy now, when I am handling a thought, till I have bounded it north, and bounded it south, and bounded it east, and bounded it west. Perhaps that accounts for the characteristic you observe in my speeches.

—*New York Independent,* September 1, 1864

We are not enemies but friends. We must not be enemies. Though passion may have strained, it must not break our bonds of affection. The mystic chords of memory, stretching from every battlefield and patriot grave to every living heart and hearth stone, all over this broad land, will yet swell the chorus of the Union, when again touched, as surely they will be, by the better angels of our nature.

—First Inaugural Address, Washington, March 4, 1861

The dogmas of the quiet past are inadequate to the stormy present. The occasion is piled high with difficulty, and we must rise with the occasion. As our case is new, so we must think anew and act anew. We must disenthrall ourselves, and then we shall save our country.

—Message to Congress, December, 1, 1862

When I hear a man preach, I like him to act as if he were fighting bees.

□

As a nation, we began by declaring that "all men are created equal." We now practically read it, "All men are created equal, except Negroes." When the Know-Nothings get control, it will read, "All men are created equal, except Negroes, and foreigners, and Catholics." When it comes to this I should prefer emigrating to some other country where they make no pretense of loving liberty—to Russia, for instance, where despotism can be taken pure, without the base alloy of hypocrisy.

—letter, 1855

If slavery is not wrong, nothing is wrong.

—letter to A. C. Hodges, April 4, 1864

I protest, now and forever, against that counterfeit logic which presumes because I do not want a Negro woman for a slave I do necessarily want her for a wife. My understanding is that I do not have to have her for either.

—debate with Douglas, 1858

As I would not be a slave, so I would not be a master. This expresses my idea of democracy. Whatever differs from this, to the extent of the difference, is no democracy.

—letter, 1858

ABOUT HIM

Inseparable from the public picture of Lincoln was his gentleness. His clemency was famous everywhere and notorious among his colleagues. Those who came in closer contact with Lincoln saw that he was overgentle and lacking in firmness in intimate relationships. They saw how incapable he was of disciplining his own children, and how overindulgent he was of his exigent wife. The true measure of this gentleness was its continuation despite provocation. Very rarely did Lincoln allow flares of indignation to escape him. . . .

His sadness impressed contemporaries, who saw the brooding brows, the sunken cheeks, the luminous eyes, the deliberate ways; and they saw his tears at Gettysburg. Those who knew Lincoln intimately found that sadness was one of the many evidences of depression; Lincoln was plagued by insomnia, feelings of inferiority, of bearing too much responsibility, of pessimism. At times the President was suicidal.

Much of Lincoln's personality was a defense formation against extreme demands for wide appreciation. By tempering his conduct with incessant thoughts of the just rather than the popular, by neglecting as far as possible to take note of the avalanches of criticism which poured upon him, Lincoln was able to erect buffers against his own yearning for constant appreciation.

—HAROLD D. LASSWELL,
Politics—Who Gets What, When, How

At first Lincoln refused to limit the visiting hours. "They do not want much," he said of the throng waiting to see him, "and they get very little. . . . I know how I would feel in their place." So people began coming before breakfast, and some still remained late at night. . . .

. . . He was lowly to the meek, dignified to the pompous, flippant or stern with the presumptuous, and courteous to everyone, even to his foes, when they came to him in good faith. He respected the views of others and listened while they talked, for he knew that in some matters they might see truth more clearly than he, and that men arrive at truth by free discussion. . . .

It would be difficult to estimate how many tired, scared, or homesick boys in the Union army who fell asleep on picket duty, ran away in battle, or slipped off without leave to visit wives or parents were spared from the death sentence by a terse telegram from Lincoln: "Suspend sentence of execution and forward record of trial for examination," or "Let him fight instead of being shot."

Corns bothered him—he wrote a testimonial for a Jewish chiropodist who also performed confidential missions for him. . . .

. . . Only cases of meanness or cruelty failed to evoke his sympathy. He was especially averse to approving the death penalty for cowardice—"leg cases" he called those in which a soldier ran away in battle—and as he remitted sentence he said wryly: "It would frighten the poor fellows too terribly to kill them." . . .

Lincoln usually read a little before he went to bed. The telegraph operators noticed that he often carried a worn copy of

Macbeth or *The Merry Wives of Windsor* under his arm when
he made his last visit to their office. . . . He often went alone to
any sort of little show or concert and even slipped away one time
to attend a magic-lantern show intended for children. . . .

A vicious battle was raging and Lincoln remarked afterward
that he supposed some people would think it indiscreet of him
to seek amusement at such a time. "But the truth is," he declared,
"I must have a change of some sort or die." . . .

When Lamon made his customary inspection of the White
House and found that the President had gone out, he left a note
of warning on his desk: "Tonight, as . . . on several previous
occasions, you went out unattended to the theater. When I say
unattended, I mean you went . . . with Charles Sumner and a
foreign minister, neither of whom could defend himself against
an assault from any ablebodied woman in the city." . . .

—Benjamin Thomas, *Abraham Lincoln: A Biography*

Do you mean to say that she saw the President [Lincoln] alone?
Do you know that I never allow the President to see any woman
alone?

—Mary Todd Lincoln, 1865

The popular conception of Mr. Lincoln as one not seeking public
honors [is] very wide of the mark. He was entirely human in this
regard, but his desire for political preferment was hedged about by
a sense of obligation to the truth which nothing could shake.
This fidelity to truth was ingrained and unchangeable.

In all the speeches I ever heard him make—and they were
many—he never even insinuated an untruth, nor did he ever fail
when stating his opponent's positions to state them fully and
fairly. He often stated his opponent's position better than his
opponent did or could. To say what was false, or even to leave
his hearers under a wrong impression, was impossible to him.
Within this high enclosure he was as ambitious of earthly honors
as any man of his time.

Furthermore, he was an adept at log-rolling or any political
game that did not involve falsity. I was Secretary of the Republican State Committee of Illinois during some years when he
was in active campaign work. He was often present at meetings

of the committee, although not a member, and took part in the committee work. His judgment was very much deferred to in such matters. He was one of the shrewdest politicians of the State. Nobody had more experience in that way, nobody knew better than he what was passing in the minds of the people. Nobody knew better how to turn things to advantage politically, and nobody was readier to take such advantage, provided it did not involve dishonorable means. He could not cheat people out of their votes any more than out of their money.

—HORACE WHITE, Introduction, Herndon and Weik,
Life of Lincoln

In all my interviews with Mr. Lincoln I was impressed with his entire freedom from popular prejudice against the colored race. He was the first great man that I talked with in the U.S. freely, who in no single instance reminded me of the difference between himself and myself, or the difference of color, and I thought that all the more remarkable because he came from a state where there were black laws.

—FREDERICK DOUGLASS,
radical black abolitionist and former slave

Lincoln wielded a greater power throughout the war than any other President of the United States prior to Franklin D. Roosevelt; a wider authority than any British ruler between Cromwell and Churchill. . . . Lincoln came near to being the ideal tyrant of whom Plato dreamed, yet, nonetheless, he was a dictator from the standpoint of American constitutional law.

—SAMUEL ELIOT MORISON,
Oxford History of the United States

In Washington the most striking thing is the absence of personal loyalty to the President. It does not exist. He has no admirers, no enthusiastic supporters, none to bet on his head.

—RICHARD HENRY DANA, 1862

In the East Room of the White House lay the body of a man, embalmed and prepared for a journey. Sweet roses, early magnolias, and the balmiest of lilies were strewn for an effect as though the flowers had begun to bloom even from his coffin. . . .

On a pillow of white silk lay the head, on plaited satin rested the body, dressed in the black suit in which the First Inaugural was delivered, with its references to "fellow citizens," to "my dissatisfied countrymen," to "better angels," as though even among angels there are the worse and the better. . . .

The services were over. The pallbearers took the silver handles. The bong of big bells on cathedrals struck and the little bells of lesser steeples chimed in, as across the spring sunshine came the tolling of all the church bells of Washington and Georgetown, and Alexandria across the river. Counting the minutes with their salutes came the hoarse boom of fort guns encircling the national capital and several batteries sent into the city.

Out of the great front door of the executive mansion for the last time went the mortal shape of Abraham Lincoln, sixteenth President of the United States.

—CARL SANDBURG, *Abraham Lincoln: The War Years*

He was a man of such high and tender humanity, of personality so appealing and pathos so melting, that almost every study of him ends in a blur of eulogy. . . .

There is a certain mystery about Lincoln, as there is about every great and simple man; a mystery too simple, it may be, to be found out.

—JOSEPH F. NEWTON, *Lincoln and Herndon*

LOGIC: ITS LIMITS

One of the most fundamental and exciting intellectual feats of this century, moreover, has been the discovery by a mathematician and logician named Kurt Gödel that logic has some built-in limitations which had previously been unsuspected.

☐

Gödel proved the absolutely stunning result (stunning in all senses) that it is impossible—actually *impossible*, not just unreasonably difficult—to prove the consistency of any set of postulates which is rich enough in content to be interesting—rich enough, that is, in the sense of leading to a useful body of results. The question, "Is there an inner flaw in this logical system?" is a question which is unanswerable!

☐

One often hears the complimentary phrase "flawless logic"; and it is hard to realize that this discipline, so long considered the one kind of thinking or reasoning beyond criticism, should have this mysterious inner flaw, which consists of the fact that you can never discover whether or not it really has a flaw.

—WARREN WEAVER, *Lady Luck*

Logic is a poor guide compared with custom. Logic, which has created in so many countries semicircular assemblies which have buildings which give to every Member, not only a seat to sit in but often a desk to write at, with a lid to bang, has proved fatal to Parliamentary Government as we know it here in its home in the land of its birth.

—WINSTON CHURCHILL

LOUIS XVI (1774–1792)

Louis XVI had, in addition, a reason for showing himself to his people. He had the fatal weakness (for a King) of wanting to be liked, and among his courtiers he had found neither affection nor esteem....

His features showed no nobility of expression. His laugh was heavy and lethargic, his face lifeless, his appearance slovenly.... He was short-sighted, overgrown, shy and awkward. An ambassador at the Court reported that he was "as wild and rustic as if he'd been brought up in a wood." He liked to work with his hands and had a forge installed in the grounds of Versailles.... His only other interest was hunting and as King he spent so much time on horseback that he would fall asleep afterwards during important conferences....

In 1789 when the King... reckoned what he had been doing since 1775, the year of his marriage, he reckoned that he had attended 400 wild boar hunts, 134 stag hunts and 324 other expeditions, accounting for 1,562 days devoted to the chase.

The elegant society of the Court offered him nothing. He had nothing to contribute to it, and soon came to despise it. He had the countryman's graceless walk, his voice at times rose to an undignified squeak and he hated dancing. Marie Antoinette, aged sixteen when she married Louis, was already a woman; he as yet but half a man. Historians have noted that though he kept a diary he wrote in it one word to describe the day after his marriage: *"Rien."* (He probably meant there was no hunting.)

—JOHN FISHER, *Six Summers in Paris*

LOVE

Love—a grave mental disease.

—PLATO

When I consider the absurd titillations of love, the brainless notions it excites...the countenance inflamed with fury and cruelty during its sweetest moments, the solemn, entranced air during an action which is downright silly, the supreme moment bathed, like pain, in sighing and fainting—then I believe with Plato that the gods made men for their amusement.

—MONTAIGNE, *Essays*

Love is the triumph of imagination over intelligence.

—H. L. MENCKEN

I want you to want me. I want you to forget right and wrong; to be as happy as the beasts, as careless as the flowers and the birds. To live to the depths of your nature as well as to the heights. Truly there are stars in the heights and they will be a garland for your forehead. But the depths are equal to the heights. Wondrous deep are the depths, very fertile is the lowest deep. There are stars there also, brighter than the stars on high. The name of the heights is Wisdom and the name of the depths is Love.

—JAMES STEPHENS, *The Crock of Gold*

A bed is love's theater.

—HONORÉ DE BALZAC

Do you know how one loves? If your love is pure and you love purity in your woman and you suddenly realize that she is a loose and immoral woman, you will love her immorality, you will love the nastiness in her which you loathe so much. This is what love is like.

—FEODOR DOSTOEVSKY, letter to V. Solovyov

In fact, all loves but one's own have an element of the tiresome.
—C. P. Snow, *The New Men*

Love is the delusion that one woman differs from another.
—H. L. Mencken

There is a satisfaction in the consciousness of being loved which to a person of delicacy and sensibility is of more importance to happiness than all the advantages which he can expect to derive from it.
—Adam Smith, *Theory of Moral Sentiments*

In how many lives does love really play a dominant part? The average taxpayer is no more capable of a grand passion than a grand opera.
—Israel Zangwill, *Romeo and Juliet*

The magic of first love is our ignorance that it can ever end.
—Benjamin Disraeli

The reason lovers are never weary of each other is because they are always talking about themselves.
—François de la Rochefoucauld

It is only with scent and silk and artifices that we raise love from an instinct to a passion.
—George Moore

Love never dies of starvation but it often dies of indigestion.
—Ninon de Lenclos

Love is said to be blind, but I know lots of fellows in love who see twice as much in their sweethearts as I can.
—Josh Billings

LOVE AND HATE

It is always possible to unite considerable numbers of men in love —so long as some still remain as objects for aggressive manifestations.
—Sigmund Freud, *Civilization and Its Discontents*

If we say I love you, it may be received with doubt, for there are times when it is hard to believe. Say I hate you, and the one spoken to believes it instantly, once for all. . . .

Love must be learned, and learned again and again; there is no end to it. Hate needs no instruction, but waits only to be provoked.

—KATHERINE ANNE PORTER, *The Days Before*

THE LOYAL OPPOSITION

. . . England invented the phrase, "Her Majesty's Opposition"; it was the first government which made a criticism of administration as much a part of the polity as administration itself.

—WALTER BAGEHOT

MARTIN LUTHER (1483–1546)

I am the son of a peasant, and the grandson and the great-grandson. My father wanted to make me burgomaster. He became a miner. I became a baccalaureate. Then I became a monk and took off the brown beret. My father didn't like it. Then I got into the pope's hair and married an apostate nun.

Who could have read all this in the stars?

□

Be a sinner and sin strongly! But more strongly believe and rejoice in Christ, who is the conqueror of sin, death and the world. So long as we are as we are, there must be sinning. This life is not the dwelling place of righteousness.

—Letters

I have risen by my pen to a position which I would not exchange for that of the Turkish sultan, taking his wealth and giving up my learning.

□

From childhood on, I knew I had to turn pale and be terror-stricken when I heard the name of Christ; for I was taught only to perceive him as a strict and wrathful judge.

□

I never work better than when I am inspired by anger; when I am angry ... my whole temperament is quickened, my understanding sharpened, and all mundane vexations and temptations depart. ...

The pope boasted that he was the head of the church, and condemned all that would not be under his power and authority; for he said, although Christ be the head of the church, yet there must be a corporal head of the church upon earth. With this I could have been content, had he but taught the gospel pure and clear and not introduced human inventions and lies into its stead. ...

Not the pope or all his shaven retinue can make me sad; for I know that they are Christ's enemies; therefore I fight against him with joyful courage.

When I am assailed with heavy tribulations, I rush out among my pigs, rather than remain alone by myself. ...

—*Table Talk*

I am panting for nothing so much as to put that mountebank [Aristotle] to public shame.

—letter to LANG, 1517

I am unable to pray without at the same time cursing. If I am prompted to say, "Hallowed be Thy name," I must add, "Cursed, damned, outraged be the name of papists." If I am prompted to say, "Thy Kingdom come," I must perforce add, "Cursed, damned, destroyed must be the papacy." Indeed, I pray thus orally every day and in my heart, without intermission.

—ERIK H. ERIKSON, *Young Man Luther*

Just as they excommunicate me on account of sacrilegious heresy of their own, I in turn excommunicate them for the sake of the truth. Christ, the judge, will see which excommunication has the most value with Him!

—*Works of Martin Luther*, Vol. VI

One would like to curse them ["the hellish Roman Church"] so that thunder and lightning would strike them, hell-fire burn them, the plague, syphilis, epilepsy, scurvy, leprosy, carbuncles, and all diseases attack them.

—PRESERVED SMITH, *The Age of the Reformation*

Who loves not women, wine and song remains a fool his whole
life long.

—Table Talk

He who despises music, as all fanatics do, does not please me. For
music is a gift of God, not a gift of men. Music drives away the
devil and makes one happy.... After theology I accord to music
the highest place and the greatest honor.

—from unfinished treatise, Concerning Music

... justification must be the result of faith alone, and eternal life
must grow out of this justification.

□

This shall be my recantation at Worms: "Previously I said the
pope is the vicar of Christ. I recant. Now I say the pope is the
adversary of Christ and the apostle of the Devil."

—Table Talk

ABOUT HIM

Luther sinned in two respects: He knocked off the crown of the
Pope and attacked the bellies of the monks.

—ERASMUS, Letters

Luther was like a man climbing in the darkness a winding staircase in the steeple of an ancient cathedral. In the blackness he
reached out to steady himself, and his hand lay hold of a rope.
He was startled to hear the clanging of a bell.

—ROLAND BAINTON, Here I Stand

No one who knows the nature of a language dares to appear in
the presence of Luther without reverence. Among no people
has one man done so much to help create their language.

—KLOPSTOCK, German poet

If we wish to find a scapegoat on whose shoulders we may lay
the miseries which Germany has brought upon the world... I
am more and more convinced that the worst evil genius of that
country is not Hitler or Bismarck or Frederick the Great, but
Martin Luther.

—DEAN INGE

In the center of the new musical movement which accompanied the Reformation stands the great figure of Martin Luther.

—PAUL HENRY LANG, *Music in Western Civilization*

... there are few men like him in history. Dogmatic, superstitious, intolerant, overbearing, and violent as he was, he yet had that inscrutable prerogative of genius of transforming what he touched into new values.

—PRESERVED SMITH, *op. cit.*

He is a theological thinker who despises philosophy, speaks of "the whore Reason," yet he himself thought out the basic existential ideas without which present philosophy would scarcely be possible.... This man gives forth a profoundly antiphilosophical atmosphere.

—KARL JASPERS, *The Way to Wisdom*

We have no right to overlook a fact which Luther was far from denying: that when he, who had once chosen silence in order to restrain his rebellious and destructive nature, finally learned to let himself go, he freed not only the greatest oratory of his time, but also the most towering temper and the greatest capacity for dirt-slinging wrath.... The problem is not how extraordinary or how pathological all this is, but whether or not we can have one Luther without the other.

☐

Luther, once free, wrote to men friends about his emotional life, including his sexuality, with a frankness clearly denoting a need to share intimacies with them. The most famous example, perhaps, is a letter written at a time when the tragicomedy of these priests' belated marriages to runaway nuns was in full swing. Luther had made a match between Spalatin and an ex-nun.... In the letter, he wished Spalatin luck for the wedding night, and promised to think of him during a parallel performance to be arranged in his own marital bed.

☐

The one matter on which professor and priest, psychiatrist and sociologist, agree is Luther's immense gift for language: his receptivity for the written word; his memory for the significant phrase; and his range of verbal expression (lyrical, biblical, satirical, and vulgar) which in English is paralleled only by Shakespeare.

□

In confession, for example, he was so meticulous in the attempt to be truthful that he spelled out every intention as well as every deed; he splintered relatively acceptable purities into smaller and smaller impurities; he reported temptations in historical sequence, starting back in childhood; and after having confessed for hours, would ask for special appointments in order to correct previous statements. . . . His superior Staupitz mocked him in a letter in which he said that Christ was not interested in such trifles and that Martin had better see to it that he have some juicy adultery or murder to confess—perhaps the murder of his parents. But nothing could drive Martin deeper into despair than his superiors' refusal to take him seriously: At such moments he became "a dead corpse," he said.

—ERIK H. ERIKSON, *op. cit.*

LYING

From considerable experience in observing witnesses on the stand, I had learned that those who are lying or trying to cover up something generally make a common mistake—they tend to overreact, to overstate their case. . . .

—RICHARD M. NIXON, *Six Crises*

NICCOLO MACHIAVELLI (1469–1527)

I desire to go to Hell, not Heaven. In Hell I shall enjoy the company of popes, kings and princes, but in Heaven there are only beggars, monks, hermits and apostles.

□

When evening comes, I return to my house, and go into my study. At the door I take off my country clothes, all caked with mud and slime, and put on court dress. And when I am thus decently re-clad, I enter into the mansions of the men of ancient days. And there I am received by my hosts with kindness, and I feast myself on that food which alone is my true nourishment, and for which I was born. I am not abashed to speak with these ancients and to question them on the reasons for their actions. And they, in their humanity, deign to answer me. And so, I forget every worry, I have no fear of poverty, I am not appalled by the thought of death: I sink my identity in that of my ancient mentors.

—December 10, 1513

ABOUT HIM

He had no outstanding vices, if we except that of lusting after women, whereby he gave relief to an exuberance of vitality and perhaps also of affection. He was, for all his poverty, extremely generous, a most loving father, scrupulously honest, a lover of his country and of freedom.

To his contemporaries he appeared exceptionally corrupt because, being a great man, he did not seek to hide that which others hid; he hid his good qualities and displayed the less good. Indeed he liked to be thought worse than he really was, to shock his equals and show he was equal to the great. He noted with some bitterness that certain cynical precepts "would not be good," if only men were good. . . . But looking about him, he was overcome by the desperate state of the good and the immanence of evil, and his spirit rebelled. Then he either gave expression to his feelings in those bitter maxims or in laughter.

He hid behind his laughter; he laughed at his own emotion, he laughed because he had looked for and believed in the noble and the good, he laughed at himself for not laughing before.

—ROBERTO RIDOLFI, *Machiavelli*

MADMEN

If you argue with a madman, it is extremely probable that you will get the worst of it; for in many ways his mind moves all the quicker for not being delayed by the things that go with good judgment. He is not hampered by a sense of humor or by charity, or by the dumb certainties of experience. He is more logical for losing certain sane affections.... The madman is not the man who has lost his reason. He is the man who has lost everything except his reason.

The madman's explanation of a thing is always complete, and often in a purely rational sense satisfactory. Or, to speak more strictly, the insane explanation, if not conclusive, is at least un-answerable.... If a man says (for instance) that men have a conspiracy against him, you cannot dispute it except by saying that all the men deny that they are conspirators; which is exactly what conspirators would do. His explanation covers the facts as much as yours.

—G. K. Chesterton, *Selected Essays*

INSANITY

The man who cannot believe his senses, and the man who cannot believe anything else, are both insane.... There is about every madman a singular sensation that his body has walked off and left the important part of him behind.

—*Ibid.*

FERDINAND MAGELLAN (1480?–1521)

HIS DEATH (APRIL 27, 1521)

The Indians perceiving their blows were ineffectual when aimed at our body or head on account of our armor, and noticing at the same time that our legs were uncovered, directed against these their arrows, javelins, and stones, and these in such abundance, that we could not guard against them.... As they knew our Captain, they chiefly aimed at him, so that his helmet was twice struck from his head. Still he did not give himself up to despair, and we continued in a very small number fighting by his side.

This combat, so unequal, lasted more than an hour. An islander at length succeeded in thrusting the end of his lance through the bars of his helmet.... He now attempted to draw his sword, but was unable, owing to his right arm being grievously wounded. The Indians, who perceived this, pressed in crowds upon him; and one of them having given him a violent cut with a sword on the left leg, he fell on his face. On this they immediately fell upon him.

Thus perished our guide, our light, and our support.... As there was not one of those who remained with him but was wounded, and as we were consequently in no condition either to afford him succor or revenge his death, we instantly made for our boats, which were on the point of putting off. To our Captain indeed did we owe our deliverance, as the instant he fell, all the islanders rushed toward the spot where he lay....

But the glory of Magellan will survive him. He was adorned with every virtue; in midst of the greatest adversity he constantly possessed an immovable firmness. At sea he subjected himself to the same privations as his men. Better skilled than anyone in the knowledge of nautical charts, he was a perfect master of navigation, as he proved in making the tour of the world, an attempt on which none before him had ventured.

—ANTONIO PIGAFETTA, *Voyage Round the World*
tr. George Sanderlin

THE MAHDI

There is an ancient tradition in the Mohammedan world, telling of a mysterious being, the last in succession of the twelve holy Imams, who, untouched by death and withdrawn into the recesses of a mountain, was destined, at the appointed hour, to come forth again among men. His title was the Mahdi, the guide; some believed that he would be the forerunner of the Messiah; others that he would be Christ himself.... Was he not also of the family of the prophet? He himself had said so; and who would disbelieve the holy man?

□

... The tall, broad-shouldered, majestic man, with the dark face and black beard and great eyes—who could doubt that he was the embodiment of a superhuman power? Fascination dwelt in every movement, every glance. The eyes painted with antimony, flashed extraordinary fires; the exquisite smile revealed, beneath the vigorous lips, white upper teeth with a V-shaped space between them—the certain sign of fortune.... Thousands followed him, thousands prostrated themselves before him; thousands, when he lifted up his voice in solemn worship, knew that the heavens were opened and that they had come near to God. Then all at once the ... elephant-tusk trumpet—would give out its enormous sound. ... The brazen war-drums would summon ... the whole host to arms. The green flag and the red flag and the black flag would rise over the multitude. The great army would move forward. ... The drunkenness, the madness, of religion would blaze on every face; and the Mahdi, immovable on his charger, would let the scene grow under his eyes in silence. ...

—Lytton Strachey, *Eminent Victorians*

MAHTO-TATONKA

Anyone can steal a squaw, and if he chooses afterwards to make an adequate present to her rightful proprietor, the easy husband for the most part rests content, his vengeance falls asleep, and all danger from that quarter is averted. Yet this is regarded as a pitiful and mean-spirited transaction. The danger is averted, but the glory of the achievement also is lost. Mahto-Tatonka proceeded after a more dashing fashion. Out of several dozen squaws whom he had stolen, he could boast that he had never paid for one, but snapping his fingers in the face of the injured husband, had defied the extremity of his indignation, and no one yet had dared to lay the finger of violence upon him. ...

Perhaps his impunity may excite some wonder. An arrowshot from a ravine, or a stab given in the dark, require no great valor, and are especially suited to the Indian genius; but Mahto-Tatonka had a strong protection. It was not alone his courage and audacious will that enabled him to career so dashingly among his compeers. His enemies did not forget that he was one of thirty warlike brethren. ... Should they wreak their anger upon him, many keen eyes would be ever upon them, and many fierce hearts thirst for their blood. The avenger would dog their footsteps everywhere. To kill Mahto-Tatonka would be an act of suicide.

—Francis Parkman, *The Oregon Trail*

MALARIA AND HISTORY

Malaria until recently was not really considered a sickness; it was looked upon by those in malarial countries as a normal sort of condition—rather as Westerners look upon the common cold. But its effects upon the evolution of the races of man have been profound. In a sense the malarial mosquito has helped keep the races of man "pure" in that it made Africa, for instance, a "white man's grave" and thwarted attempts by the genetically unprotected Europeans to colonize the continent on a large scale. In the same way it protected the people of Indonesia against Chinese invaders. But while it has protected some races it has also sapped their strength and kept them in a state of chronic sickness and thus discouraged any urge in them ... even to improve their standards of living.

How different might history have been, one wonders, if the British Isles had been constantly subjected to endemic malaria. It was malaria that eventually undermined the Roman Empire, that killed Alexander the Great, at the age of thirty-three, and that probably killed Oliver Cromwell.

—JAMES CLARKE, *Man Is the Prey*

MAN

... the narrowest hinge in my hand puts to scorn all machinery.
—WALT WHITMAN

Something has not apparently changed at all: we have carried the old jungle with us, and this is what nobody seems to understand. The jungle is in us, in our unconscious, and we have succeeded in projecting it into the outside world. ...

—C. G. JUNG, letter, November 6, 1960

Man is the only animal of which I am thoroughly and cravenly afraid. I have never thought much of the courage of a lion tamer. Inside the cage he is at least safe from other men. There is less harm in a well-fed lion. It has no ideals, no sect, no party, no nation, no class: in short, no reason for destroying anything it does not want to eat.

—GEORGE BERNARD SHAW, *Sixteen Self Sketches*

Man's chief difference from the brutes lies in the exuberant excess of his subjective propensities.

—WILLIAM JAMES, *The Will to Believe*

Why was man created on the last day? So that he can be told, when pride possesses him: God created the gnat before thee.

—Talmud, *Sanhedrin*

Most men resemble great deserted palaces: The owner occupies only a few rooms and has closed-off wings where he never ventures.

—FRANCOIS MAURIAC, *Second Thoughts*

Man: the glory, jest and riddle of the world.

—ALEXANDER POPE

I hate mankind, for I think myself one of the best of them, and I know how bad I am.

—SAMUEL JOHNSON

Whenever man forgets that man is an animal, the result is always to make him less humane.

—JOSEPH WOOD KRUTCH, *The Twelve Seasons*

The most pernicious race of little odious vermin that nature ever suffered to crawl upon ... the earth.

—JONATHAN SWIFT, *Gulliver's Travels*

Man was created a little lower than the angels, and has been getting a little lower ever since.

—JOSH BILLINGS

Man is the only animal that blushes—or needs to.

—MARK TWAIN

It is possible that our race may be an accident, in a meaningless universe, living its brief life uncared-for, on this dark, cooling star: but even so—and all the more—what marvelous creatures we are! What fairy story, what tale from the Arabian Nights of the jinns, is a hundredth part as wonderful as this true fairy story of simians!

—CLARENCE DAY, *This Simian World*

What a chimera is man! What a novelty, what a monster, what a chaos, what a contradiction, what a prodigy! ... depository of truth, and sewer of uncertainty and terror, the glory and the shame of the universe.

—BLAISE PASCAL, *Pensées*

Man is an animal that makes bargains; no other animal does this— no dog exchanges bones with another.

—ADAM SMITH

Man: the inventor of stupidity.

—REMY DE GOURMONT

Though boys throw stones at frogs in sport, the frogs die in earnest.

—PLUTARCH

The ability to make love frivolously is the chief characteristic which distinguishes human beings from the beasts.

—HEYWOOD BROUN

Man is the only animal who eats when he is not hungry, drinks when he is not thirsty, and makes love during all seasons.

—ANON.

MAN AND THE COSMOS

If you wish to reflect on our significance in the cosmos it may be salutary to look towards the constellation of Coma, hold a penny at arm's length and remember that you obscure from your vision a cluster of a thousand galaxies, 350 million light years away, and receding from us with a velocity of nearly 5,000 miles per second.

—SIR BERNARD LOVELL, "Whence," *New York Times*,
November 16, 1975

DUKE OF MARLBOROUGH (1650–1722)

Marlborough's motives often remain obscure and his character is not as sharply definable as that of Chatham, Nelson or Welling-ton. ... Marlborough kept a very strict guard on both his tongue and his pen. He liked to keep his own secret, and in keeping it from contemporaries he has kept it from posterity as well. . . .

Perhaps the secret of Marlborough's character is that there is no secret. Abnormal only in his genius, he may have been guided by motives very much like those that sway commoner folk. He loved his wife. . . . He loved his country; he was attached to her religion and free institutions. He loved money, in which he was not singular. He loved, as every true man must, to use his peculiar talents to their full; and as in his case they required a vast field for their full exercise, he was therefore ambitious. Last, but not least, he loved his fellowmen, if scrupulous humaneness and consideration for others are signs of loving one's fellows.

He was the prince of courtesy. It is true that courtesy was one of his chief weapons in political and diplomatic negotiation; but it would not have been so effective if it had not been genuine, and based on kindly feelings. . . .

The talk about his avarice, grossly exaggerated for purposes of fiction, arose in part from little, thrifty personal habits which never go down well in England. They would have passed unnoticed in Holland or France. But the English made it a crime in a man who had given them victory that he blew out unnecessary candles, and walked home when other rich men would call a coach. These habits . . . he had acquired in his penurious youth, when he was living at Charles II's Court on his ensign's pay, and they clung to him when he grew rich.

—GEORGE M. TREVELYAN,
England Under Queen Anne, Vol. I

MARRIAGE

Arnold Bennett says that the horror of marriage lies in its "dailiness." All acuteness of relationship is rubbed away by this.

—VIRGINIA WOOLF

No man is so virtuous as to marry only to have children.

—MARTIN LUTHER, *Table Talk*

Marriage is the only adventure available to the cowardly.

—VOLTAIRE

Love your wives but love them chastely. Insist on the work of the flesh only in such measure as is necessary for the procreation of children.

□

Marriage is only a relative good, and it would be better if all men were to refrain from it.... Then the number of the elect would be completed sooner, the City of God perfected earlier, and the end of the world would be upon us earlier.

—St. Augustine *The City of God*

Men and women marry with the vow to love each other. Would they not be more happy if they vowed to please one another?

—Anon.

KARL MARX (1818–1883)

No credit is due me for discovering the existence of classes in modern society, nor the struggle between them. Long before me, bourgeois historians had described the historical development of this class struggle and bourgeois economists had described the economic anatomy of the classes.

What I did was to prove that (1) the existence of classes is only connected with particular phases in the development of production; (2) the class struggle necessarily leads to the dictatorship of the proletariat; (3) this dictatorship only constitutes the transition to the abolition of all classes and to a classless society.

—Karl Marx to Joseph Weydemeyer, March 5, 1852

ABOUT HIM

Marx himself was the type of man who is made up of energy, will power and unshakable conviction, a type highly remarkable also in outward appearance. A mane of thick black hair, hairy hands, his coat buttoned crookedly, he nevertheless looked like a man who had the right and the power to command respect, even though his appearance and behavior might seem peculiar enough. His movements were clumsy, but bold and self-assured; his manners defied all the usual social conventions. But they were proud, with a tinge of contempt, and his sharp, metallic voice was remarkably suited to the radical judgments he delivered on men and things. He spoke in nothing but imperatives, the words tolerating no opposition, penetrating everything he said with a harsh tone that jarred me almost painfully. The tone expressed his firm conviction of his mission to dominate men's minds and to prescribe laws for them.... Before my eyes stood the personification of a democratic dictator, such as might float before one's mind in a moment of fantasy.

—PAVEL ANNENKOV, *Reminiscences of Marx and Engels*

Nervous, as they say, to the point of cowardice, he is extraordinarily ambitious and vain, quarrelsome, intolerant and absolutist like Jehovah, the Lord God of his ancestors, who is, like Marx himself, vengeful to the point of madness. There is no lie or calumny that he is not capable of inventing against anyone who has had the misfortune of arousing his jealousy or, which is the same thing, his hatred.

—MICHAEL BAKUNIN, *The State and Anarchy*

Jenny [Marx's wife] did not know that her husband was the father of [the maid] Lenchen's baby. As the result of an understanding reached between Marx and Engels, Jenny and the rest of the family assumed that Engels, a gay bachelor, was the father, and the secret was preserved, apparently intact, to the end of Jenny's life.

□

Marx never retracted his defamation of the Jews, and this was to have its influence on socialist thinking. On the contrary, he harbored a lifelong hostility towards them. In his *Theses on Feuerbach* (1845) ... he thought it necessary to drag in his bias, referring to the "dirty Jewish" aspect of Christianity. His private letters are replete with anti-Semitic remarks, caricatures, and crude epithets: "Levy's Jewish nose," "usurers," "Jew-boy," "nigger-Jew," etc. For reasons perhaps explainable by the German concept *Selbsthass* [self-hate], Marx's hatred of Jews was a canker which neither time nor experience ever eradicated from his soul.

—SAUL K. PADOVER,
Karl Marx: An Intimate Biography

ABOUT HIS THEORIES

It seems an extraordinary thing that Marx had no theory of foreign trade; and the lack of it has handicapped socialists from then until now. But in the era of free trade, no theory of foreign trade was necessary; or rather it was there already. Marx merely assumed that socialist communities would go on trading with each other according to the best principles of the division of labor. Indeed he even assumed that socialism would work without planning or conscious forethought; and so it would, if every man followed his own economic interest logically.

—A. J. P. TAYLOR, *From Napoleon to Lenin*

It was only after a year and more of biological work at the Normal School of Science, that I came full face upon Marxism and by that time I was equipped to estimate at its proper value its plausible, mystical and dangerous idea of reconstituting the world on a basis of mere resentment and destruction: the Class War. Overthrow the "Capitalist System" (which never was a system) was the simple panacea of that stuffy, ego-centered and malicious theorist. His snobbish hatred of the bourgeoisie amounted to a mania. Blame somebody else and be violent when things go wrong, is the natural disposition of the common man in difficulties all the world over. Marx offered to the cheapest and basest of human impulses the poses of a pretentious philosophy, and the active minds amidst the distressed masses fell to him very readily. Marxism is in no sense creative or curative. Its relation to the inevitable reconstruction of human society which is now in progress, is parasitic. It is an enfeebling mental epidemic of spite which mankind has encountered in its difficult and intricate struggle out of outworn social conditions towards a new world order. It is the malaria of the Russian effort to this day. There would have been creative revolution, and possibly creative revolution of a far finer type, if Karl Marx had never lived.

—H. G. WELLS, *Experiment in Autobiography*

(THE APPEAL OF) MARXISM

Nothing is easier to understand than the fascination exerted by [the Marxist] synthesis. . . . It is particularly understandable in the young and in those intellectual denizens of our newspaper world to whom the gods seem to have granted the gift of eternal youth. Panting with impatience to have their innings, longing to save the world from something or other, disgusted with textbooks of undescribable tedium, dissatisfied emotionally and intellectually, unable to achieve synthesis by their own effort, they find what they crave for in Marx. There it is, the key to all the most intimate secrets, the magic wand that marshals both great events and small.... They need no longer feel out of it in the great affairs of life—all at once they see through the pompous marionettes of politics and business who never know what it is all about. And who can blame them, considering available alternatives?

—JOSEPH A. SCHUMPETER,
Capitalism, Socialism and Democracy

The first volume of *Capital* is badly written, ill put together, lacking in order, logic, and homogeneity of material.... It has in a measure become the "Bible of the working classes" and the oracle of a great nation; and its name and associations will not soon be erased from men's minds.

—JACQUES BARZUN, *Darwin, Marx, Wagner*

MARXISM AS RELIGION

In one important sense, Marxism is a religion. To the believer it presents, first, a system of ultimate ends that embody the meaning of life and are absolute standards by which to judge events and actions; and, secondly, a guide to those ends which implies a plan of salvation and the indication of the evil from which mankind, or a chosen section of mankind, is to be saved. We may specify still further: Marxist socialism also belongs to that subgroup which promises paradise on this side of the grave....

The religious quality of Marxism also explains a characteristic attitude of the orthodox.... To him, as to any believer in a Faith, the opponent is not merely in error but in sin. Dissent is disapproved of not only intellectually but also morally. There cannot be any excuse for it once the Message has been revealed.

□

Preaching in the garb of analysis and analyzing with a view to heartfelt needs, this is what conquered passionate allegiance—and gave to the Marxist that supreme boon which consists in the conviction that what one is and stands for can never be defeated but must conquer victoriously in the end.

—JOSEPH A. SCHUMPETER, *op. cit.*

(*See also:* COMMUNISM)

MARY STUART, QUEEN OF SCOTS (1542–1587)
THE EXECUTION

About three hundred knights and gentlemen of the county had been admitted [to the great hall of Fotheringay Castle] to witness the execution . . . and a great wood fire was blazing in the chimney. At the upper end of the hall . . . stood the scaffold. . . . It was covered with black cloth. . . . On the scaffold was the block, black like the rest; a square black cushion was placed behind it, and behind the cushion a black chair. . . . The axe leant against the rail, and two masked figures stood like mutes on either side at the back.

The Queen of Scots swept in as if coming to take a part in some solemn pageant. Not a muscle of her face could be seen to quiver; she ascended the scaffold with absolute composure, looked round her smiling, and sat down. . . . Beale then mounted a platform and read the warrant aloud.

In the assembly Mary Stuart seemed the person least interested in the words which were assigning her to death.

She laid her crucifix on her chair. . . . The lawn veil was lifted carefully off, not to disturb her hair, and was hung upon the rail. The black robe was next removed. Below it was a petticoat of crimson velvet. The black jacket followed, and under the jacket was a bodice of crimson satin. One of her ladies handed her a pair of crimson sleeves, with which she hastily covered her arms; and thus she stood on the black scaffold with the black figures all around her, blood-red from head to foot.

Her reasons for adopting so extraordinary a costume must be left to conjecture. It is only certain that it must have been carefully studied, and that the pictorial effect must have been appalling. . . . Then she knelt on the cushion. Barbara Mowbray bound her eyes with a handkerchief.... They stepped back from off the scaffold and left her alone. On her knees she repeated the Psalm, *In te, Domine, confido,* "In thee, oh Lord, have I put my trust." ...

When the psalm was finished she felt for the block, and laying down her head, muttered: *"In manus, Domine, tuas, commendo animam meam."* The hard wood seemed to hurt her, for she placed her hands under her neck. The executioners gently removed them, lest they should deaden the blow, and then, one of them holding her slightly, the other raised the axe and struck. The scene had been too trying even for the practiced headsman of the Tower. His arm wandered. The blow fell on the knot of the handkerchief, and scarcely broke the skin. She neither spoke nor moved. He struck again, this time more effectively. The head hung by a shred of skin, which he divided without withdrawing the axe; and at once a metamorphosis was witnessed, strange as was ever wrought by wand of fabled enchanter. The coif fell off and the false plaits. The labored illusion vanished. The lady who had knelt before the block was in the maturity of grace and loveliness. The executioner, when he raised the head ... to show it to the crowd, exposed the withered features of a grizzled, wrinkled old woman.

—JAMES ANTHONY FROUDE, *A History of England from the Fall of Wolsey to the Defeat of the Armada*

THE MASSES

What maintains the cohesion of the state is superstition.... Every multitude is fickle, full of lawless desires, unreasoned passion, and violent anger. [They] must be contained by invisible terrors and pageantry.

—POLYBIUS, *The History*

The mass believes that it has the right to impose and to give force of law to notions born in the café. I doubt whether there have been other periods of history in which the multitude has come to govern more directly than in our own. That is why I speak of hyperdemocracy.

□

When the mass acts on its own, it does so only in one way, for it has no other: It lynches. It is not altogether by chance that lynch law comes from America, for America is, in a fashion, the paradise of the masses. And it will cause less surprise, nowadays, when the masses triumph, that violence should triumph and be made the one doctrine.

The multitude has suddenly become visible, installing itself in the preferential positions in society. Before, if it existed, it passed unnoticed, occupying the background of the social stage; now it has advanced to the footlights and is the principal character. There are no longer protagonists; there is only the chorus.

—ORTEGA Y GASSET, *The Revolt of the Masses*

Why babble about brutality and be indignant about tortures? The masses want that. They need something that will give them a thrill of horror.

What you tell the people in the mass, in a receptive state of fanatic devotion, will remain words received under an hypnotic influence, ineradicable, and impervious to every reasonable explanation.

—ADOLF HITLER

MATHEMATICS AND MATHEMATICIANS

So it is tempting to approach the nature of mathematical creativity by describing the nature of creative mathematicians ... [But this] approach cannot explain the fact, amusing at first and then puzzling, that nearly all mathematicians are eldest sons. The few exceptions tend to be mathematicians whose older brothers are mathematicians, too. Mathematical gifts cannot be unique to oldest sons. It must be that the discipline itself is crucial—that it provides a domain in which mental power and creativity can be wielded in a manner congenial to the special qualities of men who for a time, at least, were the only sons in their families.

☐

... The discipline is unforgiving in its contempt for the solution of almost any problems but the most profound and difficult ones. ...

The insanity and suicide levels among mathematicians are probably the highest in any of the professions. But the rewards are proportionately great. A new mathematical result, entirely new, never before conjectured or understood by anyone, nursed from the first tentative hypothesis through labyrinths of false attempted proofs, wrong approaches, unpromising directions, and months or years of difficult and delicate work—there is nothing, or almost nothing, in the world that can bring a joy and a sense of power and tranquillity to equal those of its creator.

And a great new mathematical edifice is a triumph that whispers of immortality. What is more, mathematics generates a momentum, so that any significant result points automatically to another new result, or perhaps to two or three other new results. And so it goes—goes, until the momentum all at once dissipates. Then the mathematical career is, essentially, over.... It has been said that no man should become a philosopher before the age of forty. Perhaps no man should remain a mathematician after the age of forty.

—ALFRED ADLER, *The New Yorker*, February 19, 1972

The mathematician may be compared to a designer of garments, who is utterly oblivious of the creatures whom his garments may fit.... The conic sections, invented in an attempt to solve the problem of doubling the altar of an oracle, ended by becoming the orbits followed by the planets.... The imaginary magnitudes invented by Cardan and Bombelli describe in some strange way the characteristic features of alternating currents. The absolute differential calculus, which originated as a fantasy of Riemann, became the mathematical vehicle for the theory of Relativity. And the matrices which were a complete abstraction in the days of Cayley and Sylvester appear admirably adapted to the exotic situation exhibited by the quantum theory of the atom.

—TOBIAS DANTZIG,
Number, the Language of Science

I will not go so far as to say that to construct a history of thought without profound study of the mathematical ideas of successive epochs is like omitting Hamlet from the play.... That would be claiming too much. But it is certainly analogous to cutting out the part of Ophelia. This simile is singularly exact. For Ophelia is quite essential to the play, she is very charming—and a little mad.

—ALFRED NORTH WHITEHEAD

Philosophy is written in that great book which ever lies before our eyes—I mean the universe. But we cannot understand it if we do not first learn the language and grasp the symbols in which it is written. This book is written in the mathematical language, and the symbols are triangles, circles, and other geometrical figures, without whose help it is impossible to comprehend a single word of it, without which one wanders in vain through a dark labyrinth.

—GALILEO, *Il Saggiatore*, 1610

It was Leonardo who first remarked that a science is perfect to the degree that it is mathematical. But is there any reason to assume ... that the universe must be of a kind that permits exact mathematical description?

—J. W. N. SULLIVAN, *Limitations of Science*

Mathematics is the only science where one never knows what one is talking about, nor whether what is said is true.

—BERTRAND RUSSELL

How is it that there are so many minds that are incapable of understanding mathematics? Is there not something paradoxical in this? Here is a science which appeals only to the fundamental principles of logic ... to what forms, so to speak, the skeleton of our understanding, to what we could not be deprived of without ceasing to think, and yet there are people who find it obscure, and actually they are the majority. That they should be incapable of discovery we can understand, but that they ... should remain blind when they are shown a light that seems to us to shine with a pure brilliance, it is this that is altogether miraculous.

—HENRI POINCARÉ, *Science and Method*

JAMES CLERK MAXWELL (1831–1879)

Then came the great revolution forever linked with the names Faraday, Maxwell and Hertz. The lion's share in this revolution was Maxwell's. ... If we confine our attention to the modification that he produced in our conception of the nature of Physical

Reality, we may say that, before Maxwell, Physical Reality ... was thought of as consisting in material particles, whose variations consist only in movements governed by partial differential equations. Since Maxwell's time, Physical Reality has been thought of as represented by continuous fields, governed by partial differential equations, and not capable of mechanical interpretation. This change in the conception of Reality is the most profound and the most fruitful Physics has experienced since the time of Newton. ...

—ALBERT EINSTEIN,
in *James Clerk Maxwell, a Commemoration Volume*

For to him [Maxwell] was given, after many years of quiet investigation, a success which must be numbered among the greatest of all intellectual achievements. By pure reasoning he succeeded in wresting secrets from nature, some of which were only tested a full generation later, as a result of ingenious and laborious experiments.

—MAX PLANCK, *Autobiographical Papers*

It cannot be too much emphasized that the identification of the laws of light and electromagnetism is what opened the way to relativity, by rendering optical experiments relevant to the description of the field.

—CHARLES COULTON GILLESPIE, *Edge of Objectivity*

MEDIEVAL CRUELTIES

What strikes us in this judicial cruelty and in the joy the [medieval] people felt at it, is rather brutality than perversity. Torture and executions are enjoyed by the spectators like an entertainment at a fair. The citizens of Mons bought a brigand at far too high a price, for the pleasure of seeing him quartered, "at which the people rejoiced more than if a new holy body had risen from the dead." The people of Bruges, in 1488, during the captivity of Maximilian, king of the Romans, cannot get their fill of seeing the tortures inflicted, on a high platform in the marketplace, on the magistrates suspected of treason. The unfortunates are refused the deathblow which they implore, that the people may feast again upon their torments.

—JOHAN HUIZINGA, *The Waning of the Middle Ages*

MEDIEVAL WORLD

... it was not merely the great facts of birth, marriage and death which, by the sacredness of the sacrament, were raised to the rank of mysteries; incidents of less importance, like a journey, a task, a visit, were equally attended by a thousand formalities: benedictions, ceremonies, formulae.

□

All things in life were of a proud or cruel publicity. Lepers sounded their rattles and went about in processions, beggars exhibited their deformity and their misery in churches. Every order and estate, every rank and profession, was distinguished by its costume. The great lords never moved about without a glorious display of arms and liveries, exciting fear and envy.

Executions and other public acts of justice, hawkings, marriages and funerals, were all announced by cries and processions, songs and music. The lover wore the colors of his lady; companions the emblem of their confraternity; parties and servants the badges and blazon of their lord. ... A medieval town did not lose itself in extensive suburbs of factories and villas; girded by its walls, it stood forth as a compact whole, bristling with innumerable turrets.

—Ibid.

LORD MELBOURNE (1779–1848)

All he had seen of the world confirmed him in his view that it was ruled mainly by folly, vanity, and selfishness. And when someone quoted to him an old observation of his own to the effect that man could only learn by experience, "No, no," he returned sadly, "nobody learns anything by experience; everybody does the same thing over and over again."

□

Even on serious subjects his tone was ambiguous. Its salient characteristic was irony, a mischievous, enigmatic irony, that played audaciously over the most sacred topics, leaving its hearer very much in doubt whether William Lamb thought them sacred at all. Paradox, too, was of the fiber of his talk. He loved to defend the indefensible. "What I like about the Order of the Garter," he once remarked, "is that there is no damned merit about it."

□

His philosophy hampered his power of action. It was not that he was weak, as his friends were always complaining. On the contrary, no one could act more vigorously once he was convinced he was right. The trouble was that he was seldom so convinced. He saw every question from so many sides, most problems seemed to him so hopeless of solution, that he was generally for doing nothing at all. Still less could he direct his various actions to a chosen end: He had never made up his mind as to whether any end was worth achieving. If circumstances should happen to push him into a position of power, he was perfectly ready to take it on: For men and their affairs inspired him with far too little respect for him to shrink from assuming responsibility for them. But, on the other hand, he did not think it worthwhile stirring a finger to mold circumstances to his will. Smiling, indolent, and inscrutable he lay, a pawn in the hands of fortune.

□

He was that rare phenomenon, a genuinely independent personality. From the turmoil of warring influences which, from cradle to middle age, had fought for possession of him, he had emerged dominated by none, his every opinion the honest conclusion of his own experience, his every utterance and habit, down to the way he ate, and folded his letters, the unqualified expression of his own individuality. But, though he was enslaved to nothing else, he was not master of himself. Strong enough to reject any faith that his own reason did not think convincing, he had not the strength to form a faith of his own. His spiritual security was at the mercy of circumstances.

—DAVID CECIL, *Melbourne*

MEMORY

I can remember how very dark that room was, in the dark of the moon, and how packed it was with ghostly stillness when one woke up by accident away in the night, and forgotten sins came flocking out of the secret chambers of the memory.

—MARK TWAIN, *Autobiography*

God gave us our memories so that we might have roses in December.

—James M. Barrie

Nothing so deeply imprints anything on our memory as the desire to forget it.

—Montaigne

Memory is the diary we all carry about with us.

—Oscar Wilde

A man's real possession is his memory. In nothing else is he rich, in nothing else is he poor.

—Alexander Smith

Memory is the one paradise out of which we cannot be driven.

—Sacha Guitry

The advantage of a bad memory is that one enjoys several times the same good things for the *first* time.

—Friedrich Nietzsche

It's a poor sort of memory that only works backwards.

—Lewis Carroll (Charles Lutwidge Dodgson),
Alice in Wonderland

The memory capacity of even an ordinary human mind is fabulous. We may not consider ourselves particularly adept at remembering technical data . . . but consider how many faces we can recognize, how many names call up some past incident, how many words we can spell and define. . . . It is estimated that in a lifetime, a brain can store 1,000,000,000,000,000 (a million billion) "bits" of information.

—Isaac Asimov

It is difficult, impossible, I am told, for anyone to recall his boyhood exactly as it was. It could not have been what it seems to the adult mind, since we cannot escape from what we are . . . and in going back we must take our present selves with us: The mind has taken a different color, and this is thrown back upon our past.

—W. H. Hudson, *Far Away and Long Ago*

I suppose that in the forty-five years of my existence every atom, every molecule that composes me has changed its position or danced away and beyond to become part of other things. New molecules have come from the grass and the bodies of animals to be part of me a little while, yet in this spinning, light and airy as a midge swarm in a shaft of sunlight, my memories hold, and a loved face of twenty years ago is before me still. Nor is that face, nor all my years, caught cellularly as in some cold precise photographic pattern, some gross, mechanical reproduction of the past. My memory holds the past and yet paradoxically knows, at the same time, that the past is gone and will never come again. It cherishes dead faces and silenced voices, yes, and lost evenings of childhood.

—LOREN EISELEY, *The Immense Journey*

MEN AT WAR

Out of more than thirty-seven thousand muskets which had been left on the field [Gettysburg], nearly a third were loaded with more than one cartridge. In the excitement of battle men forgot to fix percussion caps, sometimes even forgot to pull the trigger, and reloaded automatically without realizing that they had not fired. One man remarked briefly that "not all the forces attacking or attacked are fully conscious of what they are doing," and veterans were free to admit that in this as in all other battles there had been a great deal of wild, ineffective shooting. Whole regiments at times fired volleys with the line of muskets pointing vaguely toward the sky at an angle from the vertical no more than forty-five degrees, and men were often seen to fire with both eyes tightly shut.

—BRUCE CATTON, *Glory Road*

GALLIPOLI

Ship after ship, crammed with soldiers, moved slowly out of the harbor, in the lovely day, and felt again the heave of the sea ... and the beauty and the exaltation of the youth upon them made them like sacred things as they moved away.... These men had come from all parts of the British world, from Africa, Australia, Canada, India, the Mother Country, New Zealand and remote islands in the sea. . . . In a few hours at most, as they well knew, perhaps a tenth of them would have looked their last on the sun, and be part of foreign earth or dumb things that tides push. Many of them would have disappeared forever from the knowledge of man, blotted from the book of life none would know how, by a fall or chance shot in the darkness, in the blast of a shell, or alone, like a hurt beast, in some scrub or gully, far from comrades and the English speech and the English singing.

☐

All that they felt was a gladness of exultation that their young courage was to be used. They went like kings in a pageant to the imminent death.

☐

As each ship crammed with soldiers drew near the battleships, the men swung their caps and cheered again, and the sailors answered, and the noise of cheering swelled, and the men in the ships not yet moving joined in, and the men ashore, till all the life in the harbor was giving thanks that it could go to death rejoicing. All was beautiful in that gladness of men about to die, but the most moving thing was the greatness of their generous hearts.

They left the harbor very, very slowly; this tumult of cheering lasted a long time; no one who heard it will ever forget it, or think of it unshaken. It broke the hearts of all there with pity and pride; it went beyond the guard of the English heart. Presently all were out, and the fleet stood across for Tenedos, and the sun went down with marvelous color, lighting island after island and the Asian peaks, and those left behind in Mudros trimmed their lamps knowing that they had been for a little brought near to the heart of things.

—John Masefield, *Gallipoli*

MESSALINA, WIFE OF CLAUDIUS (?–48)

Narcissus rushed out, and ordered the centurions and the tribunes, who were on guard, to accomplish the deed of blood. Such, he said, was the emperor's (Claudius's) bidding. Evodus, one of the freedmen, was appointed to watch and complete the affair. Hurrying on before with all speed to the gardens, he found Messalina stretched upon the ground, while by her side sat Lepida, her mother, who, though estranged from her daughter in prosperity, was now melted to pity by her inevitable doom, and urged her not to wait for the executioner. "Life," she said, "was over; all that could be looked for was honor in death." But in that heart, utterly corrupted by profligacy, nothing noble remained. She still prolonged her tears and idle complaints, till the gates were forced open by the rush of the newcomers, and there stood at her side the tribune, sternly silent, and the freedman, overwhelming her with the copious insults of a servile tongue.

Then for the first time she understood her fate and put her hand to a dagger. In her terror she was applying it ineffectually to her throat and breast, when a blow from the tribune drove it through her. Her body was given up to her mother.

Claudius was still at the banquet when they told him that Messalina was dead, without mentioning whether it was by her own or another's hand. Nor did he ask the question, but called for the cup and finished his repast as usual. During the days which followed he showed no sign of hatred or joy or anger or sadness, in a word, of any human emotion, either when he looked on her triumphant accusers or on her weeping children. The Senate assisted his forgetfulness by decreeing that her name and her statues should be removed from all places, public or private.

—TACITUS, *Annals*, Book II

PRINCE KLEMENS LOTHAR VON METTERNICH (1773–1859)

My life has coincided with an abominable time. I came into the world too soon or too late. At the present time I do not feel I can accomplish anything. Earlier, I would have shared in the rejoicing of the time; later, I could have helped in the work of reconstruction. Today I spend my time shoring up crumbling edifices. I should have been born in 1900 with the twentieth century before me.

—*Memoires*, III, October 8, 1822

For some years now I have made a singular observation. It is that men who are diametrically opposed to me die. The explanation is quite simple, these men are mad, and it is the mad who die.

—*To the Comtesse de Lieven*, December 6, 1818

The world has need of me still if only because my place in it could not be filled by anyone else. To be what I am needs an accumulation of experience, and one could as easily replace an old tree as an old Minister.

—*Memoires*, IV, to his son Viktor, May 15, 1828

Throughout my long career as a Minister I have been among those who rule, the only one capable of ruling.

—*Memoires*, VIII, to his daughter, January 17, 1849

Canning flies, I walk. He soars to a region uninhabited by men, I take up my position on the level of human action. The resulting difference is that Canning will have on his side the romantics whereas I shall be left to the prose-writers. His role is as brilliant as a flash of lightning but lasts no longer. Mine is not dazzling but it preserves what the other consumes.... Men like Canning fall twenty times and recover themselves as often; men like myself have no need of recovery because they are not subject to falls. The first play to the gallery; the second usually bore it. To the great majority of those who see me at work I must be very boring to watch but they will have to put up with it for I will not change.

—to Neuman, June 23, 1826

I consider myself stronger than most of my contemporaries because I have an invincible hatred of words and empty phrases and my instinct is always towards action.

—*Memoires*, IV, to Gentz, August 5, 1825

Posterity will judge me. Her voice is the only one whose favor I seek, the only one to which I do not remain indifferent, and yet it is the only one I shall never hear.

—*Memoires*, III, Quoted in G. de Bertier de Sauvigny, *Metternich and His Times*

ABOUT HIM

It is certainly no mean performance to have been able to win the respect of such widely differing personalities as the Emperors Francis and Napoleon, the Czar Alexander, Castlereagh, and

Guizot. A perfect courtier with a quick, well-chosen repartee. "You are indeed young," Napoleon once remarked to him, "to represent the oldest monarchy in Europe." "Sire, my age is the same as Your Majesty's at Austerlitz."

☐

Metternich appears to us as a man of goodwill and as a man of good sense: an admirable judge of men and of the political problems of his age, experienced in all kinds of diplomatic finesse; much less doctrinaire and much more opportunist than he appears at first sight. Circumstances at least as much as his gifts assisted his career. His rise was encouraged by a situation in which finesse and patience were the only weapons that could be matched against power and genius; and finally the astonishing length of his reign is due in large part to the combination of circumstances which placed him, the conservative and cautious Minister *par excellence*, at the head of an empire, which, if it was to survive, needed above all peace and stability.

Everything that is known about his behavior, the whole judgment of those who knew him well, converges on the same conclusion: in him character was not on the same high level as intelligence.

☐

His is a vanity which, leaving the limits of ridicule far behind, assumes grandiose and fascinating dimensions.... Never before, perhaps, has verbal egotism been carried to such lengths. In speaking of himself, Metternich is inexhaustible. He misses no opportunity: conversations, official documents, love letters.

—G. DE BERTIER DE SAUVIGNY, *op. cit.*

Vain and complacent, with fatuous good looks, his first thought in a crisis was to see whether his skin-tight breeches fitted perfectly and the Order of the Golden Fleece was hanging rightly. Even his love affairs—and he had many—were calculated for their political effect. He sought influence on Napoleon through the Queen of Naples and learnt the secrets of Russia from Countess Lieven. It must have been disturbing when he whispered political gossip in bed. He never made a clever remark. His thoughts, like those of most conservatives, were banal and obvious. "Things must get worse before they get better"; "after war Eu-

rope needs peace"; "everyone has his allotted place in society."
Most men could do better than this when shaving.

□

His only answer to either liberalism or radicalism was, in fact,
repression.... Since he had no genuine conservative ideas himself,
he denied that radical ideas were genuine; and solemnly maintained that discontent everywhere was the result of "a conspiracy." ...

He had no faith in principles or ideas, despite his theoretical
posturing. Though he claimed to be a disciple of Burke, he
doubted whether historical institutions would hold against radical
ideas....

□

Metternich did not invent the Balance of Power, nor do much to
develop it. The Great Powers of Europe existed without his
assistance; and his only initiative at the Congress of Vienna was
to project an unnecessary war over Poland—a war which others
had too much sense to fight. In international affairs, too, he offered a series of platitudes. "All I ask is a moral understanding between the five Great Powers. I ask that they take no important
step, without a previous joint understanding." Even the United
Nations would work if Metternich's request were granted.

—A. J. P. TAYLOR, *From Napoleon to Lenin*

Few statesmen have received so much adulation—and abuse. To
[liberals] he was the incarnation of senseless repression. Since 1919
he has enjoyed considerable rehabilitation as a preserver of peace.
His diplomatic skill is undeniable.

—ROBERT G. D. LAFFAN, *Chambers's Encyclopedia*

He was the guiding spirit of the international congress at Vienna
(1814–15) and the chief statesman of the so-called Holy Alliance.
... His system depended upon political and religious censorship,
espionage, and the suppression of revolutionary and nationalist
movements.... The revolution of 1848 (which forced him to seek
refuge in England) was in part directed at his repressive system.

—*Columbia Encyclopedia*

MICHELANGELO (1474–1564)

A man cannot achieve excellence if he satisfies the ignorant and not those of his own craft, and if he is not "singular" or "distant." ...As to those other meek, commonplace spirits, they may be found without the need of a candle in any of the highways of the world.

□

Pope Julius set me to paint the vault of the Sistine Chapel.... The first design consisted of figures of the Apostles within the lunettes, while certain portions were to be decorated in the usual manner.

As soon as I began this work, I realized that it would be poor, and I told the pope that in my opinion the placing of the Apostles alone would have a very poor effect.

He asked why, and I replied, "Because they also were poor." He then gave me new instructions, which left me free to do as I thought best.

□

I've grown a goiter dwelling in this den [the Sistine Chapel]. My beard turns up to heaven; my nape falls in: My breastbone grows visibly like a harp; a rich embroidery adorns my face—from brush-drops thick and thin. My loins grind into my paunch like levers; my buttocks like a crupper bear my weight; my feet wander to and fro; in front, my skin grows loose and long; behind, by bending, my skin becomes more taut and strait; crosswise, I strain myself like a Syrian bow.

—from various letters and VASAR, *Lives of the Painters*

THE MIDDLE CLASS

The city which is composed of middle-class citizens is necessarily best governed; they are, as we say, the natural element of a state....

The best political community is formed by citizens of the middle class, and those states are likely to be well-administered in which the middle class is large, and larger if possible than both the other classes ... or at any rate than either singly; for the addition of the middle class turns the scale, and prevents either from being dominant.

—Aristotle, *Politics*

MILITARY MORALE

Morale cannot be produced by pampering or coddling an army and is not necessarily destroyed by hardship, danger or even calamity. Though it can survive and develop in the adversity that comes as an inescapable incident of service, it will quickly wither and die if soldiers come to believe themselves the victims of ignorance, personal ambition, or ineptitude on the part of their military leaders.

—Douglas MacArthur, Annual report to the Chief of Staff, U.S. Army, June 30, 1933

MINOAN CIVILIZATION: LINEAR SCRIPT B

When Schliemann excavated the great site of Mycenae in 1876, he was unable to find any trace of writing.... Homer himself had made no explicit reference to writing at Agamemnon's court, and most people were content to believe that the Greeks had got their first knowledge of writing from the Phoenicians, some 400 years after the time of the Trojan War.

Then, one day in 1889, Sir Arthur Evans, keeper of the Ashmolean Museum, was sent a peculiar-looking sealstone from Greece. On its four sides it was engraved with pictographic signs —animals' heads, a human arm, arrows—rather like the hieroglyphs which the Hittites had used. Evans searched Greece and the Islands for more examples of these early sealstones: Many of them he found being worn as lucky charms by the Greek peasant women. He determined that they could all, in fact, be traced to the sites of ancient cities in Crete. And before long Evans came to the site of Knossos, the great palace of the legendary Minos, who had ruled Crete before the Trojan War, when she was a prosperous island of ninety cities.

Evans began to dig there in 1899, and it took him the rest of his life to catalogue, describe, and preserve all that he found. Among the brilliant remains of this "Minoan" civilization...he found ample evidence for not one, but at least four, different systems of writing. For the pictographs which he had collected on the seal-stones, dating from about 2000 B.C., were only the crude beginnings of Minoan writing, and had before long given rise to various simplified scripts in local use throughout Crete. In the last great half-century of Knossos' prosperity, before she was destroyed about 1400 B.C., the royal scribes had reduced these systems to a highly standardized official script, which Evans called Linear Script B.

—MICHAEL VENTRIS, on BBC, in *The Listener* (London), July 10, 1952

MINORITIES AND CAPITALISM

The groups in our society that have the most at stake in the preservation and strengthening of competitive capitalism are those minority groups which can most easily become the object of the distrust and enmity of the majority—the Negroes, the Jews, the foreign-born, to mention only the most obvious. Yet, paradoxically enough, the enemies of the free market—the Socialists and Communists—have been recruited in disproportionate measure from these groups. Instead of recognizing that the existence of the market has protected them from the attitudes of their fellow countrymen, they mistakenly attribute the residual discrimination to the market.

□

No one who buys bread knows whether the wheat from which it is made was grown by a Communist or a Republican, by a constitutionalist or a Fascist, or, for that matter, by a Negro or a white. This illustrates how an impersonal market separates economic activities from political views and protects men from being discriminated against in their economic activities for reasons that are irrelevant to their productivity—whether these reasons are associated with their views or their color.

—MILTON FRIEDMAN, *Capitalism and Freedom*

MIRACLES

A miracle cannot prove what is impossible; it is only useful to confirm what is possible.

—MAIMONIDES, *Guide to the Perplexed*, III

Nothing is esteemed a miracle, if it ever happen in the common course of nature. It is no miracle that a man, seemingly in good health, should die on a sudden; because such a kind of death, though more unusual than any other, has yet been frequently observed to happen. But it is a miracle that a dead man should come to life; because that has never been observed in any age or country. There must, therefore, be a uniform experience against every miraculous event, otherwise the event would not merit that appellation. And as a uniform experience amounts to a proof, there is here a direct and full *proof*, from the nature of the fact, against the existence of any miracle.

—David Hume

The most remarkable thing about miracles is that they happen.
—G. K. Chesterton

MODERATION

Moderation and the mean are always best. We may therefore conclude that in the ownership of all gifts of fortune a middle condition will be the best. Men who are in this condition are the most ready to listen to reason. Those who belong to either extreme—the overhandsome, the overstrong, the overnoble, the overwealthy; or at the opposite end the overpoor, the overweak, the utterly ignoble—find it is hard to follow the lead of reason....
—Aristotle, *Politics*

What is the spirit of moderation? It is the temper which does not press a partisan advantage to its bitter end, which can understand and will respect the other side, which feels a unity between all citizens—real and not the factitious product of propaganda—which recognizes their common fate and their common aspirations —in a word, which has faith in the sacredness of the individual. If you ask me how such a temper and such a faith are bred and fostered, I cannot answer. They are the last flowers of civilization, delicate and easily overrun by the weeds of our sinful human nature; we may even now be witnessing their uprooting and disappearance until in the progress of the ages their seeds can once more find some friendly soil. But I am satisfied that they must have the vigor within themselves to withstand the winds and weather of an

indifferent and ruthless world; and that it is idle to seek shelter
for them in a courtroom.

—JUDGE LEARNED HAND, in Shientag,
The Personality of the Judge

MODERN AGE

A sense of insecurity...has taken up its abode in the soul of
modern man. To him is happening what was said of the Regent
during the minority of Louis XV: He had all the talents except
to make use of them. To the nineteenth century many things
seemed no longer possible, firm-fixed as was its faith in progress.
Today, by the very fact that everything seems possible to us, we
have a feeling that the worst of all is possible: retrogression, barbarism, decadence. ...

Our age is characterized by the strange presumption that it is
superior to all past time. ... We live at a time when man believes
himself fabulously capable of creation, but he does not know
what to create. Lord of all things, he is not lord of himself. He
feels lost among his own abundance. With more means at its
disposal, more knowledge, more technique than ever, it turns out
that the world today goes the same way as the worst of worlds
that have been; it simply drifts.

—ORTEGA Y GASSET, *The Revolt of the Masses*

MOGHUL PILLARS OF HEADS

The Moghuls were saved by a lucky accident after...an arrow
hit Hemu in the eye, and although it did not immediately kill him
it made him unconscious. In any battle at this period the death
of the leader meant the end of the fight, and the sight of the tiny
Hemu slumped in the howdah of his famous elephant Hawai was
enough to make his army turn tail. He was brought unconscious
before Akbar and Bairam, and in that condition was decapitated
amongst much self-congratulation about the holy duty of slaying
the infidel. His head was then sent to Kabul, and his torso to
Delhi for exposure on a gibbet. There was great slaughter of
those who had been captured from his army, and in keeping with
the custom of Jenghiz Khan and Timur [Tamurlane] a victory
pillar was built with their heads. Peter Mundy, an Englishman

traveling in the Moghul empire some seventy-five years later, found such towers still being made of the heads of "rebbells and theeves" and made a drawing of one "with heads mortered and plaistered in, leaveinge out nothing but their verie face."

—BAMBER GASCOIGNE, *The Great Moghuls*

MOHAMMED (570–632 A.D.)

About the year 610 a new prophet appeared at Mecca ... Abu-l-Qasim Muhammad of the tribe of Quraysh, who was like a new incarnation of the old Hebrew prophets. At first the people did not pay much attention to him, but after he had abandoned his native town and moved ... to al-Medina, in 622, his success was phenomenal.

No prophet was ever more successful. By the time of his death ten years later, he had managed to unite the Arabian tribes and to inspire them with a singlehearted fervor which would enable them later to conquer the world. Damascus was captured in 635; Jerusalem in 637; the conquest of Egypt was completed in 641; that of Persia in the following year; that of Spain somewhat later in 710–712. By this time ... the Prophet's followers were ruling a large belt of the world all the way from Central Asia to the Far West.

—GEORGE SARTON, *The History of Science*

(*See also:* MUSLIMS)

MONA LISA

Hers is the head upon which all "the ends of the world are come," and the eyelids are a little weary. It is a beauty wrought out from within upon the flesh, the deposit, little cell by cell, of strange thoughts and fantastic reveries and exquisite passions. Set it for a moment beside one of those white Greek goddesses or beautiful women of antiquity, and how would they be troubled by this beauty, into which the soul with all its maladies has passed. . . . She is older than the rocks among which she sits; like the vampire, she has been dead many times, and learned the secrets of the grave; and has been a diver in deep seas, and keeps their fallen day about her.

—WALTER PATER, *The Renaissance*

MONEY

No complaint...is more common than that of a scarcity of money. Money, like wine, must always be scarce with those who have neither the wherewithal to buy it nor credit to borrow it.

□

There is no art which one government sooner learns of another, than that of draining money from the pockets of the people.... To relieve the present exigency is always the object which principally interests those immediately concerned in the administration of public affairs. The future liberation of the public revenue, they leave to the care of posterity.

—ADAM SMITH, *Wealth of Nations*, Vol. IV

If you would know the value of money, try to borrow some.

—BENJAMIN FRANKLIN

I cannot afford to waste my time making money.

—LOUIS J. R. AGASSIZ

The money that men makes lives after them.

—SAMUEL BUTLER

When I was young I used to think that money was the most important thing in life; now that I am old, I know it is.

—OSCAR WILDE

Lack of money is the root of all evil.

—GEORGE BERNARD SHAW

When a fellow says, "It ain't the money but the principle of the thing," it's the money.

—FRANK MCKINNEY ("Kin") HUBBARD

MONOGAMY

The habit of choosing one mate and being faithful until death do you part is indulged in only by a select and strangely assorted band of creatures...

If we were endowed with the same biological mating pattern

as the goose, there could be no polygamy, no promiscuity, no celibacy, no harem, no group marriage, no trial marriage, and no divorce in any human community in any part of the world. To say "my ex-wife" would make no more sense than saying "my ex-sister."

—ELAINE MORGAN, *The Descent of Woman*

... if God had not ordained marriage, but had left men to associate with the first woman they met, they themselves would very speedily have become tired of this disorderly course, and have prayed for marriage, since it is the very prohibition to do wrong which most excites to wrong.

—MARTIN LUTHER, *Table Talk*

Even in civilized mankind faint traces of a monogamic instinct can sometimes be perceived.

—BERTRAND RUSSELL, *Marriage and Morals*

MONOPOLY

We have no acts of parliament against combining to lower the price of work, but many against the combining to raise it.

—ADAM SMITH, *Wealth of Nations*

When technical conditions make a monopoly the natural outcome of competitive market forces, there are only three alternatives that seem available: private monopoly, public monopoly, or public regulation. All three are bad, so we must choose among evils. Henry Simons, observing public regulation of monopoly in the United States, found the results so distasteful that he concluded public monopoly would be a lesser evil. Walter Eucken, a noted German liberal, observing public monopoly in German railroads, found the results so distasteful that he concluded public regulation would be a lesser evil. Having learned from both, I reluctantly conclude that, if tolerable, private monopoly may be the least of the evils.

—MILTON FRIEDMAN, *Capitalism and Freedom*

MICHEL EYQUEM DE MONTAIGNE (1533–1592)

I look into myself. I have no other business. I eternally meditate upon myself, control myself, circulate within myself.

☐

My hands are so clumsy that I cannot even write clearly.... I cannot fold a letter well. I could never make a pen, nor carve meat at table, nor lure a hawk, nor speak to a horse. In short, the qualities of my body are well suited to those of my soul; nothing is deft—but there is a full, firm vigor. My soul is free, entirely its own....

☐

Reader, here is a truthful book. It warns you at the outset that I have set for myself only a private goal. I have not thought of either your needs or my glory, for my powers would not be equal to such a task.

I want to be seen without affection or artistry, but simply and naturally; for it is only myself that I portray. My faults will be found here, and my plain nature, so far as discretion will allow it.

Had I lived among those people of whom it is said that they still live under the sweet freedom of nature, I assure you I would willingly picture myself to you wholly naked. And so, reader, I myself am the content of my book: there is no reason for you to spend your leisure on so frivolous a subject. Farewell, then!

—MONTAIGNE, *Essays*

MONTEZUMA II (1480?–1520)

The Great Montezuma was about forty years old, of good height and well proportioned, slender and spare of flesh, not very swarthy, but of the natural color and shade of an Indian. He did not wear his hair long, but so as just to cover his ears, his scanty black beard was well shaped and thin. His face was somewhat long, but cheerful, and he had good eyes and showed in his appearance and manner both tenderness and, when necessary, gravity. He was very neat and clean and bathed once every day in the afternoon.

He had many women as mistresses, daughters of Chieftains, and

he had two great Cacicas as his legitimate wives. He was free from
unnatural offenses. The clothes that he wore one day, he did not
put on again until four days later. He had over two hundred
Chieftains in his guard ... and when they went to speak to him
they were obliged to take off their rich mantles and put on others
of little worth ... and they had to enter barefoot with their eyes
lowered to the ground, and not to look up in his face. And they
made him three obeisances, and said: "Lord, my lord, my Great
Lord," before they came up to him. ...

—BERNAL DIAZ DEL CASTILLO,
The Discovery and Conquest of Mexico, tr. A. P.
Maudslay

MONTEZUMA II DINES

I have heard it said that they were wont to cook for him the flesh
of young boys, but as he had such a variety of dishes, made of so
many things, we could not succeed in seeing if they were of human flesh or of other things ... but I know for certain that after
our Captain censured the sacrifice of human beings, and the eating of their flesh, he ordered that such food should not be prepared
for him henceforth.

—Ibid.

MONTEZUMA II'S DEATH

Montezuma was placed by a battlement of the roof with many of
us soldiers guarding him, and he began to speak to his people,
with very affectionate expressions telling them to desist from the
war, and that we would leave Mexico. Many of the Mexican
Chieftains and Captains knew him well and at once ordered their
people to be silent and not to discharge darts, stones or arrows,
and four of them reached a spot where Montezuma could speak
to them, and they to him, and with tears they said to him: "Oh!
Señor, and our great Lord, how all your misfortunes and injury
and that of your children and relations afflicts us, we make known
to you that we have already raised one of your kinsmen to be our
Lord," and there he stated his name, that he was called Cuitlahuac,
the Lord of Ixtapalapa, and moreover they said that the war must
be carried through, and that they had vowed to their Idols not to

relax it until we were all dead, and that they prayed every day to their Huichilobos and Texcatepuca to guard him free and safe from our power, and that should it end as they desired, they would not fail to hold him in higher regard as their Lord than they did before, and they begged him to forgive them.

They had hardly finished this speech when suddenly such a shower of stones and darts were discharged that (our men who were shielding him having neglected for a moment their duty, because they saw how the attack ceased while he spoke to them) he was hit by three stones, one on the head, another on the arm and another on the leg, and although they begged him to have the wounds dressed and to take food, and spoke kind words to him about it, he would not. Indeed, when we least expected it, they came to say that he was dead. Cortes wept for him, and all of us Captains and soldiers, and there was no man among us who knew him and was intimate with him, who did not bemoan him, as though he were our good father, and it is not to be wondered at, considering how good he was.

—Ibid.

THE MOON

The great clock at Westminster shrinks into insignificance when compared with the mighty clock which the captain uses for setting his chronometer. The face of this stupendous dial is the face of the heavens. The numbers engraved on the face of a clock are replaced by the twinkling stars; while the hand which moves over the dial is the beautiful moon herself. When the captain desires to test his chronometer, he measures the distance of the moon from a neighboring star. In the Nautical Almanac he finds the Greenwich time at which the moon was three degrees from the star. Comparing this with the indications of the chronometer, he finds the required correction.

□

The moon always turns the same side towards us, and accordingly we never get a view of the other side. This is caused by the interesting circumstance that the moon takes exactly the same time to turn once round its own axis as it takes to go once round the earth. The rotation is, however, performed with uniform speed,

while the moon does not move in its orbit with a perfectly uniform velocity. The consequence is that we now get a slight
glimpse round the east limb, and now a similar glimpse round the
west limb, as if the moon were shaking its head very gently at us.
But it is only an insignificant margin of the far side of the moon
which this *liberation* permits us to examine.

□

It seems probable that a building on the moon would remain for
century after century just as it was left by the builders. There
need be no glass in the windows, for there is no wind and no rain
to keep out. There need not be fireplaces in the rooms, for fuel
cannot burn without air. Dwellers in a lunar city would find that
no dust could rise, no odors be perceived, no sounds be heard.
—Robert Ball, *The Story of the Heavens*, 1885

MORALITY

Morality rests on the inescapable exigencies of human cohabitation.
—Sigmund Freud

Fear is the mother of morality.
—Nietzsche, *Beyond Good and Evil*

Neither the individuals nor the ages most distinguished for intel-
lectual achievements have been distinguished for moral excellence.
—W. E. H. Lecky,
History of European Morals, Vol. I

Our moralists would do well to cease their upbraidings and apply
themselves to the interesting problem—"How is goodness to be
made the object of passionate desire, as attractive as fame, success,
or even adventure?" If they could excite in men an enthusiasm
for virtue, as the poets, musicians and artists excite in them enthusiasm for beauty...if they could devise a morality that has
power to charm, they would win all hearts.
—W. Macneill Dixon, *The Human Situation*

The problem is, how to construct a world in which immoral
people can do the least harm; not, how to enable moral people to
do the most good. Nothing would be more conducive to blood-

shed than to have a world of highly moral people whose morals differ, trying to work for the public good.

—MILTON FRIEDMAN, *op. cit.*

The highest possible stage in moral culture is when we recognize that we ought to control our thoughts.

—CHARLES DARWIN, *Descent of Man*

Men always attempt to avoid condemning a thing upon merely moral grounds. If I beat my grandmother to death tomorrow in the middle of Battersea Park, you may be perfectly certain that people will say everything about it except the simple and fairly obvious fact that it is wrong. Some will call it insane; that is, will accuse it of a deficiency of intelligence. This is not necessarily true at all. You could not tell whether the act was unintelligent or not unless you knew my grandmother. Some will call it vulgar, disgusting, and the rest of it; that is, they will accuse it of a lack of manners. Perhaps it does show a lack of manners; but this is scarcely its most serious disadvantage. Others will talk about the loathsome spectacle and the revolting scene; that is, they will accuse it of a deficiency of art, or aesthetic beauty. This again depends on the circumstances: In order to be quite certain that the appearance of the old lady has definitely deteriorated under the process of being beaten to death, it is necessary for the philosophical critic to be quite certain how ugly she was before. Another school of thinkers will say that the action is lacking in efficiency: that it is an uneconomic waste of a good grandmother. But that could only depend on the value, which is again an individual matter.

The only real point that is worth mentioning is that the action is wicked, because your grandmother has a right not to be beaten to death. But of this simple moral explanation modern journalism has, as I say, a standing fear. It will call the action anything else—mad, bestial, vulgar, idiotic, rather than call it sinful.

—G. K. CHESTERTON, *Selected Essays*

Morality turns on whether the pleasure precedes the pain or follows it.... Thus, it is immoral to get drunk because the headache comes after the drinking, but if the headache came first, and the drunkenness afterwards, it would be moral to get drunk.

—SAMUEL BUTLER, *Notebooks*

SIR THOMAS MORE (1478–1535)

In his *Utopia* his lawe is that the young people are to see each other stark-naked before marriage. Sir William Roper, of Eltham ... came one morning, pretty early, to my Lord with a proposall to marry one of his daughters. My Lord's daughters were then both together abed in a truckle-bed in their father's chamber asleep. He carries Sir William into the chamber and takes the Sheete by the corner and suddenly whippes it off. They lay on their Backs, and their smocks up as high as their arme-pitts. This awakened them, and immediately they turned on their bellies. Quoth Roper, I have seen both sides, and so gave a patt on the buttock, he made choice of, sayeing, Thou art mine. Here was all the trouble of the wooeing. This account I had from my honoured friend old Mrs. Tyndale.

—Aubrey's Brief Lives

MORGUE

Sign over entrance to New York City morgue:

Taceant colloquia effugiat risus hic locus est ubi mors gaudet succurrere vitae.

Let conversation cease. Let laughter flee. This place is where death delights to help life.

"MOTHER" LOVE

Love of infants for their mothers is often regarded as a sacred or mystical force, and perhaps this is why it has received so little objective study. . . .

With this question in mind, we exposed our infant monkeys to strange objects likely to frighten them, such as a mechanical teddy bear that moved forward, beating a drum. It was found that, whether the infants had nursed on the wire mother or the cloth one, they overwhelmingly sought comfort in stress from the cloth one. The infant would cling to it, rubbing its body against the toweling. With its fears thus assuaged, it would turn to look at the previously terrifying bear without the slightest sign of alarm. It might even leave the comfort of its substitute mother to approach the object that had frightened it only a minute before.

It is obvious that such behavior is analogous to that of human infants.... If a human child is taken to an unfamiliar place, for example, he will usually remain calm and happy so long as his mother is nearby, but if she leaves him, fear and panic may result. Our experiments showed a similar effect in infant monkeys. We put the monkeys in a room that was much larger than their usual cages, and in the room we placed a number of unfamiliar objects—a crumpled piece of newspaper, blocks of wood, a metal plate, and a doorknob mounted on a box. If a cloth mother was present, the monkey, at the sight of these objects, would rush wildly to her and, rubbing against the toweling, cling to her tightly. Its fear would then diminish greatly or else vanish altogether, as in the previous experiment.

If, on the other hand, the cloth mother were absent, the infant would rush across the room and throw itself head down on the floor, clutching its head and body and screaming in distress. The bare wire mother afforded no more reassurance than no mother at all—even monkeys that had known only the wire mother from birth showed no affection for her and got no comfort from her presence. Indeed, this group of monkeys showed the greatest distress of all.

—HARRY F. HARLOW, "Of Love in Infants," in
Natural History, 1960

Do incubator chickens love their mother?

—ARTHUR ("Bugs") BAER

MOTIVATION

The natural effort of every individual to better his own condition, when suffered to exert itself with freedom and security, is so powerful a principle, that it is alone, and without any assistance, not only capable of carrying on the society to wealth and prosperity, but of surmounting a hundred impertinent obstructions with which the folly of human laws too often encumbers its operations.
—ADAM SMITH, *Wealth of Nations*, Vol. V

MOTIVES IN RESEARCH

There are many highly respectable motives which may lead men
to prosecute research, but three which are much more important
than the rest. The first (without which the rest must come to
nothing) is intellectual curiosity, desire to know the truth. Then,
professional pride, anxiety to be satisfied with one's performance.... Finally, ambition, desire for reputation, and the position, even the power or the money, which it brings.

It may be fine to feel, when you have done your work, that
you have added to the happiness or alleviated the sufferings of
others, but that will not be why you did it. So if a mathematician,
or a chemist, or even a physiologist, were to tell me that the driving force in his work had been the desire to benefit humanity,
then I should not believe him (nor should I think the better of
him if I did). His dominant motives have been those which I have
stated, and in which, surely, there is nothing of which any decent man need be ashamed.

—G. H. HARDY, *A Mathematician's Apology*

MUNICH

It will take a book to examine ... the stories with which the road
to Munich was paved. Every man continued along the line he
had followed during the past six months—except that the movement gathered vertiginous speed and a ghastly momentum. In the
previous long-drawn process of attrition there was time and room
for disguise and make-believe (flimsy though it did prove). But
in the violent rush down the precipice things appear with glaring
starkness; promises and guarantees vanish overnight; sacrifices are
inflicted on the Czechs to preserve them, so they are told, from
even worse ones, which in turn are demanded from them almost
before they had time fully to envisage the former. And then the
Munich conference for which Hitler had given Mussolini directions and Chamberlain gave him thanks. Daladier and Chamberlain were treated with an inattention bordering on contempt: but
Chamberlain apparently never noticed it; and having delivered
Czechoslovakia, land and men, into Hitler's hands he took his
stand on trifles most truly within his range: claims to compen-

sation . . . currency, outstanding loans, etc. . . . Of the "pity and fear" of that night he felt nothing.

When all was over, at 1:30 A.M. the two Prime Ministers had to inform the Czech representatives of the death verdict passed on their nation, unheard. Daladier was visibly embarrassed while Chamberlain "yawned without ceasing and with no show of embarrassment". . . .

—Sir Lewis Namier,
"Peace in Our Time: The Makers of Munich," in
The Nazi Era

MURDERERS' MOTIVES

No detective worth his salt, therefore, ever bases a case against a murderer on motive alone. At best an overwhelming motive for committing a particular murder is but one pointer among many to the identity of the murderer; at worst, the motive can be so trivial or improbable as to make the rest of the evidence against the murderer appear doubtful.

There are in fact almost as many different motives for murder as there are murderers.

□

. . . "Not even the Devil knows what's in a man's mind," sums up the chief difficulty in establishing motives. A detective can usually determine how, when, where, and by whom a murder has been committed. He sometimes knows with reasonable certainty the extent to which it has been premeditated, but the motive more often than not remains the dark secret of the murderer. Moreover, motives, even when they are known, are extremely difficult to prove, and no court can ever be certain that it has heard the whole truth.

—Anthony Martienssen, *Crime and the Police*

MUSIC

Without music, life would be a mistake.

—Friedrich Nietzsche

Who hears music, feels his solitude peopled at once.

—Robert Browning

Music: cathedrals in sound.

—ALFRED BRUNEAU

Wagner has beautiful moments but awful quarter hours.

—GIACCHINO ANTONIO ROSSINI

Of all noises, I think music is the least disagreeable.

—SAMUEL JOHNSON

Berlioz says nothing in his music, but he says it magnificently.

—JAMES GIBBONS HUNEKER

Classical music is the kind that we keep hoping will turn into a tune.

—FRANK McKINNEY ("Kin") HUBBARD

Good music makes people homesick for something they never had and never will have.

—EDGAR ("Ed") HOWE

MUSLIMS

NAME

It was a long time before Christendom was even willing to give them [Muslims] a name with a religious meaning. For many centuries both Eastern and Western Christendom called the disciples of the Prophet Saracens, a word of uncertain etymology ... both pre-Islamic and pre-Christian. In the Iberian peninsula, where the Muslims whom they met came from Morocco, they called them Moors, and the people of Iberian culture ... continued to call Muslims Moors even if they met them in Ceylon or in the Philippines.

In most of Europe, Muslims were called Turks, after the main Muslim invaders, and a convert to Islam was said to have "turned Turk." ... Farther east, Muslims were Tatars, another ethnic name loosely applied to the Islamized steppe peoples who for a while dominated Russia....

The Muslims do not, and never have, called themselves Muhammedans nor their religion Muhammedanism, since Muhammad does not occupy the same place in Islam as Christ does in Christianity.

—BERNARD LEWIS,
"The Return of Islam," in *Commentary*, January 1976

BELIEFS

In Islam, religion is not, as it is in Christendom, one sector or segment of life, regulating some matters while others are excluded; it is concerned with the whole of life—not a limited but a total jurisdiction. In such a society the very idea of the separation of church and state is meaningless, since there are no two entities to be separated. Church and state, religious and political authority, are one and the same. In classical Arabic and in the other classical languages of Islam there are no pairs of terms corresponding to lay and ecclesiastical, spiritual and temporal, secular and religious, because these pairs of words express a Christian dichotomy which has no equivalent in the world of Islam. It is only in modern times, under Christian influence, that these concepts have begun to appear and that words have been coined to express them. Their meaning is still very imperfectly understood and their relevance to Muslim institutions dubious.

—*Ibid.*

A MUSLIM TABOO

A church relief official reported today that about 200,000 Bengali wives who were raped by Pakistani soldiers during the war in East Pakistan last month were now ostracized by the Moslem communities and had virtually no place to turn to.

The Rev. Kentaro Buma, Asian relief secretary of the World Council of Churches, said at a news conference that by tradition no Moslem husband will take back a wife touched by another man, even if she was subdued by force.

—Associated Press, January 17, 1976

BENITO MUSSOLINI (1883–1945)

His character and behavior as head of the government [showed] the same blend of ostentation, inconsistency and opportunistic political calculation which had always characterized his career and

which fulfilled the prophecy Sorel was supposed to have made ...
20 years earlier: " 'Mussolini is no ordinary socialist ... some day
we shall see him at the head of a mighty legion, saluting the Italian
flag with his sword ...' " He exulted in displaying his sturdy phy-
sique, in being photographed stripped to the waist ... flying a plane
or jumping on horseback. As he uttered his inflammatory speeches
his chin was always stuck well out, and the photographers were at
pains to ensure that his short stature was disguised. So likewise ...
his policies during the years of his dictatorship were always flam-
boyant ... he was right in supposing that the Italians would respond to his *braggadocio;* they were tired of appearing before the
world as a poor relative....

—EDWARD E. Y. HALES, *Chambers's Encyclopedia*

Mussolini was an intelligent, self-taught man of uncertain cultural background who wrote rough and vivid journalistic prose.
(I have never been able to ascertain how good a violinist he was.
His oldest son Vittorio told me, during the Ethiopian war, that
his father's favorite aria was "Ramona," which he played to the
accompaniment of a Victrola record.) But, even if he had been
a great Renaissance figure, a great political thinker, and a great
musician, twentieth-century "romantics" should still have asked
themselves whether the abolition of all fundamental liberties was
not an excessive price to pay for such cultural achievements.

Liberals were both "romantics" and "nativists," sometimes
simultaneously. They liked Mussolini as a man who could restore
to Italy the splendors of past centuries and make these unruly,
unreliable, noisy and dishonest Italians behave. Furthermore they
were seduced by his "progressivism." In many American minds
progress takes precedence over democracy. They would probably spurn a stationary democracy. Of course, *le problème ne se
pose pas* in the United States, where the two things always go
hand in hand, but the choice often presents itself in more backward countries, where both democracy and progress usually have
a rough time and are in contrast. The preference for progress was
encouraged by Mussolini, himself a progressive since his socialist
days; he did not always have to tell lies to liberal Americans who
interviewed him. He honestly believed like them, that progress—

in education, public works, industrial development, *autostrade*, armaments, law and order—came first.

The real importance of the precedent was that Roosevelt, like most progressive Americans, belonged to a generation which was abandoning the firm moral values and restraints of their ancestors and experimenting with unprejudiced realism. For Roosevelt, as for Mussolini, vaguely defined but "progressive" ends justified whatever means were indicated, and success was the vindication of everything. Many Italians shared this view (a much older view in Italy than in the United States). They revolted against Mussolini in the end not because he had cheated but because, being a cheat, he had lost.

—LUIGI BARZINI,
(London) *Times Literary Supplement*, October 3, 1975

MYSTERY AND SCIENCE

The most beautiful thing we can experience is the mysterious. It is the source of all true art and science. He to whom this emotion is a stranger, who can no longer pause to wonder and stand in awe, is as good as dead: His eyes are closed.

—ALBERT EINSTEIN, *The World as I See It*

Does science leave no mystery? On the contrary it proclaims mystery where others profess knowledge. There is mystery enough in the universe of sensation and in its capacity for containing those little corners of consciousness which project their own products, of order and law and reason, into an unknown and unknowable world. There is mystery enough here, only let us clearly distinguish it from ignorance within the field of possible knowledge. The one is impenetrable, the other we are daily subduing.

—KARL PEARSON, *Grammar of Science*, 1892

MYSTICISM AND REASON

... anything which is rational, is always difficult for the lay mind. But the thing which is irrational anyone can understand. That is why religion came so early into the orld and spread so far, while science came so late into the world and has not spread at all. History unanimously attests the fact that it is only mysticism which stands the smallest chance of being understood by the people. Common sense has to be kept as an esoteric secret in the dark temple of culture.

—G. K. CHESTERTON, *Heretics*

Mix a little mystery into everything, for mystery arouses veneration.

—BALTHASAR GRACIAN, *The Art of Worldly Wisdom*

MYTH

The faculty for myth is innate in the human race. It seizes with avidity upon any incidents, surprising or mysterious, in the career of those who have at all distinguished themselves from their fellows, and invents a legend to which it then attaches a fanatical belief. It is the protest of romance against the commonplace of life. The incidents of the legend become the hero's surest passport to immortality.

—W. SOMERSET MAUGHAM, *The Moon and Sixpence*

NAPOLEON BONAPARTE (1769–1821)

...Suddenly I found myself victorious, laying down the law, courted by emperors.... What enthusiasm! What shouting! "Long live the liberator of Italy!" At twenty-five! From that moment, I foresaw what I might be.... I felt the earth flee from beneath me, as if I were being carried to the sky.

□

In Egypt...I saw myself founding a religion, marching into Asia, riding an elephant, a turban on my head and in my hand the new Koran that I would have composed to suit my needs.

□

[The day after his coronation]: I came too late. . . . Look at Alexander: When he had conquered Asia and presented himself . . . as the son of Jupiter, the whole Orient believed him . . . [but] if I declared myself [divine] every fishwife would hoot when she saw me pass. The masses are too enlightened these days: Nothing great can be done any more.

☐

I . . . love power . . . as an artist. I love it as a violinist loves his violin.

☐

History I conquered rather than studied. . . . I spurned what was of no use . . . and seized upon those conclusions that pleased me.

☐

My policy is to govern men the way the great majority wants to be governed. . . . By making myself Catholic I brought the war in the Vendéc to an end. By becoming a Moslem, I established myself in Egypt. By acting ultramontane, I won the minds of the Italians. If I governed a nation of Jews, I should restore the temple of Solomon.

☐

A true master of politics is able to calculate . . . the advantages to which he may put his very faults.

☐

In politics . . . never retreat, never retrace . . . never admit a mistake.

☐

What are the lives of a million men to me?

☐

Troops are made to let themselves be killed.

☐

I have made all the calculations: Fate will do the rest.

☐

I measure my dreams with the calipers of reason.

☐

I start out by believing the worst.

☐

I defy anyone to trick me. [Only] exceptional rascals [could be] as bad as I assume them to be.

☐

All I have to do is hang gold braid on [virtuous republicans] and they are mine.

□

Vanity made the revolution; liberty was only the pretext.

□

Asked what would be said about him when he died, he answered, "Ouf!"

□

I would not hesitate to act as a coward—if it would be useful.
                              —compiled from various biographies and letters

I love no one. No, not even my brother. Joseph maybe, a little . . . [from] force of habit.
                                        —in conversation, 1800

I like only those people who are useful to me, and only so long as they are useful.
                                             —said in 1818

You must submit to every one of my whims. . . . To all your complaints I have the right to answer with an eternal "I." I am apart from everybody. I accept no one's condition.
                                             —to Josephine

Had I succeeded, I should have died with the reputation of the greatest man who ever lived. Although I failed, I shall be considered an extraordinary man. I have fought fifty battles, almost all of which I [won]. I have framed and carried into effect a code of laws that will bear my name into the most distant posterity.
                        —to O'Meara, at St. Helena, March 3, 1817

ABOUT HIM

Success in cowing the environment by willfulness forms a personality predisposed toward imperious violence. . . . Napoleon appears to have won through willfulness from the second year of his life. He grew into a quarrelsome and combative child; and when his parents, seeking to curb his truculence, sent him to a girls' school at the age of five, he was only spoiled by his teachers and schoolmates, who tolerated the eccentricities of the only boy among them. Evidently Napoleon was deeply fixated on the mother image, and resentful of the rivalry of his elder brother Joseph, whom he used to "thump and bite."

His inordinate craving for deference was but partly gratified, even by success; for the picture of an inferior self, against which he struggled, was ever with him. Among his companions at the military school at Brienne he felt hopelessly inferior, for he was but five feet five in height. He was taunted as poor and Corsican. He secretly worried lest his sexual organs were atrophied, and lived an active sexual life as a constant means of reassuring himself of his doubtful masculinity.

Throughout his life Napoleon was subject to moods of melancholy and to reveries of inferiority and isolation. To some extent these were mitigated by fantasies and claims to grandiosity: "I am no ordinary man, and laws of propriety and morals are not applicable to me." ... He sought the balm of success for his wounded ego, and he was forever licking his self-inflicted mutilations.

—HAROLD D. LASSWELL,
Politics—Who Gets What, When, How

...that singular, incomplete, but truly marvelous being...one of the strangest spectacles that can be found in the universe.

☐

He was as great as a man can be without morality.

—ALEXIS DE TOCQUEVILLE

On his face was written: Thou shalt have no other god but me.

—HEINRICH HEINE

Napoleon was, of all the men in the world, the one who most profoundly despised the human race. He had a marvelous insight into the weaker sides of human nature.

—METTERNICH

It is fashionable today to magnify Bonaparte's victories: Those who suffered by them have disappeared; we no longer hear the curses of the victims and their cries of pain and distress; we no longer see France exhausted, with only women to till her soil; we no longer see parents arrested as hostages for their sons, or the inhabitants of a village punished jointly and severally with the penalties applicable to a single deserter; we no longer see the conscription notices pasted up at street corners, and the passers-by gathering in a crowd in front of those huge death warrants, looking in consternation for the names of their children, their brothers, their friends, their neighbors. We forget that everybody bewailed the news of a victory; we forget that in the theater, the slightest remark directed against Bonaparte which had escaped the censors' notice was hailed with rapture; we forget that the people, the Court, the generals, the ministers and Napoleon's relatives were weary of his tyranny and his conquests, weary of that game which was always being won yet went on being played, of that existence which was brought into question again every morning because of the impossibility of peace.

□

He delighted in the humiliation of what he had overthrown; he slandered and wounded most of all whatever had dared to oppose him. His arrogance was equal to his good fortune: the more he humbled others, the greater he believed himself to appear. Jealous of his generals, he accused them of his own mistakes, for he considered himself infallible.

—François-René Chateaubriand, *Memoirs*

His main achievement was the revolution he brought about in the techniques of power and of manipulating men. His use of the press and propaganda, his mastery of applied psychology to make people do what he wanted them to do, his rhetoric, his bulletins, his genius at self-dramatization, his flair for pageantry, his superb exploitation of human vanity, ambition and gullibility, his genius at fanning fear and greed by turns, and, finally, his artful creation of his own legend—all this places him squarely in our own times.

—J. Christopher Herold,
The Horizon Book of the Age of Napoleon

He always asked the impossible, and sometimes it was granted him. This is the real basis of the Napoleonic legend (as it will be for the legend of Hitler)....Yet what did this wonderful human being end in? A querulous sick man on a sub-tropical island dictating a drab and meaningless record to while away the time. The memoirs of Napoleon suggest that there is something to be said for not thinking that you are God.

A. J. P. TAYLOR, *From Napoleon to Lenin*

God was bored by him.

—VICTOR HUGO

NATURE

It is hard to know whether nature is a kind parent or a harsh stepmother.

—PLINY THE ELDER

Nature does nothing uselessly.

—ARISTOTLE

God made the beauties of nature like a child playing in the sand.

—APOLLONIUS OF TYANA, c. 70 A.D.

Nature does not care whether the hunter slays the beast or the beast the hunter. She will make good compost of them both, and her ends are prospered whichever succeeds.

—JOHN BURROUGHS

I do not understand where the "beauty" and "harmony" of nature are supposed to be found. Throughout the animal kingdom, animals ruthlessly prey upon each other. Most of them are either cruelly killed by other animals or slowly die of hunger. For my part, I am unable to see any very great beauty or harmony in the tapeworm.

—BERTRAND RUSSELL,
"What Is an Agnostic?", in *Religions of America*

Our old Mother Nature has pleasant and cheery tones... when she comes in her dress of blue and gold over the eastern hilltops; but when she follows us to our beds in her suit of black velvet and diamonds... every whisper of her lips is full of mystery and fear.

—OLIVER WENDELL HOLMES,
Autocrat of the Breakfast Table

There is something in this external nature that I could never worship. There is a cruelty and a dark intention that I cannot blink.
It shines in the eye of the hawk and the humblest humming airfly
is not without its utter heartlessness and brutality.

—The Book without a Name

My congenital indifference to nature in the wild, natural scenery,
rocks, rills, woods and templed hills, hardened into permanent dis-
taste. ... I can see nature only as an enemy; a highly respected
enemy, but an enemy.

—A. J. NOCK, *Memoirs of a Superfluous Man*

There are no accidents in nature. All things are made and changed
from form to form in accordance with absolute, immutable and
unchangeable laws.

—BARUCH SPINOZA, *The Ethics* (Part I)

Wherever ... anything in nature seems to us ridiculous, or evil, it
is because we only have a partial view of things, and are in the
main ignorant of the order and coherence of nature as a whole,
and because we want everything to be arranged according to our
own reason. ...

—BARUCH SPINOZA, *Political Treatise*

DEATH

The bird, however hard the frost may be, flies briskly to his customary roosting place, and, with beak tucked into his wing, falls
asleep. He has no apprehensions; only the blood grows colder and
colder, the pulse feebler as he sleeps, and at midnight, or in the
early morning, he drops from his perch—dead.

Yesterday he lived and moved, responsive to a thousand external influences ... ; he had a various language, the inherited
knowledge of his race, and the faculty of flight, by means of
which he could shoot ... [with] marvelous certitude in all his
motions, as to be able to drop himself down from the tallest tree-
top, or out of the void air, on to a slender spray, and scarcely
cause its leaves to tremble. Now, on this morning, he lies stiff and
motionless; if you were to take him up and drop him from your

hand, he would fall to the ground like a stone or a lump of clay—
so easy and swift is the passage from life to death in wild nature!
But he was never miserable.

—W. H. Hudson, *Birds in Town and Village*

NEIGHBORS

We make our friends; we make our enemies; but God makes our
next-door neighbor. Hence he comes to us clad in all the careless
terrors of nature; he is as strange as the stars, as reckless and indifferent as the rain. He is Man, the most terrible of the beasts.

—G. K. Chesterton, *The Man Who Was Chesterton*

HORATIO NELSON (1758–1805)

The two years which followed Nelson's arrival at Naples after his
victory in the Nile were in some ways the saddest in his life and
blemished his wonderful reputation and career. Desperately in
love with Lady Hamilton—a once fabulously lovely woman whose
beauty was now fast fading and who, with her melodramatic
nature, was resolved to keep her last lover and hero constantly at
her side—he appeared everywhere with her and her aging husband, the ambassador. At her instigation he became involved in
the treacherous politics of the corrupt Neapolitan court. It was
his nature to do everything with passionate intensity, and for a
time his devotion to her almost took the place of his utter dedication to his country's service. . . .

Traveling across Europe with the Hamiltons, he was everywhere lionised as a hero, with his adored Emma beside him. But
when he reached England, though his carriage was drawn by a
cheering mob from Ludgate to the Guildhall and the City fathers
presented him with a diamond-studded sword, his wife refused
to countenance his new friends and parted from him forever,
while the King, after the briefest of greetings, turned his back on
him at a levee. In political and official circles it was assumed by
many that his career was finished.

□

At half-past ten on the night of Friday, September 13th, after
praying by the bedside of his child, Horatia, Nelson took his leave

of Merton.... Then he drove through the night over the Surrey heaths and Hampshire hills to Portsmouth ... and at two o'clock, accompanied by Canning and George Rose, who were to dine with him, went off to the *Victory*. Near the bathing machines, which he had chosen in preference to the usual landing stage, a vast crowd was waiting to see him go. "Many were in tears," wrote Southey, "and many knelt down before him and blessed him as he passed...."

—ARTHUR BRYANT, *Nelson*

HIS DEATH

By one o'clock at Trafalgar the center as well as the rear of the Franco-Spanish line was a mass of flame and billowing smoke. For nearly a mile between the two British flagships the ridge of fire and thunder continued. Codrington ... described "that grand and awful scene"—the falling masts, the ships crowded together, the broadsides crashing into blazing timbers at point blank range as rival boarding parties vainly sought an opportunity. For this was a sea battle of a pattern never previously attempted—more terrifying and more decisive.... Down in the crowded cockpit the scene of horror was so awful that the chaplain, Scott, could bear it no longer and stumbled up the companion-ladder slippery with gore, for a breath of fresh air. There, "all noise, confusion and smoke," he saw Nelson fall.

As they bore him down, his shoulder, lung and spine shot through and his golden epaulette driven deep into his body—the Admiral covered the stars on his breast with his blood-soaked handkerchief lest his men should see and be discouraged....

The last words he said were, "God and my Country."

—*Ibid.*

NERO (37–68 A.D.)

To describe the depravity of Nero is beyond the compass of this work. Many writers have given us careful accounts of all that concerned him, and anyone can learn his perversity and degenerate madness, which entailed the senseless murder of thousands. He had a lust for blood; he spared neither his closest friends nor relatives.

He was even responsible for the deaths of his mother, brothers, wife, and thousands attached to his household. . . . He was the first Roman emperor to be an open enemy of the worship of God.

—EUSEBIUS OF CAESAREA, *The Ecclesiastical History*

He castrated the boy Sporus and actually tried to make a woman of him. He married him with all the usual ceremonies, including a dowry and a bridal veil, and took him to his house attended by a great throng, and treated him as his wife. The witty jest is still current that it would have been better for the world if Nero's father had had that kind of wife.

Nero took this Sporus, dressed in the finery of empresses, riding in a litter, to the assizes of Greece, and later to Rome, through the Street of the Images, fondly kissing him from time to time.

That Nero desired illicit relations with his own mother . . . was notorious, especially after he added to his concubines a courtesan who is said to look very much like Agrippina. Even before that, so they say, whenever he rode in a litter with his mother, he had incestuous relations with her, which were betrayed by the stains on his clothing.

—SUETONIUS, *The Lives of the Twelve Caesars*

THE BURNING OF ROME

Whether it was accidental or caused by the emperor's criminal act is uncertain—both versions have supporters. Now started the most terrible and destructive fire which Rome had ever experienced. It began in the Circus, where it adjoins the hills. Breaking out in shops selling inflammable goods, and fanned by the wind, the conflagration instantly grew and swept the whole length of the Circus. There were no walled mansions or temples, or any other obstructions which could arrest it. First, the fire swept violently over the level spaces. Then it climbed the hills—but returned to ravage the lower ground again. It outstripped every countermeasure. The ancient city's narrow winding streets and irregular blocks encouraged its progress.

Terrified, shrieking women, helpless old and young, people intent on their own safety, people unselfishly supporting invalids or waiting for them, fugitives and lingerers alike—all heightened the confusion. When people looked back, menacing flames sprang up before them or outflanked them. When they escaped to a neighboring quarter, the fire followed—even districts believed remote proved to be involved. Finally, with no idea where or what to flee, they crowded on to the country roads, or lay in the fields. Some who had lost everything . . . could have escaped, but preferred to die. So did others, who had failed to rescue their loved ones. . . .

Nero was at Antium. He only returned to the city when the fire was approaching the mansion he had built . . . For the relief of the homeless, fugitive masses he threw open the Field of Mars . . . and even his own Gardens. . . . Food was brought from Ostia and neighboring towns, and the price of corn was cut. Yet these measures . . . earned no gratitude. For a rumor had spread that, while the city was burning, Nero had gone to his private stage and, comparing modern calamities with ancient, had sung of the destruction of Troy.

—TACITUS, *The Annals of Imperial Rome,*
tr. Michael Grant

KILLS HIS MOTHER

At last terrified by her violence and threats, he determined to have her life, and after thrice attempting it by poison and finding that she had made herself immune by antidotes, he tampered with the ceiling of her bedroom, contriving a mechanical device for loosening its panels and dropping them upon her while she slept. When this leaked out through some of those connected with the plot, he devised a collapsible boat, to destroy her by shipwreck or by the falling in of its cabin. Then he pretended a reconciliation and invited her in a most cordial letter to come to Baiae and celebrate the feast of Minerva with him.

On learning that everything had gone wrong and that she had escaped by swimming, driven to desperation he secretly had a dagger thrown down beside her freedman Lucius Angermus, when he joyfully brought word that she was safe and sound. He then ordered that the freedman be seized and bound, on the charge of having been hired by her to kill the Emperor, and that his mother be put to death, giving out that she had committed suicide to escape the consequences of her detected guilt. Trustworthy authorities add still more gruesome details: that he hurried off to view the corpse, handled her limbs . . . and that becoming thirsty meanwhile, he took a drink.

—SUETONIUS, *op. cit.*

PALACE

He made a palace extending all the way from the Palatine to the Esquiline, which at first he called House of Passage, but when it was burned shortly after its completion and rebuilt, the Golden House. . . . Its vestibule was high enough to contain a colossal statue of the Emperor a hundred and twenty feet high. So large was this house that it had a triple colonnade a mile long. There was a lake in it too, like a sea, surrounded with buildings to represent cities, tracts of country, tilled fields, vineyards, pastures, with great numbers of wild and domestic animals.

In the rest of the house all was overlaid with gold and adorned with jewels and mother-of-pearl. There were dining rooms with fretted ceilings of ivory, whose panels could turn and shower down flowers and were fitted with pipes for sprinkling the guests with perfumes. The main banquet hall was circular, and constantly revolved, day and night, like the heavens. . . . When the edifice was finished in this style and he dedicated it, he deigned to say nothing more in the way of approval than that he was at last beginning to be housed like a human being. . . .

—*Ibid.*

NEUROSIS AND PSYCHOSIS

Neurosis does not deny the existence of reality, it merely tries to ignore it; psychosis denies it and tries to substitute something else for it. . . .

—SIGMUND FREUD, *Collected Papers*, II

We have long observed that every neurosis has the result, and therefore probably the purpose, of forcing the patient out of real life, of alienating him from actuality. The neurotic turns away from reality because he finds it unbearable—either the whole or parts of it. The most extreme type of this alienation from reality is shown in certain cases of hallucinatory psychosis which aim at denying the existence of the particular event that occasioned the outbreak of insanity. But actually every neurotic does the same with some fragment of reality. And now we are confronted with the task of investigating the development of the relation of the neurotic and of mankind in general to reality.

—SIGMUND FREUD,
Introductory Lectures on Psychoanalysis

Everything great in the world comes from neurotics. They alone have founded our religions and composed our masterpieces. Never will the world know all it owes to them nor all that they have suffered to enrich it.

—MARCEL PROUST, *The Maxims of Marcel Proust*

A neurotic is a man who builds a castle in the air. A psychotic is the man who lives in it. And a psychiatrist is the man who collects the rent.

—LORD WEBB-JOHNSON,
British surgeon, *Look*, October 4, 1955

THE NEW LEFT

The New Left was widely accepted as a youth movement. In its leadership, at least, it was never that. At the climax of its short-lived success, in 1968–69, its literary leaders in England were aged between their mid-forties and their mid-fifties. They were already everything implied by the word middle-aged.

One may wonder if, in intellectual history, there ever was such a thing as a youth movement. The young copy; they do not invent. The Children's Crusade was not initiated by children. In Hitler Youth rallies, middle-aged men with bare knees marched out in front. And in universities in the 1960s the protest-movement was not merely captured by such men: it was their intellectual creation from the start. They wrote the books and articles, gave the lectures and edited the journals, and demonstrated in Grosvenor Square.

More than one former student militant has since revealed that he knew nothing of organized protest until he reached a university and heard it in a lecture. Enthusiasm, once kindled, might pass from student to student; but it was not invented by a student. Even the leadership of our political parties was a contributory influence here. Many wondered when, in the late 1960s, the shy, demure student of the earlier years turned into a jargon-stuffed oaf screaming abuse and obscenities. But in 1963–65 two political parties elected middle-aged leaders publicly praised for a virtue called "abrasiveness." Some of our parliamentary life, before the New Left was born, had already burned into a public model that was harsh and crude.

The middle-aged men who made and led the New Left, however, were often content to leave abrasiveness to their disciples. In England, at least, the sage at his most characteristic was bland. His literary tone was as far from the revolutionary as the artifices of style could render it. . . .

—GEORGE WATSON, *Encounter*, October 1975

NEW YORK: 1857

. . . no dumping-ground, no sewer, no vault contains more filth or in greater variety than [does] the air in certain parts of [New York] city during the long season of drought. . . . No barrier can shut it out, no social distinction can save us from it; no domestic cleanliness, no private sanitary measures can substitute a pure atmosphere for a foul one.

—*Leslie's Weekly*, 1881

Most of my friends . . . carry [revolvers] at night.

—GEORGE TEMPLETON STRONG, *Diaries*, Vol. IV

MAILING A LETTER

The first time you decide to send a card or a letter, be prepared for a shock: In New York . . . the hardest thing to find is a postage stamp. They can be had in post offices . . . or you can get them from little coin machines which can be found nearly everywhere. The machines, however, are generally either out of order or don't have the denomination you want. Furthermore, they charge a one- or two-cent commission on every transaction. Since these machines are obviously to be avoided and there is never time to go to the post office, the tourist just gives up. He is easily recognized in a New York crowd by pockets bulging with unstamped postcards.

—GIUSEPPE DICORATO,
L'Osservatore Politico Letterario (Milan)

ISAAC NEWTON (1642–1727)

I do not deal in conjectures.
                    —Conversation with his nephew, John Conduitt, in
                        L. T. More, *Isaac Newton, a Biography*

If I have ever made any valuable discoveries, it has been owing
more to patient attention, than to any other talent.... If I have
seen further, it is by standing on the shoulders of giants.
                            —letter to Robert Hooke, 1677

I do not know what I may appear to the world; but to myself I
seem to have been only like a boy, playing on the seashore, and
diverting myself, in now and then finding a smoother pebble or
a prettier shell than ordinary, whilst the great ocean of truth lay
all undiscovered before me.
                    —Portsmouth manuscripts, in Louis Trenchard More,
                                                        op. cit.

ABOUT HIM

Once, as the legend goes, a few of Newton's colleagues induced
him to propose to a certain young lady. While tenderly holding
the woman's hand during an absorbing conversation, Newton's
mind wandered into more abstract areas of thought, and instead of
raising her hand to his lips, he absent-mindedly used her little
finger as a tamp for his pipe. Aroused by her sudden exclamation
of pain from the heat of the ashes, Newton cried out: "Ah, my
dear Madam, I beg your pardon! I see it will not do! I see, I see
that I am doomed to remain a bachelor."
                                                        —*Ibid.*

Newton left his study where he had some very important papers
he had been working on, and a little dog, called Diamond, his
constant companion, upset a candle. The study caught on fire and
the papers were destroyed, though Newton returned in time to
save all but the important papers. Without striking the dog, Newton merely said: "Oh Diamond, Diamond! Thou little knowest
the mischief thou has done!"
                    —in David Brewster, *Memoirs of the Life, Writings
                        and Discoveries of Sir Isaac Newton,* Vol. II

A house in Cambridge, opposite St. John's College, was thought to be haunted. Once a few of the Fellows had rushed in, armed with pistols, to attack the ghost, and a crowd had gathered. Newton happened to pass by and seeing the sight and hearing what it was all about he said: "Oh ye fools! Will you never have any wit? Know you not that all such things are mere cheats and impostures? Fie! Fie! Go home for shame." With this he passed on to his study.

—in J. Eddleston (ed.),
Correspondence of Sir Isaac Newton

NIGHT

Night brings our troubles to the light, instead of banishing them.
—SENECA

Night conceals a world but reveals a universe.
—ROBERT BROWNING

When the great earth, abandoning day, rolls up the deeps of the heavens and the universe, a new door opens for the human spirit, and there are few so clownish that some awareness of the mystery of being does not touch them as they gaze. For a moment of night we have a glimpse of ourselves and of our world islanded in its stream of stars—pilgrims of mortality, voyaging between horizons across eternal seas of space and time.
—HENRY BESTON, *The Outermost House: A Year of Life on the Great Beach of Cape Cod*

THE NIGHT WORLD

We experience the known, but our intuitions point to things that are unknown...
...[Creators] are visionaries, seers and prophets, perhaps in touch with the nightside of life.... It is only we who have repudiated it... because we strive to construct a conscious world that is safe.... Yet even in our midst the poet now and then catches sight of the figures that people the night world—the spirits, demons and Gods. He has a presentiment of incomprehensible happenings....
—CARL GUSTAV JUNG, *Modern Man in Search of a Soul*

NIXON RESIGNS

It is less than a year that a President of the United States was forced to resign from office under the darkest of clouds and he was asked to leave the office because he lied to the American people.

I was at the White House that night to hear his resignation speech, and what impressed me more than anything else was that while one leader of our country was resigning and another was taking his place, I did not see one tank or one helmeted soldier in the street and the only uniforms I saw that night were two motorcycle policemen who were directing traffic on Pennsylvania Avenue.

Two hundred million people were able to change Presidents overnight without one bayonet being unsheathed. I believe that any country in the world that can still do that can't be all bad.

—ART BUCHWALD,
commencement address, Vassar, June 1975

NUNS IN VENICE

.... Even nuns and abbesses carried weapons; an abbess once had a poniard duel with a nun over a mutual lover, the Abbé de Pomponne; and the duel only made a scandal because it took place within the convent walls. People thought that if nuns were going to fight they should do it on unconsecrated ground!

Love affairs, when they happened, tended to be quick and not to leave regrets. Both parties preferred freedom to love-ties. They entered an affair for pleasure and made no bones about it; and when it ceased to give pleasure they escaped. Perhaps the most faithful lovers in Venice were the nuns.

—MAURICE ROWDON, The Silver Age of Venice

OBJECTIVITY

There is in each of us a stream of tendency, whether you choose to call it philosophy or not, which gives coherence and direction to thought and action. Judges cannot escape that current any more than other mortals. All their lives, forces which they do not recognize and cannot name, have been tugging at them—inherited instincts, traditional beliefs, acquired convictions; and the resultant is an outlook on life, a conception of social needs, a sense in James's phrase of "the total push and pressure of the cosmos," which, when reasons are nicely balanced, must determine where choice shall fall. In this mental background every problem finds its setting. We may try to see things as objectively as we please. None the less, we can never see them with any eyes except our own.

—JUSTICE BENJAMIN CARDOZO,
The Nature of the Judicial Process

THE OBVIOUS

It requires a very unusual mind to undertake the analysis of the obvious.

—ALFRED NORTH WHITEHEAD,
Science and the Modern World

OCTAVIUS AUGUSTUS (63 B.C.–14 A.D.)

He gave every encouragement to the men of talent of his own age, listening with courtesy to their readings, not only of poetry and history, but of speeches and dialogues as well. But he took offense at being made the subject of any composition except in serious earnest and by the most eminent writers, often charging the Praetors not to let his name be cheapened in prize declamations. ...

□

He was not indifferent to his own dreams or to those which others dreamed about him. ... It was because of a dream that every year on an appointed day he begged alms of the people, holding out his open hand to have pennies dropped in it.

Certain auspices and omens he regarded as infallible. If his shoes were put on in the wrong way in the morning, the left instead of the right, he considered it a bad sign. If there chanced to be a drizzle of rain when he was starting on a long journey by land or sea, he thought it a good omen, betokening a speedy and prosperous return. But he was especially affected by prodigies. When a palm tree sprang up between the crevices of the pavement before his house, he transplanted it to the inner court beside his household Gods. ... He was so pleased that the branches of an old oak, which had already drooped to the ground and ... became vigorous again on his arrival in the island of Capri, that he arranged with the city of Naples to give him the island in exchange for Aenaria.

—SUETONIUS, *The Lives of the Twelve Caesars*

THE OEDIPUS COMPLEX

Being in love with the one parent and hating the other are among the essential constituents of the stock of psychical impulses which is formed at that time and which is of such importance in determining the symptoms of the later neurosis. It is not my belief, however, that psychoneurotics differ sharply in this respect from other human beings who remain normal—that they are able, that is, to create something absolutely new and peculiar to themselves. It is far more probable—and this is confirmed by occasional observations on normal children—that they are only distinguished by exhibiting on a magnified scale feelings of love and hatred to their parents which occur less obviously and less intensely in the minds of most children.

This discovery is confirmed by a legend that has come down to us from classical antiquity: a legend whose profound and universal power to move can only be understood if the hypothesis I have put forward in regard to the psychology of children has an equally universal validity. What I have in mind is the legend of King Oedipus and Sophocles' drama which bears his name.

—SIGMUND FREUD, *Interpretation of Dreams*

THE OLD AND THE YOUNG

As one grows older the memories of past accomplishments and joys assume an increasing importance. Perhaps for that reason one becomes increasingly involved with tradition, ritual and ceremony which reinforce the values of the past. At weddings and graduation ceremonies the tears of the middle-aged and elderly only in part grow out of sadness. They also are tears of joy evoked by memories of past pleasures. Rituals and symbols reassure the elderly person that the things he did will continue to be done by others, that something about him will not entirely disappear with his death.

In our new world, however, he may perceive that the past counts for less and less. Young people, less in need of this function of ceremony, are more inclined to detect its irrational elements since their preoccupations are primarily those of survival in an uncertain future. So imagine the sense of regret and dismay felt by a parent who watches his child get married in a park, under water, or even naked. The parent who plans to watch his child's graduation with feelings of pride and joy is crushed when the child refuses to participate in what he describes as an irrelevant or obscene ceremony. His child's refusal to perpetuate the traditions is viewed by the parent not only as a rejection of the social order; it is viewed as a rejection of the parent himself.

—SEYMOUR HALLECK, *Think*, IBM, 1970

OPEN-MINDEDNESS

Cursed is he that does not know when to shut his mind. An open mind is all very well in its way, but it ought not to be so open that there is no keeping anything in or out of it. It should be capable of shutting its doors sometimes, or it may be found a little draughty.

—SAMUEL BUTLER, *Notebooks*

OPINION

I do not believe the people who tell me that they do not care a
row of pins for the opinion of their fellows. It is the bravado of
ignorance.

—W. Somerset Maugham, *The Summing Up*

The world is ruled by force, not opinion; but opinions use force.

—Blaise Pascal

Error of opinion may be tolerated where reason is left free to combat it.

—Thomas Jefferson, March 4, 1801

There is no process of amalgamation by which opinions, wrong
individually, can become right merely by their multitude.

—John Ruskin

Sentiments are what unites people, opinions what separates them.
Sentiments gather us together; opinions represent the principle of
variety that scatters.

—Johann Wolfgang von Goethe, letter to
F. Jacobi, January 6, 1813

The disposition of mankind, whether as rulers or as fellow-citizens,
to impose their own opinions and inclinations as a rule of conduct
on others is so energetically supported by some of the best and
by some of the worst feelings incident to human natures that it is
hardly ever kept under restraint by anything but want of power.

—John Stuart Mill, *On Liberty*

OPTIMISM

While there is a chance of the world getting through its troubles,
I hold that a reasonable man has to behave as though he was sure
of it. If at the end your cheerfulness is not justified, at any rate
you will have been cheerful.

—H. G. Wells

Strange, how her courage had revived with the sun! She saw now, as she had seen in the night, that life is never what one dreamed, that it is seldom what one desired; yet for the vital spirit and the eager mind, the future will always hold the search for buried treasure and the possibilities of high adventure.

—ELLEN GLASGOW

One lesson, and only one, history may be said to repeat with distinctness, that the world is built somehow on moral foundations; that in the long run it is well with the good; in the long run it is ill with the wicked. But this is no science; it is no more than the old doctrine taught long ago by the Hebrew prophets.

—J. A. FROUDE

A pessimist thinks all women are bad; an optimist hopes they are.

—CHAUNCEY DEPEW

ORATIONS: PERICLES

The great funeral oration of Pericles, delivered over those fallen in the war, stands out as unlike all other commemoration speeches ever spoken. There is not a trace of exaltation in it, not a word of heroic declamation. It is a piece of clear thinking and straight talking. The orator tells his audience to pray that they never have to die in battle as these did. He does not suggest or imply to the mourning parents before him that they are to be accounted happy because their sons died for Athens. He knows they are not and it does not occur to him to say anything but the truth.

—EDITH HAMILTON, *The Greek Way*

ORATORY

The aim of the sculptor is to convince us that he is a sculptor; the aim of the orator is to convince us that he is not an orator.

—G. K. CHESTERTON, *Heretics*

Oratory, phrases, the evocative power of verbal symbols must not be despised, for these are and have been one of the chief means of uniting the United States and keeping it united.

—D. W. BROGAN

The written word has never, in times of tension and doom, the strength of warm and living speech, the vocal call to arms.

—STEFAN ZWEIG

Surely whoever speaks to me in the right voice, him or her I shall follow.

—WALT WHITMAN

ORIENTAL LIFE

Life in the East is fierce, short, hazardous, and in extremes. Its elements are few and simple, not exhibiting the long range and undulation of European existence, but rapidly reaching the best and the worst. The rich feed on fruits and game—the poor, on the watermelon's peel.

All or nothing is the genius of Oriental life. Favor of the sultan, or his displeasure, is a question of Fate. A war is undertaken for an epigram or a distich, as in Europe for a duchy. The prolific sun and the sudden and rank plenty which this heat engenders, make subsistence easy.... [But] the desert, the simoon, the mirage, the lion and the plague endanger it, and life hangs on the contingency of a skin of water.

—RALPH WALDO EMERSON, *Collected Works*, Vol. VIII

ORIGINALITY

An original writer is not one who imitates nobody but one whom nobody can imitate.

—CHATEAUBRIAND

PAGAN GODS

If the Greek gods steal, by whom shall their believers swear?

—APOCRYPHA, *Ahikar*, 8:22

PAGANS

Some men had become the toys of demons and evil spirits, and they gave scope to the passionate element of their souls, and invented pleasures of even greater excess. Some could not endure these things, and considered atheism better than such worship and some, even more shameless than all these, asserted that the life of wisdom was no more than the life of pleasure, and they held pleasure to be the ultimate good.

The whole race of man was enslaved by the goddess Pleasure, or by a shameful and licentious demon, and it was overwhelmed by miseries of every kind. Its women, as our holy apostle has said, exchanged the natural function of womanhood for that which was unnatural, and the same was true of its men. They abandoned the natural love of women and burned with passion for one another. Men wrought shameful deeds with men.

Greeks and barbarians, the wise and the unlearned, indulged their lowliest appetites. They bowed in an adoration of pleasure as an irresistible and inexorable deity. Amidst songs and hymns, they performed the mysteries, the ignoble rites of shameful and licentious pleasure, so that this, above all, has been rightly abolished among us, for "belief in idols is the beginning of fornication."

Other races, too, embraced the unholy and abominable principle of pleasure.... Their whole lives were polluted by the frantic lust for women, by corruption among men, by marriage with mothers and intercourse with daughters, and wild, animal nature held sway in wickedness.

—Eusebius, *The Preparation for the Gospel*

PAIN

Let this remark of Epicurus aid thee: Pain is neither intolerable nor everlasting, if you bear in mind that it has its limits, and if you add nothing to it in imagination.

—Marcus Aurelius, *Meditations*

Pain may be purely mental, caused by the good fortune of another.

—Ambrose Bierce

PAINTERS AND PAINTING

There is an essential difference between a line and a fish. And that is that the fish can swim, eat, and be eaten. It has, then, capacities of which the line is deprived.

These capacities of the fish are necessary extras for the fish itself and for the kitchen, but not for painting. And so, not being necessary, they are superfluous.

That is why I like the line better than the fish—at least in my painting.

—WASSILY KANDINSKY

The artist does not paint what he sees, but what he must make others see.

—EDGAR DEGAS

If a painter wishes to see enchanting beauties, he has the power to produce them. If he wishes to see monstrosities, whether terrifying or absurd and laughable, or pitiful, he has the power to create them. If he wants to produce towns or deserts, or in the hot season wants cool and shady places, or in the cold season warm places, he can make them. If he wants valleys, or wants to survey vast stretches of country from a mountain, or if beyond he wants to see the horizon on the sea, he has the power to create all these. . . . Indeed, whatever exists in the universe, whether in essence, in fact, or in imagination, the painter has it first in his mind and then in his hands.

—LEONARDO DA VINCI, *Notebooks*

A man paints with his brains and not with his hands, and if he cannot have his brains clear he will come to grief.

—MICHELANGELO

We painters take the same liberties as poets and madmen take.

—PAOLO VERONESE, statement to the Inquisition, 1573

It is not bright colors but good drawing that makes figures beautiful.

—TITIAN

... Painting is the music of God, the inner reflection of his luminous perfection.

—MICHELANGELO

I have had three masters: nature, Velazquez, and Rembrandt.

—FRANCISCO DE GOYA

The Chinese have painted for two thousand years, and have not discovered that there is such a thing as chiaroscuro.

—JOHN CONSTABLE

A picture is something which requires as much knavery, trickery, and deceit as the perpetration of a crime. Paint falsely, and then add the accent of nature.

—EDGAR DEGAS

Be guided by feeling alone. It is better to be nothing, than an echo of others. A wise man has said: "When you follow another, you are always behind."

—JOHN BAPTISTE CAMILLE COROT

... When we invented cubism we had no intention whatever of inventing cubism. We wanted simply to express what was in us.

—PABLO PICASSO, interview with Christian Zervos, 1935

... I want a red to be sonorous, to sound like a bell. ... I have no rules and no methods; anyone can look at my materials or watch how I paint—he will see that I have no secrets. I look at a nude; there are myriads of tiny tints. I must find the ones that will make the flesh on my canvas live and quiver.

—PIERRE AUGUSTE RENOIR

PARACELSUS (1493–1541) (PHILIPPUS THEOPHRASTUS BOMBASTUS VON HOHENHEIM)

Was he a medieval "magus" or a modern scientist? A charlatan or a gifted healer? ... He turned magic into science [and] substituted a functional conception of physiology—the living organism—for the ancient anatomy of "humors" and "qualities."

□

One midsummer night, Paracelsus solemnly committed to the flames the famous textbook of medieval medicine, the *Canon of Avicenna*. The defiant gesture, imitating Luther's burning of the Pope's Bull, became a symbol of rebellion against pedantry and unthinking acceptance of ancient doctrines.... Medical students of that period, who hardly ever saw a patient before they graduated, were aroused by Paracelsus' battle cry: "The patients are your textbook, the sickbed is your study."

—HENRY M. PACHER, *Paracelsus*

ST. PATRICK (c.389–469)

Considering all the great things that Patrick did for Ireland, it is a little sad, in a way, that he is most famous for something that he most certainly did not do. It is true that there are no snakes in Ireland, and who can say that it is not by divine intervention that this is so? But if it is, the intervention took place long before Patrick arrived. The Irish didn't even know what a snake was until Patrick told them the story of the Garden of Eden, for there have never been any snakes in Ireland.

□

He was not—strange as it may seem—an Irishman himself. He was a Romanized Briton, born about the year 389 in a small town called Bannavem Taberniae, according to his own account. The trouble is that that information doesn't really help us much because the town has long since vanished from the face of the earth.... His full name was Patricius Magonus Sucatus. His father, Calpurnius, was a deacon, and his grandfather was a priest. This is not so scandalous as it might sound, for in those days there was no strict rule forbidding the clergy to marry.

In spite of his family background, Patrick was not, by his own admission, very religious as a youth.... When he was sixteen, Bannavem Taberniae was raided by a band of heathen Irish pirates, and he was carried off to Ireland as a slave, where he was to remain until he was twenty-two.

—RANDALL GARRETT, *A Gallery of Saints*

PEACE

War is waged that peace may be obtained.... But it is a greater glory to slay war with a word than men with a sword, and to gain and maintain peace by means of peace, not by means of war.

—St. Augustine, letter

It is madness for sheep to talk peace with a wolf.

—Thomas Fuller, 1732

To be enduring, a peace should be endurable.

—Evan Esar, *Humorous English*

Though General Sherman "War is hell!" lived on into the peace, he never said what he thought of it.

—Harry V. Wade

Better beans and bacon in peace than cakes and ale in fear.

—Aesop, "The Town Mouse and the Country Mouse"

The fateful question of the human species seems to be whether, and to what degree, the cultural process will succeed in mastering those derangements of communal life which are caused by the human instinct of aggression and self-destruction.

—Sigmund Freud, *Civilization and Its Discontents*

PEACE CORPS VS. "LUST FOR PROFIT"

Presumably, a Peace Corps volunteer who teaches an illiterate Brazilian to read without hope of profit is doing more for the illiterate Brazilian than General Electric do Brasil when it hires teachers to teach the illiterate members of its work force to read in the hope that it can reduce its supervisory costs and increase its profits. The end result is the same. Illiterate Brazilians learn to read. But the motive is different. Somehow that means that the Peace Corps volunteer has contributed to the welfare of poor Brazilians and G.E. has not. The Peace Corps volunteer was not motivated by self-interest (except to the extent that he desires

travel and adventure and instant status at minimum cost) while
G.E. was motivated by a lust for profit.

—YALE BROZEN, "Welfare without the Welfare State"
(pamphlet)

PEASANTS

Alexis de Tocqueville was almost the first to realize that once the
peasants acquired their land free of landlords and feudal dues
they would become the most conservative of all classes. This was
not grasped by Marx or by later Marxists, who went on treating
"workers and peasants" as a revolutionary combination until the
events of 1932 in the Ukraine and the present political situation
in eastern Europe revealed that the conflict between town workers
and peasants is the most ghastly as it is the most fierce of all civil
wars.

—A. J. P. TAYLOR, *From Napoleon to Lenin*

PERJURY

We may better know there is fire when we see much smoke rising
than we could know it by one or two witnesses swearing to it.
The witnesses may commit perjury, but the smoke cannot.

—ABRAHAM LINCOLN

A PERSECUTION

Early in 1685, Louis XIV sent his troops into all those towns
where the Protestants were strongest, and he ordered the frontiers
to be carefully guarded, to prevent the flight of those whom the
new persecution was intended to convert. It was a hunt carried
out in an enclosed area.

A bishop or priest or civic official marched ahead of the King's
soldiers. The leading Calvinist families were assembled and ordered to renounce their religion. Those who refused were handed
over to the soldiers, who could do whatever they wanted to them
... except kill them. Some were so horribly maltreated that they
died. Children of the refugees still cry out in horror at the sufferings their fathers endured.

It was odd to see such savage orders coming from a court famous for its manners, its graces and its charm. Behind the scenes could be detected the hand of the Marquis of Louvois, who had wanted to drown all of Holland in the sea. . . .

Paris did not participate in these persecutions, for the sound of suffering might have been heard too near the throne. It is quite all right to make men suffer, but it is painful to have to listen to their cries. . . .

Louvois thought that an official order would securely guard the frontiers and the coasts, but he was wrong. Those who apply all their skill to breaking the law are always stronger than authority.

The bribe of but a few guards ensured the escape of hosts of refugees.

Almost fifty thousand families left France in three years. They were later followed by others. They took with them all their skill, industry and wealth. Northern Germany, devoid of industries, was transformed by the arrival of the Protestants. The cloth, hats, stockings once bought from France were now made in Germany. A suburb of London was populated by French silk workers. Other Protestants brought the art of making cut glass out of France. One can still find in Germany the gold brought there by the refugees.

All told, France lost about 500,000 inhabitants, a vast amount of money, and precious skills which enriched her enemies.

—Voltaire, *The Age of Louis XIV*

PHARAOH TOMBS

When he reached the bottom of the shaft, Emile Brugsch beheld a white and yellow coffin, and upon it was the name of Neskhonsu. Further on he saw a coffin whose shape suggested the style of the XVIIth Dynasty. Scattered over the ground were boxes with funerary statues, jars, bronze libation vessels . . . and further on, the funeral tent of Queen Isimkheb . . . folded and crumpled, like a thing of no value which a priest in a hurry to get out had thrown into a corner.

All down the main corridor of the shaft, Brugsch saw the same profusion of objects, and the same careless disorder. He had to crawl. . . .

Coffins and mummies, glimpsed by the flickering light of a candle, were marked with historic names: Amenophis I, Thutmose II . . . Soqununri, Queen Ahhotpu, Ahmose Nefertari. . . .

Brugsch thought that he must be the victim of a dream; like him, I still wonder if I am not dreaming when I see and touch what were the bodies of so many illustrious personages of whom we had never expected to know more than their names.

Forty-eight hours proved enough to bring everything up from the shaft, but the task was only half finished. Now the convoy had to be conducted across the Theban plain and beyond the river to Luxor. . . .

Finally the coffins and mummies were all safe at Luxor, carefully wrapped in mats and cloth. . . . No sooner was the precious load aboard [our steamboat] than it started to return to Bulaq with its cargo of ancient kings.

. . . all the way from Luxor to Qift, from both banks of the Nile, fellah women with their hair down followed our boat, howling, while the men fired ceremonial salutes, as they do at funerals.
—GASTON MASPERO, *A Report on Deir-el-Bahari*, 1881

PHILOSOPHY AND PHILOSOPHERS

Nor shall we be philosophers, even should we have read all the arguments of Plato and Aristotle. So long as we are unable to arrive at a firm judgment of our own on the matters of which they are treating, what we are learning is not science, but history.
—RENÉ DESCARTES

Philosophers are very severe towards other philosophers because they expect too much. Even under the most favorable circumstances no mortal can be asked to seize the truth in its wholeness or at its center. As the senses open to us only partial perspectives . . . and report the facts in symbols which . . . resemble the colored signals of danger or of free way which a railway engine-driver peers at in the night, so our speculation, which is a sort of panoramic sense, approaches things peripherally and expresses them humanly.
—GEORGE SANTAYANA, *Character and Opinion in the United States*

The philosopher should be a man willing to listen to every suggestion, but determined to judge for himself. He should not be biased by appearances; have no favorite hypothesis; be of no school; and in doctrine have no master. He should not be a respecter of persons but of things. Truth should be his primary object. If to these qualities be added industry, he may indeed go and hope to walk within the veil of the temple of Nature.

—MICHAEL FARADAY, in Richard Gregory, *Discovery*

Men were first led to study philosophy by wonder. At first they felt wonder about superficial problems; afterwards they advanced gradually by perplexing themselves over greater difficulties; e.g., the behavior of the moon, the phenomena of the sun, the origination of the universe.

Now he who is perplexed and wonders believes himself to be ignorant. Hence even the lover of myths is, in a sense, the philosopher, for a myth is a tissue of wonders. Thus if they took to philosophy to escape ignorance, it is patent that they were pursuing science for the sake of knowledge itself, and not for any utilitarian applications. . . .

Just as we call a man free who exists for his own ends and not for those of another, so it is with this, which is the only free man's science: It alone of the sciences exists for its own sake. . . .

—ARISTOTLE, *Metaphysics*

Honors, monuments, all that ambition has blazoned in inscriptions or piled high in stone will speedily sink to ruin; there is nothing that the lapse of time does not dilapidate and exterminate. But the dedications of philosophy are impregnable; age cannot erase their memory or diminish their force. . . .

The philosopher's life is therefore spacious; he is not hemmed in and constricted like others. He alone is exempt from the limitations of humanity; all ages are at his service as at a god's. Has time gone by? He holds it fast in recollection. Is time now present? He utilizes it. Is it still to come? He anticipates it. The amalgamation of all time into one makes his life long.

—SENECA

. . . if we ask, "Have any ravens been seen in Iceland in 1955?" we know how to set about answering such a question—the correct answer must obviously be based on observation, and the naturalist is the expert to whom we can appeal. But when men ask questions like, "Are there any material objects in the universe (or does it, perhaps, consist rather of minds and their states)?" what steps do we take to settle this? Yet outwardly there is a similarity between the two sentences.

Or again, supposing I ask, "Did the battle of Waterloo take place in the seventeenth century?" we know how to look for the relevant evidence, but what are we to do when asked "Did the universe have a beginning in time?"

—Isaiah Berlin, *The Age of Enlightenment*

PHYSICS AND PHYSICISTS

What really exists are unchangeable particles, atoms, and their motions in empty space.

—Democritus (c.460–357 b.c.)

... in the abstract lexicon of quantum physics there is no such word as "really"... for whenever (the physicist) attempts to penetrate and spy on the "real" objective world, he changes and distorts its findings by the very process of his observations. And when he tries to divorce this "real" world from his sense perceptions he is left with nothing but a mathematical scheme.

—Lincoln Barnett, *The Universe and Dr. Einstein*

That physicist is so young—yet has contributed so little.

—Wolfgang Pauli

... no one ever directly experienced an atom, and its existence is entirely inferential. The atom was invented to explain constant combining weights in chemistry. For a long time there was no other experimental evidence of its existence, and it remained a pure invention, without physical reality, useful in discussing a certain group of phenomena.

It is one of the most fascinating things in physics to trace the accumulation of independent new physical information all pointing to the atom, until now we are as convinced of its physical reality as of our hands and feet.

—Percy W. Bridgman, *The Logic of Modern Physics*

Einstein often has said to me, "I am more a philosopher than a physicist."

—LEOPOLD INFELD, *Albert Einstein*

PABLO PICASSO (1881–1973)

Nature and art are two different things, and cannot be the same thing. Through art we express our conception of what Nature is not.

□

To me there is no past or future in art. If a work of art cannot always live in the present, it must not be considered at all.

The art of the Greeks, of the Egyptians, of the great painters who lived in other times, is not an art of the "past"; it may be more alive today than it ever was. Art does not evolve by itself; the ideas of people change, and with them their mode of expression changes, too.

□

People say, "I have no ear for music." They never say, "I have no eye for painting."

—from several letters and interviews

PLAGUE: ENGLAND

Nor had anyone any idea what caused the mortality: the pallor, the sudden shivering and retching, the dreadful scarlet blotches and black boils—"God's tokens"—the delirium and the unbearable agony that came without warning and carried off its victims in a few hours. . . .

The crops rotted in the fields, the church bells were silent, and everywhere corpses were flung, blackened and stinking, into hastily dug pits. . . .

Once established in the soil, the plague remained endemic. Dormant for perhaps a dozen years it would suddenly flare up, first in one city, then in another, at least once in a generation. For three hundred years—a period of time as great as that which divides us from the last outbreak in Charles II's reign—the red cross on the stricken door, the cart piled with corpses on its way to the plague-pit, the cry of "Bring out your dead!" formed a recurrent part of the background of English life.

During the three centuries since the Norman conquest the population of England had probably doubled. The generation born in the middle of Edward III's reign saw it halved.

—SIR ARTHUR BRYANT, *The Age of Chivalry*

PLATO (427?–347 B.C.)

... that unique man, whose name is not to come from the lips of the wicked. Theirs is not the right to praise him—he who first revealed clearly by word and by deed that he who is virtuous is happy. Alas, not one of us can equal him.

—ARISTOTLE

Out of Plato come all things that are written and debated among men of thought. Plato is philosophy and philosophy Plato.

—RALPH WALDO EMERSON, *Representative Men*

Plato never forgot the lesson of Socrates, that wisdom begins when a man finds out that he does not know what he thinks he knows.

—F. M. CORNFORD, *The Republic of Plato*

Plato himself hated nothing more than system-making.... To him philosophy meant no compact body of "results" to be learned, but a life spent in the active pursuit of truth and goodness by the light of one or two great passionate convictions.

—A. E. TAYLOR, *Plato: The Man and His Work*

With all his brilliance and subtle insight, Plato, the architect of the eternal ideas, builds what is after all a magnificent palace of half-truths.

—A. D. WINSPEAR, *The Genius of Plato's Thought*

While wading through the whimsies, the puerilites, and unintelligible jargon of this work [Plato's *Republic*] I laid it down often to ask myself how it could have been, that the world should have so long consented to give reputation to such nonsense as this?

—Thomas Jefferson to John Adams, July 5, 1814

PLATO AND POETS

Plato did not exclude all poets from the ideal city, but only Homer and those like him. This Plato did because he attributed to the gods and their offspring adultery, pederasty, theft, lying, uncontrolled anger, and those terrible vices no decent ruler would allow in his city, no family head tolerate in his wife or children or domestics.
—ERASMUS, *On Mending the Peace of the Church*

PLAY: ITS FUNCTIONS

Among the many forms of life, man is the supreme player. Only man appears to play from birth to death, although forms of human play tend to change as humans age. Some societies have discouraged or even prohibited certain forms of play, such as dancing. But the impulse to play is irrepressible, appearing unmistakably in every normal newborn child. Our closest living relatives, the apes and monkeys, also do much playing. It seems the more advanced a species is on the evolutionary scale, the more frequent and diverse are its play activities. . . .

A much more impressive case than I have set forth in these few pages may be made for the positive aspects of play: its role as a source of important inventions and esthetic creations, as a means whereby children learn adult roles, as a socially acceptable way of expressing hostile feelings and resolving conflicts, as a sanction for behavior. And its importance in still other ways, some of which we can as yet see only hazily. . . .

Once the player begins the game, the uniqueness, nonsense, triviality, distortion, or serendipity that follows may well bring secondary gains. The experience of play heightens the player's flexibility and imaginative capacity in addition to improving his physical and strategic competence. But these secondary gains are clearly indirect.

Games are in part imitative of the larger culture and therefore embody its processes and attitudes. But because play is voluntary, it admits madness as well as sanity. So that what ensues may be only partly a rehearsal for any specific cultural outcome. The primary purpose of play has a deeper importance for every individual. Playing children are motivated primarily to enjoy living. This is the major rehearsal value of play and games, for without the ability to enjoy life, the long years of adulthood can be dull and wearisome.

—Brian Sutton-Smith, in "Play," a special
supplement of *Natural History*, December 1971

POETRY

Poetry is more philosophical and of greater importance than history.

—Aristotle, *Rhetoric and Poetics*

Poets utter great and wise things which they do not themselves understand.

—Plato

Dowered with the hate of hate, the scorn of scorn, the love of love. . . .

—Tennyson, *The Poet*

We poets struggle with Non-being to force it to yield Being. We knock upon silence for an answering music.

—a Chinese poet, quoted in
Archibald MacLeish, *Poetry and Experience*

. . . Poetry should surprise by a fine excess, and not by singularity; it should strike the reader as a wording of his own highest thoughts, and appear almost a remembrance.

—John Keats to John Taylor, February 27, 1818

Perhaps no person can be a poet, or even enjoy poetry, without a certain unsoundness of mind.

—Thomas Babington Macaulay

. . . Patting and stroking are nature's anodynes. We rock our babies to sleep, we smooth the foreheads of the fretful, and we love to slide into oblivion ourselves, carrying with us the sound of rain-drops on a roof, or beneath us in the darkness the murmur of a brook. . . .

Rhythm is used, not only to lull the body, and set free the

imagination, but also, like wine itself, to excite the body. . . . These are the two primitive uses of the recurrent stimulus, and somehow they both survive in poetry. The very metrical monotony that drowses us becomes, when we are lost to coarser things, a turbulent and stimulating stream along our veins.

—MAX EASTMAN, *The Enjoyment of Poetry*

AN ANTISEPTIC VIEW

Poetry is commonly thought to be the language of emotion. On the contrary, most of what is so called proves the absence of all passionate excitement. It is a coldblooded, haggard, anxious, worrying hunt after rhymes which can be made serviceable, after images which will be effective, after phrases which are sonorous; all this under limitations which restrict the natural movements of fancy and imagination. . . .

True poetry . . . is but the ashes of a burnt-out passion. The flame was in the eye and in the cheek, the coals may be still burning in the heart, but when we come to the words it leaves behind it, a little warmth, a cinder or two just glimmering under the dead gray ashes—that is all we can look for.

—OLIVER WENDELL HOLMES, "Cacoethes Scribendi," in *Over the Teacups*

JAPAN

I had known something of Japanese poetry and basic rules, the frequent alternation of five and seven syllables and a few other points, but now that I was reading more of them . . . these poems really started growing on me. Soon I could not resist the temptation of trying my own hand at this art. So I wrote a poem.

> I am looking at a frog.
> He smiles back at me.
> Frogs' smiles always remind me of
> Eternity.

As this was definitely encouraging, I wrote another . . . :

> I am looking at a frog.
> He smiles back at me.
> Frogs' smiles always remind me of
> Snow.

And who can blame me for turning it into a trilogy?

> A frog looks at me.
> I am smiling back at him.
> My smile always reminds frogs of
> The Spring and the Moon.
> Ah, the Moon . . .

I showed my poems to some Japanese friends who declared that they were superb. . . . I was not at all certain who was pulling whose leg. But when my three poems were translated into Japanese and published in one of the leading poetry magazines, I became pensive and wistful.

I had known nothing of my power, simply because I had never tried to write Japanese poetry, just as I had never tried to play the violin. Is it possible—I ask my readers—is it possible that I am one of the greatest Japanese poets of this age?

—GEORGE MIKES, *The Land of the Rising Yen*

POLITICAL FORCE

Among the other evils which being unarmed brings you, it causes you to be despised.

—MACHIAVELLI

The use of force alone is but temporary. It may subdue for a moment, but it does not remove the necessity of subduing again; and a nation is not governed which is perpetually to be conquered.

Terror is not always the effect of force; and an armament is not a victory. If you do not succeed, you are without resource; for, conciliation failing, force remains; but, force failing, no further hope of reconciliation is left. Power and authority are sometimes bought by kindness, but they can never be begged as alms by an impoverished and defeated violence.

—EDMUND BURKE, speech,
House of Commons, March 22, 1775

POLITICAL JARGON

I hope you have all mastered the official Socialist jargon which our masters, as they call themselves, wish us to learn. You must not use the word "poor"; they are described as "lower income group."

When it comes to freezing a workman's wages the Chancellor of the Exchequer speaks of "arresting increases in personal income." ... There is a lovely one about houses and homes. They are in future to be called "accommodation units." I don't know how we are going to sing our old song, "Home Sweet Home." "Accommodation Unit, Sweet Accommodation Unit, there's no place like our Accommodation Unit."

—WINSTON CHURCHILL, speech, House of Commons

POLITICAL SYSTEMS

The only political system that can endure is one which prevents the rich from impoverishing the poor (by talent or shrewdness) and the poor from robbing the rich—by votes or through violence.

—ARISTOTLE, *Politics*

POLITICS

If they [Plato and Aristotle] wrote politics, it was like making rules for a lunatic asylum, and if they have seemed to speak of it in the grand manner, it was because they knew that the lunatics for whom they were speaking thought of themselves as kings and emperors.

—PASCAL, *Pensées*

Politics is far more complicated than physics.

—ALBERT EINSTEIN, in Robert Watson-Watt,
Man's Means to His End

... The power of politics to put things right in this world is not unlimited.... There are inherent limitations on what may be achieved by political means.... The aim of politics, as of all else, is the good life. But the good life is something which cannot be comprehended in some phrase or formula.... The most a politician can do is to ensure that some conditions in which the good life can exist are present and, more important, to prevent fools or knaves from setting up conditions which make an approach to the good life impossible except for solitaries or anchorites.... All the great evils of our time have come from men who mocked and exploited human misery by pretending that good government, that

is government according to *their* way of thinking, could offer utopia.
—QUINTIN HOGG, *The Case for Conservatism*

The need to hold together a majority in a pluralistic society produces a willingness to compromise on vital matters. . . . This practice is defended by many newspaper commentators as not only a necessity of modern political life, but also as the supreme virtue. To this contemporary school, moderation, as in the 1850s, is the most praised quality, while idealism looms up as the real enemy of the attainable good.
—PAUL H. DOUGLAS

They that are discontented under monarchy call it tyranny, and they that are displeased with aristocracy call it oligarchy; they which find themselves grieved under a democracy call it anarchy.
—HOBBES, *Leviathan*

Politics is not the science of setting up a permanently impregnable society, it is the art of knowing where to go next in the exploration of an already existing traditional kind of society. And in a society, such as ours, which has not yet lost the understanding of government as the prevention of coercion, as the power which holds in check the overmighty subject, as the protector of minorities against the power of majorities, it may well be thought that the task to which this generation is called is not the much advertised "reconstruction of society" but to provide against the new tyrannies which an immense growth in population in a wantonly productivist society are beginning to impose; and to provide against them in such a manner that the cure is not worse than the disease.
—MICHAEL OAKESHOTT, *Rationalism in Politics*

Politics is perhaps the only profession for which no preparation is thought necessary.
—ROBERT LOUIS STEVENSON, *Familiar Studies*

CORRUPTION

That he [Robert Walpole] practiced corruption on a large scale, is, we think, indisputable. But whether he deserves all the invectives which have been uttered against him on that account may be questioned. No man ought to be severely censured for not being beyond his age in virtue. To buy the votes of constituents is as immoral as to buy the votes of representatives. The candidate who gives five guineas to the freeman is as culpable as the man who gives three hundred guineas to the member. Yet we know that, in our own time, no man is thought wicked or dishonorable, no man is cut, no man is black-balled, because, under the old system of election, he was returned in the only way in which he could be returned, for East Retford, for Liverpool, or for Stafford. Walpole governed by corruption, because, in his time, it was impossible to govern otherwise.

—THOMAS BABINGTON MACAULAY, "Horace Walpole," in *Critical and Historical Essays*, Vol. I

OPTIMISTS

The optimist in politics is an inconstant and even dangerous man, because he takes no account of the great difficulties presented by his projects; these projects seem to him to possess a force of their own, which tends to bring about their realization all the more easily as they are, in his opinion, destined to produce the happiest results. He frequently thinks that small reforms in the political constitution, and, above all, in the personnel of the government, will be sufficient to direct social development in such a way as to mitigate those evils of the contemporary world which seem so harsh to the sensitive mind.... Self-interest is strongly aided by vanity and by the illusions of philosophy. The optimist passes with remarkable facility from revolutionary anger to the most ridiculous social pacificism.

—GEORGES SOREL, *Reflections on Violence*

POLLS: WHAT THEY CAN DO

Hubert Humphrey was greatly disadvantaged in the decisive California primary in 1972 by published surveys which showed him farther behind McGovern than the actual results suggested he had been. The highly reputable California Poll reported four days before the June primary that McGovern was ahead of Humphrey by 20 percent (46 percent to 25 percent), but just a few days later McGovern won by only five percent....

Humphrey's California campaign manager credited this poll with determining the outcome of the 1972 election, by cutting off campaign contributions: "It was just like turning off the water tap with one flick of the wrist. If it had been more accurate, we would have raised more money, spent more money, and we would have won. If we had won California, there are a lot of people who say we would have won the nomination and won the election."

—SEYMOUR MARTIN LIPSET, "The Wavering Polls," in
Public Interest, Spring 1976

MARCO POLO (1254?–1324)

After an absence of twenty-six years, Marco Polo and his father Nicolo and his uncle Maffeo returned from the spectacular court of Kublai Khan to their old home in Venice. Their clothes were coarse and tattered; the bundles that they carried were bound in Eastern cloths and their bronzed faces bore evidence of great hardships, long endurance, and suffering. They had almost forgotten their native tongue. Their aspect seemed foreign and their accent and entire manner bore the strange stamp of the Tartar. During these twenty-six years Venice, too, had changed and the travelers had difficulty in finding their old residence. But here at last as they entered the courtyard they were back home. Back from the Deserts of Persia, back from the lofty steeps of Pamir, from mysterious Tibet, from the dazzling court of Kublai Khan, from China, Mongolia, Burma, Siam, Sumatra, Java; back from Ceylon, where Adam has his tomb, and back from India, the land of myth and marvels. But the dogs of Venice barked as the travelers knocked on the door of their old home.

—MANUEL KOMROFF,
Introduction, *Travels of Marco Polo*

POLYGAMY

Polygamy is not in the least romantic. Polygamy is dull to the point of respectability.... Anything having the character of a Turkish harem has also something of the character of a Turkey carpet. It is not a portrait, or even a picture, but a pattern...we

know that on every side, in front as well as behind, the image is
repeated, without purpose and without finality.

G. K. Chesterton,
"The Boredom of Butterflies," *Fancies Versus Fads*

MME. DE POMPADOUR (1721–1764)

If Madame de Pompadour spent many nights poring over reports
with the head of the Paris police, it was no sign of paranoia but a
sound precaution for someone in her position. Madame de Pompadour was in a less enviable position than most royal mistresses.
She was hated by the populace because she had been one of them
and had made the leap to the aristocracy, and she was hated by the
aristocracy for being a bourgeoise who had elbowed her way
into their ranks. For centuries the kings of France had chosen
their mistresses from the nobility; indeed, it was an accepted belief
that only someone brought up to the intricacies of life at court
could possibly carry off so delicate a role. But Madame de Pompadour was ambitious, courageous, and secure in the knowledge
that the king was very much in love with her. Moreover, she believed she was fulfilling her destiny.

Jeanne-Antoinette Poisson was the only daughter of an en-
trepreneur in the food market who was not above making the
occasional shady deal, and of a mother who was more admired for
her beauty than for her virtue. When she was nine years old,
Jeanne had visited a fortune teller, a certain Madame Lebon, who
had predicted that she would one day become the mistress of
Louis XV. There are indications that not only she, but also her
parents, really believed this would happen.

—Nancy Caldwell Sorel, *Word People*

POOR NATIONS

There is always a good case, in both principle and prudence, for
the more affluent being charitable toward the poor—even to those
whose poverty is largely their own fault. Nor is there any reason
to expect, much less insist on, gratitude: Such benevolence is
supposed to be its own reward. But when the poor start "mau-
mauing" their actual or potential benefactors, where they begin

vilifying them, insulting them, demanding as of right what it is not their right to demand—then one's sense of self-respect may properly take precedence over one's self-imposed humanitarian obligations.

If the United States is to gain the respect of world opinion, it first has to demonstrate that it respects itself—its own institutions, its own way of life, the political and social philosophy that is the basis of its institutions and its way of life. Such a sense of self-respect and self-affirmation seems to be a missing element in our foreign policy. It is no wonder, therefore, that we are making such a mess of the "new cold war."

—IRVING KRISTOL, *Wall Street Journal*, July 17, 1975

POPULATION AND NUTRITION

Historically, food changes have been associated with rapid population growth. Within 100 years after the introduction of the white potato in 1750, Ireland's population nearly tripled. The recent introduction of enriched flour in Scandinavia was followed by a decrease in childhood mortality, and the Chinese population explosion in the sixteenth century was related to the expanded use of corn, sweet potatoes, and peanuts.

□

As nutrition improves, infant and childhood mortality rates decline; as mortality rates decline, parents respond by having fewer children. Parents are not enthusiastic about family planning in the presence of high infant and childhood mortality rates. Family planning implies that planning will be successful, and parents should be able to plan that their existing children will survive to adulthood. Intrauterine devices cut down on births but provide no insurance against dysentery, pneumonia, or malaria.

—ROY BROWN and JOE WRAY,
"The Starving Roots of Population Growth," in
Natural History, 1974

PORNOGRAPHY

A pornographic work represents social acts of sex, frequently of a perverse or wholly fantastic nature, often without consulting the limits of physical possibility. Such works encourage solitary fantasy, which is then usually quite harmlessly discharged in masturbation. A pornographic book is, then, an instrument for procuring a sexual catharsis, but it rarely promotes the desire to achieve this through a social mode, an act of erotic congress: The book is, in a sense, a substitute for a sexual partner. A pornograph can be either verbal or visual, but the visual stimulus is generally more intense than the verbal one. If anything that encourages sexual fantasy and leads to onanistic discharge is a pornograph, then pornographs lie all about us—underwear advertisements, the provocative photography in the nonclass Sunday papers. . . . Any depersonalized picture of a possible sexual partner represents the purest pornography you can get; how much more stimulating, though, is a real girl in a miniskirt. Women cannot help moving, and men cannot help being moved.

—ANTHONY BURGESS, *Urgent Copy*

There is no such thing as a dirty theme. There are only dirty writers.

—GEORGE JEAN NATHAN, *Testament of a Critic*

Nine-tenths of the appeal of pornography is due to the indecent feelings concerning sex which moralists inculcate in the young; the other tenth is physiological, and will occur in one way or another whatever the state of the law may be. On these grounds, although I fear that few will agree with me, I am firmly persuaded that there ought to be no law whatsoever on the subject of obscene publications.

—BERTRAND RUSSELL, *Marriage and Morals*

PRINCE GRIGORI ALEKSANDROVICH POTEMKIN (1739–1791)

In 1787 Catherine made a six-month journey to New Russia, including the Crimea—vast, recently annexed territories ruled by Potemkin as newly created Prince of Tauris. In the dark of January with the temperature well below zero the Empress set out from her palace at Tsarskoye Selo for the south and the spring. She shared with her current lover a huge sledge containing several compartments, drawn by thirty horses and escorted by nearly two hundred other sledges and vehicles. They consumed peaches and champagne in the snows, and at night great bonfires lighted their way. Within a few weeks the party was sailing down the Dnieper in a fleet of some four score vessels, Catherine traveling Cleopatra-like in one of three huge barques gorgeous in red and gold.

Now the renowned Potemkin villages swam into her ken. The great showman had forcibly uprooted the population of nearby areas to serve as a living backcloth and make it seem that his Empress was gliding through a prosperous, newly-colonized paradise—in fact a wilderness of empty steppe. Buildings had sprung up on the river banks, while other picturesque habitations further off were mere two-dimensional stage scenery. Once the Empress had passed by, the props were packed up and the dazed villagers sent home. This violent transplanting desolated entire provinces, taking a heavy toll in human life.

□

On the return journey the party witnessed a reenactment of the Battle of Poltava staged by fifty thousand soldiers on the original site.

Potemkin was in a class of his own among Catherine's lovers—huge of stature, ill-proportioned and ugly, but with great vitality. Called Cyclops, because he was blind in one eye from an assault by Alexis Orlov, according to rumor, he consumed estates, serfs, jewels, honors, titles, roubles, and women on a grandiose scale. . . . In another century Potemkin might have found his true level directing a film "epic." At Bender in 1791, when commander-in-chief against the Turks, he imported orchestras, girls and jewels in quantity, besides an entire corps de ballet and over five hundred personal servants. The grand tycoon set up court beneath the battlefield, roistering and wenching in underground halls specially excavated by his soldiers. From these orgies he would periodically emerge to defy Turkish bullets, a style of trench warfare all his own.

—RONALD HINGLEY, *The Tsars*

POVERTY

Professor Lampman has remarked [that] with $100 billion of transferred income in the United States . . . "how can we explain the fact that there is any poverty left in the United States."

The explanation lies in the fact that a major part of the transferred income does not go to the poor. It goes to people in the form of services which they are quite capable of buying for themselves and in money grants which have been described as "poverty programs for the well-to-do." The agricultural program (a poverty program for rich farmers) is an example of the latter.

—YALE BROZEN, address to Mont Pelerin Society,
September 9, 1966

Poverty is self-perpetuating because the poorest communities are poorest in the services which would eliminate it. To eliminate poverty efficiently we should invest more than proportionately in the children of the poor community. It is there that high-quality schools, strong health services, special provision for nutrition and recreation are most needed to compensate for the very low investment which families are able to make in their own offspring.

—JOHN KENNETH GALBRAITH, *The Affluent Society*

The biggest welfare fraud of all is committed each year by the U.S. Census Bureau—which persists in churning out estimates of a huge poverty population, 25 million persons in 1976, for example, compared with 36 million when the war on poverty was launched in 1964. Between those years, transfer payments leaped to $156 billion from $27 billion. Are we really to believe that only 11 million persons were raised from poverty with an expenditure of $129 billion—$11,727 a head?

The problem is that so far as the Census Bureau is concerned, the transfer payments don't count. It counts only cash income, while the transfer growth has been largely in in-kind services. The census doesn't even count food stamps, which in fact circulate as cash. So no matter how much the government spends on these programs, it can never reduce the census statistics. This is especially convenient for that brand of liberals who want, not a poverty cure but a poverty issue.

—editorial, *Wall Street Journal*, October 3, 1978

Amid all the sad statistics poured forth about the ghettos, it is worth remembering that in 1967 some 88 percent of all black American families had a television set.

—London *Economist*, May 10, 1969

THE THIRD WORLD

Far from the West having caused the poverty of the Third World, contact with the West has been the principal agent of material progress there.... The materially most advanced regions of the Third World are those with which the West established the most ... extensive contacts: the cash-crop-producing areas and *entrepot* ports of Southeast Asia, Africa, the Caribbean, and Latin America.

The level of material achievement usually diminishes as one moves away from the foci of Western impact: the poorest and most backward are the populations with few or no external contacts. ...

Wherever local conditions permitted, contact with the West most often resulted in the elimination of the worst epidemic and endemic diseases, the mitigation or disappearance of famines, and a general improvement in the material standard of living for all.

—P. T. BAUER, "Western Guilt & Third World Poverty," in *Commentary*, January 1976

POWER

Nearly all men can stand adversity, but if you want to test a man's character, give him power.

—ABRAHAM LINCOLN

The world is governed by demons, and he who lets himself in for ... power and force as means, contracts with diabolic powers; and for his action it is *not* true that good can follow only from good and evil only from evil, but that often the opposite is true. Anyone who fails to see this is, indeed, a political infant.

—MAX WEBER, *Politics as a Vocation*

The effect of power and publicity on all men is the aggravation of self, a sort of tumor that ends by killing the victim's sympathies.

—HENRY ADAMS, *The Education of Henry Adams*

There is no power without an army, no army without money, no money without agriculture, no agriculture without justice.

—ARDASHIR, King of Persia

Armed prophets succeed, but unarmed prophets come to ruin.

—MACHIAVELLI

...all spiritual power is properly founded in liberty, not in coercion.

☐

...no greater deformity can be caused by anyone than is caused by one who through contemplation of his own great power comes to believe that all things are permitted to him and infringes upon the rights of his subjects.

—NICHOLAS OF CUSA, *De Concordantia Catholica*

Power tends to corrupt; absolute power corrupts absolutely.

—JOHN, LORD ACTON, letter to Bishop Mandell
Creighton

Craving for power is not a vice of the body, consequently it knows none of the limitations imposed by a tired or satiated physiology upon gluttony, intemperance and lust. Growing with every successive satisfaction, the appetite for power can manifest itself indefinitely, without interruption by bodily fatigue or sickness.... Instead of bringing to the power-lover a merciful respite from his addictions, old age is apt to intensify them by making it easier for him to satisfy his cravings on a larger scale and in a more spectacular way. That is why, in Acton's words, "all great men are bad." ...
Except by saints, the problem of power is finally insoluble.

—ALDOUS HUXLEY, *The Perennial Philosophy*

Our key hypothesis about the power seeker is that he pursues power as a means of compensation against deprivation. Power is expected to overcome low estimates of the self, by changing either the traits of the self or the environment in which it functions.

—HAROLD D. LASSWELL, *Power and Personality*

CONCENTRATED

Conservatives believe that the deliberate policy of concentrating more and more power in the hands of the executive is to jump from the frying-pan into the fire.

—QUINTIN HOGG, *op. cit.*

The preservation and expansion of freedom are today threatened from two directions. The one threat is obvious and clear. It is the external threat coming from the evil men in the Kremlin who promise to bury us. The other threat is far more subtle. It is the internal threat coming from men of good intentions and good will who wish to reform us. Impatient with the slowness of persuasion and example to achieve the great social changes they envision, they are anxious to use the power of the state to achieve their ends and confident of their own ability to do so. Yet if they gained the power, they would fail to achieve their immediate aims and, in addition, would produce a collective state from which they would recoil in horror and of which they would be among the first victims. Concentrated power is not rendered harmless by the good intentions of those who create it.

—Milton Friedman, *Capitalism and Freedom*

[Themistocles to his wife]: Wife, the Athenians rule the Greeks, and I rule the Athenians, and thou me, and our son thee; let him then use sparingly the authority which makes him, foolish as he is, the most powerful person in Greece.

—Plutarch,
The Lives of the Noble Grecians and Romans

ITS LIMITS

When I was in Egypt, conqueror, lord, and absolute master though I was, laying down the law ... by simple decrees ... it [was] beyond my power to prevent the population from speaking freely in the coffeehouses. ... The coffeehouses were the castles of their rights, the marketplaces of their opinions.

—Napoleon

POWER AND LIBERTY

Political liberty is nothing else but the diffusion of power. ... Political liberty is impossible to the extent that power is concentrated in the hands of a few men. It does not matter whether these be popularly elected or no. Give men power and they will misuse it.

—Quintin Hogg, *op. cit.*

POWER AND VIRTUE

Political liberty is to be found only in moderate governments; and even in these it is . . . there only when there is no abuse of power. But experience shows us that every man who is invested with power is likely to abuse it, to carry his authority as far as it will go. Is it not strange . . . to say that virtue itself has need of limits?
—MONTESQUIEU, *The Spirit of the Laws*

PRAYER

Prayer is the soul's affectionate reach towards God.
—ST. AUGUSTINE

Once we hoped for Utopia; now, in a chastened mood, we can at best hope for a reprieve; pray for time and play for time. For had the dinosaur learnt the art of prayer, the only sensible petition for him would have been to go down on his scaly knees and beg, "Lord, give me another chance."
—ARTHUR KOESTLER,
"The Trail of the Dinosaur," in *Encounter*, May 1955

Dear God—
    We are going on vacation for two weeks so won't be in church. I hope you will be there when we get back. When do you take your vacation.

Donnie
—*Children's Letters to God*, compiled by Eric Marshall
and Stuart Hample

PREDICTIONS

The prediction, as it is usual, contributed to its own accomplishment.
—EDWARD GIBBON,
The Decline and Fall of the Roman Empire

Suppose a charlatan makes a hundred predictions, and chance fulfills one. The others are forgotten; the one remains a sign of God's favor, proof of a miracle.

If none of the predictions comes true, a new interpretation is placed on the words; this explanation is accepted by enthusiasts— and believed by fools.

—VOLTAIRE, *The Age of Louis XIV*

PREJUDICE

My friend Mr. Moll (for the prosecution) says, gentlemen, that this isn't a race question. This is a murder case. We don't want any prejudice; we don't want the other side to have any. Race and color have nothing to do with this case. This is a case of murder.

I insist that there is nothing but prejudice in this case; that if it was reversed and eleven white men had shot and killed a black while protecting their home and their lives against a mob of blacks, nobody would have dreamed of having them indicted. I know what I am talking about, and so do you. They would have been given medals instead. Ten colored men and one woman are in this indictment, tried by twelve jurors, gentlemen. Everyone of you are white, aren't you? At least you all think so. We haven't one colored man on this jury. We couldn't get one. One was called and he was disqualified. You twelve white men are trying a colored man on race prejudice.

Now, let me ask you whether you are not prejudiced. I want to put this square to you, gentlemen. I haven't any doubt but that every one of you is prejudiced against colored people. I want you to guard against it. I want you to do all you can to be fair in this case, and I believe you will.

All I hope for, gentlemen of the jury, is this: that you are strong enough, and honest enough, and decent enough to lay it aside in this case and decide it as you ought to. And I say, there is no man in Detroit that doesn't know that these defendants, every one of them, did right. There isn't a man in Detroit who doesn't know that the defendant did his duty, and that this case is an attempt to send him and his companions to prison because they defended their constitutional rights. It is a wicked attempt, and you are asked to be a party to it.

—CLARENCE DARROW, to the jury, *U.S. vs. Sweet* and others, Detroit, 1926; in Arthur Weinberg, *Attorney for the Damned*

I am quite sure that (bar one) I have no race prejudices, and I think I have no color prejudices nor caste prejudices, nor creed prejudices. Indeed, I know it. I can stand any society. All that I care to know is that a man is a human being—that is enough for me; he can't be any worse.

—MARK TWAIN, "Concerning the Jews," in *Harper's*,
September 1899

Racial prejudice is dangerous because it is a disease of the majority endangering minority groups.... For those who would keep any group in our nation in bondage, I have no sympathy or tolerance. ... My faith in my fellowman is too great to permit me to waste away my lifetime burning with hatred against any group.

—LYNDON JOHNSON, in the Senate, 1949, in Harry
McPherson, *A Political Education*

No wise man can have a contempt for the prejudices of others; and he should even stand in a certain awe of his own, as if they were aged parents or monitors. ...

—WILLIAM HAZLITT, *Characteristics*

THE PRESENT

No more deadly harm can be done to young minds than by depreciation of the present. The present contains all that there is. It is holy ground; for it is the past, and it is the future.

Where attainable knowledge could have changed the issue, ignorance has the guilt of vice. And the foundation of reverence is this perception, that the present holds within itself the complete sum of existence, backwards and forwards, that whole amplitude of time, which is eternity.

—ALFRED NORTH WHITEHEAD,
The Aims of Education

The fleeting now may not be just what we once dreamed it might be, but it has the advantage of being present, whereas our past is dead and our future may never be born.

—CHARLES MACOMB FLANDRAU, *Viva Mexico*

PRISONERS

... when they leave prison, society throws gasoline on the fire by inflicting restrictions and economic sanctions upon the exconvict. ... He may not be allowed to sell real estate professionally, drive a taxi, work in a night club, or take up any of a dozen other occupations. The rationale behind these controls over exconvicts is obviously fallacious—otherwise doctors would be required to have disease-free histories and teachers would have to prove that they had never made an error.

—ALBERT F. NUSSBAUM,
The American Scholar, Autumn 1971

PRISONS

Prison has a social structure, a pecking order, that is the reverse of the one outside. At the top are the big-time swindlers and bank robbers; at the bottom are the petty thieves and sexual deviates. Car thieves and check passers often pretend to be bank robbers in an effort to gain more acceptance. No one would think of claiming innocence or playing down his crimes except with outsiders. "It's okay to steal a lot if you leave a little" is prison philosophy at its zenith. Is it any wonder that, after spending years in that unhealthy environment, released prisoners often graduate to more serious crimes?

—*Ibid.*

PROGRESS

Progress is not a law of nature. The ground gained by one generation may be lost by the next. The thoughts of men may flow into the channels which lead to disaster and barbarism.

—H. A. L. FISHER, Preface, *A History of Europe*

Is it progress if a cannibal uses a knife and fork?

—STANISLAW LEC

The art of progress is to preserve order amid change and to preserve change amid order.

—ALFRED NORTH WHITEHEAD,
Great Ideas of Western Man

In creative art, as well as in critical taste, the faltering talent of Christendom can at best follow the lead of the ancient Greeks and the Chinese. In myth-making, folklore, and occult symbolism, many of the lower barbarians have achieved things beyond what the latter-day priests and poets know how to propose. In political finesse . . . more than one of the ancient peoples give evidence of a capacity to which no modern civilized nation may aspire.

To modern civilized men, especially in their intervals of sober reflection, all these things that distinguish the barbarian civilization seem of dubious value . . . futile in comparison with the achievements of science. . . . This is the one secure holding-ground of latter-day conviction, that "the increase and diffusion of knowledge among men" is indefeasibly right and good. . . . No other cultural ideal holds a similar unquestioned place in the convictions of civilized mankind.

—THORSTEIN VEBLEN,
The Place of Science in Modern Civilization

The rapid progress *true* science now makes, occasions my regretting sometimes that I was born so soon. It is impossible to imagine the height to which may be carried, in a thousand years, the power of man over matter. We may perhaps learn to deprive large masses of their gravity, and give them absolute levity, for the sake of easy transport. Agriculture may diminish its labor and double its produce; all diseases may by sure means be prevented or cured, not excepting even that of old age, and our lives lengthened at pleasure even beyond the antediluvian standard. O that moral science were in as fair a way of improvement, that men would cease to be wolves to one another, and that human beings would at length learn what they now improperly call humanity!

—BENJAMIN FRANKLIN,
letter to Joseph Priestley, February 8, 1780

PROLETARIAN CHAINS

Wrote Marx and Engels in *The Communist Manifesto:* "The proletarians have nothing to lose but their chains. They have a world to win." Who today can regard the chains of the proletarians in the Soviet Union as weaker than the chains of the proletarians in the United States, or Britain or France or Germany or any Western state?

      —MILTON FRIEDMAN, *Capitalism and Freedom*

PROPAGANDA

Propaganda, when successful, is astute in handling: Aggressiveness, Guilt, Weakness, Affection.

The organization of the community for war takes advantage of the concentrated aggressiveness which accumulates in any crisis. When another nation is presented as a threat, retaliatory impulses to destroy it are promptly evoked; but such impulses cannot find direct expression. They are partially suppressed, partially repressed, but they contribute to the trend and tone of mental life. The energy of frustrated impulses may be discharged in many paths, but men in the mass are likely to use the most primitive. One of the rudimentary modes of coping with internal stress is projection. This mechanism resolves the inner emotional difficulties by treating an impulse of the self as an attribute of the environment. Instead of recognizing the simple intensity of one's retaliatory destructiveness, one feels that the outside world is more destructive than in reality it is. This "moralizes" the murderous impulse by imputing destructiveness to the other fellow. The symbol of the "other" is elaborated into a scheming, treacherous, malevolent "influence."

      —HAROLD D. LASSWELL,
      Politics—Who Gets What, When, How

NAZI

The stresses of war, blockade, inflation, and deflation had exacted a tremendous moral toll in Germany. Multitudes had succumbed to sexual and property "temptations"; hence they were predisposed toward "purification" to remove the heavy hand of conscience. For them the Jew was the sacrificial Isaac. Indeed, the whole nineteenth century had witnessed the growth of the secular cult of nationalism, furnishing a substitute for the fading appeal of established religion. This decline of piety, however, left legacies of guilt which could be expiated by attacking the Jew, traditional enemy of Christianity.

      —*Ibid.*

REVOLUTIONARY

Revolutionary propaganda selects symbols which are calculated to detach the affections of the masses from the existing symbols of authority, to attach these affections to challenging symbols, and to direct hostilities toward existing symbols of authority. This is infinitely more complex than the psychological problem of war propaganda, since in war the destructive energies of the community are drained along familiar channels. Most of those who have a hand in revolution must face a crisis of conscience. Constituted authority perpetuates itself by shaping the consciences of those who are born within its sphere of control. Hence the great revolutions are in defiance of emotions which have been directed by nurses, teachers, guardians, and parents along "accredited" channels of expression. Revolutions are ruptures of conscience.

—HAROLD D. LASSWELL,
World Politics and Personal Insecurity

PROPERTY AND JUSTICE

It is preposterous, therefore, to imagine that we can have any idea of property without fully comprehending the nature of justice. . . . The origin of justice explains that of property.

—DAVID HUME, *Of the Origin of Justice and Property*

People who have property in a country which they may lose, and privileges which they may endanger, are generally disposed to be quiet; and even to bear much, rather than hazard all. While the government is mild and just, while important civil and religious rights are secure, such subjects will be dutiful and obedient. The waves do not rise but when the wind blows.

—BENJAMIN FRANKLIN, 1760, in Verner W. Crane,
Benjamin Franklin and a Rising People

I am conscious that an equal division of property is impracticable, but, the consequences of this enormous inequality producing so much misery to the bulk of mankind, legislators cannot invent too many devices for subdividing property, only taking care to let their subdivisions go hand in hand with the natural affections of the human mind.

—THOMAS JEFFERSON,
letter to the Reverend James Madison, 1785

The supreme power cannot take from any man part of his property without his consent; for the preservation of property [is] the end of government and that for which men enter into society....

—JOHN LOCKE, *Second Treatise*

Private property is the natural bulwark of liberty because it ensures that economic power is not entirely in the hands of the state.

—QUINTIN HOGG, *The Case for Conservatism*

PROSTITUTES: LONDON

The language of prostitutes is the language of love-making, and we all make love. But when we come to write about love, or to talk about it with people we don't know very well, we use a different language, one compounded of heavy latinisms and coy paraphrases. We say *penis* and *intercourse* as though we were so many specimens in a botanist's collection instead of men and women made of flesh and spirit. Or we say *having a good time*, as though we were children at a party, or *making time* with someone, as though we were trains running late. But as soon as we get into bed we begin to talk English like people.

□

None of the girls I met had ever had a proper ponce, though some had tried a candidate for a few days and then chucked him out. They regretted this, and wished they could be lucky enough to find a good one. One, rather drunk, even thought it would be a good plan if I took this on in my spare time. She needed someone to kick her out on the street when it was time, to make sure she had the rent ready on rent day, to keep her off the bottle, to tell her what clothes she looked nice in, and, perhaps most important of all, to help her see if she couldn't have some sort of a sex-life of her own. She thought that with a "sixty minute man" things might happen.

The ponce—in London today: always with that reservation—is neither more nor less than the whore's husband. He provides stability for her, a bit of discipline, someone to listen to her adventures. He makes love to her as much for her sake as for his own, and takes trouble over it. He is also a gauge of her prestige.

If she keeps him well in hand-made shoes and black silk shirts, then her credit goes up among the whores, and his among the ponces.

□

Some whores share a ponce with another, or even with two others. This arrangement, which is the rule in New York, is the exception in London. It does not arise because the ponce is able to subject two or three silly but reluctant women for his own gain. It arises because in the world of prostitution ... monogamy is not the rule. Add to this that in the world of prostitution chastity is by definition something which does not come in, and that many whores are at least a bit lesbian, and the multiple ponce becomes comprehensible.

□

The whore world is like a little gearwheel engaged with a big one; it goes round faster, and in the opposite direction. You can see the gears engaging on the pavements of Piccadilly; the whores stand still and the men pour past, looking, considering, pausing to haggle, passing on to the next. The counter-society or underworld is, like the society or overworld which has expressed it from its own body, class-ridden, intolerant, but free from oppression. As to the rest of us, we cherish and pay it with one hand and belabor it with the other. That's how it gets like it is. The overworld sees the whore as a social problem or a social service, according to the amount of use it makes of her. The whore judges the overworld by what she sees. First, she sees the client, whom she holds in contempt for his gullibility and in respect for his purse. Through him she sees his wife who, he inevitably tells her, is cold. To the English whore, England is a country of women as frigid as she is, or frigider, but who don't even try to pretend.

□

Well, that's prostitution, known to the whores as The Game. It is a game, too; it is a market in illusion, a shop window like the ones in Holborn where you can buy bits of rubber that look like poached eggs. It's a market where you can buy grunts and groans that are supposed to sound like love. That's all. In the last resort, the client is having his own money.

—WAYLAND YOUNG,
"Sitting on a Fortune," in *Encounter*, May 1959

PSYCHOANALYSIS

Freud explained that by giving up hypnosis and suggestion, the widening of consciousness, which had supplied the analyst with the pathogenic memories and fantasies, was now missing. Free association was a completely satisfactory substitute in that it permitted the involuntary thoughts of the patient to enter the treatment situation. This is Freud's description of this method: "Without exerting any other kind of influence, he invites them to lie down in a comfortable attitude on a sofa, while he himself sits on a chair behind them outside their field of vision. He does not even ask them to close their eyes, and avoids touching them in any way, as well as any other procedure which might be reminiscent of hypnosis. The session thus proceeds like a conversation between two people equally awake, but one of whom is spared every muscular exertion and every distracting sensory impression which might divert his attention from his own mental activity. . . . In order to secure these ideas and associations he asks the patient to 'let himself go' in what he says, "as you would do in a conversation in which you were rambling on quite disconnectedly and at random." The procedure of free association became known as the fundamental or basic rule of psychoanalysis.

Free association has remained the basic and unique method of communication for patients in psychoanalytic treatment. Interpretation is still the decisive and ultimate instrument of the psychoanalyst. These two technical procedures give psychoanalytic therapy its distinctive stamp. Other means of communication occur during the course of psychoanalytic therapy, but they are affiliated, preparatory, or secondary, and not typical of psychoanalysis.

—RALPH R. GREENSON,
The Technique and Practice of Psychoanalysis

Freud learned to look for meanings and not for reports. Every dream, every phrase, every hesitation, every gesture, every intonation, every outburst began to take on significance as possible allusions to the "traumatic" episode. Allusions to hated objects, reminiscence of a brother, failure to mention a hated sister until days had passed . . . every deviation from comprehensiveness— was scrutinized for the clue it might afford. . . . The problem was to discover the nature of the patient's conflict and to volunteer interpretations for the sake of helping the patient to dare to bring into full consciousness the unavowed impulse which had once frightened his socially adjusted self into frantic repression. This involved the interpretation of the symptom as a compromise product of the patient's ideal of conduct; and the out-of-consciousness of the sufferer possessed enough strength to procure partial gratification of the illicit and partial punishment by the conscience.

—Harold D. Lasswell, *Psychopathology and Politics*

Psychoanalysis will not judge morally, or insist on any moral standard. Its task is merely to help restore the possibility of moral choice to patients—not to make the choice for them. As the patient gains insight into his motivation and, sometimes, the effects of his behavior, he may, or may not, change his former beliefs. The physician setting a patient's broken leg does not tell him where to go, or condition his services on the patient's going his way; nor does the psychoanalyst when helping to mend a patient's injuries or crippling disease.

—Ernest van den Haag, "Genuine and Spurious Integration," in *Psychoanalysis and Social Science,* ed. H. M. Ruitenbeck

In the analytic situation an important aspect of the art of communicating to the patient is the analyst's skill in the use of silence. The analyst's silence has many meanings to the patient, depending on the patient's transference situation as well as the analyst's countertransference. Furthermore, silence is one of the greatest stresses that our patients have to bear in the analytic situation, and should therefore be administered thoughtfully in quality and quantity. Silence is both a passive and an active intervention on the part of the analyst. The patient needs our silence because he may need time for his thoughts, feelings, and fantasies to emerge from within himself. Our silence also exerts a pressure upon him to communicate and to face his utterances and emotions without distraction. He may feel our silence as supportive and warm, or as critical and cold. This may be due to his transference projections, but it may also be derived from his subliminal awareness of our countertransference reactions.

—Ralph R. Greenson, *op. cit.*

Things have changed since Freud invented psychoanalysis. Psychoanalysis now is best described as a process by means of which personality can be partially reshaped and reintegrated through the cooperation of an analyst and a patient. There is no need to assume the presence of a disease requiring cure. . . .

Sometimes [the analyst] does treat a disease, but at other times he may merely help the patient to lead a happier or more productive life or to achieve his aims. That is indeed what—sometimes— he can do for the addict, even though addiction is not a disease.
—ERNEST VAN DEN HAAG, *Punishing Criminals*

As a radical method of cure one can only say that psychoanalysis helps those who are well enough to tolerate it, and intelligent enough to gain by it over and above the cure of symptoms. As an intellectual experience, however, it is like other ascetic methods in specifically arousing and giving access to certain recesses of the mind otherwise completely removed from conscious mastery.

□

Young people in severe trouble are not fit for the couch: They want to face you, and they want you to face them, not as a facsimile of a parent, or wearing the mask of a professional helper, but as the kind of overall individual a young person can live by or will despair of. When suddenly confronted with such a conflicted young person the psychoanalyst may learn for the first time what facing a face, rather than facing a problem, really means.

□

Probably the most neglected problem in psychoanalysis is the problem of work. . . . Decades of case histories have omitted the work histories of the patients or have treated their occupation as a seemingly irrelevant area of life in which data could be disguised with the greatest impunity.
—ERIK H. ERIKSON, *Young Man Luther*

PSYCHOANALYSIS AND MORALS

Psychoanalytically, there is no intellectual ground for taking any moral line at all. It is clear, no doubt, that analysts do; and that the man who, at the end of an analysis paid up, thanked his analyst, and announced that he was off on an affair with his mother would not be regarded as cured. But the Freudian position would clearly not be condemnatory. It would have to hedge the moral question by talking in terms of a "lack of insight."

—KENNETH MINOGUE, *Encounter*, June 1973

PUBLIC ADMINISTRATION

... Almost to the end of the eighteenth century the Chinese were far in advance of the rest of the world in matters of administrative organization.... It is certainly difficult for a European to realize how long-established in China were practices that in the West we associate mainly with the modern age.

—O. B. VAN DEN SPRENKEL,
quoted by H. G. Creel, in *Midway*, Summer 1969

PUBLIC DEBT

To relieve the present exigency is always the object which principally interests those immediately concerned in the administration of public affairs. The future liberation of the public revenue, they leave to the care of posterity.

—ADAM SMITH, *Wealth of Nations*

PUBLIC OPINION

A universal feeling, whether well or ill-formed, cannot be safely disregarded.

—ABRAHAM LINCOLN, 1854

Nothing appears more surprising to those who consider human affairs with a philosophical eye than the easiness with which the many are governed by the few. When we inquire by what means this wonder is affected, we shall find that, as force is always on the side of the governed, the governors have nothing to support them but opinion. It is, therefore, on opinion only that government is founded, and this maxim extends to the most despotic and most military governments as well as to the most free and most popular.

—DAVID HUME, *Of the First Principles of Government*

Economy is necessary at all times but especially at the beginning of a reign, when public opinion is being formed.

—NAPOLEON

PUBLIC VIRTUE VS. PRIVATE VICE

What is shameful? An exact line is impossible to draw. For some it is nudity, for others homosexuality, for others pornography. And even the notion of "community standards" may be of little help, since the community itself is often divided. But what *can* be defined is a different distinction of *public* and *private*, and a wall can be set up between them. Thus, there can be a prohibition on public display of pornography, obscenity, and those prurient elements which degrade the human personality; but behind the wall, what consenting adults do is their own business.

Where does this leave us? With public virtue, and private vices. A tribute—in a different sense of the word—that hypocrisy pays to the double nature of man. A difficult formula, but perhaps the only one.

—DANIEL BELL, "The Public Household," in
The Cultural Contradictions of Capitalism

LORD RAGLAN (1788–1855)

He [Lord Raglan] was fearless to the point of recklessness. At Alma he rode far ahead of his army, right past the French skirmishers (who were no doubt amazed at the sight of this extraordinary English general in his blue frock coat, white shirt, and black cravat), and on into the Russian lines, where the view happened to be much better. Some days later, while the British army was marching around Sebastopol, the entire cavalry took a wrong turn in the woods and got lost. Lord Raglan, who believed he was following the cavalry when he was actually far ahead of it, suddenly collided with a large body of Russian infantry. He quietly told one of his staff to go find the cavalry; then he reined up and sat facing the enemy so calmly that it never occurred to the confused Russian soldiers that this was the British commander-in-chief, who with his staff had somehow lost the British army and was quite defenseless. Raglan directed the battle of Balaclava from the heights above the actual fighting, but at Inkerman he occupied a ridge with round shot whistling past and shells exploding throughout, and at Malakoff and Redan he stood in the mortar battery behind the forward trench under heavy fire . . .

Lord Raglan watched his army perish before his eyes during that winter of 1854–55. His men froze to death because the government in London refused to believe that a Crimean winter was not balmy; they starved because there was no road by which to transport those supplies that did reach the little harbor at Balaclava. His days were an endless round of orders, dispatches, instructions and letters to the parents of all the officers who had died. Because he rode around the camps as inconspicuously as possible, often after nightfall and always half-concealed in the big-sleeved cloak to which he lent his name, his men believed him aloof and unconcerned with their sufferings.

—NANCY CALDWELL SOREL, *Word People*

RATIONALISM

He was a rationalist, but he had to confess that he liked the ringing of church bells.

—ANTON CHEKHOV

It takes a long time to realize that the rational is only a small segment of the human complex, that the spirit of reason is difficult to invoke, and that there are as many dangers in the rational as in the irrational.

—ANTHONY BURGESS, *Urgent Copy*

Pure rationalism, complete immunity from prejudice, consists in refusing to see that the case before one is absolutely unique. It is always possible to treat the country of one's nativity, the house of one's fathers, the bed in which one's mother died, nay, the mother herself if need be, on a naked equality with all other specimens of so many respective genera. It shows the world in a clear frosty light from which all fuliginous mists of affection, all swamp-lights of sentimentality, are absent. Straight and immediate action becomes easy then—witness a Napoleon's or a Frederick's career.

But the question always remains, "Are not the mists and vapors *worth* retaining?" The illogical refusal to treat certain concretes by the mere law of their genus has made the drama of history. The obstinate insisting that tweedledum is *not* tweedledee is the bone and marrow of life. . . . A thing is important if any one *think* it important. . . . The sovereign road to indifference, whether to evils or to goods, lies in the thought of the higher genus.

—WILLIAM JAMES, *Principles of Psychology*

The human understanding when it has once adopted an opinion ... draws all things else to support and agree with it. And though there be a greater number and weight of instances to be found on the other side, yet these it either neglects and despises, or else ... sets aside, and rejects. . . .

It was a good answer that was made by the man who was shown hanging in a temple a picture of those who had paid their vows as having escaped shipwreck. They would have had him say whether he did not now acknowledge the power of the gods. "Aye," asked he again, "but where are they painted that were drowned after their vows?"

—FRANCIS BACON, *De Argumentis*

READERS

Readers may be divided into four classes:
1. Sponges, who absorb all they read and return it nearly in the same state, only a little dirtied.
2. Sand-glasses, who retain nothing and are content to get through a book for the sake of getting through the time.
3. Strain-bags, who retain merely the dregs of what they read.
4. Mogul diamonds, equally rare and valuable, who profit by what they read, and enable others to profit by it also.

—SAMUEL TAYLOR COLERIDGE, *Notebooks*

I divide all readers into two classes: Those who read to remember and those who read to forget.

—WILLIAM LYON PHELPS

READING

There is a great deal of difference between the eager man who wants to read a book and the tired man who wants a book to read.

—G. K. CHESTERTON

Reading—the nice and subtle happiness of reading. . . . This joy not dulled by Age, this polite and unpunished vice, this selfish, serene, life-long intoxication.

—LOGAN PEARSALL SMITH,
"Consolation," in *More Trivia*

Compared with the labor of reading through these volumes [Guicciardini's *History*] all other labor, the labor of thieves on the treadmill, of children in factories, of negroes in sugar plantations, is an agreeable recreation. There was, it is said, a criminal in Italy, who was suffered to make his choice between Guicciardini and the galleys. He chose the history. But the war of Pisa was too much for him. He changed his mind and went to the oar.

—THOMAS BABINGTON MACAULAY,
Critical and Historical Essays

REASON

Reason is a light God kindled in the soul.

—ARISTOTLE

The true triumph of reason is that it enables us to get along with those who do not possess it.

—VOLTAIRE

If you follow reason far enough it always leads to conclusions that are contrary to reason.

—SAMUEL BUTLER

Most philosophers...have exhibited a grotesque ignorance of man's life and have built up systems that are elaborate and imposing, but quite unrelated to actual human affairs. They have almost consistently neglected the actual process of thought and have set the mind off as something apart to be studied by itself....

Kant entitled his great work *A Critique of Pure Reason*. But to the modern student of mind, pure reason seems as mythical as the pure gold, transparent as glass, with which the celestial city is paved.

—JAMES HARVEY ROBINSON, *The Mind in the Making*

REASON AND IMAGINATION

The ideas tossed into consciousness by imagination are, we have said, overwhelmingly bad—untrue or unbeautiful—and must be curbed and ruddered by reason...Formal education is directed to our conscious reason, which can at least be supplied with content and practice; if the more intuitive and unconscious imagination can be cultivated, we have yet to learn the secret. There is a danger of reason stifling the imagination.... To teach rigor while preserving imagination is an unsolved challenge to education.

—RALPH W. GERARD,
The Biological Basis of Imagination

RELIGION

If men are so wicked with religion, what would they be without it?

—BENJAMIN FRANKLIN

Man...is the only animal that has the true religion—several of them.

—MARK TWAIN, *Letters from the Earth*

A fantastic faith in gods, angels and spirits. A faith without any scientific foundations, religion is being supported and maintained by the reactionary circles. It serves for the subjugation of the working people and increases the power of the exploiting bourgeois classes.

—Dictionary, U.S.S.R., 1951 Edition

We have just enough religion to make us hate, but not enough to make us love one another.

—JONATHAN SWIFT

If a people loses its religion it has no other basis for social life, no shield with which to defend itself, no fount of wisdom, no foundation, not even a form to shape its existence.

—GIOVANNI VICO, *Principles of the Laws of Society*

Religion is a thing of [our] own invention. What kind of truth is it that is true on one side of a mountain and false on the other?

—MONTAIGNE, *Essays*

I think all the great religions of the world—Buddhism, Hinduism, Christianity, Islam and Communism—both untrue and harmful. It is evident as a matter of logic that, since they disagree, not more than one of them can be true. With very few exceptions, the religion which a man accepts is that of the community in which he lives, which makes it obvious that the influence of environment is what has led him to accept the religion in question.

—BERTRAND RUSSELL, *Why I Am Not a Christian*

Religion, it seems to me, can survive only as a consciously accepted system of make-believe. People will accept certain theological statements about life and the world, will elect to perform certain rites and to follow certain rules of conduct, not because they imagine the statements to be divinely dictated, but simply because they have discovered experimentally that to live in a certain ritual rhythm, under certain ethical restraints, and as if certain metaphysical doctrines were true, is to live nobly, with style.

—ALDOUS HUXLEY, *Proper Studies*

Father religions have mother churches.

—ERIK H. ERIKSON, *Young Man Luther*

Infantile feelings are far more intense and inexhaustibly deep than are those of adults; only religious ecstasy can bring back that intensity. Thus a transport of devotion to God is the first response to the return of the Great Father.

□

One might venture to regard the obsessional neurosis as a pathological counterpart of the formation of a religion, to describe this neurosis as a private religious system, and religion as a universal obsessional neurosis.

—SIGMUND FREUD, *Collected Papers*, Vol. II

If I believe my nurse and my tutor, every other religion is false, and mine alone is the truth. But ... the earth still groans under the multitude of temples consecrated to error.... What does the history of religions teach us? That they have everywhere lighted the torch of intolerance, strewed the plains with corpses, soaked the fields with blood, burned cities, laid waste whole empires.... Are not the Turks, whose religion is a religion of blood, more tolerant than we? There are Christian churches at Constantinople, but there are no mosques in Paris.

—CLAUDE HELVÉTIUS, *De L'esprit*, 1758

RELIGION AND SCIENCE

... Science without religion is lame, religion without science is blind.

—ALBERT EINSTEIN, *The Meaning of Relativity*

When Darwin or Einstein proclaim theories which modify our ideas, it is a triumph for science. We do not go about saying that there is another defeat for science, because its old ideas have been abandoned. We know that another step of scientific insight has been gained.

Religion will not regain its old power until it can face change in the same spirit as does science.

—ALFRED NORTH WHITEHEAD,
Science and the Modern World

RESEARCH

The best person to decide what research work shall be done is the man who is doing the research, and the next best person is the head of the department, who knows the subject and the work; after that you start on increasingly worse groups, the first being the research director, who is probably wrong more than half the

time, then a committee, which is wrong most of the time, and finally, a committee of vice-presidents, which is wrong all the time.
—C. E. K. MEES, vice-president, research, Eastman Kodak Co., October 22, 1935

RESTAURANTS

NEW YORK

A friend of mine claims that he can guess the prices on the menu by the amount of light in the room—the darker the restaurant the more expensive it is. Technically, the effect is achieved by substituting little lamps or even candles for ordinary lighting. Americans think it makes the atmosphere intimate.

A pretty girl with whom I had dinner one evening confirmed this. The restaurant was full; there were at least a hundred people, to judge from the number of heads I could distinguish in the sepulchral reddish candlelight. In order to make herself heard above the clamor of voices, the girl shouted into my ear: "Very intimate, isn't it?"

—GIUSEPPE DICORATO,
L'Osservatore Politico Letterario (Milan)

THE WORST

The restaurant at Grand Santi, a small village on the banks of the Maroni River in the interior of French Guiana, will probably never win any gastronomic awards. One ugly, fly-filled room with a packed-dirt floor, it has no menu and serves whatever the owner can find for his wife to cook. Pot luck at the edge of the world's largest tropical forest can mean a ragout of peccary, spider monkey *en civet*, fricassee of flamingo, or piranha *meuniere*.

—RAYMOND SOKOLOV,
"The Melting Pot," in *Natural History*, January 1975

DAVID REUBENI (1480–1532)

Short of stature, dark-skinned, clad in striking oriental garb, Reubeni appeared in Rome on a white horse (symbolically suggestive of the Messiah's white donkey). His entourage, his flag, his personal magnetism, and above all, his plan to recapture the

Holy Land, impressed all his listeners, and he was soon granted an audience by the philo-Semitic Pope Clement VII.

The emissary of a far-off Jewish nation of warriors, Reubeni wanted the Pope's aid in securing weapons to drive the Muslims from the Holy Land—a request to which any Christian spiritual and temporal leader would be favorably disposed. Although the Pope was cautious, he sent Reubeni to the King of Portugal with letters of recommendation.

In post-expulsion Portugal, where the only Jews were Marranos, the story of David Reubeni takes a dramatic and crucial turn.... The Marranos in Portugal gathered about Reubeni and considered him a redeemer. This ferment naturally irritated the king, who began to suspect that Reubeni had come to bring the Marranos back to Judaism. When one of Reubeni's adherents in Portugal, Shlomo Molkho (the noted pseudo-Messiah), formally reembraced Judaism, Reubeni was ordered to leave the land....

It is noteworthy that Reubeni's travel diary is silent concerning his origin and his life prior to his European mission; the same silence and air of mystery surrounds much of his activity to the extent that modern scholarship is still not sure what to make of him, whether to regard him as a charlatan or a visionary....

Naive to political considerations, Reubeni was a dreamer who sought salvation in terms beyond the realistic—*i.e.*, the miraculous. Unfortunately, his end was bitter. When he came to Emperor Charles V in Germany with his new-found disciple, Shlomo Molkho, both were put in chains and returned to Italy. There Molkho was burned at the stake; and Reubeni was incarcerated in Spain, where he later died.

—CURT LEVIANT, *Masterpieces of Hebrew Literature*

REVOLUTION AND MORALS

The danger of loose morals is the gravest there is for revolutionary leaders who have passed all the earlier part of their lives in prison or exile, or simply in want and poverty.... The French Revolution collapsed because of the degeneration of the morals of its leaders, who surrounded themselves with loose women from the Palais Royal.... I am determined to bear down with a white-hot iron to burn in the bud the loosening of morals.... I'll break the

backs of all the rotten riff-raff who want to plunge our country
into corruption! I'll have no mercy on them! None of them! None
of them! ...

—Joseph Stalin,
in Budu Svanidze, *My Uncle Joseph Stalin*

REVOLUTIONS

Inferiors revolt in order that they may be equal, and equals that
they may be superior. Such is the state of mind which creates
revolution.

□

Revolutions are not about trifles, but they spring from trifles.

—Aristotle, *Politics*

In a revolution, as in a novel, the most difficult part to invent is
the end.

—Alexis de Tocqueville

The tradition of all the dead generations weighs like a nightmare
on the brain of the living. And just when they seem engaged in
revolutionizing themselves and things, in creating something that
has never yet existed ... they anxiously conjure up the spirits
of the past to their service, and borrow from them names, battle
cries and costumes, to present the new scene of world history in
time-honored disguise and borrowed language.

—Karl Marx,
The Eighteenth Brumaire of Louis Bonaparte, 1852

No man has ever seen a revolution. Mobs pouring through the
palaces, blood pouring down the gutters, the guillotine lifted
higher than the throne, a prison in ruins, a people in arms—
these things are not revolution, but the results of revolution. ...
    You cannot see a revolution: you can only see that there is a
revolution. And there never has been in the history of the world
a real revolution, brutally active and decisive, which was not
preceded by unrest and new dogmas in the region of invisible
things. All revolutions began by being abstract. Most revolutions
began by being quite pedantically abstract.

—G. K. Chesterton, *Selected Essays*

A revolution can be neither made nor stopped. The only thing that can be done is ... to give it a direction ... go along with the opinions of the masses and with events.... What the people want is almost never what the people say. Their will and needs ought to be found not ... in the people's mouth as [much as] in the ruler's heart.

—NAPOLEON

Revolution is for society what a passionate love is for the individual; those who experience it are marked forever, separated from their own past and from the rest of mankind. Some writers have captured the ecstasy of love; hardly any have rekindled the soul-purging fires of revolution. The writer of genius lives, for the most part, in a private world; it is not surprising that he deals usually with private passions. There have been some good observers of revolution—the best of them, I would guess, John Reed. Still, they observe from outside; it is like reading about the love-affair of the man next door. Two writers of the highest eminence, Lamartine and Trotsky, played the leading part in a revolution and created works of surpassing literary merit, but though their books tell us much about Lamartine and Trotsky, they do not tell us what revolution is like. The more brilliantly they write, the more the truth eludes them. For revolution calls in question the foundations of social life; it can be grasped only by one who has experienced it and yet possesses the detachment of a political psychologist.

—A. J. P. TAYLOR, *From Napoleon to Lenin*

If the peasant is in open rebellion, then he is outside the law of God.... Therefore, let everyone who can, smite, slay, and stab [the peasants], secretly or openly, remembering that nothing can be more poisonous, hurtful, or devilish than a rebel. It is just as when one must kill a mad dog; if you don't strike him, he will strike you, and the whole land with you.

—MARTIN LUTHER,
Against the Murderous and Thieving Horde

RUSSIAN

On the eve of World War I, Russia had a parliament, a viable labor movement, and ... highly vocal and popular advocates of

women's liberation [Alexandra Kolontai] and even of gay liberation. And yet that entire remarkable period is usually remembered
today as "Czarist Russia" and associated primarily with famines
and pogroms.

□

What was overthrown by Lenin and Trotsky in October of 1917
was not the Czarist regime (as 9 out of 10 foreigners believe
today), but the civil rights and democratic institutions won during
the preceding half-century, a case—if there ever was one—of
throwing out the baby with the dirty bath water. Navrozov
repeatedly refers to the October Revolution as the reinstatement
of serfdom and its extension to the entire population.
                    —SIMON KARLINSKY, *Saturday Review*, June 6, 1975

The world has never seen elections so really free, so truly
democratic. Never. History knows no other example of this
nature.

> —JOSEPH STALIN, on the election of the Supreme
> Council of the U.S.S.R., December 1937, in Boris
> Souvarine, *Stalin*

ARMAND DU PLESSIS (CARDINAL) RICHELIEU (1585–1642)

... He is an enigma only to those who fail to understand that he
was at one and the same time the supreme theorist and the supreme
pragmatist—a proclaimer of goals, but an adroit practitioner who
forever tried to take the middle way, an autocrat imperious by
instinct who was often moderate in his methods and liberal in
his achievements. His successes as a political reformer have been
exaggerated, and his diplomatic views have been largely misunderstood. In religion, government and diplomacy he was only more
or less successful, and his greatness lies in the personal influence
he wielded in all these spheres, rather than in the actual changes
he brought about. His defects of character are those of his generation; his virtues are those of Counter-Reformation Europe; and
his life is worthy of study by all who would understand the
problem of regulating human affairs.

> —KARL FEDERU, *Richelieu*

We cannot judge him [Richelieu] fairly unless we see him wholly.... He was a pioneer of religious toleration. He was a connoisseur of music, a discerning collector of art, a lover of drama and poetry ... the founder of the French Academy. But history properly remembers him above all as the man who freed France from that Spanish dominance which had resulted from the Religious Wars and which, in the League, had made France a pensioner, almost a dependency, of Spain. He achieved what Francis I and Henry IV had longed [for] and failed to do. . . .

For France itself he created unity and strength at the cost of a dictatorship and a royal absolutism that in time generated the Revolution. If it is a statesman's prime duty to make his people happy and free, Richelieu fell far short; Cardinal de Retz—a shrewd but not impartial judge—condemned him as having "established the most scandalous and dangerous tyranny that perhaps ever enslaved a state." Richelieu would have replied that the statesman is required to consider the happiness and freedom of future generations as well as of his own, that he must make his country strong to guard it against alien invasion or domination, and that for this purpose he may justly sacrifice a present generation for the security of its successors. In this sense Richelieu's Spanish rival, Olivares, rated him "the ablest minister that Christendom has possessed these last thousand years"; Chesterfield ranked him as "the ablest statesman of his time, and perhaps of any other."

—WILL and ARIEL DURANT, *The Age of Reason Begins*

ROBOT TALK

From work done at the Artificial Intelligence Laboratory of the Massachusetts Institute of Technology—a dialogue between a man and a machine:

MAN   What does the box contain?

MACHINE   The blue pyramid and the blue box.

MAN   How many blocks are not in the box?

MACHINE   Four of them.

MAN   Is at least one of them narrower than the one that I told you to pick up?

MACHINE   Yes, the red cube.

MAN   Is there a steeple?

MACHINE   Sorry, I don't know the word "steeple."

MAN   A steeple is a stack that contains two green cubes and a pyramid, for example.

MACHINE   I understand.

MAN   Are there any steeples now?

MACHINE   No.

MAN   Build one.

The machine does. It reaches out its mechanical hand, moves the cubes, and builds the structure that has just been described.

MAN   When did you pick up the pyramid?

MACHINE   While I was stacking up the red cube, the large red block, and the large green cube.

MAN   Why?

MACHINE   To get rid of it.

MAN   Why did you clear off that cube?

MACHINE   To put it on the large green cube.

—CARL SAGAN, *The Murmurs of Earth*

FRANKLIN D. ROOSEVELT (1882–1945)

I am opposed to any form of dole. I do not believe that the state has any right merely to hand out money.

□

I accuse the present administration [Hoover's] of being the greatest spending administration in peace times in all our history. On my part, I ask you very simply to assign to me the task of reducing the annual operating expenses of your national government.

□

The tendency to concentrate power at the top of a government structure is alien to our system.

□

...the cruel joke of calling on the farmers to allow twenty percent of their wheat lands to lie idle, to plow up every third row of cotton and shoot every tenth cow...

□

I believe that the individual should have full liberty of action to make the most of himself, but I do not believe that in the name of that sacred word, individualism, a few powerful interests should be permitted to make industrial cannon fodder of the lives of half the population of the United States.

□

I believe that our industrial and economic system is made for individual men and women, and not individual men and women for the benefit of the system. I believe in the sacredness of private property, which means I do not believe that it should be subjected to the ruthless manipulation of professional gamblers and the corporate system.

□

Either Stalin has been deceiving me all along, or he has not got the power I thought he had.

□

Wouldn't you be President if you could? Wouldn't anybody?

□

I should like to have it said of my first administration that in it the forces of selfishness and lust for power met their match. I should like to have it said of my second administration that these forces have met their master.

□

There is a grand word going around—boondoggling. It is a pretty good word. If we can boondoggle our way out of the Depression, that word is going to be enshrined in the hearts of American people for years to come.

□

If people like my choice of words, or my oratorical style, it is chiefly because of my constant reading of Mark Twain.

□

Ours has been a story of vigorous challenges which have been accepted and overcome—challenges of uncharted seas, of wild forests and desert plains, of raging floods and withering droughts, of foreign tyrants and domestic strife, of staggering problems—social, economic, and physical; and we have come out of them the most powerful Nation—and the freest—in all history.

—compiled from speeches, press conferences, interviews, and *The Public Papers of Franklin D. Roosevelt*

I don't know a good Russian from a bad Russian. I can tell a good Frenchman from a bad Frenchman, I can tell a good Italian from a bad Italian, I know a good Greek when I see one. But I don't understand the Russians.

—FRANCES PERKINS, *The Roosevelt I Knew*

ABOUT HIM

He is a pleasant man, who, without any important qualifications for the office, would very much like to be President.... Here is a man who has made a good governor, who might make a good Cabinet officer, but who simply does not measure up to the tremendous demands of the office of President.

—WALTER LIPPMANN,
"Today and Tomorrow," newspaper column, 1932

He demonstrated the ultimate capacity to dominate and control a supreme emergency, which is the rarest and most valuable characteristic of any statesman.

—SUMNER WELLES, *Time for Decision*

Franklin had a way, when he did not want to hear what somebody had to say, of telling stories and talking about something quite different.

□

I never heard him say that there was a problem that he thought it was impossible for human beings to solve.

—ELEANOR ROOSEVELT,
in Joseph Lash, *Eleanor and Franklin*

Meeting him is like opening a bottle of champagne.

—WINSTON CHURCHILL, *press interview*

Roosevelt knows nothing about finance, but he doesn't know that he doesn't know.

—FRANKLIN K. LANE

The frightening aspect of this method is FDR's great receptivity. So far as I know he makes no efforts to check up on anything that I or anyone else has told him.

□

One thing is sure—that the idea people get from his charming manner—that he is soft or flabby in disposition and character—is far from true. When he wants something a lot, he can be formidable; when crossed, he is hard, stubborn, resourceful, relentless.

—JOHN GUNTHER

I had supposed the President was more literate, economically speaking.

—JOHN MAYNARD KEYNES, after visiting F.D.R.; in
Frances Perkins, *op. cit.*

It was in economics that our troubles lay. For their solution his progressivism, his New Deal, was pathetically insufficient. . . . I think . . . that he will be put down as having failed in this realm of [domestic] affairs.

—REXFORD TUGWELL, *F.D.R.: Architect of an Era*

Roosevelt is in the literal sense of the term an opportunist. He has no ideas, no system, or set program in matters financial and economic. He is not doctrinaire to any degree.

—RAYMOND RECOULY,
Revue de France, Paris, August 5, 1933

The greatest autocrat in the world. . . .

—LORD RUNCIMAN,
New York Times, October 13, 1934

Practical compromise between principle and expediency . . . had been the keynote of Roosevelt's whole career in domestic American politics and, with the combination, he had worked wonders. When he attempted to apply similar methods to international relations . . . his wonder-working power abruptly vanished.

—*Survey of International Affairs*, London, 1945

No Englishman who lived through these dreadful twelve months from June 1940 to June 1941 is ever likely to forget how completely the nation's hope for ultimate victory rested on that buoyant figure in the White House. . . .

—*Economist*, London, April 21, 1945

JEAN JACQUES ROUSSEAU (1712–1778)

Those who boast of understanding all of . . . [*The Social Contract*] are cleverer than I. It is a book that should be rewritten but I no longer have either the time or the energy.

—ROUSSEAU

My situation is unique, unheard of since the beginning of time, and, I am sure, never to be paralleled. . . .

I say it without fear, if there were a single enlightened government in Europe it would have erected statues to me. . . .

If my soul were not immortal God would be unjust.

—in J. H. Huizinga, *The Making of a Saint*

ABOUT HIM

With grief and shame we find we have to admit that [Rousseau] bears about upon him the disfiguring marks of his debaucheries; who, disguised as a mountebank, drags after him from village to village, and from mountain to mountain, the unfortunate wretch whose mother he lets die of hunger: whose children he exposed on the doorsteps of a hospital, whilst rejecting the offer of a charitable person to take care of them, thus abjuring all natural sentiments, as well as those of humanity and religion. Here, then, is the man who presumes to offer advice to his fellow citizens.

—VOLTAIRE, pamphlet, *Sentiment des Citoyens*, in
Matthew Josephson, *Jean-Jacques Rousseau*

His self-portrait is a lie, brilliantly executed, but a lie.

—HEINRICH HEINE, *Confessions*

He clothed passion in the garb of philosophy, and preached the sweeping away of injustice by the perpetuation of further injustices.

—THOMAS H. HUXLEY,
On the Natural Inequality of Man

He is surely the blackest and most atrocious villain . . . in the world; and I am heartily ashamed of anything I ever wrote in his favor.

—DAVID HUME, letter to Blair, 1766

RUSSIA

["Russia], a relatively inefficient autocracy, has become an efficient totalitarian state in terms of power," said one Western diplomatic observer. "The czars were autocratic, they were stupid, they may not have recognized human rights, but they were not totalitarian. There were many areas of human rights they stayed out of." Even under the czar, he said, a dissident could find work because there was more than one employer.

—Christopher S. Wren,
"Russia in Entropy," in *Harper's*, June 1978

Was there ever a more awful spectacle in the whole history of the World than is unfolded by the agony of Russia? It is now reduced to famine of the most terrible kind—not because there is no food—there is plenty of food—but because the theories of Lenin and Trotsky have fatally and, it may be, finally, ruptured the means of intercourse between man and man, between workman and peasant, between town and country ... because they have driven man from the civilization of the twentieth century into a condition of barbarism worse than the Stone Age, and have left him the most pitiable spectacle in human experience, devoured by vermin, racked by pestilence, and deprived of hope.

—Winston Churchill, January 1921

No matter in whose hands power rests, I retain my human right to be critical of it. And I am especially suspicious, especially distrustful, of a Russian when he gets power into his hands. Not long ago a slave, he becomes the most unbridled despot as soon as he has the chance to become his neighbor's master.

—Maxim Gorky, April 23, 1917

Blind fanatics and dishonest adventurers are rushing madly, supposedly along the road to "social revolution," in reality this is the road to anarchy, to the destruction of the proletariat and of the revolution....

—Maxim Gorky, November 7, 1917

I went to Russia, had long talks with Lenin and other prominent men, and saw as much as I could of what was going on.... I thought the regime already hateful and certain to become more so. I found the source of evil in a contempt for liberty and democracy which was a natural outcome of fanaticism.

It was thought by radicals in those days that one ought to support the Russian Revolution, whatever it might be doing, since it was opposed by reactionaries, and criticism of it played into their hands. I . . . was for some time in doubt as to what I ought to do. But in the end I decided in favor of what seemed to me to be the truth. I stated publicly that I thought the Bolshevik regime abominable, and I have never seen any reason to change this opinion.

[Russia] seemed to me one vast prison in which the jailers were cruel bigots. When I found my friends applauding these men as liberators and regarding the regime they were creating as a paradise, I wondered . . . whether it was my friends or I who were mad. . . .

—BERTRAND RUSSELL, *Portraits from Memory*

The revolution is not disposed either to pity or to bury its dead.

—JOSEPH STALIN

[In response to a Red Naval proclamation stating, "For every one of our comrades murdered we shall answer with the death of hundreds and thousands of the rich."]: To me—as, probably to all those who have not yet completely lost their minds—the stern proclamation of the sailors represents not a cry for justice but the wild roar of unbridled and cowardly beasts. . . .

—MAXIM GORKY, April 1918

"SACRED COWS" IN POLITICS

Some sacred cows were regional, like dams and oil to Texas, aircraft to the Pacific coast, cotton to the South. I was shocked when Kennedy and Pastore opposed a bill levying fines for the misbranding of textiles, until I realized that sacred cows grazed in New England as elsewhere.

Others were national: pay increases for federal workers, for one. And these had to be uniform. The salaries of civil servants could not be raised unless those of postal workers were raised simultaneously. Separate treatment was once tried; when a remedial amendment was offered on the floor, the gallery was packed with postmen in shirt-sleeved blue, their weight upon the men below as palpable as a late-returning precinct. I half expected someone to speak out against this menacing pressure, so foreign to the measured deliberations of the Senate. No one did, and the amendment was overwhelmingly adopted.

—HARRY McPHERSON, *A Political Education*

THE SACRED CROCODILE

The crocodile is esteemed sacred by some of the Egyptians; by others he is treated as an enemy. Those who live near Thebes, and those who dwell around Lake Moeris, regard them with especial veneration. In each of these places they keep one crocodile in particular, who is taught to be tame and tractable. They adorn his ears with earrings of molten stone or gold, and put bracelets on his forepaws, giving him daily a set portion of bread, with a certain number of victims; and after having thus treated him with the greatest possible attention while alive, they embalm him when he dies, and bury him in a sacred repository.

—HERODOTUS, *History*

ST. PETER'S: HIGH MASS

Sitting in a scented crush of mink and sable and gold braid . . . [we] watched with a feeling of enchantment as the gates of Time seemed to have been thrown wide to admit a procession from the halls of Karnak or the Sacra Via. The Pope was borne into the Church in the state palanquin, while trumpets sounded, peacock fans waved, and the packed church shouted its head off. . . .

—H. V. MORTON, *A Traveler in Rome*

SATAN

I have no special regard for Satan; but I can at least claim that I have no prejudice against him. It may even be that I lean a little his way, on account of his not having a fair show. All religions issue bibles against him, and say the most injurious things about him, but we never hear *his* side. We have none but the evidence for the prosecution, and yet we have rendered the verdict. . . . A person who has for untold centuries maintained the imposing position of spiritual head of four-fifths of the human race, and political head of the whole of it, must be granted the possession of executive abilities of the loftiest order. In his large presence the other popes and politicians shrink to midges for the microscope. I would like to see him. I would rather see him and shake him by the tail than any other member of the European Concert.

—MARK TWAIN,
"Concerning the Jews," in *Harper's*, September 1899

A SCENE IN PARLIAMENT

Prompted by Lord Grey, William IV therefore hurried down to Westminster and cramming his crown hastily on to one side of his head, entered the Chamber and dissolved Parliament. A stormy general election followed in which the Whigs got their increased majority. Once again, the [Reform] Bill was brought in: this time it passed the Commons and proceeded to the House of Lords. On its first appearance there was the occasion of a memorable full-dress debate. The outstanding speakers were Lord Grey, who revived for the wonder and delight of a new generation the stately splendors of eighteenth century oratory; and Lord Chancellor Brougham, a master of the more trenchant modern style. His speech culminated in a peroration in which falling on his knees and with outstretched hands, he implored the peers not to throw out the Bill. Unluckily, in order to stimulate his eloquence, he had during his speech drunk a whole bottle of mulled port, with the result that once on his knees he found he was unable to get up until assisted to do so by his embarrassed colleagues.

—DAVID CECIL, *Melbourne*

HEINRICH SCHLIEMANN (1822–1890)

[He traversed] the Great Wall of China and penetrated the jungles of Peru, Mexico and Chile; he criss-crossed the United States and traipsed the deserts of Arabia.

... The German-born Schliemann traveled to California ... and made a fortune in the gold rush before returning to St. Petersburg, where he amassed enormous wealth. He was a profiteer of the Crimean War, justifying himself by saying the cash was needed to prove that Homer wrote history and Troy was a real place.... He wanted a Greek wife at his side.

After a miserable marriage with a ... Russian woman, he arranged to divorce her in the United States, at Indianapolis. While there, he began negotiations for an Hellenic bride ... [writing to] an Athenian friend, Archbishop Theoclitus Vimbos, who ... had tutored Schliemann in ancient and modern Greek.... Schliemann stated that he wanted to marry a girl of pure Greek heritage who resembled Helen of Troy, as he visualized her....

Heinrich sent his shirts and underthings from Athens to a laundry in London, by fast ship.... In his diary for March 1877, he wrote: "If I live in this country much longer, I shall have to stop my excavations because it is costing me so much to have my laundry done.... I'm hoping that my 218 shirts will be enough to last me throughout the year."

—LYNN and GREY POOLE, *One Passion, Two Loves*

SCIENCE

APPLIED

I often wish that this phrase, "applied science," had never been invented. For it suggests that there is a sort of scientific knowledge of direct practical use, which can be studied apart from another sort of scientific knowledge, which is of no practical utility, and which is termed "pure science." But there is no more complete fallacy than this.

What people call applied science is nothing but the application of pure science to particular classes of problems. It consists of deductions from those general principles, established by reasoning and observation, which constitute pure science. No one can safely make these deductions until he has a firm grasp of the principles.

—Thomas Henry Huxley, *Science and Culture*

SOME POSERS

Was there ever a time when matter did not exist?

May time have a beginning or an end?

May space or time be discontinuous?

Are there parts of nature forever beyond our detection?

May there be missing integers in the series of natural numbers as we know them?

Why does nature obey laws?

If one part of our universe could be completely isolated from the rest, would it continue to obey the same laws?

Can we be sure that our logical processes are valid?

—Percy W. Bridgman,
The Logic of Modern Physics

SCIENCE AND RESPONSIBLITIY

It is not enough that you should understand about applied science in order that your work may increase man's blessings. Concern for man himself and his fate must always form the chief interest of all technical endeavors, concern for the great unsolved problems ... in order that the creations of our mind shall be a blessing and not a curse to Mankind. Never forget this in the midst of your diagrams and equations.

—Albert Einstein,
address, California Institute of Technology, 1931

SCIENTIFIC METHOD

Even primitive men were scientists, and in certain aspects of accurate and subtle observation and deduction it would probably be hard to beat the ancient skilled hunter.

Indeed, one important contrast between the savage and the professor is simply that modern scientific methods make it possible to crystallize our experience rapidly and reliably, whereas primitive science does this clumsily, slowly, and with much attendant error. But it is, after all, well to remember that ephedrine is the active principle in an herb, Ma Huang, that has been empirically employed by native Chinese physicians for some 5000 years. Certain

African savages when they moved their villages did take with them to the new location some dirt from the floor of the old hut. Moreover, it is true that they said that they did this to avoid the anger of their gods who might not wish them to move, fooling them by continuing to live on some of the same ground. But the fact remains that by this process they brought to the new location the soil microorganisms that continued to give some degree of protection from certain ailments. We quite properly honor Fleming and Florey, but Johannes de Sancto Paulo, a medical writer of the 12th century, did prescribe moldy bread for an inflamed abscess. "We are all scientists," Thomas Huxley said, because "the method of scientific investigation is nothing but the expression of the necessary mode of working of the human mind."

—WARREN WEAVER,
"Science and People," *Science*, December 30, 1955

The main business of natural philosophy is to argue from phenomena without feigning hypotheses, and to deduce causes from effects, till we come to the very first cause ... and not only to unfold the mechanism of the world, but chiefly to resolve these and such like questions: What is there in places almost empty of matter, and whence is it that the sun and planets gravitate towards one another, without dense matter between them? Whence is it that nature doth nothing in vain; and whence arises all that order and beauty which we see in the world?

—ISAAC NEWTON, *Opticks*, 1704

It was therefore not until late in the history of mankind, not until a few seconds ago so to speak, that it was recognized that nature is understandable and that a knowledge of nature is good and can be used with benefit: that it does not involve witchcraft or a compact with the devil. What is more, any person of intelligence can understand the ideas involved and with sufficient skill learn the necessary techniques, intellectual and manual.

This idea which is now so commonplace represents an almost complete break with the past. To revere and trust the rational faculty of the mind—to allow no taboo to interfere in its operation, to have nothing immune from its examination—is a new value which has been introduced into the world. The progress of science has been the chief agent in demonstrating its importance and riveting it into the consciousness of mankind. . . .

The last world war was started in an attempt to turn back to dark reaction against the rational faculty and to introduce a new demonology into the world. It failed as will every other such attempt. Once the mind is free it will be destroyed rather than be put back in chains.

—I. I. RABI, Nobel Prize acceptance speech, 1944

THE SEA

The sea was white like a sheet of foam, like a caldron of boiling milk; there was not a break in the clouds, no—not the size of a man's hand—no, not for so much as ten seconds. There was for us no sky, there were for us no stars, no sun, no universe—nothing but angry clouds and an infuriated . . . watch, for dear life. . . .

We forgot the day of the week, the name of the month, what year it was, and whether we had ever been ashore. The sails blew away, she lay broadside on under a weather-cloth, the ocean poured over her, and we did not care. We turned those handles, and had the eyes of idiots. . . .

—JOSEPH CONRAD, *Youth*

SOUNDS

The three great elemental sounds in nature are the sound of rain, the sound of wind in a primeval wood, and the sound of the outer ocean on a beach. I have heard them all, and of the three elemental voices, that of the ocean is the most awesome, beautiful and varied. . . .

The sea has many voices. Listen to the surf, really lend it your ears, and you will hear in it a world of sounds: hollow boomings and heavy roarings, great watery tumblings and tramplings, long hissing seethes, sharp rifle-shot reports, splashes, whispers, the grinding undertone of stones, and sometimes vocal sound that might be the half-heard talk of people in the sea.

—HENRY BESTON, *The Outermost House*

You come out of sleep, out of the stuffiness below, into all the freshness of the world. During the night everything has been remade for you. The open parts of the ship, the sea itself, even the morning, have just come back from the laundry. The scrubbed planks glisten and the brasses blaze in a new morning of Creation. The winking and hissing sea has just been invented. The blue above is most delicately pale and as yet untarnished. The air is a mystery of goodness. From these shifting meadows comes the fragrance of invisible sea blossoms. Ocean and air whisper the news of their perfection. It is the morning of Time itself.

—J. B. PRIESTLEY, *Delight*

SECRET POLICE

.... It's high time to do something about the NKVD. If that madman of a Yezhov keeps on the way he's going, he'll arrest me yet for plotting against Stalin.

—JOSEPH STALIN,
in Buda Svanidze, *My Uncle Joseph Stalin*

SELF-DEFENSE

... let me tell you when a man has the right to shoot in self-defense, and in defense of his home; not when these vital things in life are in danger, but when he thinks they are. These despised blacks did not need to wait until the house was beaten down above their heads. They didn't need to wait until every window was broken. They didn't need to wait longer for that mob to grow more inflamed. There is nothing so dangerous as ignorance and bigotry when it is unleashed as it was here. The Court will tell you that these inmates of this house had the right to decide upon appearances, and if they did, even though they were mistaken, they are not guilty. I don't know but they could safely have stayed a little longer. I don't know but it would have been well enough to let this mob break a few more windowpanes. I don't know but it would have been better and been safe to let them batter down the house before they shot. I don't know. How am I to tell, and how are you to tell?

—CLARENCE DARROW, Detroit, 1926, to the jury in the
murder trial of Henry Sweet, Negro; in Arthur
Weinberg, *Attorney for the Damned*

SELF-INTEREST

The natural effort of every individual to better his own condition, when suffered to exert itself with freedom and security, is so powerful a principle, that it is alone, and without any assistance, not only capable of carrying on the society to wealth and prosperity, but of surmounting a hundred impertinent obstructions with which the folly of human laws too often encumbers its operations.

—ADAM SMITH, *Wealth of Nations*

SENSUOUSNESS

The strongest hold that the sensuous have upon others [is] that they are able to create a kind of evil, passionate glory of the flesh which those less sensuous would not know otherwise and which they can never forget once they have known it. It is a dubious but magnificent glory which the mild-mannered, the timid, the unrealized never attain. They know neither its delights nor its bitterness but exist always in a kind of half-world of mild colors and gentle and safe monotony.

—LOUIS BROMFIELD, *The Wild Country*

SENTIMENTALISM

The world is neither wise nor just, but it makes up for its folly and injustice by being damnably sentimental.

—T. H. HUXLEY, *Letter to Tyndall*

SERENDIPITY

Walpole's proposal was based upon his reading of a fairy tale entitled *The Three Princes of Serendip*. Serendip, I might interject, was the ancient name of Ceylon. "As their highnesses traveled," so Walpole wrote, "they were always making discoveries, by *accident* or *sagacity*, of things which they were not in quest of." ...

□

Probably the most astounding instance of accidental discovery in either ancient or modern history was the finding of the western hemisphere by Columbus. He sailed away from Spain firm in the faith that by going west he would learn a shorter route to the East Indies; quite unexpectedly he encountered a whole new world. It is noteworthy that he was not aware of the significance of what he had found.

□

It is reported that some frogs' legs were hanging by a copper wire from an iron balustrade in the Galvani home in Bologna; they were seen to twitch when they were swung by the wind and happened to touch the iron. Whether the twitching was first noted by Luigi Galvani, the anatomist and physiologist, or by Lucia Galvani, his talented wife, is not clear. Certainly that fortuitous occurrence late in the eighteenth century was not neglected, for it started many researches which have preserved the Galvani name in the terms "galvanize" and "galvanism."

□

Pasteur was led by chance to his method of immunization. One day an old and forgotten bacterial culture was being used for inoculating fowls. The fowls became ill but did not die. This happening was illuminative. Possibly by first using cultures that had little virulence and then repeating the injections with cultures of greater virulence, the animals could be made to develop resistance to infection gradually. His surmise proved correct. By this procedure, he was able to immunize sheep against anthrax and human beings against rabies.

□

In the late eighties of the last century, Von Mering and Minkowski were studying the functions of the pancreas in digestion. While attempting to secure more evidence they removed that organ from a number of dogs. By good luck a laboratory assistant noticed that swarms of flies gathered round the urine of these animals, a fact which he mentioned to the investigators. When the urine was analyzed, it was found to be loaded with sugar. Thus for the first time experimental diabetes was produced, and the earliest glimpse was given into a possible cause of that disease. . . .
—WALTER B. CANNON, *The Way of an Investigator*

LUCIUS SEPTIMIUS SEVERUS (146–211 A.D.)

The uncommon abilities and fortune of Severus have induced an elegant historian to compare him with the first and greatest of the Caesars [Julius]. The parallel is, at least, imperfect. Where shall we find, in the character of Severus, the commanding superiority of soul, the generous clemency, and the various genius, which could reconcile and unite the love of pleasure, the thirst of knowledge, and the fire of ambition? . . .

□

He promised only to betray, he flattered only to ruin; and however he might occasionally bind himself by oaths and treaties, his conscience, obsequious to his interest, always released him from the inconvenient obligation.

—EDWARD GIBBON,
The Decline and Fall of the Roman Empire

SHADOWS

Unnoticed, the sun occupied his sky, and the shadows of the tree stems, extraordinarily solid, fell like trenches of purple across the frosted dawn.

—E. M. FORSTER, *Howard's End*

SHOES IN VENICE: 16TH CENTURY

The height and costliness of the clog was a measure of sexual morality. In the sixteenth century it had reached its highest and most expensive; the Sumptuary Laws imposed a fine of twenty-five lire for clogs beyond the allowed measurements or of too elaborate design. Fine pearls were forbidden as a form of decoration, and even permitted embroidery could not be too rich. These shoes lasted as a form of patrician display, though there was nothing in the rest of Europe like them, until the end of the seventeenth century. And then—with the disappearance of heroes and Mediterranean hegemony—they went out so thoroughly that women seemed to have no shoes at all.

—MAURICE ROWDON, *The Silver Age of Venice*

SITTING

No one sits quite so relaxedly, expertly, beatifically as a Turk; he sits with every inch of his body; his very face sits. He sits as if he inherited the art from generations of sultans in the palace above Seraglio Point. Nothing he likes better than to invite you to sit with him in his shop or in his office with half a dozen other sitters: a few polite inquiries about age, your marriage, the sex of your children ... where and how you live, and then ... join the general silence.

—V. S. PRITCHETT, *The Offensive Traveler*

THE SKULL OF SHAIBANI

Shaibani had met his match, both in resources and tactics. By a series of ruses he was led, in 1510, into an ambush and was cornered in a cattle compound. His body was dismembered and was sent to different parts of the Persian empire for display purposes, and his skull, set in gold, was turned into a drinking cup which the Shah himself much enjoyed using.

—BAMBER GASCOIGNE, *The Great Moghuls*

SLAVE MARKET: MEDINA

[In Arab disguise, Richard Burton] was curious about the eunuchs who guarded and maintained the mosques, learning that they were generally regarded as honorable men, that they were fairly well paid, and that most of them were married, some even having three or four wives. He visited the slave market and noted the prices and condition of the merchandise: a black slave-girl for housework cost from 40 to 50 dollars, but "neat-handedness, propriety of demeanor, and skill in feminine accomplishment" might raise her price to 100 dollars ... eunuchs were quite expensive; boys were sold, but there were few male adults on the market; Abyssinian girls were prized because "their skins are always cool in the hottest weather" and they sold for between 80 and 240 dollars; white slave-girls were seldom on the market, their price being from 400 to 1,600 dollars he was told.

All such information was written into his carefully kept notebooks together with notes on diseases and their treatment, magic, architecture, family life, the character and physical features of the people, the prices of dozens of articles of food, popular sayings, the status of agriculture and a host of other subjects.

—BYRON FARWELL, *Burton*

SLAVERY

What, am I to argue that it is wrong to make men brutes, to rob them of their liberty, to work them without wages, to keep them ignorant of their relations to their fellow men, to beat them with sticks, to flay their flesh with the lash, to load their limbs with irons, to hunt them with dogs, to sell them at auction, to sunder their families, to knock out their teeth, to burn their flesh, to starve them into obedience and submission to their masters? Must I argue that a system thus marked with blood, and stained with pollution, is wrong? No! I will not. I have better employment for my time and strength than such arguments would imply.

What, then, remains to be argued? Is it that slavery is not divine; that God did not establish it; that our doctors of divinity are mistaken? There is blasphemy in the thought. That which is inhuman cannot be divine! Who can reason on such a proposition? They that can may; I cannot. The time for such argument is past.

At a time like this, scorching iron, not convincing argument, is needed. O! had I the ability, and could I reach the nation's ear, I would today pour out a fiery stream of biting ridicule, blasting reproach, withering sarcasm, and stern rebuke. For it is not light that is needed, but fire; it is not the gentle shower, but thunder. We need the storm, the whirlwind, and the earthquake. The feeling of the nation must be quickened; the conscience of the nation must be roused; the propriety of the nation must be startled; the hypocrisy of the nation must be exposed; and its crimes against God and man must be proclaimed and denounced.

—FREDERICK DOUGLASS, speech, New York, July 4, 1852

He who is no slave must consent to have no slave. Those who deny freedom to others deserve it not for themselves; and, under a just God, cannot long retain it.

—ABRAHAM LINCOLN

There must doubtless be an unhappy influence on the manners of
our people produced by the existence of slavery among us....
The man must be a prodigy who can retain his manners and morals undepraved by such circumstances.

—THOMAS JEFFERSON, *Notes on Virginia*

SLAVERY IN ROME

For a couple of centuries the great gentlemen in Rome had
been content to have their business affairs run by their slaves or
manumitted slaves. They themselves knew nothing of trade or
commerce, or money matters generally; they had no wish to understand these matters nor were they allowed to. But of course
they wanted to make money, to get rich, and to get rich quickly.
That was what they had their slaves for—the slaves they had
bought with their newly gained money.

□

...the Roman wars began to assume the character of vast slave
hunts. No general would set out without surrounding himself first
with slave merchants who made him firm offers for the booty to
be expected. Each victory meant great sums of money with which
all the debts incurred earlier could easily be redeemed. Thus the
impoverished Roman landed gentry, who until recently had tilled
their own fields, became a wealthy class within a few decades.

The Romans did not suspect at that time that this disastrous slave
policy would do them a great deal of harm in the future. Their
entire politics came to be dependent, to a certain extent, on the
slave traders. It was they who advanced money for expensive wars
and who insisted on the wars being waged ruthlessly, in a way that
would break the will of the enemy to resist. After all, they could
make profits only if the generals mercilessly turned the vanquished
into slaves. The great gentlemen, who did not look beyond their
attractive profits, evidently did not realize this at first.

The slave trade was only able to achieve such huge profits because its "merchandise" was available at such incomparably low
prices. So long as Rome waged its wars as definite wars of conquest and depredation, so long as it burst into wealthy and flourishing kingdoms and seized their treasures to finance its own war
effort, the campaigns yielded a good profit. The prisoners taken

in open battle were not nearly numerous enough to meet the costs of the extensive organization connected with the slave trade in Delos. Entire nations had to be enslaved to assure the soldiers of sufficient revenue.

—ERNST SAMHABER, *Merchants Make History*

SLEEP

The brain of man is subject to short and strange snatches of sleep. A cloud seals the city of reason or rests upon the sea of imagination; a dream that darkens as much, whether it is a nightmare of atheism or a day-dream of idolatry. And just as we have all sprung from sleep with a start and found ourselves saying some sentence that has no meaning, save in the mad tongues of the midnight, so the human mind starts from its trances of stupidity with some complete phrase upon its lips: a complete phrase which is a complete folly.

—G. K. CHESTERTON, *Selected Essays*

The witchcraft of sleep divides with truth the empire of our lives.

—RALPH WALDO EMERSON, *Works*

ADAM SMITH (1723–1790)

Adam Smith's breadth was sufficient to include all that was best in all his contemporaries, French and English; and though he undoubtedly borrowed much from others, yet the more one compares him with those who went before and those who came after him, the finer does his genius appear, the broader his knowledge and the more well-balanced his judgment.

—ALFRED MARSHALL, *Principles of Economics*

Next to Napoleon he [Smith] is now the mightiest monarch in Europe.

—ALEXANDER VON DER MARWITZ,
in Francis W. Hirst, *Adam Smith*

Fate tried to conceal him by naming him Smith.

—OLIVER WENDELL HOLMES

We study him because in him, as in Plato, we come into contact with a great original mind, which teaches us how to think and work.

—ARNOLD TOYNBEE, *The Industrial Revolution of the 18th Century in England*

This solitary Scotchman has, by the publication of one single work, contributed more toward the happiness of man than has been effected by the united abilities of all the statesmen and legislators of whom history has presented an authentic account.

—THOMAS BUCKLE

SNAKES AND IMMORTALITY

The snake must have seemed to early man to be gifted with a superior intelligence—because when they saw it sloughing its skin they must have thought it was rejuvenating itself. By changing its skin, it could remain eternally young; hence it was immortal. So the snake became in Egypt and in Greece, the symbol of immortality.

—VOLTAIRE, *Customs of Nations*

SNOWFLAKES

There is one fact of overwhelming interest about snow crystals: Snow is the only substance that crystallizes in such a variety of shapes. All other crystals have dependable ways of putting themselves together which allows one to classify them at a glance. . . .

The picture of a snow crystal's career . . . is one of a microscopic germ of matter that begins collecting water molecules on its surface. For some time this speck is blown along with the winds inside the clouds, passing through whatever variations of temperature and humidity are to be found in a horizontal plane. Then, as it gains weight, it begins to sink toward the Earth, as far as six miles below. (It is these extremely high crystals which produce halos around the moon.)

The droplets, the first step in the condensation of rain out of a cloud, tend to be much too small to fall (10,000 of them would fit in a line across the head of a pin) and fiercely independent. They do not join to make big heavy drops. . . .

Every so often one of them freezes. When that happens, the personality of the droplet, once so withdrawn and modest in its ambitions, undergoes a remarkable change. . . .Soon the droplets in the area begin to shrink as water evaporates from their surfaces and flows to the crystal. The ice crystal has turned into a kind of predator, and soon grows so fat with accumulated booty that it begins to fall toward Earth. When it strikes a layer of warm air, it melts back to water and completes its journey as a raindrop.

□

A single ice crystal might well contain some ten sextillion molecules: Considering all the ways those molecules can be arranged, the odds against any two completely identical snowflakes having fallen since the atmosphere formed some four billion years ago are enormous. But by the same analysis, no two grains of sand on the beach . . . no two hairs on the head are identical. Why all the fuss, then, over snowflakes?

Partly, perhaps, it is because snow crystals are so *similar*. For one thing, they are all six-sided. The iron law of crystal formation is that all angles must be multiples of 60 degrees. . . . By contrast, grains of sand are a chaotic riot of jumbled angles whose anarchy defeats any effort to face them squarely.

□

An international effort of some 45 years duration . . . and all the paraphernalia of modern science [have] not yet fully succeeded in bringing snow into the routine, bleached world of the textbook. The snow blossoms still harbor unpredictable, baffling, frustrating and refreshing surprises. They still lead us on.

—FRED HAPGOOD, "When Ice Crystals Fall from the Sky," in *Smithsonian*, January 1976

SOCIAL CONFLICTS

Seek the roots of disastrous conflicts between nations and classes and sects, and invariably you find a man, often gifted and resourceful, who has failed to master his own inner turmoil—a neurotic, perhaps, or an epileptic, a slave of sensuality or of pride—who diffuses the bitterness and desperation of his tortured soul among masses. . . .

—FRANCIS MEEHAN, *The Temple of the Spirit*

SOCIAL CONTROL

The recognition of the insuperable limits to his knowledge ought to teach the student [to] ... guard against becoming an accomplice in man's fatal striving to control society—a striving which makes him not only a tyrant over his fellows, but may well make him destroy a civilization which no brain has designed, but which has grown from the free efforts of millions of individuals.
—F. A. HAYEK, Nobel Memorial Lecture, 1976

SOCIALISM

I criticize doctrinaire State Socialism, not because it seeks to engage men's altruistic impulses in the service of Society, or because it departs from *Laissez-faire,* or because it takes away from man's natural liberty to make a million, or because it has courage for bold experiments. All these things I applaud. I criticize it because it misses the significance of what is actually happening; because it is, in fact, little better than a dusty survival of a plan to meet the problems of fifty years ago, based on a misunderstanding of what someone said a hundred years ago.
—JOHN MAYNARD KEYNES,
Laissez-faire and Communism

THE INTELLECTUALS

Perhaps the rise of modern political socialism is a phase in the struggle for power, not of the manual workers, but of the "intellectuals" who successfully allied themselves with the discontented manual workers in wresting power from the aristocracy and the plutocracy. Once established in power, they give special privileges to special skill.... Deference and higher money incomes go to those who perform technical and organizational functions, not to those who do manual work.
—HAROLD D. LASSWELL,
Politics—Who Gets What, When, How

ITS END

... The death of socialism is the unrealized political fact of this century. In the Soviet world we have seen the cruel falsification of the communal dreams of the nineteenth-century radicals. The "socialism" of most of the third-world countries is a deceit in that liberty and freedom are denied while new elites drive the people in the name of economic development. And in China the people are fused into a single "moral personality," embodied in the thought of Mao, so that all ego is erased and all individual voices of expression, especially in culture, are suppressed.

—Daniel Bell, "The Public Household," in
The Cultural Contradictions of Capitalism

SOCIALISM AND FREEDOM

What is essential is that the cost of advocating unpopular causes be tolerable and not prohibitive. ... In a free market society, it is enough to have the funds. The suppliers of paper are as willing to sell it to the *Daily Worker* as to the *Wall Street Journal*. In a socialist society, it would not be enough to have the funds. The hypothetical supporter of capitalism would have to persuade a government factory making paper to sell to him, the government printing press to print his pamphlets, a government post office to distribute them among the people, a government agency to rent him a hall in which to talk, and so on.

—Milton Friedman, *Capitalism and Freedom*

SOCIETY

Society requires not only that the passions of individuals should be subjected, but that even in the mass and body, as well as in the individuals, the inclinations of men should frequently be thwarted, their will controlled, and their passions brought into subjection. This can only be done by a power outside of themselves. ... In this sense the restraints on men, as well as their liberties, are to be reckoned among their rights.

—Edmund Burke,
Reflections on the Revolution in France

When men live in society, a certain average of conduct, a sacrifice of individual peculiarities going beyond a certain point, is necessary to the general welfare. If, for instance, a man is born hasty and awkward, is always having accidents and hurting himself or his neighbors, no doubt his congenital defects will be allowed for in the courts of Heaven, but his slips are no less troublesome to his neighbors than if they sprang from guilty neglect. His neighbors accordingly require him, at his proper peril, to come up to their standard, and the courts which they establish decline to take his personal equation into account.

—OLIVER WENDELL HOLMES, JR.

Anyone who either cannot lead the common life or is so self-sufficient as not to need to, and therefore does not partake of society, is either a beast or a god.

—ARISTOTLE

SOCRATES (470?–399 B.C.)

[To the court determining his fate:]

I have refused to address you in the manner which would have flattered you, repenting or weeping, throwing myself on your sympathy, saying things I consider unworthy. For I would rather die as the result of the defense I made than live as the result of the other. . . . Nothing can harm a good man, in life or in death. . . .

Now it is time to go—I to die and you to live; which of us will be the happier is not known to anyone but God.

—PLATO, *Phaedo*

ABOUT HIM

Socrates was all-glorious within . . . the most righteous man of the age . . . so pious that he did nothing without taking counsel of the gods, so just that he never did an injury to any man . . . so temperate that he never preferred pleasure to right, so wise that in the judging of good and evil he was never at fault. . . . He was the best and happiest of men. . . . His self-control was absolute; his powers of endurance were unfailing. . . . When we were cut off from our supplies and compelled to go without food, he was superior to everybody. . . . His fortitude was remarkable. There was a severe frost; everyone else wore an immense quantity of clothes, were well-shod, and had their feet swathed in felt and fleece; Socrates, with his bare feet on the ice and in ordinary dress, marched better than the other soldiers.

□

I was affected in a wonderful way in his company. No feeling of pity entered my mind as one would expect, being present at the death of a friend. He seemed to me happy in his mien and in his conversation, and he died fearlessly and nobly, I could not but believe that the divine hand was in it, leading him to the gates beyond, and that his lot would be blessed. . . . No regret seized me, as one would have expected at such an extremity.

—*Ibid.*

Socrates brought down philosophy from heaven to earth.

—CICERO

I hate this Socrates, this babbling beggar, who has meditated more than anybody else, but has never asked where he was going to get his dinner.

—EUPOLIS

Of all the men I have ever known Socrates was the most anxious to ascertain in what any of those about him was really versed.

—XENOPHON

SOUTHERN SPEECH-MAKING

In the South, there was an old tradition of politics-as-show. Speeches in the town square in later summer—before the Democratic primary that was "tantamount to election"—followed an hour or two of country music by young men whose long sideburns antedated fashion by several decades. When the time came for the candidate to speak, people thought now we'll hear a lot of self-important posturing and belaboring of the obvious; but they expected something thrilling, too, something that organized and gave voice to their discontent. There was an element of priest as well as performer in Southern political man—many of whom adopted red galluses or frock coats or long curling hair, as priests did cassocks and surplices, to set themselves apart from the multitude. (Recognition was vital if they were to be remembered on election day—I don't care what they say about me, so long as they spell my name right.)

—HARRY MCPHERSON, *A Political Education*

SOVIET BELIEFS IN CRISIS

Gadgets can be engineered, programs can be designed, institutions can be built, but belief has an organic quality, and it cannot be called into being by fiat. Once a faith is shattered, it takes a long time to grow again—for its soil is experience—and to become effective again.

In the Soviet Union where a messianic creed sought to embody itself in a people, the crisis of belief is threefold: most persons no longer believe in the creed (would one dispute the end of ideology in the Soviet Union?); there is a loss of faith in the leaders (the denigration of Stalin, and the admission of *his* crimes by his heirs, effectively broke the feet of that idol); and few persons seem to believe in "the future"—it no longer works.

—DANIEL BELL, "The Public Household," in
The Cultural Contradictions of Capitalism

SOVIET MAN

The problem for the Kremlin is that Soviet man has not turned out in accordance with the Marxist-Leninist "scientific" plan. It now has a generation brought up without contaminating bourgeois contact. This conditioned generation should be selflessly dedicated to the Communist cause and abide by the 1961 party program's moral code, including "conscientious labor for the good of society."...

Naturally none of this has happened, is happening, or is likely to happen. Soviet man is bogged down with a full human share of anxieties, selfishness, dishonesty, and guile. These take forms somewhat different from ours, but they are there.

Boredom, cynicism, and careerism seem to affect most of the new generation's privileged class, the sons and daughters of party bosses and high military officers.... These young people are scarcely models of the party program's moral code, but there they are, high in Communist society, ideological conformists or cynics, some of them parasites and many of them shrewdly able careerists.

—JOHN PATON DAVIES, JR., *Foreign and Other Affairs*

SOVIET TERROR

Stalin saw in the centralized Soviet system an instrument for the realization of the bloodiest dictatorship any tyrant ever wielded over his own people. Anyone inclined to question this is referred to "The Great Terror" by Robert Conquest (whose) conclusions, supported by ... Soviet census statistics (show) that the victims of Stalin's terror numbered 20 million. ... Even if Mr. Conquest's figure were to be halved, the atrocity is without parallel. ... Confessions were obtained by a mixture of subtle and crude forms of torture. ... Stalin killed, in one way or another, every member of the Politburo ... (and) 98 of the 130 members of the Party Central Committee, according to ... Nikita Khrushchev. ... Labor camps had a population of eight million, of whom 10% died every year only to be replaced by new batches of prisoners supplied by the secret police. About a million persons were killed outright. ... About 3.5 million ... perished in the man-made famine of 1932–1935. ... And the occupation of Eastern Europe and the Baltic, following Stalin's pact with Hitler, produced new holocausts.

—WILLIAM HENRY CHAMBERLIN, "The Bookshelf,"
Wall Street Journal, November 8, 1968

SPACE AND STARS

Leave only three wasps alive in the whole of Europe and the air of Europe will still be more crowded with wasps than space is with stars.

—JAMES JEANS

SPACE SHIPS

Some women ... should not be allowed aboard ship; weightlessness did things to their breasts that were too damn distracting. It was bad enough when they were motionless; but when they started to move, and sympathetic vibrations set in, it was more than any warm-blooded male should be asked to take. [The commander] was quite sure that at least one serious space accident had

been caused by acute crew distraction, after the transit of an up-
holstered lady officer through the control cabin.
                    —ARTHUR C. CLARKE, *Rendezvous with Rama*

SPAIN

LOVE

As has often been observed, the Spaniard does not say to a woman
te amo (I love you), but *te quiero* (I want you), which is a possessive verb implying authority over property not to be shared
with anybody and presupposing many more rights than duties. In
love as in other manifestations, the Spaniard personifies what is
objective; the surroundings, the buildings, the whole world only
exist to authenticate his feelings.
                                —FERNANDO DIAZ-PLAJA,
                        The Spaniard and the Seven Deadly Sins

LUST

In Spain lust is in the air. There is nothing clandestine about the
Spanish appreciation of sex, nothing inhibited or restrained. That
is why there are very few sexual crimes in Spain. The man responsible for sexual crimes is usually a puritan who has been
warned since childhood against the most serious sins of the flesh. . . .
                                                        —*Ibid.*

SPAIN EXPELS THE JEWS (1492)

History relates very few measures that produced so vast an amount
of calamity. In three short months, all unconverted Jews were
obliged under pain of death, to abandon the Spanish soil. Multitudes, falling into the hands of the pirates who swarmed around
the coast, were plundered of all they possessed and reduced to
slavery; multitudes died of famine or of plague, or were murdered
or tortured with horrible cruelty by the African savages. About
80,000 [Jews] took refuge in Portugal, relying on the promise of
the king. Spanish priests lashed the Portuguese into fury, and the
king was persuaded to issue an edict which threw even that of
Isabella into the shade. All the adult Jews were banished from
Portugal; but first all their children below the age of fourteen

were taken from them to be educated as Christians. Then, indeed, the cup of bitterness was filled to the brim. The serene fortitude with which the exiled people had borne so many and such grievous calamities gave way, and was replaced by the wildest paroxysms of despair. When at last, childless and broken-hearted, they sought to leave the land, they found that the ships had been purposely detained, and the allotted time having expired, they were reduced to slavery and baptized by force. A great peal of rejoicing filled the Peninsula, and proclaimed that the triumph of the Spanish priests was complete.

—W. E. H. LECKY,
History of Rationalism in Europe, Vol. II

SPRING

Spring has set in with its usual severity.

—HORACE WALPOLE

All things belonging to the earth will never change—the leaf, the blade, the flower, the wind that cries and sleeps and wakes again, the trees whose stiff arms clash and tremble in the dark, and the dust of lovers long since buried in the earth—all things proceeding from the earth to seasons, all things that lapse and change and come again upon the earth—these things will always be the same, for they come up from the earth that never changes, they go back into the earth that lasts forever. Only the earth endures, but it endures forever.

The tarantula, the adder, and the asp will also never change. Pain and death will always be the same. But under the pavements trembling like a pulse, under the buildings trembling like a cry, under the waste of time, under the hoof of the beast above the broken bones of cities, there will be something growing like a flower, something bursting from the earth again, forever deathless, faithful, coming into life again like April.

—THOMAS WOLFE, *You Can't Go Home Again*

JOSEPH STALIN (1879–1953)

Stalin: Genghis Khan with a telephone.

—Author unknown

[He was] of very small stature and ungainly build. His torso was short and narrow, while his legs and arms were too long. His left arm and shoulder seemed rather stiff. He had a quite large paunch, and his hair was sparse, though his scalp was not completely bald. His face was white, with ruddy cheeks. Later I learned that this coloration, so characteristic of those who sit long in offices, was known as the "Kremlin complexion" in high Soviet circles. His teeth were black and irregular, turned inward. Not even his mustache was thick or firm. Still the head was not a bad one; it had something of the folk, the peasantry, the pater familias about it—with those yellow eyes and a mixture of sternness and roguishness.

—MILOVAN DJILAS, *Conversations with Stalin*

The greater the sweep of events the smaller was Stalin's place in it.... There is no basis for accusing Stalin of cowardice, he was simply noncommittal. The cautious schemer preferred to stay on the fence at the crucial moment [1917]. He was waiting to see how the insurrection turned out before committing himself to a position.

—LEON TROTSKY, *Stalin*

Comrade Stalin, having become General Secretary, has concentrated an enormous power in his hands; and I am not sure that he always knows how to use that power with sufficient caution.

—LENIN, in his will, Anatole Shub, *Lenin*

Stalin is too rude, and this fault, entirely supportable in relations among us Communists, becomes insupportable in the office of General Secretary. Therefore, I propose to the comrades to find a way to remove Stalin from that position and appoint to it another man who in all respects differs from Stalin ... namely, more patient, more loyal, more polite, and more attentive to comrades, less capricious, etc.

—LENIN, in Isaac Deutscher,
Stalin: A Political Biography

Stop it, don't make a fool of yourself. Everybody knows that theory is not exactly your field.

—RYAZANOV to Stalin, at a Party meeting, 1923; in
Isaac Deutscher, *op. cit.*

Stalin originated the concept "enemy of the people." This term automatically rendered it unnecessary that the ideological errors of a man or men engaged in a controversy be proven; this term made possible the usage of the most cruel repression . . . against anyone who in any way disagreed with Stalin, against those who were only suspected of hostile intent, against those who had bad reputations.

This concept, "enemy of the people," eliminated the possibility of any kind of ideological fight or the making of one's views known on this or that issue. . . . The only proof of guilt used, against all norms of current legal science, was the "confession" of the accused himself; and, as a subsequent probing proved, "confessions" were acquired through physical pressures against the accused. . . . Many entirely innocent [people], who in the past had defended the Party line, became victims. . . .

It was determined that of the one hundred thirty-nine members and candidates of the Party's Central Committee who were elected at the Seventeenth Congress, ninety-eight persons, i.e., 70 percent, were arrested and shot [mostly in 1937–1938]. [*Indignation in the hall.*] . . .

—NIKITA KHRUSHCHEV, to Congress of All Soviets,
Moscow, February 24–25, 1956

. . . "social-facism." At the time this was the Communist Party line, laid down by Stalin and the Communist International in Moscow, that the Socialists were not the opponents of the Fascists but "their twins," and just as much "an enemy of the working class." . . .

This fateful view was one of the means by which Stalin helped Hitler climb to power, since it made an honest united front of the German working class impossible. The Communists called for "a united front from below" which was a self-defeating appeal to the rank-and-file of the Socialist Parties to abandon their leadership.

—SIDNEY HOOK,
"Memoir," in *Encounter*, January 1976

Stalin's greatness as a dissimulator was an integral part of his greatness as a statesman. So was his gift for simple, plausible, ostensibly innocuous utterance. . . . The modern age has known no greater master of the tactical art. The unassuming, quiet facade, as innocently disarming as the first move of the grand master at chess, was only a part of this brilliant, terrifying tactical mastery.

—GEORGE F. KENNAN, *Memoirs: 1925–1950*

THE STATE

What maintains the cohesion of the state is superstition.... Every multitude is fickle, full of lawless desires, unreasoned passion, and violent anger. [They] must be contained by invisible terrors and pageantry.

—POLYBIUS, *History of Rome*

It is easier to seize wealth than to produce it; and as long as the State makes the seizure of wealth a matter of legalized privilege, so long will the squabble for that privilege go on.
□
As Voltaire saw so clearly, advantage to the State's beneficiaries means disadvantage to those who are not its beneficiaries.
□
The two luxuries which a good statesman must rigorously deny himself during business hours are conscience and sentiment....

—A. J. NOCK, *Memoirs of a Superfluous Man*

The statesman who should attempt to direct private people in what manner they ought to employ their capital would not only ... assume an authority which could safely be trusted not only to no single person, but to no council or senate whatever, and which would nowhere be so dangerous as in the hands of a man who had folly and presumption enough to fancy himself fit to exercise it.

—ADAM SMITH, *Wealth of Nations*, Vol. V

STRATAGEMS

A certain man of pleasure about London received a challenge from a young gentleman of his acquaintance, and they met at the appointed place. Just before the signal for firing was given, the man of pleasure rushed up to his antagonist, embraced him, and vehemently protested that "he could not lift his arm *against his own flesh and blood!*" The young gentleman, though he had never heard any imputation cast upon his mother's character, was so much staggered that (as the ingenious man of pleasure had foreseen) no duel took place.

—Samuel Rogers, *Table Talk*

I have found that nothing so deceives your adversaries as telling them the truth.

—Bismarck

Sir Hierome challenged Sir William to fight. Sir William is extremely shortsighted, and being the challengee it belonged to him to nominate place and weapon. He nominates, for the place, a dark cellar, and the weapon to be a great carpenter's ax.

This turned the knight's challenge into ridicule, and so it came to naught.

—*Aubrey's Brief Lives*

STRIKING A MATCH

When we strike a match, there is a splutter and a flare, which are the atoms of the match and of the atmosphere performing a new sort of dance. Nothing is added to what was already there; no fresh elements or forces arrive on the gay scene. The atoms are the explosion, and the explosion is the atoms. They hurry up, they change step, they exchange partners; that is all.... When something strikes us, there is a splutter and a flare, which are the atoms of our cerebral cells performing, in the crowded ballroom of the brain, a new sort of dance; and that is all. That dance is consciousness, and consciousness is that dance. Consciousness is neither the music which accompanies the dances, nor the reaction which follows the dance: It is the dance, it is the atoms in motion.

—Stephen Paget

STUDENTS AND "RELEVANCE"

What the student cry for relevance turned out to be was the all-too familiar middle-class child's cry to be entertained, to be stimulated, above all, to be *listened to*, no matter what or how complex the subject at hand. Having become accustomed in their homes to get attention to whatever was on their minds, and of course incessant and lavish praise for their "brightness," is it not to be expected that when the children go off to the university the same attention should be given their interests and needs?

—Robert Nisbet, *Encounter*, February 1970

STUDENT UPHEAVALS: 1968–69

The issues involved in that hysteria [on American campuses in 1968 and 1969] were in large measure pseudo-issues. They were the devices of sheepdogs hearding millions of academic sheep throughout the world.

During the five academic years from 1965 to 1970, the campuses were the scene of one of the most amazing phenomena of mass psychology in modern times. . . . It can be compared only with such tragic absurdities as the children's crusades, the Holland tulip craze, and the Salem witchcraft mania. Thanks to modern communications and modern affluence, it swept up unprecedented numbers of people and achieved an unprecedented degree of world-wide simultaneity. What was said one day in New York and Berkeley about the irrelevance of higher education, or a crisis in confidence in the multiversities, or the insensitivity of administrators, was said the next week in Wichita and Laramie and the next month in Christchurch and Dunedin.

That the same things were said on all campuses on given issues, often in the same phrases, was perhaps surprising, since universities pride themselves on nonconformity and boast of thinking independently, but it was not nearly so surprising as that all campuses should talk about the same issue at the same time. Their agenda were set for them, not by them.

—W. Allen Wallis, Chancellor, University of Rochester, speech, January 18, 1971

STUPIDITY

Among men who are enamored of the mysterious, the distance between being a son of god and being a god is small. And so, as time passed, great temples were built to those presumed to have been born from the supernatural mating of a god with a human.

Volumes could be written on this question; but all they really could tell us can be said in a few words. The majority of the human race has always been and will long remain stupid and senseless. Perhaps the most senseless of all have been these people who tried to find some sense behind these absurd fables and tried to fortify folly with reason.

—VOLTAIRE, *Customs of Nations*

STYLE

Above all I seek clarity of expression, the precise and appropriate thought presented calmly and dispassionately. Any exaggeration is harmful: That is why I shun and detest superlatives. Every superlative is a mistake, it distorts the sentence. I also banish from my style the use of florid expressions. Clarity is the only eloquence permissible in politics. It is true that in certain instances this clarity finds better expression in an image and that is why I make frequent use of them. When, on reading through what I have written, I come across an obscure passage I follow the advice of an old hand, Baron Thugut. I do not attempt to replace it by a happier turn of phrase, I simply cut out anything that is not absolutely essential to the line of thought, and more often than not what remains exactly expresses what I am trying to say.

—METTERNICH, in G. de Bertier de Sauvigny, *Metternich and His Times*

Only a mediocre writer is always at his best.

—SOMERSET MAUGHAM, *The Summing Up*

SUICIDE

No man is educated who never dallied with the thought of suicide.

—WILLIAM JAMES

Who has not had friends, relations, who of their own free will have left this world? Are these to be thought of with horror as criminals? Most emphatically, no! I am rather of opinion that the clergy should be challenged to explain what right they have to go into the pulpit, or take up their pens, and stamp as a crime an action which many men whom we hold in affection and honor have committed; and to refuse an honorable burial to those who relinquish this world voluntarily. They have no biblical authority to boast of, as justifying their condemnation of suicide; nay, not even any philosophical arguments that will hold water; and it must be understood that it is arguments we want, and that we will not be put off with mere phrases or words of abuse.

If the criminal law forbids suicide, that is not an argument valid in the Church; and besides, the prohibition is ridiculous; for what penalty can frighten a man who is not afraid of death itself. If the law punishes people for trying to commit suicide, it is punishing the want of skill that makes the attempt a failure.

—ARTHUR SCHOPENHAUER, "On Pessimism," in *Essays*

SUMMER

The mists had fallen from the hills, revealing old woods wrapped in the blue doom of summer.

—RONALD FIRBANK

On the wings of the dragon-fly as he hovers an instant before he darts, there is a prismatic gleam. These wing textures are even more delicate than the minute filaments on a swallow's quill, more delicate than the pollen of a flower. They are formed of matter indeed, but how exquisitely it is resolved into the means and organs of life.

Though not often consciously recognized, perhaps this is the great pleasure of summer, to watch the earth, the dead particles, resolving themselves into the living case of life, to see the seed-leaf push aside the clod and become by degrees the perfumed flower. It is in this marvelous transformation of clods and cold matter into living things that the joy and the hope of summer reside. . . . That we could but take to the soul some of the greatness and the beauty of the summer!

—RICHARD JEFFRIES, *The Pageant of Summer*

SUN YAT-SEN (1866–1925)

What is the standing of our nation in the world? In comparison with other nations we have the greatest population and the oldest culture, of four thousand years' duration. We ought to be advancing in line with the nations of Europe and America. But the Chinese people have only family and clan groups; there is no national spirit. Consequently, in spite of four hundred million people gathered together in one China, we are in fact but a sheet of loose sand. We are the poorest and weakest state in the world, occupying the lowest position in international affairs; the rest of mankind is the carving knife and the serving dish, while we are the fish and the meat. Our position now is extremely perilous; if we do not earnestly promote nationalism and weld together our four hundred millions into a strong nation, we face a tragedy—the loss of our country and the destruction of our race.

—"The Three Principles of the People," lecture, 1924

SUPERSTITION

Men ... enriched by your sweat and misery ... made you superstitious, not that you might fear God but that you might fear them.

□

We must try to trace the way in which the human mind develops when left to its own devices. Suppose that a small community of primitive men see their fruits wither; or some of their huts destroyed by floods, or burned by lightning. Who, they ask, has caused this evil? It can not be one of their fellows, for they have all suffered equally. Therefore it must be some secret power. It has ill-treated them; therefore it must be propitiated. How can this be done? By treating it the same way one treats anyone one wants to please; that is, by giving it little presents. There is a serpent in the neighborhood; it might very well be this serpent; so some milk is left as an offering for it, near the cave in which it takes refuge. From then on it becomes sacred; it is invoked when a war breaks out with the neighboring village; and that village has chosen a different protector of its own.

□

Nature being the same everywhere, men adopted the same truths, and the same errors, above all those phenomena which are most obvious to the senses—and most stimulating to the imagination. They must all have attributed the noise and effects of thunder to the power of a superior being who lives in the sky. People living near the ocean, seeing the great tides flood their shores during a full moon, must have believed that the moon was the cause of everything that happened in the world at the times of its different phases.

In religious ceremonies, men almost all turned toward the east, not realizing that there is really neither an east nor a west, but paying homage to a sun which rose before their eyes.

—VOLTAIRE, *Customs of Nations*

In the mind of the masses superstition is no less deeply rooted than fear....

Men would never be superstitious if they could govern all their circumstances by set rules, or if they were always favored by fortune: but being frequently driven into straits where rules are useless, and often kept fluctuating pitiably between hope and fear by the uncertainty of fortune's greedily-coveted favors, they are, for the most part, very prone to credulity.

—BARUCH SPINOZA, *Tractatus Theologico-Politicus*

A famous physicist had a horseshoe nailed to the wall above the door of his laboratory. A visitor would often ask: "Do you think that horseshoe brings luck to your experiments?"

The scientist always replied, "I do not believe in superstitions—but I am told the horseshoe works even if you don't believe in it."

—a favorite story of NIELS BOHR

SWEDEN

Everything is painfully tidy. And silent. It is the silence of Sweden that really sets it apart from other countries.

Sweden's silence is something more than the absence of sound. It's a kind of tumultuous stillness, deafening in its intensity—as if within it negotiations of some primordial, unspoken sort were implacably proceeding. Trains, buses and streetcars full of speechless people rumble through the avenues of Stockholm like wheeled coffins. There are few street noises, little clatter of trade or cries of children; clean walls cry out for desecration.

Russian friends bear-hug when they get excited; the French kiss. Swedes show emotion with a firm, mute handshake, and when they do speak, the cadence of their language reduces the exchange to the tonelessness of a weather forecast. They are a nation of spectacle wipers. You ask them a question and, figuratively or literally, they pause to wipe their spectacles before they answer. Conversation thus becomes a series of pauses interrupted by words.

□

"The Swedes have their medical expenses taken care of, all of their welfare costs paid for, their rent subsidized, and so much done for them, that if they lose their car keys they promptly commit suicide," Godfrey Cambridge, the U.S. comedian, once remarked.

But even if citizens of ten other countries manage to kill themselves oftener, the Swedes must top everybody when it comes to drinking. The Swedish government liquor commission is the largest single buyer of the products of the French wine industry, and there is a saying in Scandinavia that while the Norwegians live to eat and the Danes eat to live the Swedes eat to drink. I believe it.

—PETER C. NEWMAN,
MacLean's Magazine (Toronto), November 1971

POLICE CARS: SWEDEN

The police are not taught driving, but they are taught how to drive fast with safety over any sort of road surface and in any weather. Their cars are kept in excellent condition and they seldom have to abandon a chase because of engine failure or other breakdowns. The police therefore consider that their drivers are far more experienced in high-speed driving than the majority of criminals. Their method for stopping escaping criminals is based on this assumption and on the fact that, because they also have the psychological advantage which the hunter always has over the hunted, they are much less likely to get excited and to make mistakes which, in high-speed driving, might be fatal.

Instead, therefore, of using shock tactics such as crashing into the criminal's car or trying to puncture his tires with gun fire, the police simply "tail" the escaping car. If he refuses to stop, they make no effort to overtake him or to edge him into the side of the road; they simply keep close behind the criminal where he can see them in his driving mirror and they follow every move he makes. If he slows down, the police slow down, if he accelerates, the police accelerate, aiming always to keep themselves in full view of the criminal. Sooner or later, the criminal loses his head and either stops of his own accord or begins to take greater risks than he should and eventually crashes. All the police then have to do is to step in and pick up the pieces without further risk to themselves or their cars.

—ANTHONY MARTIENSSEN, *Crime and the Police*

TAHITI

It is not upward and inward that Tahiti looks, but outward to the sea. And its seascapes are dazzling in their loveliness. Only the beaches—as on so many Pacific islands—are apt to be disappointing to the visitor; for they are neither numerous nor well cared for, and on most the sand is dark brown or black. But all the rest is a prismatic dream: the gleaming emerald of the shore line; the lighter green of the lagoon, darkening, turning to azure and then sapphire blue as it deepens seaward; the white frieze of breakers on the girdling reef; and beyond the reef, nine miles across the shining water from the northwest coast, the neighbor island of Mooréa thrusting its incredible silhouette of dome and spire—now green, now purple, now black, now sunset red—into the ocean sky.

—JAMES RAMSEY ULLMAN,
Where the Bong Tree Grows

FREE LOVE

One amusement or custom more I must mention, though I must confess I do not expect to be believed, as it is founded upon a custom so inhuman and contrary to the principles of human nature. It is this: that more than one half of the better sort of the inhabitants have entered into a resolution of enjoying free liberty in love, without being troubled or disturbed by its consequences. These mix and cohabit together with the utmost freedom, and the children who are so unfortunate as to be thus begot are smothered at the moment of their birth. Many of these people contract intimacies and live together as man and wife for years, in the course of which the children that are born are destroyed. They are so far from concealing it that they rather look upon it as a branch of freedom upon which they value themselves. They are called *Arreoys*, and have meetings among themselves, where the men amuse themselves with wrestling, etc., and the women in dancing the indecent dance before-mentioned, in the course of which they give full liberty to their desires, but I believe keep up to the appearance of decency.

—JAMES COOK, *A Voyage to the Pacific Ocean*, 1770

CHARLES MAURICE DE TALLEYRAND (1754–1838)

Paternal care had not yet come into fashion; the fashion was indeed the very reverse, when I was a child. Thus, my early years were spent cheerlessly [away from my parents] in an outlying district of Paris.

At the age of four, I accidentally fell from the top of a cupboard and dislocated my foot. The woman to whose care I had been entrusted only told my parents about this several months afterwards. . . . The dislocation was too old to be remedied; and my other foot, having had to bear alone the whole weight of my body, had grown weaker. Thus I remained lame for life.

This accident exerted a great influence on my life. It led my parents to think I was unfit for a military career; . . . they were thus induced to seek some other profession which, in their eyes, would be best calculated to serve the interests of the family. For, in great families, the *family* was much more cared for than its individual members, especially the younger members, who were still unknown. These considerations are painful . . . so I will not dwell on them. . . . On taking leave of my grandmother I shed tears, and so did she, so great was her affection. I had been painfully impressed by having been so hurriedly despatched to college, without having been taken to my father and mother. I was then eight and the eyes of my parents had not yet rested on me. . . .

I felt isolated, helpless, and always shut up in myself: I do not complain, for I believe that my early meditations developed and strengthened my thinking powers. My sad and cheerless child-hood accustomed me to think more deeply than I should have done—had my early life been filled with happiness. . . .

I am, perhaps, the only man of distinguished birth, belonging to a large and esteemed family, who did not, for one week in his life, enjoy the sweetness of being under his father's roof.

All the care and attention paid me only impressed me with the idea that, my lame foot rendering me incapable of serving in the army, I must necessarily enter holy orders, no other career was open to a man of my name. . . .

I spent three years at Saint-Sulpice, and hardly spoke during the whole time. People thought I was supercilious and often reproached me. This seemed to me to point out how little they knew me, so I deigned no reply. They then said my arrogance was beyond all endurance. . . .

The library at Saint-Sulpice had been enriched by gifts from Cardinal de Fleury; its works were numerous and carefully selected. I spent my days reading the great historians, the private lives of statesmen and moralists, and a few poets.

A good library affords true comfort to all the dispositions of the soul. . . . I was self-taught, in lonely silence.

The only good principle is to have none.

—*Memoirs of the Prince de Talleyrand*

ABOUT HIM

Monsieur de Talleyrand had an exceptional brain. I was near enough to him to study him closely and to realize that he was intended for destructive purposes rather than to preserve. Being a priest, he was yet compelled by his temperament to oppose religion: noble by birth, he argued in favor of the abolition of the nobility. Under the Republic he plotted against the Republic. Under the Empire he was constantly plotting against the Emperor: finally under the Bourbons he worked for the overthrow of the legitimate dynasty. *To prevent the accomplishment of anything definite*, that was the greatest talent of that statesman. Napoleon had the same opinion of him and he was right. In the course of a conversation, held after one of M. de Talleyrand's numerous resignations from the Ministry, the Emperor said to me: 'When I want to do something I do not make use of the *prince de Bénévent:* I turn to him when I want to do nothing without appearing to want to.' In private life M. de Talleyrand was a safe and pleasant person with whom to do business. [*Memoires,* I, pp. 70–71]

□

The prince de Talleyrand is at one and the same time the friend of political peace and the enemy of tranquility. He lives on intrigues and on diplomatic complications. His counsels are always dangerous to follow, not because of their impractical aspects, but because even when they are practical they still conceal some moral danger and the possibility of some material surrender of principle. [to Newman, December 11, 1832]

□

[When Talleyrand was asked by Louis XVIII how he had managed to ruin so many governments]: There is something about me, Sire, which brings bad-luck...to governments... which neglect me.

—METTERNICH, in G. de Bertier de Sauvigny,
Metternich and His Times

TARIFFS

Some of these measures, which may have produced short run benefits for a selected group in the past, may now damage the very people they once benefited. Textile workers for example, may have had a rise in wage rates (relative to what they otherwise would have been paid) after the passage of tariff legislation imposing import duties on textiles. However, wage rates earned by textile workers in the United States today are lower than they would be in the absence of tariffs. Our export industries today are high wage industries. To the extent that tariffs limit the dollar earnings of those who could otherwise sell more to the United States, they have limited demand for U.S. exports. This limits the number of jobs at high wage rates in the export industries.

—YALE BROZEN,
address to Mont Pelerin Society, September 9, 1966

498   LEO ROSTEN

TEACHING

I love to teach. I love to teach as a painter loves to paint, as a musician loves to play, as a singer loves to sing, as a strong man rejoices to run a race. Teaching is an art—an art so great and so difficult to master that a man or a woman can spend a long life at it, without realizing much more than his limitations and mistakes and his distances from the ideal.

—WILLIAM LYON PHELPS

To discharge the duties of a professor means to be willing to make ... ideas accessible to anyone, anywhere, at any time. It means to consider scholarship not as a property, but as a devotion, a sacrament....

It means to be willing to pursue an idea wherever it may lead, not departing from its pursuit for any consideration of gain, prestige, or advantage, until one has found out that the line of thought has run out.... It means that if the line of research cannot be compassed within a single lifetime, to be content with doing what one humanly can do, even though it means leaving to others to reap where one has sown.

—NORBERT WIENER,
Boston Sunday Herald, October 30, 1960

THEODORA (508?–548)

[Justinian's] beautiful consort, Theodora, was perhaps of even lower origins (she was the daughter of a bear-tamer at the hippodrome). All agree that she was a powerful personality, and in spite of the rather poor press she received from the prejudiced Procopius, there is no doubt that she had a certain influence over Justinian. In fact the relationship of Theodora and Justinian recalls the association of Pericles and Aspasia. Though Justinian seems to have maintained his own policies in most matters, his determined wife often followed her own desires in such matters as the support of the Monophysite clergy. Perhaps her most decisive act was her intervention in the resolution of the court council that the emperor should flee Constantinople during the Nika rebellion of 532. Had Justinian followed the decision to flee, his reign would have terminated before the consummation of the works for which it is famous.

—SPEROS VRYONIS, JR., *Byzantium and Europe*

THEODOSIUS THE GREAT (c.346–395)

He was a Spaniard, the first of the Spanish Inquisitors, who at the end of the fourth century carried forward the work of Constantine and made Christianity—and a particular form of Christianity—the official religion of the State.... Centuries later, the Spaniards would bash down the pagan idols of Mexico and Peru and demand that all men be made to believe the remarkable doctrine of the Immaculate Conception. Theodosius set fanatical mobs to bash down the pagan temples of the East and required all his subjects to believe the no less remarkable doctrine of the Trinity. But behind this ideological bigotry Theodosius held the Roman Empire together. He reunited East and West and defended both against barbarians and usurpers. He was the last great emperor of the West. . . .

—HUGH TREVOR-ROPER, *The Rise of Christian Europe*

THEOLOGY

Most theology, like most fiction, is essentially autobiography. Aquinas, Calvin, Barth, Tillich, worked out their systems in their own ways and lived them in their lives. And if you press them far enough, even at the most cerebral and forbidding, you find an experience of flesh and blood, a human face smiling or frowning or weeping or covering its eyes before something that happened once . . . maybe no more than a child falling sick, a thunderstorm, a dream, and yet it made . . . a difference which no theology can ever entirely convey or entirely conceal.

—FREDERICH BUECHNER, *The Alphabet of Grace*

ST. THÉRÈSE (THÉRÈSE MARTIN) (1873–1897)

Before she died, she said, "I have never given the good God anything but love, and it will be with love that He will repay me. After my death, I will let fall a shower of roses."

On September 30, 1897, she was dead.

—RANDALL GARRETT, *A Gallery of the Saints*

THE THIRD WORLD

Our appreciation of the difficulties facing the Third World has been impaired by certain misconceptions deriving from our anti-colonial and liberal past... uncritically applied to the Third World. We have come to believe, for example, that much of the misery and degradation so typical of life in the Third World is a result of what we have done or failed to do.

We have frequently accepted at face value, and sometimes even eagerly, the Third World's accusations of callousness and exploitation and tried to atone for our alleged sins with foreign aid. In some cases our aid has improved the lot of the recipients; in most cases it has been a waste of human and national resources; occasionally it has made matters worse. What we have not understood is that the main roots of the Third World's misery and degradation lie within its own politics.

These roots are impervious to foreign aid and can only be remedied by governments able and willing to put the Third World's house in order. More likely than not, these will be foreign governments acting directly or through native surrogates. What the Third World seems headed for is not self-sufficient sovereign governments but a new colonialism, however disguised.
—Hans J. Morgenthau,
The New Leader, April 26, 1976

... the West supports governments whose domestic policies impoverish their own peoples and often inflict extreme hardship both on ethnic minorities and on the indigenous population. President Amin's massive and explicit persecution and expulsion of Asians is only one of many instances. Another is Tanzania (Mr. McNamara's favorite African country, as it has rightly been called) which receives large-scale Western aid while it forcibly herds millions of people into collectivized villages, often destroying their households to make them move. Western aid has conferred respectability on governments like these and helped them conceal temporarily from their own people the economic consequences of their policies.
—P. T. Bauer, "Western Guilt and Third World
Poverty," in *Commentary*, January 1976

THOUGHT PROCESS

Since the word "understand" has several meanings, the definitions that will be best understood by some are not those that will be best suited to others. We have those who seek to create an image, and those who restrict themselves to combining empty forms, perfectly intelligible, but purely intelligible, and deprived by abstraction of all matter.

—HENRI POINCARÉ *Science and Method*

Anyone who has ever attempted pure scientific or philosophic thought, knows how one can hold a problem momentarily in one's mind and apply all one's powers of concentration to piercing through it, and how it will dissolve and escape and you find that what you are surveying is a blank. I believe that Newton could hold a problem in his mind for hours and days and weeks until it surrendered to him its secret.

—JOHN MAYNARD KEYNES, *Essays in Persuasion*

The working of our mind in productive thinking is ... not based on steady application only. It is most probably connected with changes of cathexis which may take the character of sudden, as it were eruptive, processes. The part attributed to chance would then properly be described as rationalization. But this description ... does not take into account one further element: that of the excitement sometimes connected with productive thinking, even if that excitement is less noticeable. ... Such excitement is of a libidinal nature.

—ERNST KRIS, *Psychoanalytic Explorations in Art*

TIBERIUS (42 B.C.–37 A.D.)

At Capri they still point out the scene of his executions, from which he used to order that those who had been condemned after long and exquisite tortures be cast headlong into the sea before his eyes. A band of marines waited below for the bodies and broke their bones with boat hooks and oars, to prevent any breath of life from remaining in them. ...

He would trick men into drinking copious draughts of wine, and then tying up their private parts, would torment them by the torture of the cords and the stoppage of their water. Had not death prevented him, and Thrasyllus induced him to put off some things through hope of a longer life, it is believed that still more would have perished, and that he would not even have spared the rest of his grandsons; for he had his suspicions of Gaius and detested Tiberius as the fruit of adultery. And this is highly probable, for he used at times to call Priam happy, because he had outlived all his kindred.

—Suetonius, *The Lives of the Twelve Caesars*

TIDAL WAVE

On the morning of April 1, 1946, residents of the Hawaiian Islands awoke to an astonishing scene. In the town of Hilo almost every house on the side of the main street facing Hilo Bay was smashed against the buildings on the other side. At the Wailuku River a steel span of the railroad bridge had been torn from its foundations and tossed 300 yards upstream. Heavy masses of coral, up to four feet wide, were strewn on the beaches. Enormous sections of rock, weighing several tons, had been wrenched from the bottom of the sea and thrown onto reefs. Houses were overturned, railroad tracks ripped from their roadbeds, coastal highways buried, beaches washed away. The waters off the islands were dotted with floating houses, debris and people. The catastrophe, stealing upon Hawaii suddenly and totally unexpectedly, cost the islands 159 lives and $25,000,000 in property damage.

Its cause was the phenomenon commonly known as a "tidal wave," though it has nothing to do with the tidal forces of the moon or sun. More than 2,000 miles from the Hawaiian Islands, somewhere in the Aleutians, the sea bottom had shifted. The disturbance had generated waves which moved swiftly but almost imperceptibly across the ocean and piled up with fantastic force on the Hawaiian coast.

Scientists have generally adopted the name "tsunami," from the Japanese, for the misnamed tidal wave. It ranks among the most terrifying phenomena known to man and has been responsible for some of the worst disasters in human history.

—JOSEPH BERNSTEIN,
"Tsunamis," in *Scientific American*, 1954

TIME-WASTERS

... He who cannot persuade himself to withdraw from society, must be content to pay a tribute of his time to a multitude of tyrants; to the loiterer, who makes appointments which he never keeps; to the consulter, who asks advice which he never takes; to the boaster, who blusters only to be praised; to the complainer, who whines only to be pitied; to the projector, whose happiness is to entertain his friends with expectations which all but himself know to be vain; to the economist, who tells of bargains and settlements; to the politician, who predicts the fate of battles and breach of alliances; to the usurer, who compares the different funds; and to the talker, who talks only because he loves to be talking.

—SAMUEL JOHNSON, *The Idler*

TIMUR (1336–1405) (TAMERLAND or TAMBERLAINE*)

Timur definitely wanted to be thought of as closely connected with the Mongols—he was most proud of his title *Gurgan*, son-in-law to the Mongol royal family, which he acquired by marrying a princess descended from Jenghiz Khan, and the genealogy carved on his tomb in Samarkand laboriously traces for him a common ancestor with Jenghiz Khan in one Buzanchar, himself descended from a legendary virgin who was ravished by a moonbeam.

□

When the thousands of prisoners were assembled outside the city, the craftsmen among them were handed over to Timur. He was particularly interested in Delhi's famous stonemasons, who, like the elephants, were destined for Samarkand. It was his invariable policy, after capturing any sophisticated town, to send

* English version of Timur Lenk, meaning "Timur the Lame."

the skilled men back to Samarkand, where they would provide
the art and architecture to embellish his capital city.

☐

Timur, having laid waste Lahore, was already recrossing the
Indus. He had been in the country less than six months and he
left behind him a carnage unprecedented in India's history. Famine
was the inevitable result of the destruction caused by his troops;
plague followed equally certainly from the corpses they left behind them. It was said that in Delhi nothing moved, not even a
bird, for two months.

☐

Timur's departure in 1399 proved, thankfully, the last that Delhi
would see of his family for over a century. When they returned
they came to stay, but the family character had changed. Apart
from the ability to win battles, the only quality they seemed to
inherit from their gruesome ancestor was his liking for learned
men and his passion for beautifying his capital city. Their form
of patronage had less of slavery in it than his; and the desire to
create, subsidiary in his life, became almost paramount in theirs.
Where his ambition was to terrify the world, theirs seemed more
to impress it. He brought Delhi a shattering disaster. They, instead, gave Muslim India her period of greatest splendor.

—BAMBER GASCOIGNE, *The Great Moghuls*

TODAY AND TOMORROW

We are tomorrow's past. Even now we slip away like those pictures painted on the moving dials of antique clocks—a ship, a
cottage, a sun, a moon, a nosegay. The dial turns, the ship rides
up and sinks again, the yellow painted sun has set, and we, that
were the new thing, gather magic as we go.

—MARY WEBB, *Precious Bane*

All passes; nothing lasts: The moment that we put our hand upon
it it melts away like smoke, is gone forever, and the snake is eating
at our heart again; we see then what we are and what our lives
must come to.

—THOMAS WOLFE, *Of Time and the River*

TOLERANCE

The first thing to learn in intercourse with others is noninterference with their own peculiar ways of being happy, provided those ways do not assume to interfere by violence with ours.... The pretension to dogmatize about them in each other is the root of most human injustices and cruelties, and the trait in human character most likely to make the angels weep.

—WILLIAM JAMES, a speech to psychology teachers

The Jew is the emblem of civil and religious toleration. "Love the stranger and the sojourner," Moses commands, "because you have been strangers in the land of Egypt." And this was said in those remote and savage times when the principal ambition of the races and nations consisted in crushing and enslaving one another.

—LEO TOLSTOY

Tolerance always has limits—it cannot tolerate what is itself actively intolerant.

—SIDNEY HOOK,
Pragmatism and the Tragic Sense of Life

The various modes of worship which prevailed in the Roman world were all considered by the people as equally true, by the philosopher as equally false, and by the magistrate as equally useful. And thus toleration produced not only mutual indulgence but even religious concord.

—EDWARD GIBBON,
The Decline and Fall of the Roman Empire

TORTURE: CHINA, 1860

...Much has been made of the vandalism of Lord Elgin for burning down the Imperial Summer Palace outside Peking in 1860, but it is often forgotten that this was a reprisal for the unforgivable murder of envoys from his force who were first sent to the Chinese capital under a white flag. The envoys were bound with thin ropes that were wetted to make them tighten, and thrown down in an open courtyard. If they spoke or cried out in their torment, they were stamped on, and if they begged for food, their mouths were filled with ordure. The cords slowly cut into the flesh, as day followed ghastly day, until gangrene set in; and of the thirty-eight unfortunate men, more than half died and were left to rot among the living.

—DENNIS BLOODWORTH, *The Chinese Looking Glass*

TOTALITARIANISM

Stalin may have been a coarser, crueller, and viler man than Lenin or Trotsky. But it was not this that was decisive. Give absolute power ... to a tightly disciplined clique of professional revolutionaries who claim to possess the final scientific truth about human society, who regard men and women as clay to be moulded to the purposes of history, and who have consciously abandoned ... all absolute and moral standards, and you can get only one result—totalitarianism. Whether the leader's name is Ulyanov [Lenin] or Bronstein [Trotsky] or Djugashvili [Stalin] matters a good deal less.

—HUGH SETON-WATSON, *Encounter*, April 1954

TRADE, ABSENCE OF

Why was it that in Central Europe at this very early date there was this extensive commerce to which archaeological finds testify? How was it that trade was known in the Old World so early when, many centuries later, there was still none in the New? And why did the Spaniards and even the Portuguese fail to notice this peculiarity of America; why did they never complain of it?

—E. SAMHABER, *Merchants Make History*

TRADE UNIONS: ENGLAND

Only the trade union leaders look and sound as men of power should look and sound in an age when privilege is a mark not of divine grace—as it used to be—but of the devil's handiwork. ... Not only, in short, do they have the increased economic power which ... is a factor common to all trade-union movement today in a free society—but also this intangible advantage of embodying the one style of leadership in Britain today which avoids appearing both anachronistic and illegitimate.

—P. WORSTHORNE, *Encounter*, January 1976

TRAGEDY

In a true tragedy, both parties must be right.

—HEGEL

TRANSLATION

Why should I swim the Charles River when there is a bridge?

—RALPH WALDO EMERSON

TRAVEL

With me traveling is frankly a vice. The temptation to indulge in it is one which I find almost as hard to resist as the temptation to read promiscuously, omnivorously, and without purpose. . . .

We read and travel, not that we may broaden and enrich our minds, but that we may pleasantly forget they exist. We love reading and traveling because they are the most delightful of all the many substitutes for thought. Sophisticated and somewhat refined substitutes. That is why they are not every man's diversion. The congenital reader or traveler is one of those most fastidious spirits who cannot find the distractions they require in betting, mah-jong, drink, golf or fox-trots.

There exist a few, a very few, who travel and, for that matter, who read, with purpose and a definite system. This is a morally admirable class. And it is the class to which, in general, the people who achieve something in the world belong.

—ALDOUS HUXLEY, *Along the Road*

Never go anywhere without your wife. If your wife won't go, because the concert or canning season is on, or something of the sort, take your sister or your mother or your cousin. The American woman is indispensable in getting the tickets and reservations, packing and unpacking, mixing Bromo-Seltzers, fending off beautiful ladies who are traveling alone, and making herself useful generally. Hers is also the only sex that can successfully close a wardrobe trunk. If a man closes a wardrobe trunk, there is always a sharp snapping sound, caused by the breaking of something that will not bend, such as the handle of a mirror, or the stem of a Dunhill pipe, or the stopper of a perfume bottle. If a woman is deprived of her Chanel No. 5 during say, a nineteen-day cruise, she will become irritable, and there is nothing more exasperating on a cruise, or anywhere else, than an irritable female companion.

—JAMES THURBER, *Thurber Country*

TREES

A PLACE IN THE SUN

In some exuberant rain forests of the tropics there grows a strange variety of plants known as strangler trees. Such a plant starts by seeding itself and growing like a vine on the trunk or branches of an ordinary forest tree. Climbing over its host, the strangler enfolds it in a thick mass of roots, strangles it to death, and finally stands on its own as an independent tree!

The reason for the origin of the strangler trees (of which there are a number of species) is plain. In the dense tropical forest the competition for sunlight is keen. A young plant sprouting on the dark forest floor has a poor chance of survival unless it can somehow break through the canopy overhead. The stranglers have solved the problem by climbing on other trees. And the whole life history of these outlandish trees seems beautifully contrived to accomplish their objective: to seize a place in the sun in the midst of a dense tropical forest.

—THEODOSIUS DOBZHANSKY and JOAO MURCA-PIRES,
"Strangler Trees," in *Scientific American*, January 1954

IN THE WIND

I am sitting under tall trees, with a great wind boiling like surf about the tops of them, so that their living load of leaves rocks and roars in something that is at once exultation and agony. I feel, in fact, as if I were actually sitting at the bottom of the sea among mere anchors and ropes, while over my head and over the green twilight of water sounded the everlasting rush of waves and the toil and crash of shipwreck of tremendous ships. The wind tugs at the trees as if it might pluck them root and all out of the earth like tufts of grass. Or, to try yet another desperate figure of speech for this unspeakable energy, the trees are straining and tearing and lashing as if they were a tribe of dragons each tied by the tail.

—G. K. Chesterton, *Selected Essays*

LEON TROTSKY (1879–1940)

A dictator lurks in every forceful writer. Power over words leads easily to a longing for power over men. Trotsky could never resist a challenge. He wrote *The Defence of Terrorism* at the height of his labors during the civil war; and he justified the conquest of Georgia against the Social Democrats of western Europe, though he had himself opposed it. Now in 1921 he preached the militarization of labor and permanent dictatorship of the Communist party. Lenin restrained him. But the weapons which Trotsky forged then were soon to be turned against him by Stalin.

□

The man of action in Trotsky was always second to the man of words, even at the greatest moments of decision. He was never happy over a victory until he had written about it; and in later years literary triumph seemed almost to atone with him for the bitterness of defeat. Bernard Shaw said that, as a political pamphleteer, he "surpassed Junius and Burke," what is even more to the point, he is the only Marxist who has possessed literary genius.

□

It was the same on a more gigantic scale in 1917. The Bolsheviks did not carry Trotsky to power; he carried them. Lenin made the party resolve on insurrection, but he was still in hiding when it broke out and at first could not believe in its success. The seizure of power in October was Trotsky's work; and Lenin acknowledged this immediately afterwards, with supreme generosity, when he proposed that Trotsky be put at the head of the new revolutionary government. One may even ask—what did Lenin and the Bolsheviks do during the civil war? They held on clumsily to the reins of civil power in Moscow. It was Trotsky who created the armies; chose the officers; determined the strategy; and inspired the soldiers. Every interference by the

Soviet government was a mistake; and the greatest mistake was
the campaign against Poland, which Trotsky opposed. The achievement was not only one of organization. It was the impact of a
fiery personality, the sparks from which flew round the world.
                        —A. J. P. TAYLOR, *From Napoleon to Lenin*

[At the Congress of the Third International] Lenin . . . was followed by Trotsky, who spoke for seven and a half hours in
Russian, German, and French until it seemed that the entire
revolution was to be drowned in a flood of words.
                                    —ROBERT PAYNE, *Lenin*

HARRY S. TRUMAN (1884–1972)

At 75, Truman was asked by a Missouri boy: "Mr. President,
was you popular when you was a boy?"

"Why, no," Truman answered. "I was never popular. The
popular boys were the ones who were good at games and had
big, tight fists. I was never like that. Without my glasses I was
blind as a bat, and to tell the truth, I was kind of a sissy. If there
was any danger of getting into a fight, I always ran. I guess that's
why I'm here today."

□

Three things can ruin a man—money, power, and women. I never
had any money, I never wanted power, and the only woman in
my life is up at the house right now.

□

I fired [General Douglas] MacArthur because he wouldn't respect the authority of the President. I didn't fire him because
he was a dumb son of a bitch, although he was, but that's not
against the law for generals. If it was, half to three-quarters of
them would be in jail.

□

Being President is like riding a tiger. You have to keep on riding
or be swallowed. The fantastic, crowded month of 1945 [when
he took office] taught me that either a President is constantly
on top of events or—if he hesitates—events soon will be on top
of him. I felt that I could never let up for a moment.

□

A leader is a man who must have the ability to get other people to do what they don't want to do—and like it.

□

Henry Wallace wanted to be a great man, but he didn't know how to go about it.

□

Slanders, lies, character assassination—these things are a threat to every single citizen everywhere in this country. When even one American—who has done nothing wrong—is forced by fear to shut his mind and close his mouth—then all Americans are in peril. It is the job of all of us—of every American who loves his country and his freedom—to rise up and put a stop to this terrible business. [Speech to American Legion, 1951]

□

Nixon is a shifty-eyed goddamn liar, and people knew it. He's one of the few in the history of this country to run for high office talking out of both sides of his mouth at the same time—and lying out of both sides.

□

The biggest power the President has is the power to persuade people.

—compiled from various interviews and newspaper accounts

ABOUT HIM

I have read over and over again that he was an *ordinary* man. . . . I consider him one of the most extraordinary human beings who ever lived.

—DEAN ACHESON, in a television interview, 1973

I don't care how the thing is explained. It defies all common sense to send that roughneck ward politician back to the White House.

—Senator ROBERT TAFT, during the 1948 election campaign

He never put on airs.

—MRS. TRUMAN

I must confess, sir ... I loathed your taking the place of Franklin Roosevelt. I misjudged you badly. Since that time, you, more than any other man, have saved Western civilization.

—WINSTON CHURCHILL
to Truman at Potsdam Conference, July 17, 1945

TRUTH

The dictum that truth always triumphs over persecution is one of those pleasant falsehoods which men repeat after one another till they pass into commonplaces, but which all experience refutes. History teems with instances of truth put down by persecution. If not suppressed forever, it may be thrown back for centuries. ...

No reasonable person can doubt that Christianity might have been extirpated in the Roman Empire. It spread, and became predominant, because the persecutions were only occasional, lasting but a short time, and separated by long intervals of almost undisturbed propagandism.

□

It is a piece of idle sentimentality that truth, merely as truth, has any inherent power ... of prevailing against the dungeon and the stake.

□

The real advantage which truth has consists in this, that when an opinion is true, it may be extinguished once, twice, or many times, but in the course of ages there will generally be found persons to rediscover it, until some one of its reappearances falls on a time when from favorable circumstances it escapes persecution until it has made such head as to withstand all subsequent attempts to suppress it.

—JOHN STUART MILL, *On Liberty*

The least initial deviation from the truth is multiplied later a thousandfold.

□

Plato is dear to me but dearer still is truth.

—ARISTOTLE

Truth is beautiful—without doubt; but so are lies.

—RALPH WALDO EMERSON

No one can disprove the proposition that ten thousand angels can dance on the point of a pin, but that does not make it true.

—J. B. S. Haldane

If man were forced to demonstrate for himself all the truths of which he makes daily use, his task would never end. He would exhaust his strength in preparatory demonstrations without ever advancing beyond them... [so] he is reduced to take on trust a host of facts and opinions which he has not had either the time or the power to verify.

—Alexis de Tocqueville, *Notes*

A lie stands on one leg, truth on two.

—Benjamin Franklin

When you add to the truth, you subtract from it.

—Talmud: *Sanhedrin*

TURKISH AND CHRISTIAN MANNERS

There is a great contradiction in the manners of the Turks; they are at once brutal and charitable; covetous, yet never guilty of theft; their idle manner of living never leads them either to gaming or intemperance; very few of them use their privilege of having a number of wives, and enjoying several slaves; and there is not a great city in Europe where there are less common women. Invincibly attached to their own religion, they hate and despise the Christians, and look upon them as idolaters; and yet they suffer, and even protect them throughout the empire and in their capital; they permit them to make processions in the vast quarter which is set apart for them in Constantinople; and four Janissaries march before the procession through all the streets, to preserve them from insults. The Turks are haughty, they know nothing of nobility; they are brave, but have not adopted the custom of dueling. This is a good quality, which they have in common with all the Asiatics, which arises from their never bearing arms but when they go to war. This likewise was the custom with the Greeks and Romans. ...

The contrary practice was introduced among Christians only in the times of barbarism and chivalry, when it was made a point of duty and honor to walk abroad with spurs at their heels, and to sit at table, or say their prayers, with a sword by their sides. The Christian nobility was distinguished by this custom, which was soon followed, as I have already observed, by the scum of the people, and placed in the rank of those follies which do not appear such because we are conversant with them everyday.

—VOLTAIRE, *Ancient & Modern History*, tr. T. Smollett, T. Francklin, others, 1762

MARK TWAIN (1835–1910)

I was born the 30th of November, 1835, in the almost invisible village of Florida, Monroe County, Missouri. My parents removed to Missouri in the early 1830's; I do not remember just when, for I was not born then and cared nothing for such things. The village contained a hundred people and I increased the population by one percent. It is more than many of the best men in history have done for a town.

☐

My first visit to the school was when I was seven. A strapping girl of fifteen, in the customary sunbonnet and calico dress, asked me if I "used tobacco"—meaning did I chew it. I said no. It roused her scorn. She reported me to the crowd and said: "Here is a boy seven years old who can't chaw tobacco."

By the looks and comments which this produced I realized that I was a degraded object; and I determined to reform. But I only made myself sick; I was not able to learn to chew tobacco, I learned to smoke fairly well but that did not conciliate anybody and I remained a poor thing and characterless.

☐

When I was younger, I could remember anything, whether it had happened or not; but my faculties are decaying now and soon I shall be able to remember only the things that never happened. It is sad to go to pieces like this but we all have to do it.

☐

In my time I have had desires to be a pirate myself. The reader, if he will look deep in his secret heart, will find—but never mind what he will find. I am not writing his autobiography but mine.

☐

Confession may be good for my soul but it's bad for my reputation.

□

Of the various protections against temptation, cowardice is the surest.

—Autobiography

TWEEDLEDUM AND TWEEDLEDEE

The obstinate insisting that tweedledum is *not* tweedledee is the bone and marrow of life. Look at the Jews and the Scots, with their miserable factions and sectarian disputes, their loyalties and patriotisms and exclusions—their annals now become a classic heritage, because men of genius took part and sang in them.

—WILLIAM JAMES, *Principles of Psychology*, Vol. II

TWILIGHT

As he stands musing in the April twilight, he hears that fine, elusive stir and rustle made by the angleworms reaching out from their holes for leaves and grasses; he hears the whistling wings of the woodcock as it goes swiftly by him in the dusk;...he hears at night the roar of the distant waterfall, and the rumble of the train miles across country when the air is "hollow." ... When the mercury is at zero or lower, he notes how the passing trains hiss and simmer as if the rails or wheels were red-hot.

—JOHN BURROUGHS, *Leaf and Tendril*

TYRANTS

The greatest crimes are caused by surfeit, not by want. Men do not become tyrants so as not to suffer cold.

—ARISTOTLE, *Politics*

Tyrants are incorrigible because they are proud, because they love flattery, and will not restore ill-gotten gains. ... They hearken not unto the poor, and neither do they condemn the rich. ... They corrupt voters, and farm out taxes to aggravate the burdens of the people. ... The tyrant is wont to occupy the people with shows and festivals, in order that they may think of their own

pastimes and not of his designs, and, growing unused to the conduct of the commonwealth, may leave the reins of government
in his hands.

—SAVONAROLA,
in John Addington Symonds, *Italian Literature*

UMBRELLAS AND PARASOLS

... nobody seems to have thought of the thing as a protection
against the rain. Early peoples did not bother about the rain. . . .

Civilizations developed in hot climates where . . . "the sun an-
nihilates, shade is a luxury, and rain a blessing." The first sun-
shade was probably the large leaf of some tropical plant, the stalk
of which supplied the handle. But umbrellas, in the sense of something specially made for the purpose, were known in China twelve
centuries before Christ.

They were not merely utilitarian. . . . They were a symbol of
dignity and high office. All over the East they were an attribute
of royalty. Nimrod had an umbrella held over his head when he
commanded his troops in battle. In Siam the royal audience
chamber had no furniture except three umbrellas, while the
monarch of a neighboring kingdom signed himself "King of the
White Elephants and Lord of the Twenty-Four Umbrellas."

□

The Ancient Greeks and Romans had had umbrellas too, for
purely utilitarian purposes, but they were only used by women,
and the idea that there was something effeminate in an umbrella
persisted for many centuries.

□

The umbrella is still with us, but what has happened to the
parasol? From the early 19th century to World War I ladies did
everything they could to preserve the whiteness of their skins. . . .

And then, in the 1920's everything changed. White skins went out of fashion and the object of every young woman was to get herself as "brown all over" as decency allowed.

—JAMES LAVER, "The Umbrella," in *Wheeler's Review* (London), 4th quarter, 1971

THE UNCONSCIOUS: "OUR INNER AFRICA"

The unconscious is really the largest realm in our minds ... our inner Africa, whose unknown boundaries may extend far away. ... The whole great realm of memory, only appears to it illuminated in small areas while the entire remaining world stays invisible in the shadows. May there not be a second half-world of our "mental moon" which never turns toward consciousness?

The most powerful thing in poets ... is precisely the unconscious.... So a great one, like Shakespeare, will enfold and present jewels which he could no more see than he could see his own heart in his body.... If one dares to say anything about the unconscious and unfathomable, one can only seek to determine its existence, not its depths.

—JEAN PAUL RICHTER, *Works*, 1841

Some of my poetry came to me as if it were dictated to me—and without any apparent thought or intention or premeditation on my part.

—WILLIAM BLAKE

The key to the understanding of the character of the conscious life lies in the region of the unconscious.

—C. G. CARUS, *Psyche*, 1846

One must therefore first distinguish an unconscious and a conscious region in the life of the mind, which are nonetheless intimately interconnected in such a manner that what enters conscious presentations only develops itself from the flowing depths of dark feelings and activities and sinks back into them again. This unconscious, but rich and indeed inexhaustible background always accompanies our clearly conscious mental life, which in comparison is relatively meager. But we can learn of the depth of its range, and what hidden treasures it contains, when we turn our attention to these phenomena of dreams, of insight, and so on.

—I. H. FICHTE, *Psychologie*, 1864

Outside consciousness there rolls a vast tide of life which is perhaps more important to us than the little isle of our thoughts which lies within our ken.... Each is necessary to the other.... Between our unconscious and our conscious existence, there is a free and constant, but unobserved traffic forever carried on.

—E. S. DALLAS, *Gay Science*, 1866

... the brain, through unconscious cerebration, produces results which might never have been produced by thought.

—W. B. CARPENTER,
Principles of Mental Physiology, 1874

UNDERDEVELOPED COUNTRIES

While it is difficult to save people from others, it is well nigh impossible to save them from themselves.... No wave of reforms swept the hemisphere below the Rio Grande. And to the Kennedy administration's irritation, the Latins persisted in being themselves. When military *coups d'état*, traditional as fiestas in Latin America, occurred in a number of countries, Washington cracked down on some of the resulting juntas, apparently accepted others, but sounded off about all of them. It was an erratic performance, inspiring neither admiration nor awe. Worst of all, it was ineffectual, a defiance of diplomacy as the art of the possible.

The result of Washington's public feuds with the military and those commanding capital resources in Latin America was to encourage the demagogues. This meant, inevitably ... inflation, and the flight of domestic capital....

In underdeveloped societies the key factor in blocking Communist take-overs is not economic or social but political. That is to say, it is an ability and will to govern. There are few underdeveloped regimes with this capacity.

—JOHN PATON DAVIES, JR., *Foreign and Other Affairs*

UNDER WATER

I continue to go down, slipping over rays of sunlight half strangled by shadow. A silky silence broken by the rhythm of my breathing: a comic gurgling, like pipe bubbles, accompanies my exploration of this endless blue silk.

I roll over on my side for the pleasure of lying on a bed of water. At the same time I bask in my loneliness: The sea surface seems far away. Someone overhead is throwing pearls into the sea. No, I am wrong, these pearls are born of my breath.

—PHILIPPE DIOLÉ, *Undersea Adventure*

UNHAPPINESS

Who is unhappy at having only one mouth? And who is not unhappy at having only one eye? Probably no man ever ventured to mourn at not having three eyes. But anyone is inconsolable at having none.

—BLAISE PASCAL, *Pensées*

Our possibilities of happiness are limited from the start by our very constitution. It is much less difficult to be unhappy. Suffering comes from three quarters: from our own body, which is destined to decay and dissolution, and cannot even dispense with anxiety and pain as danger-signals; from the outer world, which can rage against us with the most powerful and pitiless forces of ·destruction; and finally from our relations with other men. The unhappiness which has this last origin we find perhaps more painful than any other; we tend to regard it more or less as a gratuitous addition, although it cannot be any less an inevitable fate than the suffering that proceeds from other sources.

—SIGMUND FREUD, *Civilization and Its Discontents*

UNIONS

Trade unions have a cause which excuses excess, or at any rate seems to render it understandable and even tolerable. Educated opinion does not approve of the extent to which [trade unions] bully society at large. There is a lot of tut-tutting and even indignation. But it is not wholehearted indignation because however immoral some of the methods used by the trade unions are felt to be, their basic aim—improving the lot of working people—is still felt to be work of almost religious significance. . . .

It is impossible to exaggerate the value to the trade unions of this moral legitimacy which no other major organized group enjoys to anything like the same extent, since moral legitimacy, paradoxically enough, enables the trade unions to get away with immoral behavior—racketeering, corruption, violence, intimidation and things which come close to bloody insurrection.

—PEREGRINE WORSTHORNE, *Encounter*, January 1976

VALENTINES

In pre-Christian times the lottery technique was employed at the feast of Juno Februaria [February 15]. On that day it was thought that the birds chose their mates for the season. By a form of sympathetic magic boys and girls would draw lots for one another. It was a feast welcomed uproariously by the raffish and surreptitiously by the shy.

When Christianity took over from paganism, despite some thunderings against this heathen custom, the date was shifted to February 14, and the honor given to Valentinus, a priest who was condemned by Emperor Claudius II to be beaten, stoned and then beheaded. While awaiting execution he is said to have formed a friendship with the blind daughter of his jailor, to whom he wrote a note on the eve of his death, signed "From your Valentine." The date was February 14, A.D. 270.

Whether true or not, this legend added a further element to the Valentine sentiment: the expression not merely of sexual love, marital or extramarital, but of affection.

—ARTHUR CALDER-MARSHALL in
The Saturday Book #26, ed. John Hadfield

VANITY

There is not in the world such a smoother of wrinkles as is [found] in every man's imagination with regard to the blemishes of his own character.

—ADAM SMITH, *Theory of Moral Sentiments*

VENICE

Attila the Hun is supposed to have said that no grass would ever grow where his horse had passed, and perhaps the Venetians went where no grass grew with this in mind. It was a magical thing to want to plant a city in an immense pool of water, on sand formed by endless river deposits. It was certainly a magical thing to achieve. Sixty churches fell down before they got it right.

... The sandy shelf of what we now call the Lido barred heavy seas from the pool or *laguna*. Yet in that lagoon there were certain deep channels navigable by boats. If you got there first you naturally found out where these were, and memorized them. Invaders, not knowing them, floundered in the sand. And if they did find a deep entrance to the heart of the lagoon where your settlement lay, you simply blocked it. There lay the key to Venice's survival behind natural barriers for well over a thousand years.

—MAURICE ROWDON, *The Silver Age of Venice*

It is the fairest place, I think, in all the world ... lofty palaces faced with white marble from Istria, inlaid with porphyry and serpentine. Within, they have gilt ceilings, ornate chimney pieces, bedsteads of gold, their portals the same, all gloriously furnished. This is the most triumphant city I have ever seen.

—PHILIPPE DE COMMYNES,
(1447?–1511), French Ambassador

The mask became Venice's passport to pleasure. It personified a mysterious quality that she had always had: Something that seemed to whisper from the sea, winding its way round buildings, at your side in the alleys, lying flat and dazzling out in the lagoon, its air seeping through your closed bed-curtains at night. The appearance of the sea at every corner was always her strangest

secret, bringing a reminder of infinity wherever one went, floating one drowsily from place to place, its light changing every
hour. Venice is never simply another human city, simply mortal,
here and now.

—MAURICE ROWDON, *The Silver Age of Venice*

VIENNA (1716)

'Tis the established custom for every lady to have two husbands,
one that bears the name, and another that performs the duties.
And these engagements are so well known that it would be a
downright affront, and publicly resented, if you invited a woman
of quality to dinner without at the same time inviting her two
attendants, . . . lover and husband, between whom she always sits
in state with great gravity. . . . A woman looks out for a lover as
soon as she is married, as part of her equipage.

—LADY MARY WORTLEY MONTAGU, *Letters*, Vol. I, 1716

VIETNAM

Throughout his career, Ho [Chi Minh] showed greater skill in
handling foreigners than in dealing with his own people, with
whom his contacts, thanks to whole decades in exile or the isolation of people's war, were shortlived and at arm's length. It is
often overlooked that the issue he chose for the people's war was
not perpetuation of colonial rule in Vietnam, already renounced
by France in principle, but whether France ought to transfer a
monopoly of power, irreversibly, to the Communist Party. At
every stage in the struggle there were more Vietnamese fighting
against Ho than with him.

The effect of Mao Tse-tung's conquest of South China in 1949
was not simply to make easier the direct arming of Ho's forces
and the great victory of the Chinese artillery at Dien Bien Phu in
1954, but also to make any outcome of the conflict short of the
establishment of communist rule in northern Indochina, on a permanent basis, unacceptable to the communist block.

Ho understood this strategic fact better than his enemies and
planned his peace strategy at Geneva in 1954 to secure, without
arduous conquest, a state from which he could never again be

dislodged and, without prior consultation of their wishes, a huge population to labor for his takeover of the rest of the country. "Unification" meant unification under the Party, and ... the arrangements Ho insisted on for supervision of the elections prescribed in the agreement were calculated to procure that result exclusively—that was why his opponents declined to participate, to the uncomprehending disgust of many Western commentators.

The second Vietnam War was fought wholly on the territory of the South, for, as the People's Government of China warned in 1965, an invasion of the Democratic Republic by ground troops would have been opposed by Chinese "volunteers" as had happened in Korea. And the true reason for the failure of the Americans to deter Hanoi's invasion of Laos, Cambodia, and South Vietnam down the Ho Chi Minh Trail—an invasion disguised and denied at the time, advertised and glorified today—was that they could not discover a scale of bombing which would have achieved this object without inflicting such destruction that the continuation of Communist Party rule would have been jeopardized, at the risk of Chinese military reaction.

It required little propaganda effort from Hanoi to convince the liberal world that communist soldiers were freedom fighters. . . .

The rise of the communist power in Indochina is a tale of exquisitely cynical political craftsmanship, subtler than the ponderous generalship of Mao Tse-tung.

—DENNIS DUNCANSON,
Times Literary Supplement, September 19, 1975

VOLTAIRE (FRANÇOIS MARIE AROUET DE) (1694–1778)

It was my destiny to run from king to king, although I loved liberty even to idolatry. The King of Prussia [Frederick the Great], whom I had frequently given to understand I would never quit Madame du Châtelet for, entrapped me, now that he was rid of his rival. He enjoyed at that time a peace which he had purchased with victory; and his leisure hours were devoted to making verses, or writing the history of his country and campaigns. He was well convinced that in reality his verse and prose were superior to my verse and prose, as to their essence; though as to the form he thought there was a certain something that I might give to his writings; and there was no kind of flattery, no seduction, he did not employ to engage me to come.

Who could resist a monarch, a hero, a poet, a musician, a philosopher, who pretended too to love me, and whom I thought I also loved? I set out once more for Potsdam, in the month of June 1750.

—*Autobiography: A Collection* (London, 1826)

Christianity must be divine, since it has lasted 1700 years despite the fact that it is so full of villainy and nonsense.

☐

I am very fond of truth, but not at all of martyrdom.

—letter to d'Alembert, February 1776

I have never made but one prayer to God, a very short one: "O Lord, make my enemies ridiculous." And God granted it.

—letter to M. Damiliville, May 16, 1767

I advise you to go on living solely to enrage those who are paying your annuities. It is the only pleasure I have left.

—letter to Madame du Deffand

Let us work without disputing; for it is the only way to render life tolerable.

—*Candide*

I have an instinct for loving the truth; but it is only an instinct.

☐

My trade is to say what I think.

☐

I have no scepter, but I have a pen.

☐

I die adoring God, loving my friends, not hating my enemies and detesting superstition.

—compiled from various books, letters, biographies

ABOUT HIM

The most terrible of all intellectual weapons ever wielded by man [was] the mockery of Voltaire.

—TALLEYRAND

Voltaire has sent me from Berlin his *Histoire du siècle de Louis XIV*....Lord Bolingbroke had just taught me how history should be read; Voltaire shows me how it should be written.... It is the history of the human understanding, written by a man of genius for the use of intelligent men....Free from religious, philosophical, political, and national prejudices beyond any historian I have ever met with, he relates all those matters as truly and as impartially as certain regards, which must always be observed, will allow him.

—Lord Chesterfield, letter, April 13, 1752

He was an age. To name Voltaire is to characterize the entire eighteenth century.

—Victor Hugo

Italy had a Renaissance, Germany had a Reformation, but France had Voltaire.

—Will Durant, *The Age of Voltaire*

[On Voltaire's funeral carriage]: He prepared us for freedom.

WAR

War is waged so that peace may prevail...but it is a greater glory to slay war with a word than men with a sword, and to gain peace by means of peace and not by means of war.

—St. Augustine, *The City of God*

In war, where in defense one has to hew, stab, and burn, there is sheer wrath and vengeance, but it does not come from the heart of man but from the judgment and command of God.

—Martin Luther, *Table Talk*

...I am tired and sick of war. Its glory is all moonshine. Only those who have never fired a shot nor heard the shrieks and groans of the wounded cry aloud for blood, more vengeance, more desolation. War is Hell.

—GENERAL WILLIAM TECUMSEH SHERMAN, letter,
in Lloyd Lewis, *Sherman*

The theory that war is a biological necessity, that it is nature's method of controlling population and assuring the survival of the strong and the elimination of the weak, is inaccurate and insupportable. Within the last century, when wars have been common all over the world, the human population of the earth has almost doubled.

—FAIRFIELD OSBORN, *Our Plundered Planet*

Great quarrels, it has been said, often arise from small occasions but never from small causes.

□

Nothing in war ever goes right except by accident.

□

There is only one thing certain about war: It is full of disappointments and full of mistakes.

□

War, which used to be cruel and magnificent, is now cruel and squalid.

□

Success cannot be guaranteed. There are no safe battles.

□

Any clever person can make plans for winning a war if he has no responsibility for carrying them out.

—WINSTON CHURCHILL,
compiled from his speeches and writings

Man lives by habits indeed, but what he lives for is thrills and excitements. The only relief from habit's tediousness is periodical excitement. From time immemorial wars have been, especially for noncombatants, the supremely thrilling excitement.

—WILLIAM JAMES, *Memories and Studies*

A man who has nothing for which he is willing to fight, nothing which he cares about more than his personal safety is a miserable creature who has no chance of being free, unless made and kept so by the exertions of better men than himself.

—JOHN STUART MILL

It was in such circumstances that I realized what months of trench warfare (1917) sitting about waiting to be killed, had not taught me and never could teach me, that war, moving war, can be exciting and even enjoyable—however disgusting in retrospect. I can honestly say that I relished nearly every minute of it; and that when at last I was wounded and had to leave the field, I felt a sense of bitter deprivation.

Doubtless this was partly due to the mere relief from waiting for the unknown: this was something tangible. But partly, I am sure, it was due to something much deeper—the intellectual and emotional appeal of certain kinds of warfare as such. Certainly it enabled me to understand, what I should not have understood before, why war with all its horrors and injustices and its danger to all that civilization stands for, has yet persisted so long.

—LORD ROBBINS, *Autobiography of an Economist*

THE FUTURE

Whether we like it or not, future wars are likely. This brusque way of stating the matter is decidedly unwelcome to many if not most of us. We are so scandalized by slaughter and suffering that it is impossible to look forward to future bloodshed with equanimity. However, our present problem is not primarily to testify to our preferences but to preview the shape of things to come.

□

Mankind is caught in what appears at first sight to be a vicious circle. If we expect war, we may create an atmosphere favorable to a so-called "preventive war." If we do not expect war, we invite aggression. Strictly speaking, however, the expectation of violence implies no vicious circle. It is but one among the many variables affecting war. It contributes to war only when its magnitudes are very low or very high, when people exaggerate the inevitability of war or on the other hand exaggerate the inevitability of peace. Only an attitude that is firm, poised, and disciplined fits the facts or contributes to a just and lasting peace.

—HAROLD D. LASSWELL,
World Politics Faces Economics

HOLY

When ye encounter the unbelievers, strike off their heads until ye have made a great slaughter among them. Verily, if God pleased, He could take vengeance on them without your assistance, but He doth command you to fight His battles.

—The Koran, XLVII

IN LUXURY

On October 13th Mrs. Duberly saw an elegant and fairy-like vessel glide into Balaclava Harbor. It was Lord Cardigan's yacht, the *Dryad*, and it brought out from England not only Lord Cardigan's French cook, but also his great friend, Mr. Hubert de Burgh. . . . That night Cardigan dined in his yacht, and from October 15th, by special permission of Lord Raglan, he dined and slept aboard every night. The distance from the yacht to the Light Cavalry camp was several miles, but Cardigan did not relinquish his command. The Brigade Major came down to the yacht every evening, and a stream of orderlies spurred the wretched, overworked horses up and down the precipitous hill, soon knee-deep in mud, that led from the harbor to the heights. The Army was outraged. What— was Lord Cardigan to escape the hardship and discomfort, the icy winds, the insufficient food, the vermin, the mud? Was he to be allowed to command the Light Brigade from a luxurious yacht with a French cook, and sleep every night in a feather bed? His friends remonstrated with him, but Cardigan brushed them aside. Lord Raglan had given him permission. That was enough.

—Cecil Woodham-Smith, *The Reason Why*

TRIBAL: AFRICA

Many Britons were appalled at the ferocity of tribal war and the heavy losses of life which it entailed. . . .

The killing of women and children and the application of torture were especially repugnant to Britons, yet they were typical practices of African raiding parties. . . .

What this meant in human terms can be given in the words of a European observer who visited the Batoka country after a Matabele raid:

"They had plundered the fields, burnt the villages, mutilated and massacred the men, impaled the women, hung up little children by the feet and roasted them, satisfied their thirst for carnage, and committed nameless atrocities which the pen refuses to describe."

—H. A. C. CAIRNS, quote from F. Coillard,
On the Threshold of Central Africa (1902)

WAR AND THE U.N.

The Washington–Moscow "hot line" does not run through [the Secretary-General's] office. And were the U.N. to disappear from the scene, the world would no more plunge into a big war than it is likely to do with the world organization in existence.

The 1962 confrontation between the United States and the Soviet Union over Cuba confirmed this. Washington and Moscow worked out the clash between themselves. Neither could yield decisions regarding its vital security to any third party, least of all to the world organization. The U.N. was dragged into the affair after the crisis had passed its peak. All that happened as a result of this was its public humiliation by Castro.

—JOHN PATON DAVIES, JR., *Foreign and Other Affairs*

GEORGE WASHINGTON (1732-1799)

That I have foibles, and perhaps many of them, I shall not deny. I should esteem myself as the world also would, vain and empty, were I to arrogate perfection.... But this I know, and it is the highest consolation I am capable of feeling, that no man that was ever employed in a public capacity has endeavoured to discharge the trust reposed in him with greater honesty and more zeal for the country's interest, than I have done.

—GEORGE WASHINGTON to Robert Dinwiddie, 1757

My movements to the chair of Government will be accompanied by feelings not unlike those of a culprit who is going to the place of his execution: so unwilling am I, in the evening of a life nearly consumed in public cares, to quit a peaceful abode for an ocean of difficulties without that competency of political skill, abilities and inclination which is necessary to manage the Helm.

—to Henry Knox, April, 1789

Nothing short of independence, it appears to me, can possibly do. A peace on any other terms, would, if I may be allowed the expression, be a peace of war.

—1788, in John C. Fitzpatrick,
George Washington Himself

I have often thought how much happier I should have been ... if I could have justified the measure to posterity and my own conscience, had I retired to the back country and lived in a wigwam.

—1776

I can only say that there is not a man living, who wishes more sincerely than I do to see the plan adopted for the abolition of it [slavery]; but there is only one proper and effectual mode by which it can be accomplished and this is by legislative authority. . . .

Envious of none, I am determined to be pleased with all; . . . I will move gently down the stream of life, until I sleep with my fathers.

—letter to Lafayette, February 1, 1784

ABOUT HIM

He errs, as other men do, but he errs with integrity.

—Thomas Jefferson, letter to W. B. Giles, 1795

That Washington was not a scholar is certain. That he is too illiterate, unlearned, unread for his station and reputation is equally past dispute.

—John Adams, 1782

Long ago, when he was only a boy, he had copied out a set of rules to help in forming his manners and his character. . . . The last of the rules he still remembered. *Keep alive in your breast that little spark of celestial fire called Conscience.*

—Gilbert Highet, *People, Places and Books*

In the company of two or three intimate friends, he was talkative, and when a little excited was sometimes fluent and even eloquent. . . . The story so often repeated of his never laughing ... is wholly untrue; no man seemed more to enjoy gay conversation, though he took little part in it himself.

—James Madison,
in John Tebbel, *George Washington's America*

As to you, sir, treacherous in private friendship and a hypocrite in public life, the world will be puzzled to decide whether you are an apostate or an imposter, whether you have abandoned good principles, or whether you ever had any.

—THOMAS PAINE, letter to Washington, July 30, 1796

He has a dignity which forbids familiarity, mixed with an easy affability which creates love and reverence.

—ABIGAIL ADAMS

He preserves in battle the character of humanity which makes him so loved by his soldiers in camp.

—MARQUIS DE BARBE-MARBOIS, French staff officer

Washington is the last person you'd ever suspect of ever having been a young man.

—SAMUEL ELIOT MORISON

He ... was born with clothes on, his hair powdered, and made a stately bow on his first appearance in the world.

—NATHANIEL HAWTHORNE

Washington was the only truly "indispensable man." With his towering prestige, unfaltering leadership, and sterling character, he was perhaps the only man in the history of the presidency bigger than the Government itself. . . . He made no major mistakes —something that cannot be said of any of his successors. . . . If we must rank Presidents, Washington, in my judgment, deserves the place at the very top.

—THOMAS A. BAILEY,
historian, in *Presidential Greatness*

He is the purest figure in history.

—GLADSTONE

In Washington, America found a leader who could be induced by no earthly motive to tell a falsehood, or to break an engagement, or to commit any dishonorable act.

—W. E. H. LECKY,
History of England in the Eighteenth Century, Vol. I

His mind was great and powerful, without being of the very first order; his penetration strong, though not so acute as that of a Newton, Bacon, or Locke; and as far as he saw, no judgment was ever sounder. It was slow in operation, being little aided by invention or imagination, but sure in conclusion.

—THOMAS JEFFERSON,
letter to Walter Jones, January 1814

He was a great and good man. In all history few men who possessed unassailable power have used that power so gently and self-effacingly for what their best instincts told them was the welfare of their neighbors and all mankind.

No American is more completely misunderstood. . . . He is generally believed to have been, by birth and training, a rich, conservative, British-oriented Virginia aristocrat. As a matter of fact, he was, for the environment in which he moved, poor during his young manhood. He never set foot in England, or, indeed, any part of Europe. When at seventeen he began making his own living, it was as a surveyor, defining tracts of forest on the fringes of settlement. Soon the wilderness claimed him, first as an envoy seeking out the French in frozen primeval woods and then, for almost five years, as an Indian fighter.

. . . he had less formal education than did Jackson, than Lincoln even. Both Jackson and Lincoln studied law, while Washington's total schooling hardly went beyond what we should consider the elementary grades.

In all his long life, Washington never heard of Sulgrave Manor, the ancient British house far back in his lineage. . . . By the time he was born, the family had lost all memory of their British origin. The first settler, John Washington, was an impoverished adventurer who reached Virginia in 1675. The "Wild West" was then on the Atlantic seacoast, and John might have been a character—not the hero—in a modern Western. He was implicated in the murder of five Indian ambassadors . . .

—JAMES THOMAS FLEXNER,
Washington: Indispensable Man

Washington lived for all nations and for all centuries. . . . History offers few examples of such renown. Great from the outset of his

career, patriotic before his country had become a nation, brilliant and universal despite the passions and political resentments that would gladly have checked his career, his fame is imperishable. . . ."
—TALLEYRAND,
in N. W. Stephenson, *George Washington*, Vol. II

Washington did not turn out to be a brilliant tactician. Yet he inspired confidence, and he persisted stubbornly despite the many setbacks he suffered. His courage, tenacity, honesty, and dignity were in the long run more vital to success than was military genius.
—RICHARD HOFSTADTER, *The American Republic*, Vol. I

THE "WASP": HIS DECLINE

A few years ago the most frequently denounced person in America was the WASP. You probably remember him, the white Anglo-Saxon Protestant who was evil because he symbolized the ruling Establishment, which everyone knew was responsible for all our ills.

Now it turns out that the much put-upon WASP actually seems to be having a tough time in comparison with other religious-ethnic groups. A recent analysis for the National Opinion Research Center places the WASP behind Jews, and Irish-, Italian-, German- and Polish-American Catholics in education, income and occupation. Maybe it's overstating things to describe the WASP as "mired" in sixth place in the Establishment pecking order, but his standing is much less lofty than most of us were led to believe. . . .

Like much of the social protest of the past decade, this crusade was badly misdirected, for as it turns out WASPs are not so much a threat as an endangered species.
—editorial, *Wall Street Journal*, November 5, 1975

WEATHER: WASHINGTON

I have traveled extensively. I have sweated through the Red Sea with a following wind and a sky like burnished steel. I have sweated through steamy tropical forests and across arid burning deserts, but never yet, in any equatorial hell, have I sweated as I sweated in Washington in September 1925. The city felt as though it were dying. There was no breeze, no air, not even much sun. Just a dull haze of breathless discomfort through which the noble buildings could be discerned, gasping, like nude old gentlemen in a steam room. The pavements felt like gray nougat, and the least exertion soaked one to the skin.

—NÖEL COWARD, *First Person Singular*

WELFARE STATE

The most influential groups promoting the ... welfare state are not those who believe in the welfare state because of ideals [about] the improvement of the lot of the poor and the distressed. The promotion of the brotherhood of man by compressing the differences among them into a semblance of economic equality is not what has attracted the most powerful groups supporting intervention. They are a disparate lot, each interested in enhancing its own material status ... at great expense to others. ...

Taxicab owners, in the name of improving the condition of taxicab drivers, persuade city councils to limit entry into the taxicab business. ... Real estate operators, contractors, and building trade unions, in their passion to improve the housing and condition of slum dwellers, eagerly promote governmental appropriations for urban renewal. Railroad, trucking, and barge line interests ... support transportation regulation with indefatigable zeal.

The special interests, from sheep rancher to stockbroker, find the welfare statists to be handy, if unwitting, allies. These allies serve as front men and as a smoke screen to obscure their intent and the damage they do to the general welfare when they use the state to serve their special welfares.

□

Minimum wage laws hurt the poor by costing them jobs; agricultural price-support programs hurt the poor by raising the prices of their food; transportation regulation hurts the poor by preventing industry from moving to disadvantaged regions where the poor live and increases the cost to the poor of migrating to the regions where better paying jobs can be found; union-supporting legislation hurts the poor by permitting union power to grow to the point where it can be and is used to restrict the entrance of the poor into higher paying occupations; urban renewal appropriations hurt the poor by forcing the slum dweller out of low-priced housing into higher priced housing; regulation of the field price of natural gas increases its price and the price paid by the poor for cooking and heating fuel; usury laws make it more difficult and expensive for the poor to obtain loans; subsidizing subway fares benefits property owners in midtown locations rather than the poor who ride the subways. Where is the welfare statist who opposes these measures and calls for their abolition?

—Yale Brozen,
address to Mont Pelerin Society, September 9, 1966

It's not that big government *per se* is undesirable, just as bigness in any organization is not undesirable *per se*. Big Government becomes Bad Government because of what it does to our economy and what it does to our personal freedoms. To an extent far greater than it is commonly realized, the practices and policies of American government are at the root of many of the difficulties we are experiencing today.... In 1963 the federal government sponsored 160 different grant programs. Then along came the Great Society, and today we have more than 900 different grant programs, a hodgepodge so immense that the government has been compelled to print a catalog of programs to keep track— and the catalog is thicker than the Manhattan telephone directory.

—William E. Simon,
Saturday Review, July 12, 1975

There are, after all, two natural equilibriums for the welfare state: one in which the majority benefits at the expense of the minority, and the other in which the minority benefits at the expense of the majority. Once the welfare state reaches a certain relative size, the first is ruled out by the facts of life, and the second by the nature of democracy. That leaves only the borderline situation in which half try to gain from the other half. That circumstance... so weakens government as to imperil democracy itself.

—Warren Nutter,
Wall Street Journal, January 10, 1975

THE WESTERN MOVIE

To make fun of the Western is also to draw attention to its greatness. This naive greatness is recognized in Westerns by simple
men in every clime—despite differences of language, landscape,
custom, and dress. The epic and tragic hero is a universal character. The Civil War is part of nineteenth century history, the Western has turned it into the Trojan War of the most modern epics.
The migration to the West is our Odyssey.

—ANDRÉ BAZIN, French critic

WESTERN TOWNS

Contrary to the sanitized view that Hollywood gives us, Western
towns were actually quite dirty, and so were the cowpokes who
frequented them. The horses—everybody had at least one—
created steamy cesspools around the hitching posts, where flies
plagued man and beast and a vile odor abounded. . . .

Leadville, Colorado, reported a morass on its Main Street 18
inches deep in which the wooden sidewalks formed a "sort of
raft," an ideal nest for rats. This mess seeped into pools to be
pumped up as drinking water so putrid "it made liquor drinking a
virtue."

—OTTO L. BETTMAN, *The Good Old Days*

WHISTLER'S MOTHER

As music is the poetry of sound, so is painting the poetry of sight.
The subject-matter has nothing to do with harmony of sound or
of color.

Art should be independent of all clap-trap—it should stand
alone, and appeal to the artistic sense of eye or ear, without con-
founding this with emotions entirely foreign to it, such as devotion,
pity, love, patriotism. . . . All these have no kind of concern with
it; that is why I insist on calling my works "arrangements" and
"harmonies."

Take the picture of my mother, exhibited at the Royal Academy
as an *Arrangement in Grey and Black*. Now that is what it is. To

me it is interesting as a picture of my mother; but what can or ought the public to care about the identity?

—James McNeill Whistler

WHITE MAN'S MAGIC

Awe was also fostered by deliberately playing on African ignorance with respect to much of the gadgetry of western civilization such as mirrors, watches, and umbrellas. The fright of an African who attempted to catch the second hand of a watch was unmistakable—his limbs actually trembled, according to Duff Macdonald. It was this type of fear which led Samuel Baker to assert that "savages" could be ruled by either "force" or "humbug." Although not averse to force, humbug played a prominent part in Baker's African experiences. His supplies for the post of governor of Equatoria included musical boxes, a magic lantern, a magnetic battery, wheels of life, fireworks, and silver balls that mirrored surrounding scenes. The magnetic battery was put to good use, and *Ismailia* is replete with accounts of chiefs and elders reeling over backwards after experiencing the wonders of the white man's civilization. . . .

Versions of this gimmick approach became almost standard in the repertoire of many travelers. There was the pipe bowl which could be filled with gunpowder and ceremoniously handed to a hostile chief who, after the inevitable explosion, looked upon the white "as something almost superhuman," and respected accordingly—the giving of sniffs of concentrated ammonia to chiefs and councilors which evoked the satisfying retort, "Oh, these white men know everything, the Arabs are dirt compared to them!"—and the firing of rockets at night to shed an aura of magic protection over the camp of the traveler.

—H. A. R. Cairns, *Prelude to Imperialism*

OSCAR WILDE (1856–1900)

The gods had given me almost everything. But I let myself be lured into long spells of senseless and sensual ease. I amused myself with being a *flâneur*, a dandy, a man of fashion. I surrounded myself with the smaller natures and the meaner minds. I became the spendthrift of my own genius, and to waste an eternal youth gave me a curious joy. Tired of being on the heights, I deliberately went to the depths in search for new sensation. What the paradox was to me in the sphere of thought, perversity became to me in the sphere of passion. Desire, at the end, was a malady, or a madness, or both. I grew careless of the lives of others. I took pleasure where it pleased me, and passed on. I forgot that every little action of the common day makes or unmakes character, and that therefore what one has done in the secret chamber one has some day to cry aloud on the housetop. I ceased to be lord over myself. I was no longer the captain of my soul, and did not know it. I allowed pleasure to dominate me. I ended in horrible disgrace. There is only one thing for me now, absolute humility.

I have lain in prison for nearly two years. Out of my nature has come wild despair; an abandonment to grief that was piteous even to look at; terrible and impotent rage; bitterness and scorn; anguish that wept aloud; misery that could find no voice; sorrow that was dumb. I have passed through every possible mood of suffering. Better than Wordsworth himself I know what Wordsworth meant when he said:

> Suffering is permanent, obscure, and dark,
> And has the nature of infinity.

□

Reason does not help me. It tells me that the laws under which I am convicted are wrong and unjust laws, and the system under which I have suffered a wrong and unjust system. But, somehow, I have got to make both of these things just and right to me. ... I have got to make everything that has happened to me good for me. The plank bed, the loathsome food, the hard ropes shredded into oakum till one's finger tips grow dull with pain, the menial offices with which each day begins and finishes, the harsh orders that routine seems to necessitate, the dreadful dress that makes sorrow grotesque to look at, the silence, the solitude, the shame—each and all of these things I have to transform into a spiritual experience. There is not a single degradation of the body which I must not try and make into a spiritualizing of the soul.

□

Society, as we have constituted it, will have no place for me, has none to offer; but Nature, whose sweet rains fall on unjust and just alike, will have clefts in the rocks where I may hide, and secret valleys in whose silence I may weep undisturbed. She will hang the night with stars so that I may walk abroad in the darkness without stumbling, and send the wind over my footprints so that none may track me to my hurt: She will cleanse me in great waters, and with bitter herbs make me whole.

—De Profundis

THE WIND

Everyday since the earth was, the wind has sighed and sung around it, gathering up the laughter and tears of all creatures and taking them into its ageless liberty. More mysterious than the invisible wind is the wind that is simply felt, blowing where there are no trees in which to watch it, pressing upon one with tireless, invincible force. There are few things that bring such awe and delight; for it is stronger than a thousand strong horses, shadowless and secret as a god.

*—*MARY WEBB, *The Spring of Joy*

WISDOM

The height of wisdom is to take things as they are . . . to endure what we cannot evade.

*—*MONTAIGNE, *Essays*

The wise man does not expose himself needlessly to danger, since there are few things for which he cares sufficiently; but he is willing, in great crises, to give even his life—knowing that under certain conditions it is not worthwhile to live.

*—*ARISTOTLE

What is all wisdom save a collection of platitudes? Take fifty of our current proverbial sayings—they are so trite, so threadbare, that we can hardly bring our lips to utter them. Nonetheless they embody the concentrated experience of the race, and the man who orders his life according to their teaching cannot go far wrong. How easy that seems! Has anyone ever done so? Never.

*—*NORMAN DOUGLAS, *South Wind*

Wisdom comes by disillusionment.

—George Santayana

In our sleep, pain which cannot forget falls drop by drop upon the heart until, in our own despair, against our will, comes wisdom through the awful grace of God.

—Robert F. Kennedy

How I wish that somewhere there existed an island for those who are wise and of goodwill.

—Albert Einstein

WITS

Broadly speaking ... the wit of Swift was that of hate, of Johnson argument, of Sheridan ridicule, of Smith gaiety, of Disraeli epigram, of Labouchere detachment, of Whistler malice, of Gilbert absurdity ... of Wilde frivolity, of Shaw criticism, of Belloc pugnacity, of Beerbohm urbanity, of Chesterton analogy.

□

Wits have one thing in common with bores: they recognize at sight and avoid one another, fearing competition. The wit, like the bore, must have an audience, and dislikes being kept on his toes by too-keen rivalry. A little emulation is helpful, a contest of equals to be deplored.

—Hesketh Pearson, *Lives of the Wits*

MAJOR-GENERAL JAMES WOLFE (1727–1759)

For full two hours the procession of boats, borne on the current, steered silently down the St. Lawrence. The stars were visible, but the night was moonless and sufficiently dark. The general was in one of the foremost boats, and near him was a young midshipman, John Robison, afterwards professor of natural philosophy in the University of Edinburgh. He used to tell in his later life how Wolfe, with a low voice, repeated Gray's "Elegy in a Country Churchyard" to the officers about him. Among the rest was the verse which his own fate was soon to illustrate:

The paths of glory lead but to the grave.

"Gentlemen," he said, as his recital ended, "I would rather have written those lines than take Quebec."

—FRANCIS PARKMAN, *Montcalm and Wolfe*

WOMEN

When they are intelligent, I prefer their conversation to that of men: One finds in it a certain gentleness that is lacking in us; and besides that, they express themselves with more clarity and give a more pleasant turn to their speech.

—ROCHEFOUCAULD

One rarely finds idealists among women, for they feel instinctively the central, unconscious motive of the idealist is a hatred of his fellow creatures. It is a curious thing that when most women hate they hate individuals and not people in mass. On the other hand, men frequently acquire a sort of abstract, mass hatred.

—W. E. WOODWARD,
The Gift of Life: An Autobiography

The church had two opposite attitudes: on the one hand, woman was the Temptress, who led monks and others into sin; on the other hand, she was capable of saintliness to an almost greater degree than man. Theologically, the two types were represented by Eve and the Virgin.

—BERTRAND RUSSELL, *Unpopular Essays*

Julie received me with that affection which only a sister can show. I felt safe and protected when I was enfolded in her arms, her ribbons, her lace and her bouquet of roses. Nothing can take the place of a woman's loyalty, delicacy and devotion; a man is forgotten by his brothers and friends and misjudged by his companions, but never by his mother, his sister or his wife. When Harold was killed in the battle of Hastings, his men could not recognize him among all the dead; they had to seek the help of a girl he loved.

—CHATEAUBRIAND, *Memoirs*

In situations where they would feel exposed to shame or embarrassment, women will lie much more readily than men. The male is more truthful about facts and less so about emotions. He will not

hesitate to lie about his feelings. He will swear that he loves a girl
when he only desires her.

—Theodor Reik, *Of Love and Lust*

WOMEN'S LIBERATION (1848)

We are assembled to protest against a form of government existing without the consent of the governed—to declare our right to
be free as man is free, to be represented in the government which
we are taxed to support, to have such disgraceful laws as give
man the power to chastise and imprison his wife, to take the wages
which she earns, the property which she inherits, and, in case of
separation, the children of her love; laws which make her the
mere dependent on his bounty. It is to protest against such unjust
laws as these that we are assembled today, and to have them, if
possible, forever erased from our statute books, deeming them a
shame and a disgrace to a Christian republic in the nineteenth
century.

—Elizabeth Cady Stanton,
speech in New York, July 19, 1848

WORDS

The difference between the right word and the almost right word
is the difference between lightning and the lightning bug.

—Mark Twain

In my girlhood days I loved to play with language. I love "the
fairy way of writing." Wise words and wanton would fable for
my fancy, and many a sage and merry word was caught and imprisoned within these pages. Some words I chose for their sound
and some for their looks; some seemed to have a color and others
appeared so real that it was as if they could be touched, and I loved
the feeling. To all I have given something of myself. It matters
not who used them first or what strange country they came from,
they are now mine, mine as I am my own.

—*The Book Without a Name: Being the Journal of an
Unmarried English Lady to Her Natural Son*

The word *Papa* gives a pretty form to the lips. *Papa, potatoes,
poultry, prunes* and *prism* are all very good words for the lips.

—Charles Dickens

We want words to do more than they can.... We expect them to help us to grip and dissect that which in ultimate essence is as un-grippable as shadow.... What we should read is not the words but the man whom we feel to be behind the words.

—SAMUEL BUTLER, *The Notebooks*

He who wants to persuade should put his trust not in the right argument, but in the right word. The power of sound has always been greater than the power of sense.

—JOSEPH CONRAD, *A Personal Record*

... The things one loves, lives and dies for are not, in the last analysis, completely expressible in words. To write or to speak is almost inevitably to lie a little. It is an attempt to clothe an intangible form; to compress an immeasurable into a mold. And in the act of compression, how Truth is mangled and torn!

—ANNE MORROW LINDBERGH, *The Wave of the Future*

WORDS AND HORROR

[The horror] had power to drive me out of my conception of existence, out of that shelter each of us makes for himself to creep under in moments of danger, as a tortoise withdraws within its shell. For a moment I had a view of a world that seemed to wear a vast and dismal aspect of disorder ... but still—it was only a moment: I went back into my shell directly ... I seemed to have lost all my words in the chaos of dark thoughts I had contemplated for a second or two beyond the pale. These came back, too, very soon, for words also belong to the sheltering conception of light and order which is our refuge.

—JOSEPH CONRAD, *Lord Jim*

WORK

More men die of worry than of work, because more men worry than work.

—ROBERT FROST

Employment is nature's physician, and is essential to human happiness.

—GALEN

You can't eat for eight hours a day nor drink for eight hours a day nor make love for eight hours—all you can do for eight hours is work.

—WILLIAM FAULKNER

I am a great believer in luck, and I find the harder I work the more I have of it.

—STEPHEN LEACOCK

WORSHIP

... This craving for *community* of worship is the chief misery of every man ... and of all humanity from the beginning of time. For the sake of common worship they've slain each other with the sword. They have set up gods and challenged one another. "Put away your gods and come and worship ours or we will kill you and your gods!" And so it will be to the end of the world even when gods disappear from the earth; they will fall down before idols just the same.

—FEODOR DOSTOEVSKY, *The Brothers Karamazov*

WRITERS AND WRITING

... if the invention of the ship was thought so noble, which carrieth riches and commodities from place to place ... how much more are letters to be magnified, which, as ships, pass through the vast sea of time, and make ages so distant to participate of the wisdom, illuminations, and inventions the one of the other?

—FRANCIS BACON, *Advancement of Learning*, Book I

A transition from an author's book to his conversation is too often like an entrance into a large city after a distant prospect. Remotely, we see nothing but spires of temples and turrets of palaces, and imagine it the residence of splendor, grandeur, and magnificence; but when we have passed the gates, we find it perplexed with narrow passages, disgraced with despicable cottages, embarrassed with obstructions, and clouded with smoke.

—SAMUEL JOHNSON, *The Rambler*

... Other men are known to posterity only though the medium of history, which [grows] faint and obscure; but the intercourse between the author and his fellowmen is ever new, active, and immediate.... Well may posterity be grateful to his memory; for he has left it an inheritance not of empty names and sounding actions, but whole treasures of wisdom, bright gems of thought, and golden veins of language.

—WASHINGTON IRVING, *The Sketch Book*

What things there are to write, if one could only write them! My mind is full of gleaming thoughts; gay moods and mysterious, moth-like meditations hover in my imagination fanning their painted wings. They would make my fortune if I could catch them; but always the rarest, those freaked with azure and the deepest crimson, flutter away beyond my reach.

—LOGAN PEARSALL SMITH, "Things to Write," in *Trivia*

Long before it was a Play; when it only was a confused mass of thoughts, trembling over one another in the dark; when the fancy was yet in its first work, moving the sleeping images of things towards the light, these to be distinguished, and then either chosen or rejected by the judgment.

—JOHN DRYDEN

... it is with the common run of men that we writers have to deal; kings, dictators, commercial magnates are from our point of view very unsatisfactory. The ordinary is the writer's richer field. Its unexpectedness, its singularity, its infinite variety afford unending material. The great man is too often all of a piece; it is the little man that is a bundle of contradictory elements. He is inexhaustible.

—SOMERSET MAUGHAM, *The Summing Up*

Writing a book was an adventure. To begin with it was a toy, an amusement; then it became a mistress, and then a master, and then a tyrant.

—WINSTON CHURCHILL, November 2, 1949

YOUTH

Turbulent gangs of untidy boys and girls roamed [Germany, 1910–1914].... In bombastic words they announced the gospel of a golden age. All preceding generations, they emphasized, were simply idiotic; their incapacity has converted the earth into a hell. But the rising generation is no longer willing to endure gerontocracy, the supremacy of impotent and imbecile senility. Henceforth brilliant youths will rule. They will destroy everything that is old and useless, they will reject all that was dear to their parents, they will substitute new, real and substantial values ... for the antiquated and false ones....

The inflated verbiage of these adolescents was only a poor disguise for their lack of any ideas and of any definite program. They had nothing to say but this: We are young and therefore chosen; we are ingenious because we are young; we are the carriers of the future; we are the deadly foes of the rotten bourgeois and Philistines. And if somebody was not afraid to ask them what their plans were, they knew only one answer: Our leaders will solve all problems.

The chiefs of this youth movement were mentally unbalanced neurotics. Many of them were affected by a morbid sexuality; they were either profligate or homosexual.... Their names are long since forgotten; the only trace they left were some books and poems preaching sexual perversity....

—LUDWIG VON MISES, *Bureaucracy*

[Youth] have exalted notions, because they have not yet been humbled by life or learnt its necessary limitations.... They would always rather do noble deeds than useful ones: their lives are governed more by feeling than by reasoning.... All their mistakes are in the direction of doing things excessively and vehemently.... They love too much, they hate too much; they think they know everything; that is why they overdo everything.

—Aristotle, *Politics*

It is the mistake of youth to think imagination a substitute for experience; it is the mistake of age to think experience a substitute for intelligence.

—Lyman Bryson

Z

ZADIG

He [Zadig] was as wise as it is possible for man to be; for he sought to live with the wise. Instructed in the sciences of the ancient Chaldeans, he understood the principles of natural philosophy, such as they were then supposed to be; and knew as much of metaphysics as hath ever been known in any age, that is, little or nothing at all. He was firmly persuaded, notwithstanding the new philosophy of the times, that the year consisted of three hundred and sixty-five days and six hours, and that the sun was in the center of the world. But when the principal magi told him, with a haughty and contemptuous air, that his sentiments were of a dangerous tendency, and that it was to be an enemy to the state to believe that the sun revolved round its own axis, and that the year had twelve months, he held his tongue with great modesty and meekness.

—Voltaire, *Zadig: An Oriental History*, tr. T. Smollett, T. Francklin, others, 1762

When the moon shall have faded out from the sky, and the sun shall shine at noonday a dull cherry red, and the seas shall be frozen over, and the icecap shall have crept downward to the equator from either pole ... when all the cities shall have long been dead and crumbled into dust, and all life shall be on the last verge of extinction on this globe; then, on a bit of lichen, growing on the bald rocks beside the eternal snows of Panama, shall be seated a tiny insect, preening its antennae in the glow of the worn-out sun, the sole survivor of animal life on this our earth—a melancholy bug.

—W. J. HOLLAND, *The Math Book*

(*continued from page iv*)

The Origins of Psychoanalysis: Letters to Wilhelm Fliess, Drafts and Notes: 1887–1902, by Sigmund Freud, edited by Marie Bonaparte, Anna Freud, and Ernst Kris; authorized translation by Eric Mosbacker and James Strachey; introduction by Ernst Kris. Copyright 1954 by Basic Books, Inc., Publishers, New York.

Punishing Criminals: Concerning a Very Old and Painful Question by Ernest van den Haag. Copyright © 1975 by Basic Books, Inc., Publishers, New York. *Rationalism in Politics and Other Essays* by Michael Oakeshott. Copyright © 1962 by Michael Oakeshott.

B. T. Batsford, Ltd., for excerpts from *Our Experience of Language* by Walter Nash.

The Bobbs-Merrill Co. Inc., and Constable and Company, Ltd., for excerpts from *Melbourne* by David Cecil. Copyright © 1939, 1954, 1966 by David Cecil.

Curtis Brown, Ltd., and Houghton Mifflin Company for excerpts from *The Age of Enlightenment* by Isaiah Berlin. Copyright © 1956 by Isaiah Berlin.

Curtis Brown, Ltd., on behalf of Anthony Martienssen for Excerpts from *Crime and the Police* by Anthony Martienssen.

Yale Brozen for excerpts from an address to Mont Pelerin Society, September 9, 1966, by Yale Brozen, Graduate School of Business, University of Chicago.

Cambridge University Press for excerpts from:
Leonardo Da Vinci by Kenneth Clark.
The Cambridge Modern History, vol. 1, selection by Richard Garnett.

Bradford Cannon, executor of the estate of Walter B. Cannon, for excerpts from *The Way of an Investigator* by Walter B. Cannon.

Mrs. Gordon Mathias and Chatto & Windus, Ltd., for excerpt from *The Worst Journey in the World* by Apsley Cherry-Garrard.

William Collins Sons & Co., Ltd., and Sir Arthur Bryant for excerpts from:
Nelson by Sir Arthur Bryant. Copyright © 1970 by Sir Arthur Bryant.
Queen Elizabeth I by Milton Waldman.

Commentary, Bernard Lewis, and P. T. Bauer for articles appearing in *Commentary*. Copyright © 1976 by the American Jewish Committee.

Coward, McCann & Geoghegan, Inc., for excerpts from *Eminent Victorians* by Lytton Strachey. Copyright © 1972 by Alex Strachey and George Weidenfeld & Nicolson, Ltd.

Thomas Y. Crowell Company, Inc., for excerpts from *One Passion, Two Loves* by Lynn Poole. Copyright © 1966 by Lynn and Gray Poole.

Crown Publishers, Inc., for excerpts from *Design of the Universe* by Fritz Kahn. Copyright 1954 by Fritz Kahn.

dall'Oglio, editore for excerpt from *The Borgias* by Clemente Fusero.

Darton, Longman and Todd, Ltd., for excerpts from *Metternich and His Times* by G. de Bertier de Sauvigny. English translation published and © 1962 by Darton, Longman and Todd, Ltd.

John Day Co. for excerpt from *The Importance of Living* by Lin Yutang. Copyright 1937 by John Day Co., renewed 1965 by Lin Yutang.

Andre Deutsch, Ltd., for excerpts from *Ian Fleming Introduces Jamaica* by Morris Cargill, 1966.

Doubleday & Co., Inc., for excerpts from:
Glory Road by Bruce Catton. Copyright 1952 by Bruce Catton.
The Hidden Dimension by Edward T. Hall. Copyright © 1966 by Edward T. Hall.
Great Cities of the Ancient World by L. Sprague de Camp. Copyright © 1972 by L. Sprague de Camp.
The People's Almanac by David Wallechinsky and Irving Wallace. Copyright © 1975 by David Wallace and Irving Wallace.
Comedy by Wylie Sypher, which contains "Laughter" by Henri Bergson. Copyright © 1956 by Wylie Sypher.

Doubleday & Co., Inc., and Sir Arthur Bryant for excerpts from *The Age of Chivalry: The Atlantic Saga* by Sir Arthur Bryant. Copyright © 1963 by Arthur Bryant.

Gerald Duckworth Co., Ltd., for excerpts from *Queen Elizabeth* by Charles Williams.

Dover Publications, Inc., for excerpts from *Isaac Newton* by Louis Trenchard More, 1962.

E. P. Dutton for excerpts from:
A History of England from the Accession of James II by Thomas Babington Macaulay. An Everyman's Library Edition.
Confessions by Jean Jacques Rousseau. An Everyman's Library Edition.

Dennis J. Duncanson for excerpts from an article that appeared in the *Times Literary Supplement*, September 19, 1975. Copyright © 1975 by Dennis J. Duncanson.

The Estate of Albert Einstein for excerpts from *Out of My Later Years* by Albert Einstein. Copyright 1950 the Philosophical Library, courtesy the Estate of Albert Einstein.

Encounter, Ltd., for excerpts © 1954, 1957, 1958, 1970, 1974, 1975, 1976 from articles by the following authors:
Frank Gibney, Sidney Hook, Melvin Lasky, Kenneth Minogue, Robert Nisbet, Hugh Seton-Watson, H. R. Trevor-Roper, George Watson, Peregrine Worsthorne.

Elsevier Scientific Publishing Company for excerpts from William Faulkner, Nobel Prize Acceptance Speech, December 14, 1950.

Erik H. Erikson for excerpts from *Psychoanalysis and Social Science* edited by H. M. Ruitenbeck, published by E. P. Dutton. Copyright © 1962 by Erik H. Erikson.

Esquire magazine for excerpt by Malcolm Muggeridge in *Esquire*, October 1975. Copyright © 1975 by Esquire Magazine, Inc.

Farrar, Straus & Giroux, Inc., for excerpts from:
The Discovery and Conquest of Mexico by Bernal Diaz del Castillo, translated by A. P. Maudslay. Copyright © 1956 by Farrar, Straus & Cudahy, Inc. (now Farrar, Straus & Giroux, Inc.).
The Selected Writings of John Jay Chapman edited and with an introduction by Jacques Barzun. Copyright © 1957 by Farrar, Straus & Cudahy, Inc. (now Farrar, Straus & Giroux, Inc.). Introduction copyright © 1957 by Jacques Barzun.

Farrar, Straus & Giroux, Inc., and Martin Secker & Warburg, Ltd., for excerpts from *The Chinese Looking Glass* by Dennis Bloodworth. Copyright © 1966, 1967 by Dennis Bloodworth.

W. H. Freedman & Company, Publishers, for excerpts from an article in *Scientific American*, "Strangler Trees" by Theodosius Dobzhansky and Joao Murca-Pires, January 1954.

Funk & Wagnalls, Inc., a division of Harper & Row, Publishers, Inc., for excerpts from *The English Spirit: Essays in Literature and History* by A. L. Rowse. Published by Macmillan, Ltd., 1944. Revised edition published by Funk & Wagnalls, Inc., 1967.

Gambit and Andre Deutsch, Ltd., for excerpts from *The Land of the Rising Yen* by George Mikes. Published by Andre Deutsch, Ltd., 1970.

Lord Hailsham [Quintin Hogg] for excerpts from *The Case for Conservatism* by Quintin Hogg. Published by Penguin, Ltd.

Hamish Hamilton, Ltd., for excerpts from *From Napoleon to Lenin* by A. J. P. Taylor. Copyright © 1963 by A. J. P. Taylor.

Hamish Hamilton, Ltd., and McGraw-Hill Book Company for excerpts from *The Reason Why* by Cecil Woodham-Smith.

The Hamlyn Publishing Group, Ltd., for excerpts from:
The World's Strangest Customs by E. Royston Pike.
The River War by Winston Churchill.

Centuries of Childhood by Philippe Aries, translated by Robert Baldick. Copyright © 1962 by Jonathan Cape, Ltd.

Prejudices: Fourth Series by H. L. Mencken. Copyright 1924 by Alfred A. Knopf, Inc., and renewed 1952 by H. L. Mencken.

Salah and His American by Leland Hall. Copyright 1933 by Leland Hall and renewed 1961 by John H. Finn, Finn & Brownell, executor of Leland Hall.

Notes on Democracy by H. L. Mencken. Copyright 1926 by Alfred A. Knopf, Inc., and renewed 1954 by H. L. Mencken.

Picked-up Pieces, "Laughter in the Shell of Safety" by John Updike. Copyright © 1966–1975 by John Updike.

A Mencken Chrestomathy by H. L. Mencken. Copyright 1926 by Alfred A. Knopf, Inc.; renewal copyright 1954 by H. L. Mencken.

Irving Kristol for excerpts from articles in the *Wall Street Journal*, July 17, 1975, and September 11, 1975.

Ktav Publishing House, Inc., for excerpt from *Masterpieces of Hebrew Literature* by Curt Leviant, 1969.

Harold D. Lasswell for excerpts from:
Psychopathology and Politics by Harold D. Lasswell. Published by McGraw-Hill Book Company.
Politics—Who Gets What, When, How by Harold D. Lasswell. Published by McGraw-Hill Book Company.

Little, Brown & Company in association with The Atlantic Monthly Press for excerpts from *John Paul Jones: A Sailor's Biography* by Samuel Eliot Morison. Copyright © 1959 by Samuel Eliot Morison.

Little, Brown & Company for excerpt from *Admiral of the Ocean Sea* by Samuel Eliot Morison.

Liveright Publishing Corporation for excerpts from *The Travels of Marco Polo* revised from Marsden's translation and edited by Manuel Komroff. Copyright 1926 by Boni & Liveright, Inc. Copyright 1930 by Horace Liveright. Copyright renewed 1953 by Manuel Komroff.

Longman Group, Ltd., for excerpts from:
England Under Queen Anne, vol. 1, by G. M. Trevelyan.
Critical and Historical Essays by T. B. Macaulay.

Harry McPherson for excerpts from *A Political Education* by Harry McPherson. Published by Little, Brown & Company. Copyright © 1972 by Harry McPherson.

Macmillan, Inc., for excerpts from:
The Tsars by Ronald Hingley. Copyright © 1968 by Ronald Hingley.
Gallipoli by John Masefield. Copyright 1916, 1925 by John Masefield; renewed 1944, 1953 by John Masefield.
Science and the Modern World by Alfred North Whitehead. Copyright 1925 by Macmillan, Inc.; renewed 1953 by Evelyn Whitehead.
Modes of Thought by Alfred North Whitehead. Copyright 1938 by Macmillan, Inc.; renewed 1966 by T. North Whitehead.
The Aims of Education by Alfred North Whitehead. Copyright 1929 by Macmillan, Inc.; renewed 1957 by Evelyn Whitehead.
The Logic of Modern Physics by Percy W. Bridgman. Copyright 1927 by Macmillan, Inc.; renewed 1955 by Percy W. Bridgman.
The Method of Freedom by Walter Lippmann. Copyright 1934 and renewed 1962 by Walter Lippmann.
Science and the Social Order by Bernard Barber.
Naming Day in Eden by Noah Jonathan Jacobs. Copyright © 1958, 1969 by Noah Jonathan Jacobs.
A Dictionary of Angels edited by Gustav Davidson. Copyright © 1967 by Gustav Davidson.

Macmillan Administration, Ltd., London and Basingstoke, for excerpt from *Science and Culture* by Thomas Henry Huxley.

McGraw-Hill Book Company for excerpts from:
Word People by Nancy Caldwell Sorel. Text copyright © 1970 by Nancy Caldwell Sorel. Illustrations copyright © by Edward Sorel.
Karl Marx: An Intimate Biography by Saul K. Padover. Copyright © 1978 by Saul K. Padover

Robert Payne for excerpt from *The Life and Death of Lenin* by Robert Payne. Copyright © 1964 by Robert Payne. Published by Simon & Schuster, Inc.

Penguin Books, Ltd., for excerpts from *Tacitus: Annals of Imperial Rome* translated by Michael Grant (Penguin Classics, revised edition 1971). Copyright © 1956, 1959, 1971 by Michael Grant Publications, Ltd.

A. D. Peters & Co., Ltd., for excerpt from "The English Aristocracy" by Nancy Mitford, published in *Encounter*, Fall 1955.

Pitman Publishing, Ltd., for excerpts from *Intimate Letters of England's Kings* by Margaret Sanders, Museum Press, 1957.

Prentice-Hall, Inc., for excerpt from *Disraeli: A Picture of the Victorian Age*, by André Maurois, translated by Hamish Miles, edited by Monica D. Ryan. Copyright 1936 by Prentice-Hall. Renewed 1964 by Prentice-Hall.

Sir Victor S. Pritchett for excerpt from *The Offensive Traveler* by Victor S. Pritchett. Published by Alfred A. Knopf, Inc. Copyright © 1964 by V. S. Pritchett.

G. P. Putnam's Sons for excerpt from *An Almanac for Moderns* by Donald Culross Peattie. Copyright 1935 by Donald Culross Peattie.

Random House, Inc., for excerpts from:
The Immense Journey by Loren Eiseley. Copyright © 1957 by Loren Eiseley.
The Good Old Days—They Were Terrible! by Otto L. Bettman. Copyright © 1974 by Otto L. Bettman.

Reader's Digest Press for excerpt from the Introduction to *The Autobiography of Benjamin Franklin*, vol. 1, Reader's Digest Family Treasury of Great Biographies.

David Riesman for excerpts from a lecture given at Antioch College entitled "The Oral Tradition, The Written Word, and the Screen Image."

Routledge & Kegan Paul, Ltd., for excerpts from:
Travels in Asia and Africa by Ibn Battuta.
Prelude to Imperialism by H. A. C. Cairns. Published 1965. Copyright © 1965 by H. A. C. Cairns.

Carl Sagan for excerpts from:
Dialogue with a Computer and Robot Talk, copyright © 1977 by Carl Sagan. Published in "In Praise of Robots" by Carl Sagan, *Natural History*, January 1975; and in *The Murmurs of Earth: Science in the Age of Space*, Random House, New York, 1978.
The Galactic Telephone, copyright © 1973 by Carl Sagan. Published in "Wraparound," *Harper's*, December 1973.
Other Worlds by Carl Sagan. Published by Bantam Books, Inc.

Charles Scribner's Sons for excerpts from:
The World Crisis by Winston Churchill. Copyright 1923 by Charles Scribner's Sons.
Albert Einstein by Leopold Infeld. Copyright 1950 by Leopold Infeld.
A History of England from the Fall of Wolsey to the Defeat of the Spanish Armada by James Anthony Froude.

Charles Scribner's Sons and the Hamlyn Publishing Group, Ltd., for excerpts from *My Early Life: A Roving Commission* by Winston Churchill. Copyright 1930 by Charles Scribner's Sons.

Ilse Samhaber for excerpts from *Merchants Make History* by Ernst Samhaber. Copyright Ilse Samhaber. Published by the John Day Co., Inc., 1964.

George Sanderlin for excerpts from *First Around the World: A Journal of Magellan's Voyage* by Antonio Pigafetta, translated by George Sanderlin. Published by Harper & Row, Publishers, Inc., 1964.

The Seabury Press, Inc., for excerpts from *The Alphabet of Grace* by Frederick Buechner. Copyright © 1970 by Frederick Buechner.

Saturday Review for excerpt by Simon Karlinsky in the *Saturday Review*, June 14, 1975.

Frances Schwartz Literary Agency for excerpt from *Paracelsus* by Henry M. Pachter, with permission from the publisher, Henry Schuman, Inc. Copyright 1951.

Simon & Schuster, Inc., for excerpts from:
The Renaissance by Will Durant. Copyright 1953 by Will Durant.
Easter in Sicily by Herbert Kubly. Copyright © 1956 by Herbert Kubly.
The Mountain People by Colin Turnbull. Copyright © 1973 by Colin M. Turnbull.

Simon & Schuster, Inc., and George Allen & Unwin, Ltd., for excerpts from:
Why I Am Not a Christian by Bertrand Russell. Copyright © 1957 by George Allen & Unwin, Ltd.
Unpopular Essays by Bertrand Russell. Copyright 1950 by Bertrand Russell.
Portraits from Memory by Bertrand Russell. Copyright © 1951, 1952, 1953, 1956 by Bertrand Russell.
Autobiography of Bertrand Russell by Bertrand Russell. Copyright © 1969 by George Allen & Unwin, Ltd.

St. Martin's Press, Inc., for excerpts from *The Waning of the Middle Ages* by J. Huizinga.

Smithsonian magazine for excerpts. Copyright © 1975 Smithsonian Institution, from *Smithsonian* magazine, January 1976.

Lord [C. P.] Snow for excerpt from *Variety of Men* by C. P. Snow. Published by Charles Scribner's Sons and Macmillan, Ltd. Copyright © 1967 by C. P. Snow.

Stein and Day Publishers and Hodder & Stoughton, Ltd., for excerpts from *The English* by David Frost and Antony Jay (published in the United Kingdom, the British Commonwealth, and Canada under the title *To England with Love*). Copyright © 1968 by David Frost and Antony Jay.

Stein and Day Publishers and André Deutsch, Ltd., for excerpts from *Man Is the Prey* by James Clarke. Copyright © 1969 by James Clarke.

Thames and Hudson, Ltd., for excerpts from *Byzantium and Europe* by Speros Vryonis, Jr.

W. H. Thorpe for an excerpt published in the *Times Literary Supplement*, October 3, 1975, by W. H. Thorpe.

Mrs. James Thurber for excerpt, "The Pleasure Cruise—And How to Survive It," in *Thurber Country*, published by Simon & Schuster, Inc. Originally printed in *Holiday*. Copyright 1953 by James Thurber.

Time-Life Books for excerpt from *Japan*, Life World Library. Copyright © 1961, 1968 by Time, Inc.

Charles E. Tuttle Co., Inc., for excerpts from *Japan Unmasked* and *Japanese Are Like That* by Ichiro Kawasaki.

University of Chicago Press for excerpts from:
Capitalism and the Historians by F. A. Hayek.
Capitalism and Freedom by Milton Friedman.
Public and Private Enterprise by John Jewkes.

Ernest van den Haag for excerpts from:
"Psychoanalysis and Utopia," Freud Memorial Lecture, Philadelphia Association for Psychoanalysis, May 22, 1964.
"Genuine and Spurious Integration," in *Psychoanalysis and Social Science* edited by H. M. Ruitenbeck.
The Fabric of Society by Ralph Ross and Ernest van den Haag, Harcourt, Brace and Co., 1957.

Lois Ventris for excerpts from a talk by Michael Ventris, broadcast by the British Broadcasting Corporation, in *The Listener*, July 10, 1952.

The *Wall Street Journal* for excerpts from the following articles: "Social Security," May 26, 1965; "The Age of Discontent," December 21, 1971; "The WASPS," November 5, 1975. Copyright © 1965, 1971, 1975 by Dow Jones & Company, Inc. All Rights Reserved.

W. Allen Wallis for excerpt from a speech given at the University of Rochester, January 18, 1971.

A. P. Watt & Son for excerpts from *Oliver Cromwell* by John Buchan. With permission of Susan, Lady Tweedsmuir.

A. P. Watt & Son and the estate of the late G. K. Chesterton for excerpts from:

Selected Essays by G. K. Chesterton.

Heretics by G. K. Chesterton.

George Weidenfeld & Nicolson, Ltd., for excerpts from *The Silver Age of Venice* by Maurice Rowdon.

Yale University Press for excerpts from:

Bureaucracy by Ludwig von Mises.

The Nature of the Judicial Process by Justice Benjamin Cardozo.

Wayland Young for excerpts from "Sitting on a Fortune," published in *Encounter* magazine. Copyright © 1959 by Wayland Young.

INDEX